Where the South Lost the War

Where the South Lost the War

An Analysis of the
Fort Henry–Fort Donelson Campaign

February 1862

Kendall D. Gott

STACKPOLE
BOOKS

Published by
STACKPOLE BOOKS
5067 Ritter Road
Mechanicsburg, PA 17055
www.stackpolebooks.com

Printed in the United States of America

10 9 8 7 6 5 4 3 2 1

FIRST EDITION

Library of Congress Cataloging-in-Publication Data

Gott, Kendall D.
   Where the South lost the war : an analysis of the Fort Henry-Fort Donelson campaign, February 1862 / by Kendall D. Gott.— 1st ed.
       p. cm.
   Includes bibliographical references (p.) and index.
   ISBN 0-8117-0049-6
   1. Fort Henry, Battle of, Tenn., 1862. 2. Fort Donelson, Battle of, Tenn., 1862. I. Title.
E472.96.G68 2003
973.7'31—dc21
                                                                    2002156349

To my father, Richard W. Gott,
who started it all.

ABOUT THE AUTHOR

KENDALL D. GOTT RETIRED FROM THE U.S. ARMY IN 2000, HAVING served as an armor/cavalry and military intelligence officer, and was a certified army historian. His combat experience consists of the Persian Gulf War and two subsequent bombing campaigns of Iraq. His unpublished work, "In Glory's Shadow: In Service with the 2nd Armored Cavalry Regiment during the Persian Gulf War," details his experiences and is held at the Combined Arms Library at Fort Leavenworth, Kansas. He graduated from Western Illinois University in 1983 with a bachelor's degree in history and earned a master's degree in military history through the Command and General Staff College at Fort Leavenworth, Kansas, in 1998. He was an adjunct professor of American and World History at Augusta State University and Georgia Military College for three years before returning to Kansas. He is now a military historian in the Combat Studies Institute, which is a branch of the Command and General Staff College.

CONTENTS

List of Maps ix

Preface and Acknowledgments xi

Introduction xv

Chapter One From Plowshares to Swords,
            March–August 1861 1

Chapter Two Gunboats on Western Waters,
            1861 21

Chapter Three Autumn of Blunders,
              September–December 1861 35

Chapter Four Prelude to Battle,
             January 1862. 59

Chapter Five The Battle of Fort Henry,
             February 2–6, 1862. 75

Chapter Six The Tennessee River Raid,
            February 6–12, 1862 107

Chapter Seven Gathering of the Hosts,
              February 7–11, 1862 115

Chapter Eight   First Contact,
                  Tuesday, February 12, 1862 143

Chapter Nine   Opening Round,
                  Wednesday, February 13, 1862 157

Chapter Ten   The Vise Tightens,
                  Thursday, February 14, 1862 171

Chapter Eleven   The Confederate Attack,
                  Saturday Morning, February 15, 1862 . 191

Chapter Twelve   The Afternoon of Decision,
                  Saturday, February 15, 1862 219

Chapter Thirteen A Disgraceful Surrender,
                  Sunday, February 16, 1862 251

Chapter Fourteen The Final Analysis 271

Appendix A   Order of Battle and Casualties 281

Appendix B   Auxiliary Vessels 289

                  Notes 291

                  Bibliography 319

                  Index 333

LIST OF MAPS

1. Area of Operations, 1861 10
2. Area of Operations, September 1861 42
3. Area of Operations, January 1862 66
4. Fort Henry, February 4–5, 1862 90
5. Fort Henry, February 6, 1862 99
6. Tennessee River Raid, February 6–12, 1862 112
7. Grant's Advance on Fort Donelson, February 12, 1862 . . 146
8. Fort Donelson, February 12, 1862 151
9. Fort Donelson, February 13, 1862 163
10. Fort Donelson, February 14, 1862 176
11. Fort Donelson Water Batteries, February 13–16, 1862 . . 180
12. Fort Donelson, 6:00 A.M., February 15, 1862 193
13. Fort Donelson, 10:00 A.M., February 15, 1862 208
14. Fort Donelson, 12:00 P.M., February 15, 1862 214
15. Fort Donelson, 2:00 P.M., February 15, 1862 227
16. Fort Donelson, 3:00 P.M., February 15, 1862 233
17. Fort Donelson, 6:00 P.M., February 15, 1862 236

PREFACE AND ACKNOWLEDGMENTS

FOR MY ELEVENTH BIRTHDAY, MY FATHER GAVE ME A HARDBACK EDITION of Bruce Catton's *This Hallowed Ground*. The narrative was beyond my reading comprehension at the time, but it had a number of pictures and illustrations. These captured my imagination, and I studied them for hours on end. Little did he know that this began a life-long interest in history and the War Between the States.

My father had bought the book after a family vacation in which we passed through the Gettysburg battlefield en route to our destination. This was my first exposure to the Civil War, and I remember the cannon the best. My two sisters were not impressed in the least. Whenever we would even talk about visiting an old battlefield they would exclaim, "They all look alike—just a field with a cannon and a pile of cannonballs." My parents and I endured their whining and sulking, but we visited Vicksburg, Shiloh, Mobile Bay, and Fort Sumter while traveling on one vacation or another. They would never fail to point out their astute observation from Gettysburg.

My particular interest in the Fort Henry-Fort Donelson campaign was sparked during the summer of 1971. As a young Boy Scout, my troop trekked some 300 miles in a borrowed school bus each year to the Land Between the Lakes recreation area, which lies between the Tennessee and Cumberland Rivers. One day was set aside for the hiking the trails around Fort Donelson. It seemed we hiked for fifty miles, but it couldn't have been over twelve. After a couple of visits, I had the park memorized and became the designated trail guide for the troop.

It was at Fort Donelson where the images in Catton's book were superimposed on the terrain. For the first time, I could picture Foote's ironclads on the river, the Confederates in the trenches, and Grant's army swarming over the hills and forests beyond. I would later see other Civil War battlefields, but that was my favorite. Although from Illinois, I felt a degree of sympathy and respect for the Confederate soldiers. Miserably led by their senior officers, they fought to the brink of victory. On the other hand, the midwesterners of my home state were far from home and fighting for a cause they believed in.

I have chosen a variation of the campaign analysis model used by the Command and General Staff College at Fort Leavenworth, Kansas. By doing so, I have attempted not only to tell the historical narrative, but also to describe the rationale behind the strategies and decisions. This campaign was fought early in the war but is one of the foremost examples of the different styles of senior-level command.

In my research for this work, I relied most heavily upon primary source material—firsthand accounts from men in position to see and influence events. Many officers and men recorded their experiences during the campaign and often submitted their work for publication in newspapers, magazines, and books. One must use firsthand accounts with caution, however, as individuals often had a limited view of events, and many were not particularly objective in their recordings. Many officers had careers to salvage after the campaign, and others were eager to gain promotions. What I found particularly interesting was that the personal letters were virtually identical to later published accounts of the events. Obviously these men referred back to their earlier correspondence, but more telling, they stuck to their stories.

Government documents were also extremely helpful, particularly the *West Point Atlas* and the Fort Donelson battlefield maps drawn by the distinguished park historian Edwin Bearss. These two sources were the foundation for the maps presented in this work. The result is an approximation of unit locations at various times in the campaign to aid in the reader's understanding of this complex campaign. Of course, no book on the Civil War is complete without use of *The Official Records of the Union and Confederate Armies* and its naval counterpart.

No matter how hard one may try, no writer is an island. I am deeply indebted to the staff of the Fort Donelson Military Park. Robert Wallace, Jimmy Jobe, William "Buzz" Bazar, and Susan Hawkins are the epitome of the Department of the Interior park rangers. Friendly and expert in their field, they gave me a greater understanding of the campaign and were instrumental in my research of the Fort Henry and Fort Heiman sites.

Susan Gordon is the archivist and Kassie Hassler is a librarian at the Tennessee State Library and Archives, and they were also key contributors to this effort. They painstakingly searched through the voluminous files to find many of the pictures and portraits that appear in this book. Thanks go to

Frank A. Arre and James M. Milburn of the Naval Historical Foundation, as well as to the library staffs at the Combined Arms Research Library at Fort Leavenworth, Kansas, the Woodford Library at Fort Gordon, Georgia; and the Military History Institute at Carlisle Barracks, Pennsylvania, for their assistance in procuring rare books and materials. Other individuals who assisted in this endeavor are Velma V. Gee, James P. Guy, Dennis Hutchinson, and David Sullivan, who provided biographical information on ancestors who fought at Fort Donelson. Special thanks go to James T. Sibert of the U.S. Army Corps of Engineers, Nashville District, and to Dr. Russell K. Brown and John Stanfield. Last but certainly not least, thanks to William C. Davis for his advice and assistance, as well as for the chance to make this work become a reality.

I also must acknowledge the support and encouragement given by my two sons, David and Ryan, who good-naturedly endured the hours I spent in this endeavor with nary a word of complaint.

Few things have survived my family's nomadic existence over the years, but on the bookshelf in my den rests a worn and battered copy of *This Hallowed Ground*.

INTRODUCTION

THE FORT HENRY–FORT DONELSON CAMPAIGN WAS SMALL FOR CIVIL WAR battles, but size is misleading. The campaign on the Tennessee and Cumberland Rivers was the first significant victory for the Union during the American Civil War. After a string of defeats for the North, the final victory at Fort Donelson had far-reaching repercussions. Gen. Ulysses S. Grant's successful campaign was a great morale boost for the North, and an equally devastating one for the South. In ten days the Confederate defenses in the West were shattered, necessitating the abandonment of most of Tennessee and the state capital of Nashville. Union gunboats were also able then to ascend the Tennessee and Cumberland Rivers to wreak havoc deep into the Confederate heartland. The southern disasters at Fort Henry and Fort Donelson signaled the beginning of the dismemberment and ultimate defeat of the Confederate States of America. It was here, so early in the war, that the inexorable decline of the Confederacy began.

The Fort Henry–Fort Donelson campaign is somewhat overlooked by many historians, yet it deserves careful and deliberate study. It was indeed a small affair when compared with campaigns waged later in the war, which also incurred far greater casualties. Many also look upon the campaign as a no-win situation for the South. Outgunned and surrounded by land and a powerful ironclad fleet on the river, how could the Confederates ever have had a chance of resisting Grant's onslaught?

Although the odds were seemingly against the Confederates, defeat by Grant's army and the vaunted ironclad fleet was never assured. In fact, the Confederates had options that would have prevented the disaster, or at least lessened its impact. The Confederates lost the campaign not because of any shortcomings of its soldiers, but because of the ineptitude of department commander Albert Sidney Johnston and the senior commanders at the scene. There were indeed opportunities to avoid the disaster, even after General Grant's army invested Fort Donelson.

The Fort Henry–Fort Donelson campaign is a story of contrasts in command as well as mobilization, logistics, technology, and human endurance. The story embraces the competition for power and control at higher command levels and the utter collapse of Confederate leadership during the campaign. It shatters the contemporary myth of Gen. Albert Sidney Johnston as the preeminent military leader at the beginning of the war. Poor decisions and ultimately two generals passing command of their army after throwing away victory illustrate the spectacle of impotent Confederate generalship. In so many ways, Fort Donelson was a brilliantly missed opportunity for the Confederacy to smash an uncertain Union strategic thrust by an untested Union commander, Ulysses S. Grant.[1]

The Fort Henry–Fort Donelson campaign featured six Confederate general officers that directly influenced events and were responsible for its disastrous conclusion. At the top, Gen. Albert Sidney Johnston commanded the Western Department during the campaign and was directly responsible for the assignment of troops and general officers to the beleaguered bastions.[2] Gen. Lloyd Tilghman was a gallant example under fire at Fort Henry, but by his surrender, he left Fort Donelson without a strong leader for three critical days. The senior officer at Fort Donelson during the battle was Brig. Gen. John Floyd, a former governor of Virginia and secretary of war for the Buchanan administration with no military experience. Next in line was Gideon Pillow. The second of three commanding brigadier generals at the fort, Pillow had been a major general during the Mexican War but by many accounts was an inept field commander. The third brigadier general at Fort Donelson was Simon Buckner, a junior officer in the Mexican War who had just resigned his post as commander of the Kentucky State Guard in favor of a commission in the Confederate army. Buckner was arguably the most technically proficient brigadier at Fort Donelson. Forgotten by many, there was a fourth general officer within the defenses of Fort Donelson by the name of Bushrod Johnson, who had little if any impact on the decision-making process of the senior officers.

Excluding Albert Sidney Johnston, who was not present at Fort Donelson during the battle, the combined experience of the four brigadiers in command far exceeded that of their adversary, Ulysses S. Grant. Grant had left the army as a junior officer shortly after the Mexican War and had just recently returned to active duty after years of failing in one private venture after another. At first glance, it would appear logical that the Confederates would have the edge in leadership. After all, they were fighting on their home ground; in their unified command, the experience of the combined officers should have further added to their advantage.

Unfortunately for the Confederates, Johnston never firmly assigned command to any of the four generals at Fort Donelson, and the result was disastrous. Due to past personal hostilities and present indecision, the Confederate command took a grave situation and turned it into an absolute fiasco. The South never recovered its loss in the West.

This book also closely examines the command of the Union forces and their preparations for the campaign. Here we see an unknown and untested Ulysses S. Grant overcome the political maneuverings of his superiors and forge a victorious army on the field of battle. This campaign also features the first use of a naval force on the western rivers of the United States, and the use of ironclad gunboats against earthen fortifications. The close cooperation between the services in this campaign would have few parallels in military history.

The narrative begins in the summer of 1861 and follows the military preparations up to the onset of the campaign in order to give their strategic and operational rationale. This campaign analysis describes the initial efforts of Tennessee to defend her borders, then follows the efforts of the Confederate command to build a credible defense against a vast host forming in the North under the command of Generals Grant, Buell, and Halleck, as well as the myriad of frustrations that hampered its efforts. Finally, the battles at Fort Henry and Fort Donelson are presented in detail at the tactical level of war, but the outcome and effect are again presented at the operational and strategic level.

There are a number of personal accounts that would fill volumes. They are extraordinarily interesting, and I wish that it were possible to add them all. Several are presented to add a human dimension to this work. They are all footnoted, and I encourage interested readers to seek out these sources for the full accounts.

CHAPTER ONE

From Plowshares to Swords

March–August 1861

THE NEW CONFEDERATE STATES OF AMERICA HAD BUT ONE OBJECTIVE IN April 1861: to establish itself as a full-standing independent nation. To achieve this goal it did not require the conquest of the North. The new nation had only to maintain its existence and gain world recognition.

After secession and the outbreak of war, the new Confederacy was presented with the daunting task of defending itself from an invading army over a vast frontier that stretched from the Atlantic seaboard westward over the Appalachians, across the fields of Tennessee, and into the Great Plains. The new nation also had to guard an extended coastline against a nation with an established navy. The new Confederate president, Jefferson Davis, made an early decision to rigidly defend as much territory as possible, rejecting a more flexible defense like those used in the American Revolution or the War of 1812.

The sheer size of the country was the chief problem in defending the South, and the poor transportation and communications networks compounded it. In the western states, there were a few reinforced turnpikes. The majority of highways were mainly ordinary dirt roads, meaning they were good in the summer and bottomless mud in the winter. The railroads played a key role in this war, but within the Southern rail network, there was a great diversity in gauges, which hindered long-haul distances. The rivers were available to carry supplies and troops, but most of the boats that plied them before the war were laid up by their owners in Northern river ports. The few Southern boats that carried goods to market often had to pass through hostile territory, where they might be intercepted by enemy gunboats or blocked by land batteries. This was particularly the case for farmers and planters living along the Cumberland and Tennessee Rivers.

For communications, the telegraph was in fairly common use but was not yet mobile enough to keep pace with a moving army. Long-distance communications initially required a heavy reliance on the postal service and couriers. As a result, the reality confronting President Davis was the waging of war across half a continent, with little ability to direct it at an operational level from faraway Richmond. Jefferson Davis needed a system to coordinate the defense of the far-off reaches of the Confederacy.

Davis decided to divide the South into geographic departments to give a semblance of control and facilitate the raising, equipping, and supplying of forces. These departments varied in size and importance, and over the years of war, they were consolidated or divided as the need arose. In theory, each would have a field army, and the general officer in charge had a considerable amount of autonomy. He was expected to maintain his own administrative bureau for supply and to raise, equip, and train his own forces, thus eliminating the need for long-haul shipments. The department commander was free to contact the governors within his department concerning military matters without going through the central government in Richmond.[1] He was also expected to prepare for the defense of his department by building fortifications at key points and assigning units to guard them.

The area of conflict for the Fort Henry–Fort Donelson campaign fell into the Western Department, or Department Number 2, as it was often called. This was the largest department in the Confederacy and was bordered on the east by the Appalachians and extended onto the plains west of the Mississippi. This vast area was as well suited to military operations as about any in the South. The roads were of uncertain quality, though, so the few railroads became strategically important for moving armies and supplies. Provisions existed on the many farms and plantations throughout the region, which could thus sustain armies moving through it.[2]

The most important features in this vast department were three large rivers. The farthest west was the Mississippi; next was the Tennessee, which ran north from Florence, Alabama, to Paducah, Kentucky; and farther to the east was the Cumberland, which began in eastern Kentucky and flowed south into Tennessee past Nashville, before curving north to join the Ohio near Paducah. In 1861, the inland rivers of the United States were the principal means of transportation for cotton, iron, tobacco, food, and manufactured goods between the cities of the North and the South. The Mississippi and the port of New Orleans were the most economical means for midwesterners to get their products to overseas markets, since the railroads were still in their infancy and could not yet match the steamboats' established infrastructure and hauling capacity.[3] Because these rivers generally ran north-south, they were useless as bulwarks of defense, but they were ideal routes for an invading army.

Many in the South recognized this and saw the danger in allowing the enemy to gain control of the rivers. Loss of the Tennessee River would allow a Union gunboat fleet to isolate western Tennessee from the East and penetrate virtually all the way to Florence, Alabama. Any advance up that river would also threaten the city of Memphis and the vital rail center at Corinth, Mississippi. Loss of the Cumberland River would spell doom for the key supply and manufacturing center of Nashville. Federal control of the Mississippi would effectively split the South in two and reopen river traffic to the Midwest, linking the Northern farmers to the profitable European markets, as well as relieving political pressure on the Lincoln administration. Therefore, the defense of the great Southern rivers was key to the ultimate survival of the Confederacy, and as soon as Tennessee seceded, the state's governor, Isham Harris, ordered likely spots along the streams fortified and blocked.

Yet not everyone had a full appreciation of the strategic importance of the inland rivers. Far away in Richmond, President Jefferson Davis had a different outlook. A study of his dispatches to the Western Department commander in the *Official Records* shows clearly that the eastern theater was the main priority for the receipt of arms and troops.[4] There the South planned to defend its capital from the expected efforts of the North to capture it. It was also from Virginia that the South could most quickly invade the North, possibly capturing Washington, D.C., and ending the war.

The South raised and equipped regiments as fast as it could during the spring and summer of 1861. When Richmond established a quota for volunteers for each state, a flood of men eager to join up overwhelmed the makeshift recruiting offices. Separate companies formed in towns, cities, and counties under local officers. These were then consolidated into regiments and placed initially under state control. The Confederate government also authorized the creation of a Regular army by an act of Congress in March 1861, but it was a very small organization, consisting of staff departments, a few regiments, and an engineer corps.

In the campaign area of operations, Tennessee also scrambled to raise an army, but there were immediate problems. At the outbreak of war, the state of Tennessee had only 10,161 muskets and rifles, 350 carbines, four pieces of artillery, and a small number of pistols and sabers. Of the muskets, only 1,680 had the modern percussion locks; the rest were archaic flintlocks. Of these, 4,300 were unserviceable, as were two of the artillery guns. There were also 1,815 muskets and rifles and some 200 pistols and sabers in the hands of the volunteer militia companies.[5] This amount was but a fraction of the number required to defend the state or even arm the mass of recruits joining the service at that time. The disparity between the number of weapons and recruits was such that many men were told to go home. The other states of the new Confederacy faced very similar circumstances.

Basic supplies to field an army were also in short supply. Uniforms, accoutrements, tents, blankets, and all the other items an army needed did not exist or were in critically small numbers. Particularly at this early stage in the war, each state acquired and stored supplies in depots for its own indigenous forces. Facilities to manufacture equipment, ammunition, and powder were built to help meet the demand, and depots were created to store the implements of war. The new soldiers wore mainly civilian clothes, however, their only insignia being black stripes on their pants or some other added facings. Many of the officers were more affluent and bought the regulation gray uniform. Others wore the Federal army blue, the only difference from the enemy being the great profusion of gold lace added to denote Confederate rank. Pay was often irregular, and the men were obliged to defray the expenses of equipping themselves from the beginning.[6]

The depots and manufacturing facilities were situated in cities with available manpower, and along rivers or at railroad terminals to facilitate transportation of raw materials and delivery of finished products. The chief manufacturing centers in the Western Department during this time were in Nashville and Memphis. The former became not only vital to the western theater, but also an important supplier to the armies in the East.[7] With its war production and railroads linking the East and West, Nashville was a city the South could not afford to lose.

Tennessee collected the scattered locally raised regiments and consolidated them into the Provisional Army for the defense of the state, appointing a commander by the name of Gideon J. Pillow. An influential man in Tennessee, Pillow had been a general officer during the Mexican War. He had no formal military training and owed his appointment in that war and subsequent promotion to major general to the fact that he was a former law partner to then president James K. Polk. His performance then was clearly a matter of opinion, which was generally unfavorable. He was not especially popular with his fellow officers or his commander, Winfield Scott, who considered him insubordinate.[8] In fact, Pillow's writings and accusations were instrumental in ruining Scott's presidential aspirations, and Pillow subsequently had no shortage of personal enemies.

Despite how his fellow officers viewed him, Pillow was a man of great personal magnetism. He was dashing, tireless, fearless in battle, and often inspired troops to perform heroic acts. But he had his share of personality faults. A product of the planter society of the South, Pillow was stereotypically arrogant, rash, dominant, and aggressive. He had a prejudice against the West Point-trained professional officers corps, who never accepted him as an equal. These are not necessarily poor military qualities, but in addition, he lacked sound judgment to direct his seemingly boundless energy.[9] Pillow, with all his strengths and shortcomings, was a key player in the following months, as well as during the Fort Henry–Fort Donelson campaign.

Major General Pillow established his headquarters at Memphis and began the arduous process of raising and organizing the Provisional Army of Tennessee. Companies of men reported to Camps Cheatham, Maury, Weakley, Lillard, and Trousdale, and several other points across the state to form into regiments. Before the end of May, twenty-four infantry regiments, ten artillery companies, and one regiment of cavalry were armed, equipped, and ready to take the field. Three of the infantry regiments were transferred to service in Virginia and were no longer available for the state's defense. No one kept records, but there were at least double this number of men who wanted to enlist but were turned away. It was generally thought that their services were not yet required, since it was supposed to be a short war.

Across the South, this scenario played out as the arsenals of the states were emptied. Units were also formed without state-issued arms, as frequently the Southern recruit simply showed up with his own gun. As a result, regiments had a myriad of arms, including hunting rifles, shotguns, and even antiquated flintlock muskets. The guns were welcome, but they compounded the difficulty of supplying ammunition. Other weapons came through the blockade, and gunsmiths began to turn out more. No matter, there were never enough to go around. Some units were without arms at all, and their procurement distracted their officers from training and drill.[10] Up to the Fort Henry–Fort Donelson campaign, the Southern volunteer typically was miserably armed and equipped. The exceptions were old militia companies or state guard units, which generally were armed and equipped fairly well. Most of these units formed the nucleus of the state provisional armies and were later consolidated into the Confederate army.

Along with the challenges of raising troops, procuring arms and supplies, and organizing defenses, the armies also needed leaders. In the democratic spirit and tradition of the day, men elected their own company and regimental officers. The president, for a number of reasons and motives, appointed Confederate general officers. Officers that were elected or appointed were not always selected for their merit or martial potential. Men of political clout but little military training or ability made their way into the service. Contrary to a common misconception that large numbers of officers were merely political appointees, however, the majority of Confederate general officers were military and professional men.[11] Indeed, experienced officers with a West Point diploma were valuable commodities and became the core of the Confederate senior commanders. They also brought with them the traditions and regulations of the service from their former army.

General Pillow raised, organized, and stationed the new troops but also saw the importance of the Mississippi River and the likelihood of the enemy trying to seize it. With Governor Harris's approval, four substantial earthworks were begun along the length of the eastern bank to defend it. Meanwhile, only token forces were assigned to the Tennessee and Cumberland Rivers, as well as eastern Tennessee.

Tennessee was but one piece of the larger pie. The Confederate army operated within the departmental system of command, and one of the most important tasks facing a department commander was establishing effective control of his forces. Means of communication were usually limited and slow, and couriers or mail were the norm. The telegraph was a revolutionary marvel, but its use at this time was restricted to existing lines. A commander of forces spread over several states generally needed to place his headquarters centrally to communicate efficiently.

The nature of command reflected the nature of communication over the vast distances. Orders often gave subordinates a great deal of discretion, leaving the officer on the scene to make decisions as he saw fit. This system had the merit of being flexible, but it relied on the competency and good judgment of the subordinate.

Interestingly, in the first months of the war, no single department commander was assigned for the western Confederacy. The raising and organization of units had been purely a state responsibility, but that was about to change.

Leonidas Polk, a bishop of the Episcopal Church, was visiting Tennessee with plans to build a university in Sewanee. During his visit, he encountered Governor Harris, who discussed at length the coming war and the state's inadequate defenses. Harris knew that Polk was an old West Point classmate of Jefferson Davis and asked him to go to Richmond on his behalf. Harris hoped Polk could speak directly to the president on the subject of obtaining arms and to impress upon him the need to defend the Mississippi Valley. Polk did, in fact, go to his old friend in Richmond, where he found Davis under the heavy burden of multiplying tasks that confronted him daily.

The pleas for reinforcements and action in the West were persistent and increasingly louder over the early months of the new Confederacy. Few thought the defenses were adequate, and the people of the western states feared an invasion from the North. Powerful men lived along the rivers, and they had a great interest in seeing their property and interests protected from a marauding army. Soon Davis was receiving inquiries from the state governors and the increasingly hostile press. The demand for troops and materiel for defending the western states conflicted with Davis's priority toward the East, particularly the army guarding Richmond.

Polk sympathized with his old friend and agreed with the system of departments to defend the nation. Trying to be helpful, he recommended that Davis give either Albert Sidney Johnston or Robert E. Lee the command in the West. Neither officer was available, but Davis immediately saw the bishop as the man he wanted to command the new Western Department. After prayerful consideration, Polk accepted the post.[12]

So the command of the vast Confederate Western Department was initially given to Leonidas Polk. A West Point graduate of the class of 1827, he had resigned his army commission soon after graduation in order to enter the Episcopalian ministry. Polk then rose in the church leadership over the years to become the missionary bishop of the Southwest, but now he chose a more militant role to play. Jefferson Davis appointed him major general on June 25, 1861, in spite of his scant military experience, and placed him in this very senior position and vital command.[13] Upon arriving at his headquarters in Memphis on July 4, General Polk found orders awaiting him to receive the Provisional Army of Tennessee into Confederate service.

Gideon Pillow had been the commander of the Provisional Army of Tennessee, but with the adoption of the departmental system, he was a man without a job. Governor Harris urged Richmond to give all of Tennessee's officers in the old Provisional Army commissions of equal rank in the Confederate service when possible. Even Polk recommended the appointment of Pillow as a major general, but Davis was hesitant. Apparently he was well acquainted with Pillow's history and personality.[14] After many weeks, and ultimately bowing to political pressure, Davis finally appointed Pillow a *brigadier* general on July 9, 1861, placing him under the direct command of General Polk. Davis did this in essence to keep Pillow on a short leash. He did not want Pillow to launch one of the half-baked offensives he had been clamoring for since taking command of Tennessee's Provisional Army.[15] Pillow, who had a strong sense of pride, took the news rather badly. He had been a major general in the last war and for the beginning of this one, and he took this demotion as an insult. This increasingly became a source of humiliation and bitter resentment, which erupted into open conflict with his superiors as the months wore on.

Confederate general officers had but one system of insignia to distinguish themselves from the field and company officers. By the regulations, a brigadier and a full general wore the same uniform. It was important to clearly establish just what rank a general officer held, as well as his date of rank, when two met on a battlefield, for this determined which was in command.

One of the U.S. Army regulations adopted by the Confederate armies dealt with the situation when two officers of the same rank were assigned to the same unit or locality. This regulation set up a system to determine which was senior in position:

> When commissions are of the same date, the rank is to be decided between officers of the same regiment or corps by the order of appointment. Between officers of different regiments or corps, First: By rank in actual service when appointed; Second: By former rank and service in the Army or Marine Corps; Third: By lottery among such as [had] not been in military service of the United States. In case of equality or rank by virtue of a brevet commission, reference is had to commissions, not brevet.[16]

This short passage would have a major impact on the conduct of Confederate operations during the Fort Henry–Fort Donelson campaign, where no less than four brigadier generals arrived on the scene.

Whereas the South's primary objectives were independence and defense of its territory, the North sought to restore the Union. Although it was a more straightforward objective, the achievement of this goal would require four years of bloody warfare. The North could not place its hope on the remote possibility of peaceful reunification, either. This would require the total defeat of all enemy forces under arms and the complete occupation of the areas in rebellion.

When the Southern states seceded, the Lincoln administration instantly recognized that control of the inland waterways was key to the Northern economy, as well as to the survival of the Confederacy. The famous "Anaconda Plan," devised by Gen. Winfield Scott, became the Federals' grand design to win the war. This strategy had three elements designed to weaken the South for eventual reconciliation or ultimate military defeat. The first two elements were the creation of an army to operate against the Confederate capital of Richmond and a naval blockade to cut the South off from European markets and any military aid. The third element was based on gaining control of the inland rivers, thus splitting the Confederate States in two or more parts. The plan was derided in the press and elsewhere, being compared to the snake that slowly crushes its prey. Most official and unofficial military planners looked instead for a rapid drive on to Richmond for a quick and easy victory. Although initially denigrated by many, the "Anaconda Plan" eventually became the blueprint for the war after the battle at Bull Run, where it became apparent that the war was not about to end as quickly as many had believed or hoped.

The control of the inland rivers was not only a sound military strategy, but also an economic necessity for the North. Although railroads were becoming more efficient, the rivers were still the primary means of getting the products of the Midwest to market through the port of New Orleans. Access to this key port was denied when the Southern states seceded. Midwestern farmers and manufacturers in turn put pressure to do someting about it on their Congressmen, who passed their concerns on to President Lincoln. The increasingly frustrated president repeatedly urged his generals to advance.

The U.S. Army had about 16,000 men, including the militia of the Northern states, at the outbreak of war. In May 1861, Congress authorized the expansion of the Regular army by 20,000 men, but the popularity of state organizations was such that it was never able to attain its authorized strength.

The Northern recruits enlisted into the military service with a zeal equal to that of their Southern counterparts, and their story is much the same. Arms, equipment, and uniforms were all in short supply at the outbreak of war, and the armories were soon emptied. Brigadier General William T. Sherman lamented: "Thousands on thousands of men could be had from the states north of the Ohio, but arms and accoutrements are wanting. These are promised, but are very slow in coming."[17] Just as in the South, men reported to points across the North, such as Camp Butler, Bird's Point, Cairo, Camp Dunlap, St. Louis Arsenal, and dozens of others. And also as in the South, many men too were turned away.

The Northern armies also needed supply depots, and Cairo, Illinois, would become the main base of operations for the coming campaign. Its location at the juncture of the Ohio and Mississippi Rivers made it an important river port, and it was also the terminus of the Illinois Central Railroad. This combination made it a vital and strategic point. Fortified, Cairo could help block the flow of supplies to the South from the rivers

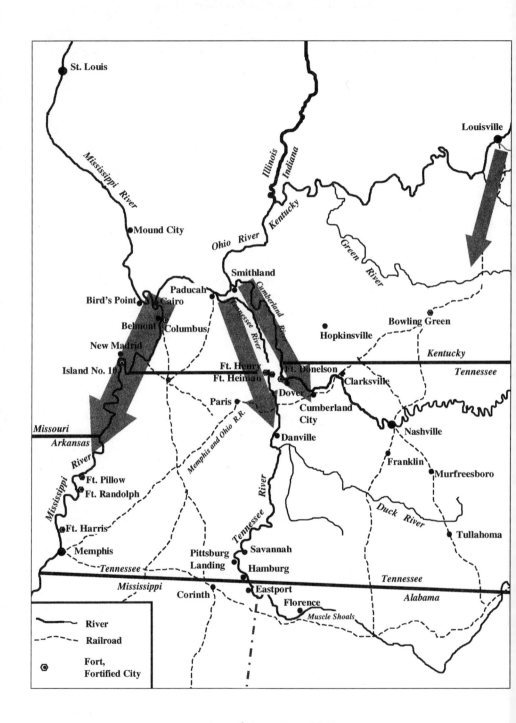

Area of Operations, 1861

and serve as an advance base of operations for the invading armies of the North. Governor Richard Yates of Illinois quickly saw the importance of this town and sent Wood's Illinois Battery there, as well as several infantry regiments. The population of Cairo thus exploded as troops arrived in a continuous stream. The few streets quickly turned to mud under the heavy military traffic, and officers struggled to establish a semblance of order. Newspaper correspondents in need of stories to satisfy impatient editors loitered about headquarters and at the many saloons and wrote of impending attacks and expeditions.

Cairo was never known to be a particularly cheerful place, and the war didn't improve anyone's disposition. The area is still called "Little Egypt" because of the annual flooding of the rivers and because of the numerous lakes in the area. The numerous dikes built to control the floods were ready-made parapets for defense, but the mosquito-infested marshes, along with the poor sanitary conditions and close confines of camp, led to epidemics of malaria, measles, and other diseases, which decimated the ranks. This situation would not improve drastically until the arrival of a particular general officer named Grant, who would spend many weeks instilling discipline and enforcing basic hygiene.

Located so far south, many of the local residents had strong sympathies with the new Confederacy. A veteran of Wood's Battery remembered, "Our reception by the citizens was not the most cordial, and it was plainly evident that they would have been better pleased if the occupying forces had come from the opposite direction."[18] Wood's Battery was assigned the duty of halting all southward-bound boats, which were then inspected for contraband goods before being permitted to go on their way. Being land-bound, the battery had but one way to stop a boat—a well-placed shot across the bow. This crude but simple technique usually persuaded the boat captains to land at the pier for inspection. The flow of war materiel from the North to the South via the Mississippi dropped to a trickle as a result.

The infantry regiments not involved with building fortifications settled into a dull routine of constant drilling, guard duty, and inspections. Camp life bore down on many men, as post commanders made it difficult to leave camp and also began to enforce strict order and silence in the ranks. Some changes, though, were made from time to time for special occasions or visitors. Letters from home, the rare pass, and competition among units for official recognition were also diversions from the routine.

The central figure for the campaign is known to history as Ulysses S. Grant. He was born in Point Pleasant, Ohio, on April 27, 1822, and named Hiram Ulysses Grant. A year later, his family moved to Georgetown, where he was raised. Grant attended the local grammar school and then Maysville Seminary, as well as the Presbyterian Academy at Ripley, Ohio. Grant's family moved to Galena, Illinois, and in 1839 his father secured an appointment for him at the U.S. Military Academy at West Point. Through an administrative error that he found impossible to rectify, Grant was listed on the muster roll as "Ulysses Simpson," a name by which he was known for the rest of his life.

Ulysses S. Grant graduated in 1843 in the middle of his class, twenty-first out of a class of thirty-nine. He was commissioned as a brevet second lieutenant upon graduation and assigned to the 4th Infantry Regiment. Stationed at Jefferson Barracks near St. Louis, he remained there until the regiment was ordered to the Southwest in 1844. During the first phases of the Mexican War, he fought with distinction at the battles of Palo Alto, Resaca, and Monterrey. In 1847, the 4th Infantry was transferred to Winfield Scott's army and fought at Veracruz, Cerro Gordo, Contreras, and Churubusco. Grant was promoted to first lieutenant for gallantry, and after the battle of Chapultepec, he was brevetted captain.

After the war with Mexico, Grant was stationed in the remote Northwest, far from his wife and family. Boredom set in, and he turned to drink to break the monotony of army life on the frontier. To make matters worse, Grant did not find favor with his commanding officer. After several months, he resigned his commission and returned to civilian life, the specter of a drinking problem surrounding him for the rest of his life. He tried his hand at farming and worked for his father's tanning business in Galena but was generally considered a failure.

The outbreak of war in 1861 was a salvation of sorts for Grant, who immediately helped raised a company of volunteers and escorted it to Springfield. He longed for a colonel's commission, frustrated that men of less experience were receiving them with perceived relative ease. Obtaining a commission would not have been difficult, with his West Point diploma and war record, but Grant hated political maneuvering and refused to take part in it.[19] As fate would have it, Governor Yates saw promise in Grant and made him the state adjutant, his duties being swearing companies and regiments into service. Perhaps Grant would have remained in this position had not the colonel of the rowdy 21st Illinois been relieved for incompetence. The men of this unit had come to know Grant, and with the governor's blessing, they elected him as their colonel. Grant quickly instituted a code of strict discipline and drilled the troops into an effective unit.

Grant did not stay a colonel for long, though. The Lincoln administration allowed each state an allotment of general officer appointments, and

Congressman Elihu B. Washburne of Galena sat on the selection board. Being an influential man who knew Grant's family, Washburne helped secure the rank of brigadier general of volunteers for his district's native son in August, but the promotion's effective date of rank was retroactive to May. The congressman was well aware of Grant's former drinking habits and assigned a man named John Rawlings to Grant's staff specifically to keep an eye on the new general. Rawlings soon became his chief of staff and loyally followed him throughout the war, acting as his conscience with constant nagging and insistence on sobriety. Grant did not know of the proceedings in advance and found out about his promotion from the newspapers. When his promotion became official, he was given command of the District of Southeast Missouri. Placing his headquarters in Cairo, he began to bring order out of the mud and chaos. Grant also fortified the outposts of Bird's Point and Fort Holt to screen the river from enemy attack.

But Grant was not in an autonomous position; he reported to Maj. Gen. John C. Frémont. Frémont had been a popular figure in America prior to the Civil War, famous for his explorations of the western territories, which earned him the nickname "the Pathfinder." After the outbreak of war, President Lincoln made him a major general and sent him to command the Army of the West. Frémont established his headquarters in St. Louis and focused his attention on raising an army and securing Missouri for the Union. Under his tutelage, regiments were quickly raised and dispatched to various trouble spots throughout the department, thus securing the state for the Union. Frémont did not manage the large number of lucrative government contracts wisely, however, and corruption became a legacy of his tenure.

In the early months of the war, the border states of Missouri, Kentucky, and Maryland were precariously close to secession from the Union. The catastrophic loss of Maryland was averted by its quick occupation by all available Federal forces. Missouri was secured for the Union within the year. Kentucky, however, provided a key element in the formation of initial strategy for both sides, as it teetered between secession and remaining in the Union.

Kentucky Governor Beriah Magoffin correctly saw that his state would be a battleground should it declare allegiance to either belligerent. Not wishing to antagonize either side, he declared that his state would remain neutral in the conflict and told both to stay out. The general assumption became that if one side violated Kentucky's neutrality, it would push the state into the other's camp. Rich in resources and manpower, Kentucky was a prize each side wanted for itself.

It was in the South's best interests to keep Kentucky neutral as long as possible, for as long as Kentucky remained so, much of the western Confederacy was shielded from attack. With Kentucky blocked, the only remaining avenues from the North into the seceded states were through Virginia, the seacoast, or the fringe states of Missouri and Arkansas. In this situation the North could do little but build up its forces and either wait for a reason or fabricate a pretext to occupy Kentucky. In the meantime, the Confederacy struggled to form a nation and an army to defend it.

As a whole, the leaders of Kentucky tried to maintain a status of neutrality, regardless of political affiliation and in spite of being deeply divided in their sentiments. The pro-Southern governor and the pro-Northern legislature formally proclaimed this policy of neutrality in a joint resolution. Representatives of Kentucky then met with delegates from both governments and received assurances that they would respect the neutrality of the state.[20] Few actually believed that this balance could last long, but for the moment it did keep open warfare from ravaging the countryside.

A key figure in Kentucky at this time and later during the Fort Henry–Fort Donelson campaign was a well-known and highly respected man named Simon Bolivar Buckner. He was born on April 21, 1823, in Hart County, Kentucky. He attended the academy at Hopkinsville, and then graduated from West Point in 1844. Buckner remained at West Point for two years after graduation as an assistant instructor of ethics. He left the academy at the beginning of the Mexican War, was assigned to the front as a quartermaster, and was promoted twice for gallantry. After the war, Buckner returned to West Point and taught tactics for two years, but quit that post and returned to the infantry.

Buckner also happened to be an old friend of Ulysses S. Grant, having met him at West Point and graduating a year later. They fought in proximity to each other in Mexico and served a short time together in the Colorado Territory. When Grant resigned penniless from the army in 1854, it was Buckner who helped his friend in need. Grant was short of cash and unable to pay his bills, and the New York City hotel in which he was staying held his bags. Buckner, who happened to be in town at the time, covered Grant's expenses until his father sent him the money to pay the hotel. This act of kindness was never forgotten.[21]

More significantly, while serving in Mexico, Buckner became involved in a feud between Winfield Scott and his rivals over policy and credit for battlefield actions. General Scott was Buckner's true hero, and the young officer defended him against all attacks. During the 1856 senatorial race in Tennessee, one of the candidates had been a senior officer during the war and took every opportunity on the campaign trail to brag about his own achievements and deride Winfield Scott. Buckner would not let this go unchallenged. He wrote a series of editorials under the pen name "Citizen" to the *Republican Banner* of Nashville. The articles were masterpieces of gibes, ridicule, irony, and sarcasm that made the man appear to be a pompous and arrogant fool, at best.[22] These letters, commonly attributed to Buckner even at the time, subsequently ruined the candidate's political aspirations. Although a few years passed before Buckner and the candidate met again, there were still hard feelings over the impact of Buckner's caustic pen. The 1856 senatorial candidate of Tennessee was none other than Gideon Pillow, former head of the Provisional Army of Tennessee and now serving under General Polk in Columbus. To say these men despised each other is probably an understatement.

Buckner followed Grant out of the army in 1855 and moved to Chicago to sell real estate. Returning to his native Kentucky in 1860, he joined the Kentucky State Guard and quickly rose through the ranks to become its inspector general. He proved himself to be an excellent organizer, although he was known to be very meticulous and deliberate in his decisions. His talents were recognized by the Lincoln administration, which offered Buckner a commission as a brigadier general in August 1861. He respectfully declined.[23]

The Kentucky State Guard was made up of a number of local militia companies originally formed to quell slave insurrections, but under Buckner's tutelage, they became much more. With constant practice, these units became highly respected for their high state of drill and discipline. Issued distinctive military uniforms, camp equipment, and standardized weapons, the State Guard rivaled and even surpassed many units of the U.S. Army at the time.[24] The State Guard was not only a military organization, but a quasipolitical one as well. Many a Kentucky gentleman used the State Guard as a stepping-stone to office. Virtually all of the officers and most of the men in the ranks had a deep sympathy for the South. In fact, the North probably respected Kentucky's neutrality because of a reluctance to combat the State Guard more than for purely political reasons. The State Guard had only about 4,000 men, but it was organized and ready, while the Union men in the state had neither arms nor organization to oppose it.

As much as they respected Kentucky's neutrality, neither side was going to let it get in the way of recruiting men and purchasing articles of war. Just across the borders each side set up camps to receive a number of men from Kentucky who came to enlist. By July 1861, this pretense was largely dropped by the Union, which set up Camp Robinson in the center of the state. The Confederates then established Camp Boone about three miles from the Tennessee line. Both sites featured large flat fields, which were ideal for learning the fine art of drill and maneuvers on a nineteenth-century battlefield. Except for these generally unarmed recruits there were no military forces from either belligerent in the state.

By the end of July, it was becoming clear that Kentucky would not secede from the Union and the influence of the South began to slip. The pro-Union legislature gained firm control of the state and disbanded the pro-Southern State Guard. These well-trained and equipped militia units were required to turn in their weapons and gear, which were then issued to the loyal Home Guard. These were warning signals to the Confederacy that the good times were soon to come to a close. If the long line of defense in the West was to be successfully maintained, much had to be done, and quickly.

Even with the neutral Kentucky to the north, Tennessee governor Isham Harris was rightly concerned about the security of the borders of his state. He did not believe the neutrality could last and ordered likely spots along the rivers fortified and blocked after Lincoln's first call for volunteers. He appointed the sixty-year-old state's attorney, Daniel S. Donelson, brigadier general and sent him to build fortifications on the rivers of middle Tennessee. These were to be as close to the border of Kentucky as possible without violating its neutrality.[25] Donelson formed a surveying team and sent it to select defensible ground dominating the Tennessee and Cumberland Rivers. Adna Anderson, who was a well-known civil engineer and receiver of the Edgefield & Kentucky Railroad, headed this team. Major William F. Foster was detached from the 1st Tennessee Infantry Regiment to assist him. Foster was a surveyor and topographer by trade and went to the rivers ahead of Anderson, who was organizing yet another group in Nashville to conduct a more thorough examination.[26]

The two engineers set to work in earnest on May 10. They initially did find suitable ground to simultaneously cover the Tennessee and Cumberland Rivers, but it was located in neutral Kentucky. They then focused on surveying possible sites along the Cumberland River, looking at the high ridges and deep hollows near the Kentucky border. In mid-May, on the west bank of the river not far below the town of Dover, Anderson laid out the water battery of Fort Donelson twelve miles from the Kentucky line. The new fort was named in honor of Gen. Daniel S. Donelson, who, along with Col. Bushrod Johnson of the Corps of Engineers, approved of the site. Construction was begun by a large force of men brought from the nearby Cumberland Iron Works.[27]

Dover, Tennessee, held little military value itself. It stood upon a bluff on the west bank of the Cumberland River and was the seat of Stewart County. Forty miles from the mouth of the Cumberland, it was connected to Nashville by a road that passed through Charlotte. The region around Dover did boast of being one of the leading iron producers in the South, though. Furnaces to melt ore and timber mills to fuel them dotted the landscape. Steamboats used the landing at Dover to transport the iron and locally grown subsistence crops to market.

The two engineers then made their way to the Tennessee River, a scant twelve miles to the west of Dover. They again carefully studied the terrain and conducted several surveys along a great length of the river. Since Fort Donelson was being built on the western bank of the Cumberland, they decided that it would be wise to build this fort on the east bank of the Tennessee. In case of trouble, men from one could move to the assistance of the other without having to cross a river.[28] This arrangement also meant an economy of limited manpower. It was unlikely that both forts would be attacked simultaneously, so in effect, only one garrison would be needed to man both of them.

The east bank of the Tennessee was low and swampy, however, not high and dry like the west bank of the Cumberland. Anderson chose a spot at the mouth of Standing Rock Creek, nearly opposite the mouth of the Sandy River. In his surveys, Foster wrote that the team carefully calculated the high-water levels and potential flood conditions. Probably because of a lack of manpower, as there were no cities or towns at this remote location, work was not immediately started on this site. As events turned out, any work started here would have been wasted.

General Donelson wanted a more defensible site downstream in Kentucky, but this would have violated that state's respected neutrality. He apparently did a survey of sorts on his own and finally decided on Kirkman's Old Landing, even though it was on low ground dominated by hills across the river.[29] Its one redeeming feature was an unobstructed field of fire that covered two miles down river. Foster and Anderson strongly objected to this site, and Col. Bushrod Johnson was called in to settle the matter.

Bushrod Johnson was another man who would play an active role in the coming campaign. He had graduated from West Point in 1840 and served without distinction during the Mexican War. He resigned his commission after a scandal in his Quartermaster Department and had taken an instructor post at the Western Military Academy at Nashville. Although a native of Ohio, when war began this luckless man cast his lot with the

South.[30] Johnson served for a time as General Pillow's recruiting officer but was later put in charge of the Tennessee Corps of Engineers. In this position, he sat in final judgment of sites selected for fortifications.

To the surprise and lasting disgust of Anderson and Foster, Johnson agreed with Donelson's choice. He evidently felt that the two-mile field of fire the site had down river would offset any disadvantage of the nearby terrain. Many later came to regret Colonel Johnson's decision. As head of the Tennessee Corps of Engineers, Johnson ordered work to commence. The site was named Fort Henry, in honor of Sen. Gustavus A. Henry.

The engineers had but one purpose in mind when they originally laid out the forts, and that was to halt river traffic. The selection of the sites is telling in this regard. The first fortifications at Fort Donelson were gun positions simply gouged out of the hillside. Fort Henry was positioned to cover a long length of the river. Neither site was chosen with much consideration of an infantry attack. Only later were additional fortifications built to protect these water batteries.

In mid-June, the 10th Tennessee Infantry, commanded by Adolphus Heiman, arrived on the scene and began building the walls of Fort Henry. The work was pushed so that the first gun was mounted and test-fired with a blank shell on July 12. Initially, six smoothbore 32-pounders and one 6-pounder cannon were installed. The ammunition on hand was so poor that it was necessary to add special quick-burning powder to each charge, creating the hazard of a premature blast to endanger the gun crews. The men eventually made embrasures for seventeen cannons.[31]

Despite this initial surge of activity, the work on Forts Henry and Donelson ground to a virtual halt, particularly after a few guns were mounted. This was mostly because the Mississippi River forts received priority for men and cannons. The few engineer officers on temporary assignment at Fort Henry were there in support of Fort Donelson as well. Further contributing to the lack of progress was a scourge of camp diseases and general discontentment among the men.[32]

Overall, the summer of 1861 showed few signs of promise for the Confederate command in the West. Leonidas Polk was not up to the daunting task of department commander and neglected the defenses of the Tennessee and Cumberland Rivers almost from the onset. The dynamic Gideon Pillow, who was also demonstrating he was unsuited for senior command, easily swayed Polk. Both of these gentlemen were essentially political appointees, regardless of their past military experiences. Yet despite the indications of incompetence, Jefferson Davis kept both men in their positions, one out of friendship, the other out of political expediency. He also maintained priority for the eastern theater in regard to troops and ordnance. The Western Department was truly treated as a secondary effort.

Some historians have argued that Jefferson Davis should have followed a more flexible defense, such as George Washington did during the Revolution. In that earlier war, Washington sought a war of attrition by falling back into the hinterland, then striking British columns at the place and time of his choosing, particularly in the rear or against the line of supply. The strategy in such a war is to trade space for time, wearing down the opponent in the process. The South was well known for its swamps, mountains, and forests, places generally considered ideal to conduct such operations. Davis and his generals were well versed in the exploits of Washington, yet few called for this strategy at this stage in the war, favoring a more conventional approach. Later in the war, the strategy of trading space for time was used at the tactical level, albeit with poor results. For example, during the campaign for Atlanta, Gen. Joseph Johnston masterfully avoided a decisive battle with his stronger opponent, Gen. William T. Sherman. Even though Johnston kept his army intact all the way back to the gates of the city, Sherman's army was bloodied yet still very effective. In the end, the key city of Atlanta was lost. Consider too that that campaign was waged over the best defensive terrain the South had to offer.

Politically, President Davis was desperately trying to achieve recognition of the Confederacy by England and France. A new nation trying to achieve world recognition would not have a strong case if invaders overran large tracts of its territory. The power elite of the South were the planters and slaveowners, and none of these men wanted to see their holdings overrun by an invading army. These men also realized very early on that Northern armies provided ample opportunities for slaves to escape, most of whom probably would not return. They wielded considerable influence as a voting bloc and gave substantial material assistance to the war effort as well. Davis could not ignore their calls to defend their states.

Economically, Jefferson Davis was also in a quandary. Munitions factories, food-producing regions, and areas with raw materials were widely scattered across the South. This was particularly true for the most vital production regions of Tennessee, Alabama, and Georgia. In a war in which space was traded for time, what area could be given up? About 90 percent of the South's copper supply would be lost if eastern Tennessee were abandoned. The loss of the Cumberland River basin would surrender the government's only operational powder mill during the summer of 1861. A severe shortage of salt and lead would result from the loss of the lower Appalachian Valley of Virginia. A Federal seizure of western Tennessee would result in the loss of the South's largest iron producer.[33] If, while trading space for time any of these regions were lost or its facilities destroyed, the South's ability to wage war would be crippled. Supply from overseas through the blockade was erratic enough from the start that it could not adequately compensate for the loss.

Finally, Jefferson Davis and his advising generals were all products of West Point and the Mexican War. These men were not trained to fight a guerrilla war, and their experiences were very conventional. They formed a military force and devised a strategy that mirrored their training and experience. The Confederacy did produce a number of legendary guerrilla fighters and raiders; these were not a product of a devised strategy or training, but of opportunity and local expediency.

The South's strategy of defending as much territory as possible was a result of these factors, and this strategy certainly had its weaknesses. From the start, there were just not enough men, ships, or cannons to defend it all. The strategy also tied down a large number of forces. Units guarding key ports or facilities were not available to the field armies, and seldom were they enough to resist a determined Federal attack on their own. Yet despite the drawbacks, and even the end result, the South had little other choice. Since it did not have the martial resources to conquer the North, it was automatically on the defensive. The Confederacy had to hold on to as much ground as it could, even if this meant surrendering the strategic initiative to the enemy.[34]

Davis's favoritism of the eastern theater in this period is well established. Supplies and war materiel were often stripped from the West and sent to Virginia. Certainly he had to defend the Confederate capital, but Davis could not ignore the security of the western states. He was not contemplating any grand offensives to inflict a military defeat on the North, choosing instead to remain on the defensive. As such, he could hold Virginia with the troops on hand and continue the war. On the other hand, with the lack of troops and defenses in the West, he could lose these states, and ultimately the war. As history shows, the war was not lost in the eastern theater; it was decided in the West.

As for the North, the situation was turning in its favor. There was no threat of a large-scale invasion of the Midwest, and other than a few small forts to guard the rivers, massive defensive works were not needed. This allowed men like Grant to focus on raising and training their forces to maneuver and fight on an open battlefield, to be an offensive army.

CHAPTER TWO

Gunboats
on Western Waters

1861

AT THE BEGINNING OF THE CIVIL WAR, THERE WERE ABOUT NINETY VES-
sels in the U.S. navy, including receiving ships, vessels in mothballs, and various ships both in and out of commission. Just over sixty were considered
warships, and they varied in vintage and tonnage. Of these only a third
were fit for sea, and those were off patrolling distant stations. None were
suited for combat on the inland rivers of the western United States, and it
was impossible for them in any case to ascend the Confederate-held Mississippi River in order to support the army in its plan to strike deep into the
South. The North would have to build an inland navy from scratch.

At this time, the inland waterways supported a thriving economy as
steamboats carried all sorts of goods and produce. The first order of business for military planners was to find out just what facilities and materials
were available for war purposes. The War Department ordered a study to
ascertain just that in May 1861. The study showed that on the Mississippi
and Ohio Rivers, there were about 500 steamboats of various types. There
were also at least 400 coal barges and 200 freight barges. Since secession and
war had virtually halted all river traffic, most of these vessels were idle and
available for purchase or leasing.[1]

The river study also showed that facilities for building boats and maintaining those in service existed on the Ohio River, at Mound City, Illinois;
Madison and New Albany, Indiana; Cincinnati, Ohio; Wheeling, Virginia;
and Pittsburgh, Pennsylvania. There were also yards on the Mississippi,
notably at St. Louis.

Supplying any fleet with coal was a potential problem. Although there were plenty of barges to haul it, the nearest supply above Cairo was at Caseyville, over 100 miles up the Ohio, and low water in summer restricted its transport. Pittsburgh coal was rated the best, but it was located even farther upstream.[2] The report found favor with Gen. Winfield Scott in Washington, who forwarded it to staff officers in the War Department. It was accompanied by an outline of the rivers, describing the narrow channels and shallow water that were so characteristic of the region.

War planners now had something to work with. It was obvious that a new type of warship was needed for service on the western waters, a type specifically designed to operate in a unique environment. John Lenthall, chief of the navy's bureau of construction, submitted a design of a shallow-draft side-wheel vessel. This and all other designs were forwarded to Samuel M. Pook, an experienced naval architect and contractor, for review. Building a boat from the keel up would take time, however, and the Union needed armed boats right away to help stop contraband war materials flowing to the South from merchants in the North. But if the war continued, armed vessels were also needed to protect key river ports from raids and, sooner or later, accompany the army in cutting its way through the heart of the South.

As vital as this was to the war effort, in reality the navy wasn't too excited about building gunboats for the inland rivers. The brass saw little chance of any of the ship-to-ship fighting or deep-water sailing that were the traditions of the U.S. Navy. It was clear, too, that the naval war in the West would be totally in support of army operations. Because of the navy's reluctance and the total lack of naval facilities in the West, the building of the first gunboats would be by civilian contract under the auspices of the War Department, not the navy.

Early in the war, Gen. John Frémont, who commanded in the West, was one of the first leaders to recognize the need for armed boats on the rivers and requested a naval officer to serve as his point man in the matter. Commander John Rodgers was ordered west by the War Department in May. His mission was to build a gunboat fleet from scratch.

A career naval officer, Rodgers felt that the building of an inland fleet was the job of the navy, not the army or the War Department. Letting his pride of service cloud his judgment, and stretching his limited authority up to the breaking point, he found three river steamboats in Cincinnati that might prove suitable: the *Conestoga, Lexington,* and *Tyler.* On May 20, the navy dispatched naval architect Samuel Pook on temporary assignment to Cincinnati to assist Rodgers in determining their worth. Pook inspected the hulls of the three steamboats, and based on his assessment, Rodgers bought them for $62,000. They apparently were a bargain, for they cost the original owners $97,000 total to build.[3] Since river traffic had virtually ceased due to the war, the immediate financial future did not look good to the boat owners, and many were facing bankruptcy. So when a navy officer happened along offering two-thirds of their value, it is not surprising that the boats were sold.

Rodgers sent the bill of sale to the Navy Department, and in return for his efforts, Naval Secretary Gideon Welles sent it back with an official reprimand. The secretary reminded the junior officer that his job was to aid and advise the army. Actual purchases were to be under its purview and certainly at the army's expense. The navy would provide nothing more than cannons and crews. Rodgers countered that Gen. George McClellan, commanding the Department of the Ohio, had authorized the purchases, but the flap resulted in a stain on the commander's reputation that would take years to remove.

The three boats were fairly new freight-passenger steamers. The *Lexington* was less than a year old, having made only one trip to New Orleans before the war stopped legal trade. They were all roughly 180 feet long, 40 feet across, and had a draft of 6 feet. They were side-wheelers, each wheel driven independently by a single-cylinder engine. This made them very maneuverable, and their top speed averaged between seven and ten knots. The three boats were taken to shipyards in Cincinnati for their conversion to gunboats.[4]

The top decks were removed, and in their place were built two decks with five inches of oak timbers. The machinery and boilers were also lowered into their holds below the waterline. This arrangement provided protection against musket balls, but anything heavier would pass through as thought it were cutting through butter. Because of their wooden structures and shoddy workmanship, these boats were often called "timberclads" or "bandboxes."

Commander Rodgers oversaw the work and was not altogether pleased. When the carpenters departed the *Lexington* and *Conestoga,* they left curious defects that defied common sense. They left but one ladder to get onto the top deck on the *Lexington,* and only two on the *Conestoga,* and there was no means to get to the lookout house located aft. On the *Tyler,* one could not traverse the length of the boat without walking over the boilers. The deck hatches leading into the pilothouse were small, through which only an "active" (thin) man could enter. Worse, the carpenters left only temporary deck braces in place; these were not only in the way of the guns, but they were also threatening to collapse, bringing down the pilothouse through the deck. The joint work was of poor quality, and the staterooms and cabins were not up to the specifications of the contract. The captain's "round-house" would not do at all, consisting of only a zinc pipe leading from the seat to the outside at a forty-five-degree angle.[5]

There was some discussion as to the appropriateness of one boat's name. The *Tyler* was named for the former president of the United States, who at that time was fully supporting the secession of the South. Commander Rodgers changed her name to the *Taylor,* but she continued to be known by her original name in most of the official reports.[6]

Eventually all of the defects were corrected, and Rodgers now had three boats for service. Painted an ominous black, they were actually no threat at all to the South at this point, since they still needed guns and crews. Getting guns was not an easy task, nor was it a part of the bargain the navy could dodge. On June 18, Rodgers received authorization to go to the depot at Erie, Pennsylvania, to select from the ordnance available. There was not much to choose from. When eventually fitted out, the new gunboats were armed with odd assortment of old 32-pounder and 8-inch naval guns. Experienced gunners were sent from the navy to train the new crews.[7]

Building and arming the boats proved easier than manning them, perhaps the greatest challenge of all. Most of the rivermen had long since joined the army, and the few that remained had little enthusiasm for serving the war under navy discipline on a gunboat. Filling the technical positions was even harder, particularly pilots. It was far more lucrative (and less dangerous) to find employment as a steamboat pilot under contract. Originally, mechanics and engineers were to come from the Atlantic fleet, but it was realized that perhaps it was better that they came from the West. These western men would know the engine types particular to the region. Thomas Merritt, who was the superintendent of building gunboat engines, was made engineer in chief of the fleet and recruited a number of his associates for the service.[8] The only bright spot in recruitment was the number of officer volunteers. These men usually came from the idle steamboats and already knew the rivers. What they didn't know about naval affairs they learned quickly. Overall, though, the frustrating process of recruiting enough men absorbed a large part of the fleet commander's time and energy.

To make up the shortfall, the War Department looked to the army. Many soldiers, perhaps tired of marching and drilling in all types of weather, seemed eager to volunteer for gunboat services. However, most unit commanders were unwilling to grant transfers, which would thin their ranks of good men. When whole units were detached, the boat captains wanted the men, but not their army officers.

The last daunting task Commander Rodgers faced was getting the gunboats down the Ohio to their new base at Cairo. By August, the river was at low ebb, with only three feet of water in some stretches. This situation threatened to maroon the boats in Cincinnati all winter. During a fortunate rise, they were taken down to Louisville, but they were detained again by the shoals just south of the city. After another rise, the timberclads were dragged over the shoals near New Albany, Indiana, and reached Cairo, Illinois, on August 16. Their hull repair and fitting out was then completed, and they then began their illustrious wartime careers.[9]

The three timberclad gunboats, essentially modified steamboats mounting some cannons, were not a technological leap forward in naval warfare, but they proved invaluable the first year of the war. When commissioned, they were the fastest and most heavily armed vessels on the rivers and either swept away the opposition or scared it off. They were also used to escort steamboats, halt contraband traffic, and perform vital reconnaissance patrols. The three wooden gunboats did much to confirm the value of armed craft on the rivers to the War Department and further justified the efforts to build a more formidable river fleet.

Yet the timberclads had a serious liability, which was the lack of armor protection. Without iron plating, the oaken sides could protect the crew and machinery against only small-arms fire. Even a small cannon hidden along the riverbank could inflict serious or fatal damage, and a head-on encounter against a Confederate ironclad would mean disaster. Because the boats were so vulnerable to enemy fire, they usually kept their distance from known enemy fortifications, firing only at long range.

While Commander Rodgers set upon his work, another man on the rivers began a major contribution to the war effort. James B. Eads of St. Louis had made his fame and fortune on the Mississippi River prior to the war. One of the most powerful and influential engineers on the Mississippi, he achieved his station in life by sheer will and hard work salvaging wrecked boats, using a series of recovery vessels and a diving bell he designed and built himself. With the hazards of river navigation of the mid-nineteenth century bringing countless contracts, Eads amassed enough wealth salvaging wrecks and cargo to retire at the age of thirty-seven.[10]

He may have been retired, but he was not inactive. After the outbreak of war, Eads began a campaign to forward the ideas of building a fleet of gunboats to secure the lower Mississippi for the Union. Using well-placed friends in Washington, he traveled there and presented his plans to Lincoln's cabinet on April 29. Eads gained the support from all but Secretary of War Simon Cameron. Secretary of the Navy Gideon Welles, however, saw merit in Eads's proposals and asked him to submit them to him in detail.[11]

As a key element of the plan, the St. Louis riverman urged the establishment of an operational naval base at Cairo, Illinois. With strong river batteries and a fleet of gunboats, control and security of the upper Mississippi and Ohio were assured. This would also block or control the main avenue of commerce in the West. The Tennessee and Cumberland Rivers could still support enemy traffic, but only during high water; however, the proposed batteries and boats at Cairo would neutralize the effectiveness of even this commercial traffic.

At this meeting, Eads incidentally also offered the sale of his *Submarine No. 7* for conversion into a cotton-clad gunboat. The concept was to place $2,000 to $3,000 worth of cotton bales on her deck to protect a battery of 32-pounder cannons. Commander Rodgers later rejected the idea, but this vessel was eventually bought and converted into the *Benton,* rated as the most powerful gunboat in the western fleet during the war.[12]

Although impressed, Naval Secretary Welles deferred making an immediate decision in order to have Eads present his proposal to a board of officers. These officers approved of the plans and forwarded Eads's technical drawings to architect Samuel Pook for study. Meanwhile, Secretary of War Cameron reversed his policies and assigned all work on inland vessels to the army. Disgusted by the chaos of Washington in the early weeks of the war, James Eads returned to St. Louis, but later made two more frustrating visits to the capital. Cameron was finally persuaded to act somewhat by the secretary of the navy, and the matter of building an inland navy was passed to Gen. George B. McClellan, who commanded in the West by that time.

Except for the conversion of the three timberclads, nearly three months passed before any further work was done on inland gunboats. Finally on August 3, 1861, Congress authorized Welles to appoint a board of three skillful naval officers to investigate the plans and specifications that were submitted for the construction or completing of ironclad steamships or steam batteries. Commodore Joseph Smith, Capt. Hiram Paulding, and Commander Charles H. Davis were appointed to the Ironclad Board five days later. This was a small step in the right direction, but it could not produce results quickly enough for Eads.

But James Eads did not have to wait for any decisions from this bureaucratic board of officers, for his persistence paid off. The day before the board met, the War Department finally approved a contract to build gunboats. Advertisements went out across the Midwest, and it turned out that Eads had four competitors. The prominent Missourian calculated his costs and cut his profit margin to the bare minimum. When all the proposals were considered, Eads did indeed have the lowest bid and was awarded a contract for the construction of seven shallow-draft ironclad river gunboats. It was a complicated contract, but the bottom line was that Eads promised to deliver the gunboats in sixty-five days and would pay a stiff penalty for each day they were late. The government was to pay installments to Eads in order to buy materials and lease facilities.

This was a mammoth undertaking, even for a man of Eads's experience. He had to start from scratch. He had never built a gunboat or worked with plate iron before, and he lacked the financial capital to begin construction. Further, the shops to supply the iron and the timber had been idle since the war, and many of the workers were now in the army. Remarkably, within two weeks of the awarding of the contract, Eads had four bondsmen to assure payments and over 4,000 men in eight states at work around the clock cutting timber, rolling iron plate, and making machinery. Shops in Cincinnati and Pittsburgh began to hammer out thirty-five boilers and twenty-one engines.[13] Eads also kept the telegraph lines alive with subcontracts and orders, as he called in every favor that was owed him.

Eads centered his operation at the Union Marine Works in Carondelet, Missouri, near St. Louis. This facility consisted of a series of tracks and cranes that could transport ships in or out of the water, up a shallow slope, then up into one of the sheds where 800 artisans, laborers, and shipwrights were employed. The facility was built in the 1850s by Primus Emerson and used in the past by Eads under lease. Eads also had a rolling mill, twenty-one sawmills, and two foundries working overtime in support of the operation. It was estimated that the boats needed fifteen million feet of white oak and eight hundred tons of iron plating, in addition to bolts, nails, engines, and boilers. Four keels were laid in short order, but even the impressive operation at Carondelet could not make all seven gunboats in the time allotted. Eads subcontracted the Hamelton and Collier Company to build the other three boats at Mound City, Illinois.[14]

James Eads wanted the boats named after Union military leaders. But he was overruled; the new gunboats would bear the names of cities along the Mississippi and Ohio Rivers. Hence, these boats would be known officially as "city-class" gunboats on the naval rosters. The boats of the class were the *Cairo, Carondelet, Cincinnati, Louisville, Mound City, St. Louis* and *Pittsburg*. Five of these boats would take part in the coming campaign.

After forty-five days, the first hull was ready for launching. On October 12, 1861, the *St. Louis* slid into the brown waters of the Mississippi as a large crowd watched. Her sisters followed over the next few days. By being further along in her construction, the *St. Louis* was the first fitted out and was officially commissioned on January 31, 1862. She was the first operational ironclad in the Western Hemisphere, beating the more famous USS *Monitor* by over a month.[15]

What made the rapid construction of the new ironclads possible was a combination of Eads's organizational skills and financial clout, the labor of thousands of men, and the simple design of the boats themselves. Many people of the day found it hard to describe the vessels, having never seen their likes on the rivers before. Made from plans designed in large part by naval architect Samuel Pook, the ironclads were often called "Pook turtles." As they were virtually identical in size and appearance, identification bands were painted on the smokestacks to tell them apart. A general description would say each boat resembled a raft with an iron shed on top. The rectangular casemate had sloped sides, which enclosed the machinery, guns, and paddle wheel to protect them all from enemy fire. The topsides were painted black, below the waterline was red, and the interiors were white.

The new boats were 175 feet long and 51 feet wide and averaged in tonnage at 512. Their shallow draft and paddle wheels allowed them to operate virtually anywhere on the western waters. Five fire-tube boilers and two reciprocating steam engines provided power for each boat, which relied on natural draft. This configuration generated a top speed of only six knots, although this varied slightly by boat. The paddle wheels were located amidships forward of the extreme stern, and protected by the casemates. Although they had two rudders, with the paddle-wheel arrangement and wide beam, the boats would never be called fleet or nimble in their ability to maneuver. They were not particularly fuel-efficient either. The boilers operated at a respectable 140 pounds per square inch steam pressure, but they consumed almost a ton of coal per hour. Surprisingly, the high consumption of coal was not generally considered a liability. Cruising range was less important than it was for the deep-water navy, since this theater of operations measured distances in hundreds of miles not thousands. Also, coal barges could easily accompany the fleet and most often did.

For protection, the hulls and superstructures generally were built of white oak. The casemate sloped at a forty-five-degree angle and ranged in thickness from twenty-six inches on the forward surfaces to nineteen inches aft. Over this was fixed 122 tons of charcoal iron. Each two-inch-thick armor plate was thirteen inches wide by eight to eleven feet long. The armor protection was not complete, though. It was arranged on the forward slope of the casemate and down only two-thirds of its length. The aft third of the casemate was without armor and particularly vulnerable. So, too, were the machinery and boilers. The pilothouse was armored, but the decks were not. As a result, the city-class boats could stand up to shot against their forward quarter, but were vulnerable to their rear and from plunging shot, fired from above. The crews thus had great incentive to keep their boats facing the enemy.

The city-class ironclads were armed with an assortment of cannons that varied from boat to boat. During the war, the vessels received new weapons with each refit. During the Fort Henry–Fort Donelson campaign, each boat had a collection of 32-pounders, 8-inch Dahlgrens, obsolete army rifled 42-pounders, and smaller 12-pounders. These were arranged to fire with three forward, four to each broadside, and two aft. The heaviest cannons were placed forward. It was soon found, though, that the guns had a limited ability to elevate their muzzles, restricting their ability to engage targets and fortifications along the high bluffs on the western rivers.

Although the boats were built in a remarkably short time, James Eads did not meet the deadlines that were called for in the contract. Obviously this was a very ambitious undertaking, but work was slowed when Eads had trouble collecting the promised government payment installments. Without the money up front, he had difficulty obtaining materials and had to reach into his own pocket to make up the difference. There were also a number of modifications and additions that slowed progress. In the end, Eads won the dispute and was paid in full, but the process took months.

While the city-class boats took shape, another was readied to join the growing fleet. By order of General Frémont, the 251-ton *New Era* was purchased from the Wiggins Ferry Company in St. Louis on September 20, 1861, for $20,000. Originally built in 1856, she was first converted into a wooden gunboat, then later returned to the yards for conversion into an ironclad. She would be the only ironclad gunboat in the Fort Henry–Fort Donelson campaign that was not of the city class, although her general appearance was similar.

One of her first missions was a reconnaissance of Fort Henry on November 6, 1861. Upon her return, Commander William "Dirty Bill" Porter assumed command and renamed her the *Essex*, after his father's old ship. He also oversaw her extensive conversion into an ironclad. She was greatly enlarged into a center-wheel steamer but retained her original two engines and four boilers. Her length was 159 feet; beam, 47 feet, 6 inches; depth, 5 feet, 10 inches; and draft, about 6 feet. In her early days as a wooden gunboat, this draft prohibited her from taking an active part in the river reconnoiters during the low waters of summer and autumn, so she served most of that time on the Ohio in the vicinity of Paducah.[16]

The armor of the *Essex* was thinner than that of the city-class boats. The forward casemate eventually had only one inch of iron plate placed over thirty inches of oak, with an inch of gutta-percha resin sandwiched in between. The resin was supposed to help absorb the impact of heavy shot, but later it did not stand up well to the hot and humid climate of the Deep South. In the high humidity, it melted or rotted away. The sides had one inch of iron plate over just sixteen inches of oak and the resin. During the campaign, the *Essex* carried three 9-inch Dahlgren smoothbores forward, one 10-inch Dahlgren smoothbore in the stern pivot, and one 32-pounder and one 12-pounder howitzer in the broadside.

As a whole, the river ironclads were not a significant leap forward in naval technology either, but they certainly were in naval capability. Yet they, too, had limitations. The boilers and machinery operated within very narrow safety limits, and the furnaces relied upon a natural draft, rather than having fans to assist the draft through the fires. As a result, the ironclads were chronically short of power to move their heavy bulks in the untamed currents of the western waters.

The gunboats' firepower was generally adequate in size and amount, but certain models of cannons proved unreliable and even unsafe. A primary example is the mounting of old army 42-pounders in the city-class boats. These guns were obsolete for the day and prone to bursting when fired. They were originally cast as smoothbores, and when they were later rifled, they lost the metal cut away for the grooves. They were then called upon to endure the increased strain of firing projectiles with less strength than had been allowed for a round ball of about half the weight.[17] Later in the war, when the crews received replacements many of the old 42s were simply heaved overboard. As the war progressed, the boats received newer and better guns with each refit, but their basic effectiveness remained essentially the same.

The armor plate also had limitations. It was placed to protect the front and only two-thirds of the length of Eads's ironclads. The rear third of these boats had no armor at all, and neither did the upper decks. The ironclads were designed and expected to fight head-on, showing only the armored surfaces to the enemy. The slope of the armor was intended to protect the boats from enemy fire traveling in a low arc, causing it to glance off. This would mean fire primarily from enemy gunboats and floating batteries. This design was not unreasonable in the narrow confines of the western rivers. However, fire from longer ranges or from the bluffs along the river would require the armor to absorb the entire mass of the strike, so heavy shot placed squarely on the armor stood a good chance of penetrating, if fired at the right angle. And the lack of armor on the upper deck made the boats particularly vulnerable to shot lobbed from above. Plunging fire from cannons placed on high riverbanks above could easily penetrate the thin wooden deck of the casemate and bring calamity to the crew and machinery within. One shot into a boiler would disable the boat, and the crew would be killed by hot steam.

An event about as significant as the building of the gunboats was the arrival of the man who would lead them into their first battle. Through the summer and autumn, Commander Rodgers was doing all that was possible to build a river fleet. Shortly after the contract was signed to build the ironclads with Eads, General Frémont placed a request to the War Department for a replacement for the diligent commander. From the East, a veteran officer by the name of Andrew Hull Foote headed to his new assignment.

Andrew Foote was born in New Haven, Connecticut, on September 12, 1806, his father being the former governor and a U.S. senator. Foote won appointment to West Point in 1822, but after a few months, at age sixteen, he entered the U.S. Navy as an acting midshipman. His first cruise was on the *Grampus* in the squadron of Commodore David Porter, which was sent to break up piracy in the West Indies. Foote spent eighteen years at sea around the globe.

He served a tour of duty onshore in Philadelphia as an instructor, then was sent to sea again as a lieutenant on the *Cumberland*. After another brief tour onshore, he was given command of the brig *Perry* and patrolled the coast of Africa. Later, while in command of the *Portsmouth,* he won the praise and admiration of his superiors by distinguished service in China. There, four forts in the Canton River fired on his ship. In response, Foote landed a force and carried them by storm.

Foote insisted on total abstinence for the crews, mandatory religious services and observance of the Sabbath, and he himself rarely swore. By sheer will and personality, he enforced these unconventional rules without a mutiny. He also was a prolific writer and wrote of his many experiences in Africa and Japan. It was said that he could preach, fight, or pray with equal facility.

At the outbreak of war, Foote was the executive officer of the Brooklyn Naval Yard. He was promoted to captain in July 1861. A month later, he was ordered to the rivers of the West. This time, to avoid any misunderstanding about who was responsible for the river fleet, Captain Foote's orders specifically stated that he must make requisitions from the War Department through the ranking army general. Whatever the army could not furnish, the navy would then endeavor to supply, but placing priority on the deep-water navy.[18]

Captain Foote arrived in St. Louis and officially and amicably replaced Rodgers on September 5. Foote asked him to stay on, but with the arrival of more senior naval officers, Rodgers applied for and received a transfer to the Atlantic fleet in mid-September. In the months prior to the campaign, Foote remained mostly in St. Louis, where he supervised the building of the new gunboats and orchestrated the recruitment of crews and requisition of ordnance and supplies.[19]

Since the river gunboats were a project of the War Department, Foote took his orders at first from General Frémont. When operating on the rivers, both he and the commanders of the operational gunboats took orders from either the army district commander or the ranking officer in the field. Remarkably, this arrangement caused no serious problems, primarily because of the cooperative spirit among individual officers. Foote in particular took a liking to Gen. Ulysses S. Grant in Cairo, and their spirit of cooperation became legendary. It was also a key factor in the coming campaign. What made this arrangement easier for Foote was a swift promotion to flag rank, putting him on par with the numerous brigadier generals of the army.

Foote had a number of challenges, but his major concern was recruiting enough men for the new boats being built by Eads. Like Rodgers before him, finding officers did not present much of a problem. Regular navy officers would command the boats, and he brought along a number of young officers from the Atlantic fleet to do so. The other officers were men formerly in the employ of river steamers, who became volunteer officers. Finding crewmen was another matter; they were in critically short supply. Flag Officer Foote sent countless letters to the Navy and War Departments on the subject and sent Lt. Leonard Paulding to Chicago to recruit all the men he could find.[20]

Finding suitable men for the gunboat fleet was a constant challenge up to and beyond the campaign. The result of the combined efforts of Foote, Paulding, and the Navy Department was an interesting cross section of American society. Men recruited for the crews included seasoned veterans from the navy, riverboat hands, and mariners from the Great Lakes. Others, sometimes the majority of a boat's crew, were army artillerymen and even infantry units detailed for the task.

Each new boat needed a minimum of about 175 men, but by October, Foote had but 100 men total. There was some relief the next month when an additional 500 showed up from the East. That meant he needed 1,100 more, but even as late as January 1862, Foote had but 589 present for duty. The boats were almost ready, but he didn't have enough recruits to man them.

During this same time, there also was a dubious experiment in the building of heavy mortar boats designed to shell fortifications into submission. They were just large enough to carry a 13-inch mortar and its crew, but they had no means of locomotion. This necessitated towing them into position. President Lincoln had a personal interest in the project, and many senior officers had high expectations of their performance. But after many months of frustrating labor, they still were not ready for the Fort Henry–Fort Donelson campaign.

Despite the limitations of the boats and initial lack of crews, the Western Flotilla served successfully throughout the war, chiefly because the gunboats were generally better than anything the Confederates could launch, and far more numerous. Besides the battles for Memphis and New Orleans and the fight with the short-lived CSS *Arkansas,* there were few instances where the South seriously challenged the Union dominance of the western rivers. With no substantial fleet on those waters, the Confederates had to rely upon fixed fortifications and hidden batteries to combat the Union river fleet.

Meanwhile, using the gunboats as escort, Union strategists could plan on carrying large numbers of troops and then supplying them by boat. As long as there was enough water, armies could move at will throughout the year, avoiding the poor roads that turned to mud after a heavy rain. This capability is also what made the Fort Henry–Fort Donelson campaign possible.

CHAPTER THREE

Autumn of Blunders

September–December 1861

DESPITE THE ENORMITY OF THE SITUATION FOR THE CONFEDERATES IN THE West and the slow progress in building defenses, all was not lost. During the long months of summer. a man had crossed the western frontier from his post in California to answer his new nation's call. Albert Sidney Johnston had arrived.

A key Confederate figure in the coming campaign, Albert Sidney Johnston graduated from West Point in 1826 near the top of his class and served with competence in the Black Hawk War. He eventually resigned from the army after eight years to tend to an ailing wife. When she died of tuberculosis two years later, Johnston moved to Texas and enlisted in the new republic's army. He quickly rose through the ranks and within a year was made its commanding general. Thereafter, Johnston served for two years as the Lone Star Republic's secretary of war. In this position, he gained valuable experience in directing fractious volunteer units, as well as defending a vast frontier with wholly inadequate resources. During the Mexican War, Johnston initially commanded a Texas regiment, then was made the inspector general of all volunteer troops in Zachary Taylor's army. Taylor was so impressed by his performance that he later said Johnston was "the best soldier he had ever commanded."[1] Johnston fought alongside West Point classmate and good friend Jefferson Davis.

After the war, Johnston tried for three unsuccessful years to earn a living at planting. Giving it up for good, he rejoined the U.S. Army and received command of the famous 2nd Cavalry Regiment. Sent west, Johnston earned a reputation as a fierce fighter and a great leader of men. In 1857, he was detached from the regiment and promoted to brevet brigadier general. He led an expedition against the Mormons in Utah, then was sent to California in 1860 to assume direction of the Pacific Coast Department. Johnston's renown soared to great heights, and many considered him the army's best general and the likely heir to the aging General in Chief Winfield Scott.[2]

This was not to be, though. When Texas seceded, Johnston resigned his commission and decided to see his old friend Jefferson Davis. He was still in California, however, and had to spend the next few months traveling over the Great Plains. When Johnston arrived in Richmond on September 5, Davis was ecstatic. He saw that Johnston was the solution to his problems in the West. General Polk had earlier expressed this sentiment to Davis, asking him to place Johnston in command of the Western Department, and many others in government echoed the bishop-general in Memphis.[3] At their first meeting, Davis immediately commissioned Albert Sidney Johnston as a full general, with his date of rank retroactive to May 30. This act made him the second-highest-ranking officer in the Confederacy.

Johnston was indeed to command the Western Department, and Jefferson Davis gave him the mission of defending the western half of the Confederacy from invasion from the North. Johnston was charged with forming a great army to defend this vast department and bringing about order and efficiency. It was a daunting task, but Johnston seemed a man big enough for the job. He had shown that he could mold the individualistic men of the West into armies that could fight. He had also served at the highest levels of command in Texas and had run an Army department, even if for only a short time. As a result, he had gained an aura of success. "I hoped and expected that I had others who would prove to be generals," Davis explained, "but I knew I had one, and that was Sidney Johnston." Many others thought so, too, and believed that he would be the greatest general of the South.[4] Johnston quickly left Richmond for Nashville and his new assignment. He was on the train en route to his new post when he got some unexpected news. Troops from his department had invaded Kentucky.

General Polk had been busy building the forts to block the Mississippi and had occupied and fortified the town of New Madrid, Missouri, in July 1861. They were good sites from which to prevent Union invaders from descending the river, but the bishop-general was looking at still another site farther upstream. Polk specifically had his eye on Columbus, Kentucky, which was situated on a high bluff over the river and was an even more formidable obstacle than New Madrid. Kentucky was still neutral, however, and no one in Richmond had authorized any such move.

Working behind the scenes was Polk's subordinate, Gen. Gideon Pillow. Pillow was impatient for action and felt the Federals were about to occupy

Columbus themselves. Some today believe he simply wanted a significant victory to secure a promotion. He incessantly bombarded General Polk with proposals and requests for authorization to occupy the town. Over time, Polk was eventually convinced that it was indeed vital to seize Columbus and Paducah as well, in spite of any repercussions of a breach of Kentucky neutrality.[5] Using slight Union violations of Kentucky neutrality as a pretext, Pillow executed Polk's plan and occupied Columbus on September 3, 1861. There Pillow began to entrench, expecting a Union attack at any moment. This unauthorized expedition effectively ended Kentucky's neutrality and set the wheels in motion for a Federal invasion of Tennessee.

Up to this time, Kentucky was at least sympathetic toward the Confederacy, but the occupation of Columbus prompted a strong rebuke from the formerly friendly Governor Magoffin. In a resolution passed by the state legislature, he wrote: "In obedience to the subjoined resolution . . . the Government of the Confederate States, the State of Tennessee, and all others concerned, are hereby informed that Kentucky expects the Confederate or Tennessee troops to be withdrawn from her soil unconditionally."[6]

In Richmond, the Confederate government was caught completely off guard by Polk's authorized occupation of Columbus. The reaction was confused and indecisive. The secretary of war ordered the forces withdrawn immediately, but Polk persuaded Davis to let him stay.[7] Davis was particularly embarrassed, since he had sent a letter to Governor Magoffin the previous week reaffirming Kentucky's neutrality. But the Confederate president now reasoned that since the neutrality was irreparably breached, military considerations overruled political ones. The fact that the ultimatum was ignored infuriated the governor and many people of the state, and in the end, it pushed Kentucky irrevocably into the Union hands. Now, without a neutral Kentucky to act as a buffer zone, the weak Confederate line was exposed to attack.

If Richmond was indecisive, a certain Kentuckian was not. During the months of Kentucky neutrality, Simon Bolivar Buckner tried to keep Union and Confederate forces out of the state with a fair degree of success. That was until General Pillow's occupation of Columbus. Buckner had used the time to prepare for the eventuality of casting his lot with the South by selling his property in the North and getting his personal affairs in order. He had hoped that Kentucky would join the Confederacy, but when that possibility became highly unlikely, he went south to Nashville to offer his services. He wrote to authorities in Richmond in September to inquire about the possibility of receiving an officer's commission. He did not have to wait long.[8]

Word of Pillow's invasion reached General Johnston when his train reached Chattanooga. He unknowingly echoed Davis's view that since Kentucky's neutrality was effectively over, military considerations now had priority. Johnston met with Gen. Felix K. Zollicoffer, in command of eastern Tennessee, and ordered him to occupy the Cumberland Gap, the historic gateway into the region. Johnston was misinformed of Pillow's movements, however, and therefore was operating under false assumptions. Johnston thought Pillow was closing in on Paducah and the strategic mouths of the Tennessee and Cumberland Rivers, not realizing that he had stopped and was fortifying Columbus. With Columbus *and* Paducah occupied, Johnston reasoned, the left flank of his department was anchored and the western rivers blocked. Zollicoffer would be the anchor on the east flank. What then remained was to secure the center of the line by moving north from Nashville and occupying Bowling Green, thus blocking the railroad that ran up to Louisville.[9] Johnston scraped together about 4,000 troops that were stationed around Nashville. He then sent the small army north by rail to Bowling Green, occupying it on September 18. The man in command of this little army was Simon Bolivar Buckner.

While waiting for his commission in Nashville, Buckner was "drafted" by General Johnston. He did not have a Confederate commission yet, but Buckner was still technically a brigadier general in the Kentucky State Guard. Johnston formally appointed him a brigadier in the Confederate service, with final approval to come from Richmond a few weeks later. Buckner's first mission was completed quickly, and Bowling Green was occupied without military opposition. The city itself wasn't much, but it was at the crossing of the Louisville and Nashville Railroad over the Big Barren River. A little to the south branched the Memphis and Ohio Railroad from the Louisville and Nashville. This accident of geography made Bowling Green a gateway through which all armies approaching Nashville from the North must pass.[10]

But there was a glitch to General Johnston's hastily devised plan. Up in Cairo, Gen. Ulysses S. Grant had been anxious to advance and considered the Confederate invasion of Kentucky a blessing. The day after Pillow marched into Columbus, Grant packed some transports with two regiments and occupied Paducah, sealing the strategic mouth of the Tennessee River. A Confederate officer by the name of Lloyd Tilghman was in the city with his staff and a company of recruits when Grant's flotilla arrived. The startled officer gathered up his soldiers and departed by rail in great haste. Tilghman would offer a little more resistance the next time they met. Interestingly, this operation by General Grant was completely on his own initiative.

He did send a telegram to General Frémont asking for permission prior to departing Cairo, though. Grant returned a few days later to find an answer giving him permission lying on his desk. He also found a reprimand for directly contacting the Kentucky legislature without going through proper channels.[11]

The race to occupy Kentucky was on, and the Confederates had already lost. For although Columbus was a powerful position, without Paducah a Union thrust down the Tennessee River could cut the Memphis and Ohio Railroad and isolate it. Fortunately for Grant, Johnston did not believe his own forces were strong enough to push the invaders across the river, and instead focused his attention on building an army. In the meantime General Grant sent any spare forces he had to occupy as many key points in the state as possible.

Brigadier General Charles F. Smith was brought into the district and assumed command of the forces Grant placed in Paducah on September 7. He quickly sent four companies to occupy Smithland, thus sealing the Cumberland. Smith was an old army veteran, having been on continuous service for the last thirty years. In fact, most of the West Pointers knew him from their cadet years, while he served there as a highly respected instructor and commandant.

Smith had won a brevet promotion to colonel during the Mexican War for gallantry and had only recently been promoted to brigadier general. As such, he was Grant's junior and under his departmental command. This situation caused some bad feelings among the career officers, who considered it an injustice that a regular officer was placed under a volunteer general who had received his promotion through congressional favors. Sensitive to these feelings, Grant was gracious to Smith and always treated him with the deep respect he was due. Smith, on the other hand, seemed proud of his former cadet and gratified with his success. To his utmost credit, Smith was always supportive and never jealous of Grant.

Grant's basic leadership style quickly became apparent during this period and would not change much over the course of the war. His methods were always simple, direct, and to the point. He did virtually everything with a specific purpose in mind and on his own. Grant had a very small staff, and even when he later became general in chief commanding more than half a million men, his staff consisted of only fourteen officers, which was no larger than those of some division commanders. He did not rely on his staff, but upon himself. He wrote nearly all of his documents with his own hand and seldom dictated any. He took time to hear all friendly suggestions with unvarying politeness, and then did exactly as he saw fit. Grant also trusted his subordinate commanders thoroughly, giving only general directions, not hampering them with petty instructions.[12]

More telling, Grant showed in his bold movements, such as at Paducah, that he never worried too much of what the enemy was going to do to him. Instead, he thought in terms of what he meant to do to the enemy. As a result, his seniors sometimes thought of him as rash, because he didn't share their fears.

After sending Buckner off to Bowling Green with every man he could find, General Johnston set up his headquarters and focused upon the daunting task of defending the western Confederacy. To do this, there were about 7,000 men under Polk at Columbus, the 4,000 with Buckner at Bowling Green, and about that many under Zollicoffer at the Cumberland Gap. Most of these units were insufficiently armed and as green as they came. These regiments were also far too few in numbers to wage an effective defense. Johnston sent two emissaries to the governors of Alabama and Georgia to ask for arms for the new units being raised in his department, and wrote an urgent appeal to his friend Jefferson Davis. These combined efforts were mostly in vain. To help alleviate the shortage, Governor Harris issued an appeal across Tennessee for the people to bring in all of their weapons for purchase by the state.[13] This measure did not bring forth a substantial number of weapons. Those that were obtained were of a wide variety of calibers, which further aggravated the ammunition problem.

The procurement of arms and raising troops took a lion's share of Johnston's time. As a result, he did not often leave his headquarters in order to inspect the defenses in his department. Instead, he sent trusted subordinates to make inspections and report back to him. Most of the officers assigned to his headquarters had received their commissions from the states before his arrival, so he had to rely on the past judgment of the states in selecting quality officers of talent.

By the end of September, Johnston moved his headquarters from Nashville to what was essentially the front line in Bowling Green. There he began to see disaster coming. From the beginning, he had too much territory to defend and too few men with which to defend it, even though the numbers were improving somewhat. At the anchor of the Confederate line in the west, Polk held Columbus with 12,000 men, while Forts Henry and Donelson were still unfinished and undermanned, with no more than 4,000 men between them. There were only 15,000 soldiers at Bowling Green, the strong point in the center of the line, and only a small garrison at Clarksville, a key railroad junction to the southeast. Zollicoffer and his small army of 8,000 held the east flank of the line at the Cumberland Gap.[14]

Although the number of troops was increasing, when compared with those of the enemy, the situation looked grim. Beyond this thin gray line, Johnston believed that General Buell was about to march on Bowling Green from Louisville with 80,000 men. This estimate was far too high, and of the forty-five thousand troops Buell did have, about one-third were not ready for action. Buell was also not confident that he could move south without significant reinforcements, but his aggressive patrols kept the garrison at Bowling Green, and Johnston in particular, on edge. Over in Cairo, Grant had about 20,000 men at his disposal, and he was anxious to use them. He wasn't authorized to advance, but he would keep the Confederates alert by his patrols and gunboat reconnoiters up the inland rivers.[15]

In desperation, Johnston turned to psychological warfare to hold off an enemy invasion. Statements doubling or tripling his strength appeared in all the Southern newspapers, and editors hinted at imminent offensives to liberate Kentucky. Johnston also kept his regiments marching about and active for all to see, which gave the impression of larger numbers than actually were present. The effects were mixed. Buell was frozen into inaction and pleaded for reinforcements to stop the anticipated Rebel hordes. This was to Johnston's advantage, in that it gave him time to raise an army and prepare defenses, but there was also a downside. A false sense of security fell over the Confederacy. Johnston's calls for reinforcements went largely unheeded because it was felt that any available troops could be put to better use elsewhere.[16]

As Albert Sidney Johnston labored to build an army, his enemy was in motion. In St. Louis, Frémont learned that the Confederates planned to reinforce their forces in Arkansas and strike. To prevent this, he ordered Grant in Cairo to make a feint toward Columbus to tie down the Confederates there. Initially, Grant sent about 3,000 men under Col. Richard Oglesby into southeastern Missouri to relieve pressure on Frémont. Grant was soon informed, though, that a large number of Confederate reinforcements were moving into Missouri that were on a collision course with Oglesby's column. Grant immediately sent reinforcements to Oglesby with additional orders for him to stop and rendezvous with Grant, and he also ordered Gen. Charles F. Smith in Paducah to march into southwestern Kentucky. Grant himself loaded five regiments of infantry on transports and with the two gunboats, *Lexington* and *Tyler,* steamed toward Columbus as well. His overall objective was to pin down the forces he was told were moving toward Oglesby.[17]

On November 7, 1861, Grant landed his force on the western bank of the Mississippi, where he encountered a Confederate force of about equal

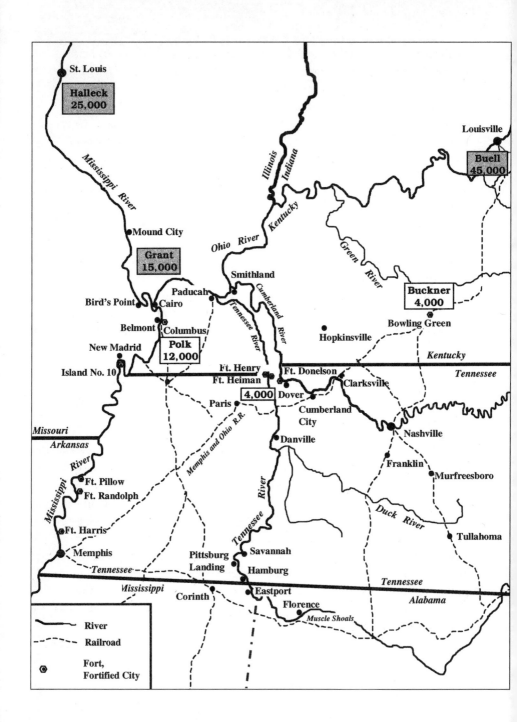

Area of Operations, September 1861

number. The two sides quickly drew up in opposing parallel lines of battle and blazed away at each other. The Confederate commander was none other than Gideon Pillow, who provided a gallant example, but his placement of his troops was unwise. The two opposing sides advanced and receded, but the Confederates gave way in the end, retreating until they were under the protection of the heavy guns of Columbus. There Pillow eventually rallied his troops, and when reinforced from Columbus, he went on the offensive. In a bold move, Pillow directed further reinforcements from across the river to land above Grant, thus threatening to cut off his route of escape.

After their victory, the green troops of Grant's tiny army had broken ranks to loot and pillage the captured Confederate camp, in spite of the best efforts of the officers to keep them in the ranks. When it was clear the enemy was returning in force, Grant ordered the camp burned to stop the looting. The tactical victory for the Federals became a fighting retreat back to the boats, with the Confederates in hot pursuit. The Federals were able to remove two captured cannons with their caissons, a wagon, twenty horses, and some prisoners, but at the landing, one regiment was unaccounted for, being separated by the terrain. Grant rode back in haste to look for it but found only a mob of howling Confederates moving at the double-quick. Spinning around, he made it back to the boats, narrowly avoiding death or capture. The missing regiment was later located and picked up farther upstream.[18]

Grant seemed to try to downplay the whole affair, probably uncomfortable with the high number of casualties. Each side thought it had won a victory, but little actual damage was done. Grant wrote: "We drove the Rebels completely from Belmont, burned their tents and carried off their artillery. For want of horses to draw them we had to leave all but two pieces on the field. The victory was complete. Our loss is not far from 250 killed, wounded, and missing. The Rebel loss must have been from 500–600, including 130 prisoners brought from the field."[19]

The battle of Belmont was inconclusive, but it showed that Grant was willing to fight and was not going to wait for summer to do it. Gideon Pillow handled himself courageously but was rash in his attacks and showed little appreciation for the terrain. Although he had the opportunity to defend from a covered position, he chose instead to form his lines in an open cornfield. There he received Grant's attack, and then launched an all-or-nothing bayonet charge against his foe, which was wisely using the timber for cover. Such tactics needlessly threw away the lives of the men he commanded. Yet it was Pillow and his conspicuous gallantry that rallied the routed Confederates and ultimately drove off the invaders.[20]

The Belmont operation also had another direct impact on the coming campaign. While Grant pushed down the Mississippi, Gen. C. F. Smith's feint into Kentucky took him toward Fort Henry to tie down any Confederate forces there and to keep a jittery Polk guessing as to where an attack may come. An added benefit to Smith's operations was the opportunity to conduct excellent reconnoiters of the river defenses. Smith's report reveals that the Federals were beginning to recognize that Fort Henry was not that formidable: "It is a strong earthwork on the water front, but not nearly so on the land side. It has three 24 or 32-pounders, one or two 8-inch Columbiads, and the remainder of field guns, in all from fourteen to sixteen." Smith also mentions "Fort Gavock or Fort MacGavock or something else," but he did not know anything about its armament.[21] He was referring to Fort Donelson, where Randal McGavock of the 10th Tennessee often commanded on a temporary basis.

A few days after the battle at Belmont, Polk was injured during the test-firing of a cannon. Flush from his "victory," Pillow assumed command at Columbus during Polk's long period of convalescence. With this golden opportunity, Pillow was anything but idle. He continued to strengthen the defenses at Columbus and kept the telegraph wires buzzing with messages. On November 25, he wired headquarters reporting that 15,000 reinforcements had reached Cairo and a host of others were in St. Louis, which were all about to descend the river. A week later, Pillow was calling for an advance on Cairo. Buried in the message traffic was an ominous note: "I think they will simply make a demonstration against this position [Columbus] to hold the force here. Will use their large water power to capture Fort Henry and pass up and take possession of the Tennessee bridge and separate [Bowling Green] and General Polk."[22] By now, though, what little credibility Pillow still had was worn very thin.

When Polk returned to duty on December 7, Pillow found himself subordinate again, and under a man he considered unqualified. The issue came to a head when Pillow complained both privately and publicly that Polk had failed to support him at Belmont and that Jefferson Davis had intentionally and systematically slighted him from the onset. Shortly after Christmas, Pillow resigned from the service in frustration and returned home.

In the weeks after Belmont, there was a major change in command of the Union armies in the West. General Frémont had finally pushed past the limits of Washington's tolerance. His financial dealings were highly suspect, and he had also taken it upon himself to issue a proclamation emancipating slaves in Missouri. The wayward general had clearly gone too far, and President Lincoln came under fire from leaders of the vital border states. A messenger bearing the order of recall finally caught up with Frémont during his campaign against Gen. Sterling Price in southwestern Missouri. Major General David Hunter assumed temporary command until the arrival of Maj. Gen. Henry W. Halleck on November 20.

Henry Halleck was forty-six years old at this time, and a native of Westernville, New York. He had attended Union College and was schooled in Napoleonic tactics at the U.S. Military Academy, graduating third in his class in 1839. He published *Elements of Military Art and Science* in 1846 and was sent to California during the war with Mexico. Halleck arrived too late to see combat, but he was active in building fortifications and served as secretary of state to the military governor. By 1854, he resigned his captain's commission to practice law and to finish a work titled *International Law*. His scholarly pursuits earned him the nickname "Old Brains," which would later become derogatory in nature. Halleck's Mexican War reputation led to his appointment as a major general, dating from August 19, 1861. He was chosen to command the Department of the Missouri chiefly because of his renowned administrative skills, so that he could untangle the chaotic mess of fraud and disorder that Frémont had created. Once he straightened out the problems from his headquarters in St. Louis, Halleck then settled down to more routine administrative duties. General Halleck would have a profound impact on the life and career of Ulysses S. Grant.[23]

For Grant, this meant political and personal obstacles to overcome. Although he had impressive credentials, Henry Halleck was not an easy man to work for. The nature of his job and his personality often provoked antagonism, hatred, and contempt. Halleck's strengths were organizing, coordinating, planning, and managing. He could also advise and suggest, and he sometimes ordered subordinates where and when to make a move, but he never was comfortable doing it himself. Halleck seldom worked openly, and as a department commander, he was always at headquarters, separated and aloof from the men. His decisions were the result of neither snap judgments nor friendly discussion, but calculated thinking. He was also prone to violent hatred and never cultivated close relationships. Overall, he generated no love, confidence, or respect.[24]

As the Union armies grew, Lincoln wanted them to advance; the questions were where and how. Just who authored the plan for the attack on Forts Henry and Donelson is still a matter of speculation. It seems that just about everyone involved sought to take at least some of the credit. One of the earliest anecdotes takes place in December, when Halleck supposedly discussed the option with his chief of staff, George Cullum, and William T. Sherman. Assuming the role of an instructor, Halleck pointed to a map on his table and took a pencil in hand, asking, "Where is the rebel line?" Cullum took the pencil and drew a line through Bowling Green, Forts Henry and Donelson, and Columbus, the three concentrations of the Confederates in the West. Halleck quizzed his students: "Now, where is the proper place to break it?" Almost in unison, both Cullum and Sherman replied, "Naturally the center." The Confederates had the advantage of interior lines—that is, the ability to quickly shift forces—and striking the center was the best way to offset this, according to the textbook. By striking the center, the attacker could fan out and disrupt the defense, or it could reinforce or retreat as necessary. Halleck took the pencil from Cullum and drew a perpendicular line across the first one. It bisected at the point of Fort Henry. Halleck declared, "That's the true line of operations."[25]

In another story, the lowly Col. Charles Whittlesey of the 20th Ohio sent a letter to Halleck even earlier, in November. It suggested a "movement by land between the Tennessee and Cumberland Rivers, the flanks to be covered by gunboats and supplies carried by transports."[26] Countless others on both sides of the conflict certainly thought of such a movement in slightly different variations. To the professional and armchair generals alike, a strike up the Tennessee or Cumberland was a fairly obvious way to wreak havoc on the Confederates. What most people expected, though, was for the Confederates to be ready for such a move by massing large numbers of troops against any force trying to pull it off. It would be pretty audacious, too, for a Union army to strike off on its own deep into hostile territory and expect to take and hold a prepared fortification.

Now Halleck was not known for his bold and daring moves, and he was not ready for one of them, at least yet. He was still busy pacifying Missouri, and he did not have enough troops to conduct the scale of operation envisioned. Repeated requests to advance were denied to an increasingly frustrated Grant.

Over in Louisville, Halleck's new rival was under the scrutiny of the president. Brigadier General Don Carlos Buell took command of the Department of the Ohio just a week before Halleck's arrival and was also under pressure to advance. Lincoln particularly wanted the liberation of the strongly loyal counties of eastern Tennessee, but Buell was in no mood to operate independently in that rugged terrain. Poor roads, lack of a functional railroad, and an outrageous overestimation of the Confederate abilities stalled any such movement. In the meantime, Buell wrote to his "dear friend" George McClellan proposing various movements and offensives, each of which called for numbers of men that were impossible to assemble at the time. It was clear Buell had no real intention of any advance from his base at Louisville for weeks or months to come.

Halleck was also hesitant to advance, for he felt he had no reliable general to lead an expedition. Grant was a West Point graduate who had done a good job so far in organizing his forces and maintaining discipline. This did not convince Halleck that he was a suitable field commander, though. It also was no secret that Grant had left the army because of his drinking problem, and that he had been a failure in just about everything afterward. In truth, Grant was where he was in great part because of a combination of luck and the support of his protégé, Congressman Washburne of Galena, Illinois. Because of this wide cultural and professional rift, Halleck and Grant did not get along well. Halleck thought of Grant as brave but reckless, and Grant probably felt overshadowed and ignored by his boss. Halleck was also one of many who believed Gen. Charles F. Smith had been unjustly put under Grant and blamed him for it.

In contrast to his senior officers, Grant was willing to advance. He long realized the significance of the Tennessee River and thought the quickest and surest way to strike the Confederates was up this waterway, with Fort Henry as the target. He also saw great potential in using ironclad gunboats to assist in the endeavor. Intelligence reports and gunboat reconnaissance showed that the twin forts upriver were still incomplete.[27] The center of the Confederate line clearly was weakest here, and a bold thrust up the river seemed to have a good chance of success. Such a move would support the Union's grand strategy of retaking the Mississippi River by threatening the Confederate fortress at Columbus and subsequently the city of Memphis. A push farther up the Tennessee River could also reach the vital rail center at Corinth, Mississippi.

What strengthened Grant's hand was the arrival of Andrew Hull Foote of the navy in September. From the start, they understood one another and made a great team. In a command structure that was virtually sure to bring about conflict and friction between the services, these two cooperated fully, conducting operations and devising strategy. Foote also gave Grant a higher level of credibility with headquarters, as he often echoed his sentiments.

While strategy was discussed in the North, General Johnston's letters at the time constantly urged his subordinates to construct the fortifications promptly and called upon the bureaus to provide the proper armament. But the needs for ordnance were much greater than the ability to supply it. By the end of September, only the defenses at Columbus were ready. Albert

Sidney Johnston was painfully aware of the peril of invasion and did what he could with what he had on hand, but even casual observation showed that the weak points of the defensive line were the Tennessee and Cumberland Rivers. In fact, the construction of Forts Henry and Donelson was far behind schedule. These forts had received little attention since their conception in the early summer months, and Fort Donelson had even been completely abandoned for several weeks. It was not until September 17 that trained engineers arrived to oversee their construction.[28]

Despite the quick approval of the sites selected, work on Forts Henry and Donelson was very slow. From the onset, there was a shortage of just about everything, particularly manpower. There were few soldiers on hand, and many of these felt it was beneath their dignity to wield a pick or shovel. The ones willing to dig refused to work side by side with the slaves that were brought in from the few plantations in the area and from northern Alabama, and sickness and disease ravaged the ranks of the soldiers. Also, there was no firm command structure to focus the work and inspire the men. Command of the forts changed hands frequently, with the arrival of an officer of senior rank to the previous one in charge. Commanders and the engineers bickered constantly, and what work was done was often counterproductive. As a result, even though months had passed since their conception, both Fort Henry and Fort Donelson were little more than name only. They were completely incapable of stopping anything more dangerous than an unarmed steamboat.

A portent of events to come, problems with the location of Fort Henry surfaced early. Lieutenant Colonel Milton Haynes, former artillery chief of the Provisional Army of Tennessee, conferred with one of his officers, Capt. Jesse Taylor, who was then running a camp of artillery instruction near Nashville and had raised a battery of artillery. Haynes relayed Governor Harris's concern that there were no trained artillerists at the forts and asked him to take command of the batteries. Arriving in the summer, Taylor did not like what he saw. He found that Fort Henry was virtually ringed by high hills that were well within rifle range. For artillery, there were but six smoothbore 32-pounders and one 6-pounder iron gun. He also noticed how low the fort was situated near the river, which did not allow for delivery of deadly plunging fire on attacking vessels. Taylor formally questioned the decision of the site's selection, and Nashville responded that "competent engineers" had made the choice. He later stumbled upon a watermark left on a tree, and after carefully finding such marks above, below, and to the rear of the fort, he surmised the river would be a more dangerous foe than the Federals. Taylor confirmed his worst fears with local residents, who told him the highest point in the fort would be submerged under two feet of water during a normal winter rise.[29]

Taylor again passed his findings to authorities in Nashville, who replied that he should take the matter up with General Polk. This report eventually got to the bishop-general, who sent the concern up to department headquarters.

Although he had visited all other major forts and commands during his first three months in the West, for some unfathomable reason, Johnston never once went in person to inspect Forts Henry and Donelson to check their progress. Instead, the commanding general sent subordinate officers to the sites and read their reports. When told of Fort Henry's deficiencies, he promptly sent one of his junior officers to the site.

The chief engineer of Johnston's staff, Lt. Joseph Dixon, reported that the batteries of Fort Henry were nearly completed, and that although the fort was not in the most favorable position, it was indeed a strong work. Instead of abandoning it and building elsewhere, Dixon recommended that work continue on the fort, and that additional protective trenches be built to the east to repel an infantry attack. He also recommended building a small fort on the commanding ground on the opposite bank of the river to offset any disadvantage of the terrain.[30]

Fort Donelson also was far behind schedule, with even less work done since the initial survey. A few separate companies that would later form the nucleus of the 49th Tennessee did arrive in the late summer to resume work on the fortifications. Dixon felt another site was preferred, but here too he recommended that work continue on the existing fortification.

On October 15, Maj. Jeremy F. Gilmer reported to Johnston at Bowling Green and superseded Dixon as chief engineer for the department. Dixon remained at Forts Henry and Donelson to oversee construction. After the purchase of a horse, Gilmer inspected Fort Henry and instantly saw the deficiencies of the location. But he agreed that the work was far too advanced to begin a new fortification. He did recommend an increase in the number of guns, which was gradually done.

Finished there, Gilmer made his way over to Fort Donelson, and after consulting with Dixon, he concluded that work should continue there too. He also supervised the emplacement of river obstacles. Three barges over 100 feet long, filled with 1,200 tons of stone, were sunk downstream of the guns and farther down at Ingram's Shoals. The engineers believed these would effectively block the passage of vessels in ordinary levels of water up to ten feet of floodwaters. Gilmer was not satisfied with the armament at Fort Donelson, and recommended that the number of cannons be doubled.[31]

The major then went to establish a subsequent defensive line along the Cumberland to fall back upon in case of disaster. His orders from Johnston were as follows:

> Arrange the works for the defense and obstruction of the river at Donelson, Clarksville, and Nashville, and to intrust [sic] the construction to subordinates. You are to spare no cost, procuring barges, steamboats, and whatever else may aid in the work. . . . Arrange a plan of defensive works for Nashville, and urge them forward by all means you can command. If you find that the work of the troops will be useful, report at once here the numbers you can use, that they may be sent to you.[32]

Gilmer rode his new horse upstream and began the process of fortifying Clarksville. He marked out a small fieldwork positioned to cover the river and the landward approaches to the Hopkinsville bridges and directed the mounting of four 32-pounder guns. Named Fort Defiance, this position was never finished. The only effect this fort had was to give Johnston the false impression that there were subsequent defensive positions along the Cumberland. His work done here for the moment, Gilmer rode to Nashville to organize its defenses. Even in the large city, there was a labor shortage for digging the fortifications, and no heavy cannons were available. Slave labor was also in short supply, as the owners were unwilling to sign labor contracts.[33]

There was some noticeable improvement for Fort Donelson, though. The month of October brought the bulk of the 10th Tennessee, with their tools and experience in construction on Fort Henry. Colonel Heiman essentially passed command of the regiment to Lt. Col. Randal W. McGavock and assumed overall command of Forts Henry and Donelson. Maney's Tennessee Battery also arrived at this time, with its four 6-pounder smoothbore guns, to cover the landward side. In addition, the initial five companies of what became the 50th Tennessee arrived in Dover. With no trained heavy artillerymen on site, Company A of this regiment was detailed to man the big guns on the river.[34]

By the end of October, the heavy armaments at Fort Donelson were still not enough to repel any serious attack. The garrison mounted two 32-pounder carronades, as well as three 32-pounders in a temporary position. The carronades were obsolete even at the outbreak of the war and effective only against wooden boats at short range. The three 32-pounder guns on the hill did not have the required trajectory to be effective against the ironclads now known to be under construction up north. Eventually these guns were moved a short distance down the face of the hill, where the gun line is located today. These five guns of dubious value were all that stood between the Federals and Nashville. Two wrought-iron 9-pounder guns also had been brought to Fort Donelson, but these "railroad guns," recently forged in Clarksville, were of such questionable quality that they were set aside. They were later mounted in the fort proper for use in the landward defenses, but there was no ammunition for them.

But fortunately for the Confederates, Fort Donelson was quite the enigma, and the enemy did not know its weaknesses. In Paducah, Gen. C. F. Smith had no information whatsoever on the fort, including its name. This ignorance came from an inability to get a good look at the work. In this time of low water, the barges sunk by Major Gilmer effectively blocked the channel for the moment and prevented a gunboat reconnoiter.[35]

Conversely, over on the Tennessee, the work on Fort Henry did not go unnoticed or unseen. On October 14, the *Conestoga* went up the river on patrol. Her skipper, Lt. Ledyard Phelps, described it as a respectable earthwork, mounting heavy guns with outerworks, and a garrison of probably 1,700 to 1,800 men. Other reports specified that there were twenty guns and 2,000 men. Phelps had heard that the Confederates were also building three ironclad gunboats up the river, but the guns of Fort Henry kept him from investigating farther upstream. After the Belmont operation, Smith sent a spy to see what progress was being made on the rumored ironclad gunboats up the river beyond, but he apparently was captured.

During this period of preparation, the daily routine for the soldiers at Forts Henry and Donelson was filled with half-hearted digging of fortifications and rudimentary drill on the guns. When a sentry posted on the river saw a trail of smoke, the long roll of the drums brought the men under arms with the rapidity of zealots. The excitement subsided when the smoke disappeared, and the men returned to their duties. Discipline was irregular as well. As winter approached, the men built log huts inside and around the forts, which were generally very comfortable. Some 400 of these huts were erected within the perimeter of Fort Donelson proper and within close proximity in the hollows to the south. The interior of Fort Donelson had fairly steep slopes, but heavy rains and the tramping of hundreds of feet caused a sea of mud.

Friends and family members in the surrounding area sent the men good things to eat and other comfort items by nearly every boat. Men whose families lived nearby also had routine visitors, which were constant distractions to digging and drill. At Fort Donelson, there was another diversion in the form of an establishment run by "Lady Peggy." Her house was located across the cold waters of the Cumberland, but that did little to hinder those disposed to pay it a call. The men used small boats by night until Heiman ordered all small craft destroyed. He was probably not a popular man after issuing this order.[36]

Johnston was kept apprised of the work at both forts, but the reports were generally negative in nature. Dixon submitted one on November 23, however, saying that the lower water battery positions of Fort Donelson were complete and the process of mounting the guns would soon commence. Dixon also ordered the felling of trees to form an obstruction to enhance the landward defenses. The main concern, though, was acquiring enough men to build and defend the post. At this time, there were but 200 men at Fort Donelson, the remainder either sick or on leave. Another concern was confusion over who was in command. Dixon was receiving conflicting orders and asked whether he fell under the authority of the chief engineer of the department or General Pillow in Columbus. He received no defining answer.[37]

What was needed at the river forts was firm leadership and unity of control over the defensive preparations. This finally occurred in late November, but not exactly as a planned event. In Columbus, Polk expressed a desire to resign, and Johnston was looking for a new commander. He submitted to the War Department a *Major* A. P. Stewart for promotion to brigadier general, but his request was denied. In his reply, the secretary of war pointed out that a Colonel Tilghman was in Johnston's command, who was in command of a brigade at Hopkinsville and an engineer of some distinction. The denial of his choice stung Johnston as a rebuke, but he accepted the officer. The new general did not go to Columbus, though, since Jefferson Davis persuaded Polk to remain on active duty. Instead, Tilghman assumed command of both Fort Henry and Fort Donelson. He arrived at his new post in early December.[38]

Lloyd Tilghman graduated from West Point in 1836 and resigned from the army the same year. Until the Civil War, he was employed as a construction engineer on a number of railroads throughout the South. He served in the Mexican War as a captain of volunteers in command of the Maryland and District of Columbia Battalion. A member of the Kentucky State Guard, Tilghman followed his commander, Simon Buckner, and cast his lot with the South. As a Kentuckian and an engineer, he was apparently a good choice to supervise both forts.

General Tilghman inspected his new command, and to say the least, he did not like what he saw on the Tennessee and Cumberland Rivers. His reports echoed the concerns of others regarding the Fort Henry site, and work was far behind schedule on Fort Donelson. On November 29, he called for more heavy artillery and lamented that his force was largely unarmed and had no hope of procuring any weapons.[39] Heavy guns would arrive over several weeks in pairs, but there were no muskets to be had.

Receiving no reply to his requests for arms from Johnston, the new commander went over his head and right to the top of the organization. Tilghman wrote a plea directly to Jefferson Davis, which was personally carried to Richmond by Col. James E. Bailey, commander of the 49th Tennessee. Bailey's mission was to act as Tilghman's emissary to secure arms specifically for Forts Henry and Donelson. He was chosen because he was a former member of the Tennessee Military and Financial Board and was familiar with the problem and procedures to fix them. The meeting with Jefferson Davis turned out to be a failure and apparently raised the ire of the president. Twelve days later, a Colonel Liddle arrived on a similar mission on behalf of Albert Sidney Johnston. The poor, unsuspecting colonel caught Davis's fury: "My God! Why did General Johnston send you to me for arms and reinforcements when he must know that I have neither? He has plenty of men in Tennessee, and they must have arms of some kind, shotguns, rifles, even pikes could be used."[40]

Meanwhile, overlapping authority, unclear command channels, and conflicting orders became a daily nightmare for Tilghman, who himself contributed to this by constantly interfering with engineer Dixon, giving advice and countermanding his orders to work crews. On November 28, for instance, Tilghman directed that the blocking of the river by employing trees lashed together be stopped. Also, since the two forts nominally fell under the command at Columbus, they felt the effects of orders emanating from there, too. In temporary command there, General Pillow published directives that brought work to a virtual halt. Pillow wanted the engineers to survey a site for a supporting fortification immediately, at the expense of ongoing work, and suggested that slaves and whites work side by side digging the trenches and batteries. The engineers and white laborers exploded in rage at the notion, and only on appeal by Johnston did the work resume.[41]

In frustration, Major Gilmer directly appealed to Johnston to countermand Tilghman's orders, protesting that the subordinate brigadiers in the department were interfering with engineering work. Tilghman did receive a rebuke for hindering the engineers, but the problems of friction between the engineers and conflicting orders were never fully resolved.[42]

Engineers and fellow brigadiers were not the only command issues Tilghman faced. Remembered today mostly for his chivalry and gallantry during the coming campaign, Lloyd Tilghman was not a particularly popular man with the soldiers and officers of his command. Colonel Stacker, the original commander of the 50th Tennessee, resigned to avoid serving under him. The new commander, Col. Cyrus A. Sugg, apparently didn't like him either. Colonel John W. Head of the 30th Tennessee also intended to resign and said just that in front of his troops during a dress parade. He did not follow through with this threat, however, and apparently achieved some sort of reconciliation with Tilghman.[43] Overall, morale was not good.

At last Tilghman did get some good news, in that the 27th Alabama was on its way to Fort Henry with some 500 slaves for labor. Tilghman's plan was to use them all for building a small fortification on Stewart's Hill, which dominated Fort Henry on the Kentucky side. This hill was within easy musket range of the fort, and holding it would prevent an enemy from forcing the evacuation of the bastion. The regiment landed the day after Christmas and spent the next few days pitching tents and building bunks for their new camp. The camp was named Fort Heiman in honor of the commander of the 10th Tennessee and of Fort Henry when Tilghman was absent. Little or no work was done on the fort's construction, though, and most of the next month was spent in routine camp duties. The rations consisted primarily of beef and cornmeal, but food and other luxuries were sent from home on regular steamboat runs.[44] There was no artillery at the site, and Fort Heiman was in no way prepared for what was to come.

The last significant event of 1861 was the assumption of direct command of the army at Bowling Green by Albert Sidney Johnston. In so doing, he narrowed his focus to the enemy to his immediate front and lost sight of the big picture. Instead of the more detached view of a departmental commander, Johnston was thinking more and more as a mere army commander. Losing sight of his flanks, Johnston became fixated on the enemy army in Louisville under Don Carlos Buell.

The view to Johnston's front was bleak, and was made more so by the poor intelligence he had on the army at Louisville under General Buell. In December, Johnston reported to Richmond that the enemy was crossing the Green River in "overwhelming numbers." These and other reports wildly inflating Buell's size and capabilities raised some questions at the War Department. The secretary of war replied that he did not understand Johnston's messages and reminded him that Columbus and Cumberland Gap appeared secure, and that only his direct front was threatened. Richmond also questioned the force ratios between Johnston and the enemy, not believing the situation was so grim. In the end, Johnston was told to just do the best he can.[45]

As the year 1861 closed, the Confederate military situation in the West was weak but at least stable. This situation was about to change.

In summary, the violation of Kentucky neutrality in September 1861 was a grievous error on the part of the Confederates. In so doing, the state was politically shoved into the welcoming arms of the North. As long as both sides respected Kentucky's neutrality, the Confederacy had an invaluable buffer zone that blocked any major Federal advance into the heart of the South. Without it, Johnston's weak defenses were open to eventual discovery and penetration as the Federals made bolder reconnaissance patrols and movements.

The Polk-Pillow invasion of Kentucky far exceeded the discretion normally allowed field commanders. That these men did so without asking permission from higher headquarters is stunning and prevented a coordinated effort to occupy all of Kentucky. The loss of Kentucky as a buffer zone was hardly offset by what was gained. In his shortsightedness, Polk took the city of Columbus but forfeited most of the state.

Militarily, the Confederates did not have much to gain by invading Kentucky in the first place. Columbus did have advantages against a river assault but was vulnerable to a flank attack. The advance of the Confederate line to Bowling Green put some distance between Nashville and the front line, but Bowling Green also formed an easily flanked salient. If the Confederates were determined to keep Kentucky, they also would have had to seize Paducah, Smithland, and Louisville. From these points, Southern cannons could have dominated the Ohio River, disrupting steamboat traffic carrying goods and troops. This was beyond the capabilities of the South, however, which did not have enough men to hold this ground at the threshold of the North's front door. Any of these advanced points were vulnerable to being locally turned and cut off from supplies and reinforcements. The Confederates also would have been faced with an extended supply line over territory of questionable allegiance, while the Federals would have enjoyed very short ones over friendly country.

At this time there was a chronic shortage of small arms all across the Confederacy, which lasted well beyond the campaign. Efforts to rectify this took up far too much of Johnston's time and energy. His staff apparently assisted, but the commanding general often had to implore governors and fellow generals in person to secure even a small number of serviceable weapons. As for artillery, the Confederates certainly could have done a better job in allocating the available guns. In Columbus, there was abundance, with tier after tier of guns trained on the river and multiple batteries facing the landward approaches. The Bowling Green defenses also boasted a large number of cannons. In contrast, Forts Henry and Donelson appeared anemic. By the end of the year, only a combined total of a dozen or so guns were present at the two forts. These vital fortifications were truly treated as the backwater of the department's defenses.

Forts Henry and Donelson during this period also suffered from neglect caused by a lack of command focus and a chronic shortage of labor and materials. Late in the year, Johnston finally assigned a general officer to command them—a man who would presumably be a clear figure of authority over the handful of field officers present with their regiments. However, Lloyd Tilghman was abrasive and caused disharmony among his subordinate commanders and engineers. Although an engineer by training, he did not bring about the improvements Johnston was hoping for. Two other officers, both of whom were in Bowling Green with Johnston, had been available for the assignment: Simon Buckner and William Hardee. Both of these men were proficient and capable leaders.

A recurring trend is that Johnston never found the time to inspect the river defenses in person. Instead, he relied on his staff and an occasional politician to do it for him. He also put his faith and trust regarding these vital defenses in a man he didn't know, and who was not his first choice to command, Lloyd Tilghman. In spite of conflicting reports and noted problems, Johnston still never found the time to form a personal view of the situation. This was a key blunder on his part, for Johnston proceeded to devise strategy and plan operations based on faulty data or no data at all.

It is easy to conclude that Johnston just did not appreciate the danger of a Union advance up the Tennessee or the Cumberland. In fact, though, he had a very clear vision of the threat. On October 31, he wrote to Polk in Columbus:

> Your front, and particularly your right flank requires incessant watching, and may at any moment demand all the force at your disposal. The Cumberland and Tennessee rivers afford lines of transportation by which an army may turn your right with ease and rapidity, and any surplus you may be able to spare from your left flank on the Mississippi can well be used to secure you against such movements.[46]

In light of this statement it is perplexing that he did not take more interest in the state of readiness of Forts Henry and Donelson.

Through the end of 1861, the Confederate line in the West held, but it was not due to the strength of the defenses. It was mainly because the Union commanders were hesitant to move, believing the crafted propaganda of inflated Confederate strength. General Albert Sidney Johnston deserves much of the credit on this point. Through guile and bravado, Johnston led his enemy to believe he was far stronger than he was. But the long gray line was anything but strong. Work to complete the forts was slow, and the delivery of supplies and personnel was even slower. The Confederates were fortunate that the Federals had not yet seriously advanced, for it would have exposed their weakness.

The South had adopted the strategy of a static defense and was essentially waiting for a Federal advance to respond to. If Grant's swift movement to Belmont was an indication, the Confederates would not have to wait long.

CHAPTER FOUR

Prelude to Battle

January 1862

In Washington, President Lincoln was impatient. In a few months, the war would be a year old, and there had been little success to show for it. In every department generals worked to train their new regiments and forge them into an army. No one wanted to repeat the summer disaster at Bull Run. Building armies took time, though, and Lincoln's was politically limited. Congress and the American people were restless and wanted to see some results from all the drilling and marching, not to mention expense. Lincoln needed the armies to move and gain victories.

The main Confederate army in Virginia seemed as strong as ever, so Lincoln focused on possible gains in the West. For weeks, Lincoln and McClellan pressured Halleck to advance and to do so in coordination with Buell in Louisville. Lincoln went so far as to sign an executive order declaring Washington's Birthday as the day all Union armies were to simultaneously advance. However, both of these department commanders had refined stalling and procrastination to a fine art. When McClellan took ill, Lincoln himself stepped in to prod Halleck and Buell, but still to no avail. Buell cited poor roads and a lack of a functional railroad. Halleck just was not to be rushed, replying that "too much waste would ruin everything."[1]

If Halleck was characteristically slow and methodical, it did not mean he failed to realize that Lincoln's patience had limits. Since Buell was either unwilling or unable to cooperate, perhaps Halleck might show at least some activity in his department and reduce the pressure from above. Missouri was a fluid battlefield at the moment and all possible was being done there. There was, however, a mobile army centered at Cairo with a commander anxious to advance. Thus orders went to Grant on January 6, 1862, to make a reconnaissance of southwestern Kentucky. He was to lead the bulk of his forces in a demonstration toward Columbus, as well as the Cumberland, but by no means was Grant to bring on an engagement. Halleck wanted to show some activity but was not quite ready to commit to a full-scale battle just yet.

Characteristically, Grant was ready at a drop of a hat. Within three days, orders were sent, supplies were issued, and a brigade of 7,000 men under Gen. John McClernand left Cairo and trudged south.

A key participant in the coming campaign, John A. McClernand was a lawyer-politician from southern Illinois who had served three terms in the state legislature and one in the U.S. Congress as a Democrat. In 1854, he returned to Illinois, where he set up his practice in Springfield and Jacksonville, and in 1859, he was again elected to Congress, serving until the outbreak of war. His military experience consisted of a short stint as a militia private in the war against the Fox Indians in 1835.

Despite McClernand's scant military experience and Democratic loyalties, Lincoln appointed him to brigadier general in May 1861. In the early months of the war, McClernand proved valuable in securing the loyalty of southern Illinois and raising a number of regiments from that region. He was never fully accepted into the brotherhood of general officers by his West Point peers, however. His open disdain of them did not help in this regard, nor did his propensity for long speeches or attempts to grab the credit for successful operations. For the present, Grant himself tolerated McClernand, but it was clear he had little respect for the man or his martial abilities.

As McClernand's men marched south, another brigade, under General Eleazer A. Paine, marched from Bird's Point to observe Columbus from the opposite bank. Still another brigade under Brig. Gen. C. F. Smith moved from Paducah to Mayfield, Kentucky, toward Columbus. A handful of gunboats under the command of William Porter of the *Essex* steamed down the Ohio River to the Mississippi to within two miles of Columbus in support of the operation.[2]

Once all of the troops were in motion, Grant saddled up and joined his small army. Just after his departure, a telegram from Halleck arrived at headquarters telling Grant to delay the movement until further notice. It was too late to stop the scattered columns, but it was a clear lesson to Grant that his boss could get cold feet at the last minute.

The soldiers considered this a welcome break from the monotonous routine of drill in garrison and building fortifications. This was the sort of adventure that many had signed up for some months ago. This reconnaissance could also turn into a fight, too, since no one knew how Polk in

Columbus would react. Danger became a second thought, though, as the winter weather turned foul. Daniel Ambrose of the 7th Illinois later wrote: "Soon it commenced to rain, and through mud and rain we march all day. Taking a circuitous route through swamp and woods, we arrive in the evening, and we go into camp. . . . We find it difficult to keep the campfires burning since our camp is in the creek bottom and the water is standing around us. The creek is rising very high and it is still raining."[3]

The blue columns pushed on southward through the endless rain and bottomless mud, and reached their objectives by January 17. Surprising to many, there was no major reaction from the Confederates. After a few days, the reconnaissance was complete, and the units were recalled to return to their garrisons for drying out.

The expedition was the largest Grant had orchestrated in his department since the battle of Belmont, and it had three great benefits: First, it provided valuable intelligence on the strength and disposition of the Confederate forces in southwestern Kentucky. Second, it trained the commanders on the complexities of coordinating logistics and handling their men in the field. A third benefit was bestowed upon Halleck, who briefly felt some of the pressure removed for inactivity.

Up the Tennessee River, the Confederate engineers were still working on completing and improving the defenses. At Forts Henry and Donelson, work focused on mounting additional cannons and protecting the water batteries. Federal gunboats were still considered the greatest threat, and measures to defend against them were the priority. At this time Lt. Col. Milton A. Haynes arrived at Fort Henry. This artillery officer was on detached service as an instructor to assist in teaching the gunners their trade. Finishing there, he organized the water batteries at Fort Donelson into a battalion and made a requisition to General Polk in Columbus for two more artillery instructors. Haynes then trained these crews to fire at targets at the predetermined ranges of 1,000, 1,500, and 2,000 yards. When not drilling, every man fit for duty in the composite battalion worked at filling sandbags and other chores.[4]

Now the forts finally took shape. Fort Henry became a five-sided, open-bastioned work rising out of the marshes that covered about ten acres. Its walls were impressive at normal water levels, rising some twenty feet from the water's edge. They were about twenty feet thick at the base and sloped upward to about ten feet thick at the parapet. Seventeen guns were mounted on solid platforms. Eleven covered the river, and the other six were positioned to repel a landward attack. Two heavy guns, a 10-inch Columbiad and a 24-pounder rifled cannon, were the most effective weapons of the water battery. The rest consisted of seven 32-pounder smoothbores. Although two 42-pounders were mounted, there was no ammunition for either.

The ground immediately surrounding Fort Henry was indeed a low marsh, and even at normal stages of the river, water flowed around three sides of the bastion. An access road was built by piling stones, logs, and dirt through the swamp, and entry to Fort Henry was gained by crossing an archaic drawbridge. Within easy musket range to the east was a long ridge that rose above the fort. There the Confederates constructed rifle pits of about four feet high and four to six feet thick to protect the garrison from the landward approaches. By the end of January, they constructed yet another ring of rifle pits to keep any attacker even farther from the fort.

A final touch to the river defenses here was the employment of a new weapon to the Americas. At Fort Henry, the Confederates anchored several metal cylinders filed with gunpowder, which were rigged to explode on contact with a boat. In their day they were called torpedoes, but years later they became known as mines. For the time being, they were used to block the main channel downstream of Fort Henry. In January, the low water in the secondary channel prevented navigation.

The fifteen-acre Fort Donelson was also nearing completion, with the assistance of a force of slaves brought up from Alabama. Unlike the bastion on the Tennessee, the water batteries on the Cumberland were not part of the fort proper. Instead, the batteries were placed on the river while the fort was situated on the hill behind to protect them. The lower water battery mounted eight 32-pounder smoothbore guns in a straight line thirty feet above the water's edge. On the far left of the line was a 10-inch Columbiad. The upper water battery was located a short distance upstream, consisting of the two obsolete 32-pounder carronades and a very lethal 6.5-inch rifled gun.[5] This rifled gun and the massive Columbiad were the two primary weapons of Fort Donelson but were not yet mounted or ready for firing.

Ammunition for the water batteries at Fort Donelson was stored in bombproof magazines. The lower battery magazine had the capacity to hold 100 rounds for the each of the eight 32-pounders and was connected to the guns by construction of a covered way. The dimensions of the upper battery magazine are lost to history, but it apparently was somewhat similar in size and capacity.

The walls of Fort Donelson proper were about ten feet high and just about as thick at their base. The fort seemed defensible from the western and northern approaches, which were covered by the positioning of an 8-inch siege howitzer on a salient in the wall. From the south, or from the direction of Dover, Fort Donelson was still vulnerable, since it was built on the slope of a hill and the rear walls extended into a gully. From the opposite hill across Indian Creek, the garrison was open and exposed. To protect this weakness, the Confederates built a small strong point and possibly mounted one of the 9-pounder nondescript "railroad guns" on this hill. Beyond Fort Donelson to the landward side was a series of ridges and hills that would pose a real threat if an enemy force occupied them. This was not yet a major concern, for the fort's primary design was to halt river traffic. Besides, the small garrison was not large enough to man any outer works even if they were built at this time.

As at Fort Henry, additional river obstructions were added, but apparently none of the underwater torpedoes. Instead, after much bickering between Tilghman and the engineers, a floating obstruction was finally emplaced about 900 yards downstream from the water batteries.[6] This ingenious barrier was made by anchoring full-length trees by the roots and allowing the tops to float in the current. But these new obstacles were placed in the ordinary stages of water, and it seems little thought was given to the winter floods, which would surely come.

Developments at Fort Henry did not go unnoticed as the Federal gunboats kept an eye on the Tennessee. Gunboat patrols had inched up the rivers on occasion since their discovery back in October, but in January there were three separate reconnoiters aimed at Fort Henry. These were made by the wooden gunboats *Conestoga* and *Lexington* under the overall command of Lieutenant Phelps of the U.S. Navy. What the intrepid navy man saw yielded fairly accurate intelligence on the construction and armament of the fort and confirmed the navigation of the river.

Fort Henry was also being assessed from the land, albeit from the Kentucky shore. During Grant's reconnaissance into Kentucky, a large force under Gen. C. F. Smith made it as far as Crown Point before turning back. This was dangerously close to the site of little Fort Heiman, guarding the bluffs overlooking Fort Henry. It was still essentially an armed camp and had only a few troops of the 27th Alabama on hand. In Columbus, Polk shuffled and recalled units in order to meet the threat, which never fully materialized. Had Smith's force occupied Fort Heiman at this time, it would have forced the premature evacuation of Fort Henry.

On the Cumberland, Fort Donelson continued to be a mystery to the Federals. No one north of the Ohio River knew much about the fort, including the number of guns, obstructions, or how many troops were there. There was a general assumption, though, that it was weaker than Fort Henry.

In spite of the progress made during the month, many Confederates might have agreed with the Federal assessments of the forts' weakness. Differences of opinion between Tilghman and the engineers still slowed the work, and some key cannons remained unmounted. A visitor to Fort Henry noted this and even observed a slave work party remaining idle awaiting instructions. Hearing rumors of this, Governor Harris sent Col. Bushrod Johnson of his engineering staff to the Tennessee and Cumberland Rivers to find out the status of the forts. This officer—ironically, the one who had made the final decision of Fort Henry's location—reported that its ability to hold back any enemy advance was doubtful. Johnson's disparaging report caught Governor Harris's ear, and with another twist of irony, Bushrod Johnson was put in temporary command of the fort on January 21st with orders to improve its state of readiness.

Two more gloomy telegrams were soon on their way to the governor. "Forces weakened here by detachments withdrawn. Cavalry and infantry ought to be sought. Can arm temporarily 500 more infantry. Need field artillery." Two days later, the colonel asked Governor Harris for "equipment for 536 sporting rifles and thirty-five muskets." In a letter dated January 26th, Johnson reported the arrival of the balance of the 53rd Tennessee, commanded by Col. Alfred Abernathy. Apparently not impressed with this or any other unit at the fort, Johnson wrote: "One more regiment of new troops will be as many of that description as will be desired here. Should still be pleased to get one good regiment of old troops. . . . Fort Donelson is our weakest point. I trust it will be duly strengthened." Just where this crack regiment was to be found and a myriad of other details would quickly become moot for Colonel Johnson. Within days, he was recalled to Nashville, where he received word that a long-sought promotion to brigadier general was approved.[7]

Over the past few months, Gen. Albert Sidney Johnston had convinced his enemies that his defenses were strong, but enemy patrols and advances were exposing the weaknesses of the extended line. The first crack in the departmental defense came not on the western rivers, but in eastern Tennessee. On January 19, 1862, Brig. Gen. George H. Thomas routed Gen. Felix Zollicoffer's Confederates guarding the Cumberland Gap at the battle of Mill Springs. As tactically complete as the Confederate defeat had been, it did not turn out to be strategically disastrous. Crossing the Cumberland, Thomas entered a region more barren of provisions than the one he left. Although he put his men on half rations, intending to move to Knoxville, poor weather and roads halted his advance. The Federals eventually withdrew, and what was left of the Confederate right wing finally came to a rest at Chestnut Mound, about sixty miles from Nashville.[8]

Zollicoffer was killed in the battle of Mill Springs, and the army in eastern Tennessee needed a new commander. Shortly after Christmas, Gideon Pillow had resigned his commission in frustration and returned home. Pillow was a man of action, however, and could not tolerate sitting idle. With the death of Zollicoffer, Senator Henry suggested that Pillow be placed in charge of the Confederate forces in eastern Tennessee. Pillow clumsily let it be known he was interested in the command and withdrew his resignation. Apparently General Johnston was not enthusiastic about the return of Pillow, for he did not assign him to field command, but to the supply depot at Clarksville.[9] Although he was less than pleased with his new assignment, Pillow was back in uniform and used his great energy and organizational skills to transform the depot into the best on the Cumberland River. He also put special emphasis on the stockpiling of supplies and ammunition at Fort Donelson. Pillow still yearned for a combat command.

In Bowling Green, Albert Sidney Johnston knew he did not have much time before the Union armies were set in motion. Gunboats were ranging up the rivers, probing Fort Henry, and the rising rivers themselves allowed clear navigation over the obstructions placed in the low water back in autumn. Spring was only weeks away. By now there were 12,000 men in Columbus, Forts Henry and Donelson had about 5,000 men combined, Bowling Green had 22,000, and 3,000 more were scattered about the department. As long as the line held, though, Johnston could use the railroads to shift forces to endangered points.

Even with the advantage of mobility, Johnston was still desperately short of troops. Grant was known to have around 20,000 men at Cairo, and Buell was thought to have over 70,000 (there actually were about 56,000). If the North launched a simultaneous advance, Johnston simply did not have enough men to meet more than one column. In such an eventuality, the Confederates would have to strike and destroy one column before the other could come to its aid. Bringing together enough men to do the job would seriously weaken one or more sectors.

Since taking command in September, Johnston had called repeatedly on Richmond to send more troops and arms to his department. With a campaign closing in western Virginia, the War Department finally felt it could shift some forces his way. By mid-January, a single brigade under the command of Brig. Gen. John B. Floyd began to arrive in Bowing Green.[10] This force was only a fraction of what Johnston had requested; however, the commander of this brigade would play a key role in the coming campaign.

Born in Virginia in 1806, John B. Floyd attended the college of South Carolina. After graduating in 1826, he practiced law and was active in Virginia politics, serving in the state legislature and as governor. After sup-

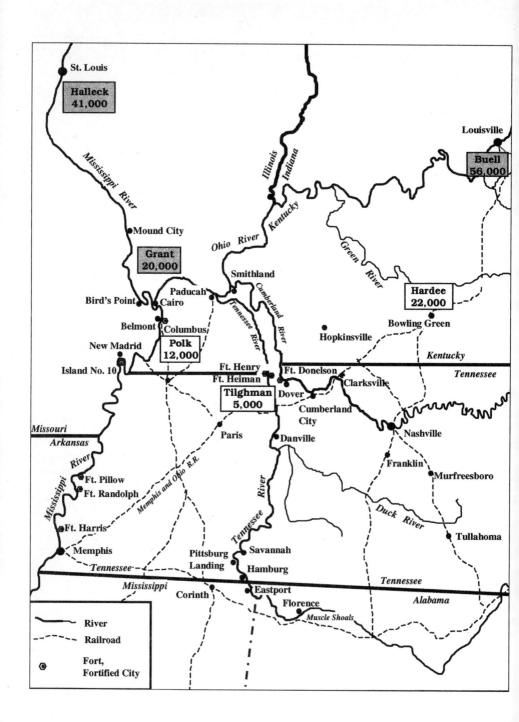

Area of Operations, January 1862

porting James Buchanan in his candidacy for president, Floyd was appointed as secretary of war but resigned when the Southern states began seceding. He served in that capacity for almost a year but resigned when the Southern states began seceding. As the country split apart, Floyd was indicted on a number of charges, including shipping arms to the South prior to the war, deploying the bulk of the army to the western frontier, and withdrawing a large sum of bonds from the Department of the Interior. He returned to Washington to face the charges and was cleared of any wrongdoing by a congressional committee.[11] Although cleared of the allegations, Floyd continued to believe that if captured, he would be taken to Washington and tried for treason.

John Floyd left Washington for good in January 1861 and was commissioned a brigadier general in the Confederate army in May of that year. He was a politician by trade with no formal military training, however, and his only war experience was serving for a few inglorious months in the western Virginia campaign under Robert E. Lee. There, Floyd became embroiled with a fellow brigadier over the placement of troops. Floyd was tactically wrong, but the other brigadier was junior in seniority. The latter was subsequently recalled to Richmond, according to the protocol of the day. Floyd and his brigade were then sent to the western theater.[12] Because of his seniority, Floyd's responsibilities would greatly increase in the coming weeks. In training, background, and temperament, he was completely out of his element.

Although authorities in Richmond would not send any other troops to the threatened department, there was a national hero on the way. In the last weeks of January, President Jefferson Davis had finally shown active concern with the situation in the West. He had grown tired of the governors and generals clamoring for troops, cannons, and supplies. Convinced that no forces could be spared from the eastern theater, he did have a general in mind who could. Pierre Gustave Toutant Beauregard had commanded the Confederate forces at Fort Sumter and Bull Run. Although successful to date, he had earned Davis's ire as a result of his close ties to antiadministration politicians in Congress and his free-flowing pen. Beauregard was offered command of the forces at Columbus and a position as wing commander of Gen. Albert Sidney Johnston's army.

General P. G. T. Beauregard had graduated second in his class at West Point and was an engineer on Winfield Scott's staff during the Mexican War, where he received two brevets for gallantry. He was popular with the troops and had shown himself so far to be an able commander in the field. He was now suffering from an inflammation of the throat, however, a condition for which he had undergone surgery prior to leaving Virginia. He was not in good health and perhaps not fit enough for active field duty. Also, some of his friends advised him not to accept the assignment, believing that he would essentially be giving up command of the South's principal army and put out to pasture. With vague assurances that he would be heavily reinforced to begin an offensive, and that he would eventually return to Virginia, Beauregard left Richmond on January 23 with a small number of his personal staff. Prior to departure, he received a situation briefing from the secretary of war that gave the number of the effective force in the western theater as about 70,000 men. This optimistic figure wasn't even close.[13]

Beauregard's new assignment solved two problems for Jefferson Davis. There was friction between Davis and Beauregard, and his new assignment would put some distance between the two. Also, the general was very popular after Fort Sumter and the battle at Manassas, and this popularity would be effective in rallying public confidence in the West. Beauregard was an able engineer, and since the strategy in the West was defensive, the general could apply his skill in fortifications. Just maybe Davis had found a solution to the constant outcry in the Western Department.[14]

On January 20, General Halleck communicated his proposed strategy to General McClellan in Washington. He argued that unity in the West was essential for success, and that General Buell's army should be placed under his command. Leaving only a small holding force to tie down Johnston at Bowling Green, the combined armies of the main attack would advance up the Tennessee and Cumberland Rivers.

Not surprisingly, Buell had a contrasting plan of his own, proposing that Halleck's forces move up the Tennessee and Cumberland Rivers with 20,000 men and the gunboat flotilla. Meanwhile, he would advance against Bowling Green and Nashville using the railroad to supply his army of some 56,000 effectives. If successful, the combined weight of the advance would compel Albert Sidney Johnston to fall back without a fight.

For all of the advice and political pressure, McClellan would not give approval for either plan. Instead, he only urged his old friend Buell to advance into loyal eastern Tennessee and cut communications connecting Nashville to Richmond, via the East Tennessee and Georgia Railroad.[15] Poor roads continued to hinder operations in that area, and Buell felt unable to move in that direction. Instead of advancing, McClellan, Halleck, and Buell kept the telegraph operators busy with proposals and counterproposals. The rivalry between the department commanders was evident, and McClellan would not take a firm stand behind either man's subsequent plans. Meanwhile, an exasperated President Lincoln heard nothing from his field commanders except reasons why they could not advance.

As a district commander located in Cairo, Gen. Ulysses S. Grant could afford a much narrower view and sharper focus. The fact that he had received no Confederate resistance in his reconnaissance through western Kentucky, combined with the reports of Fort Henry's weakness, convinced Grant that the time was right for an advance up the Tennessee. He then began a persistent campaign to persuade Halleck to authorize such a move, but his commander seemed cool at best regarding the idea. During a rare lull in his schedule, Halleck finally agreed to a personal meeting with Grant to discuss the matter.

Grant arrived in St. Louis with his own ideas of advancing up the Tennessee and taking Fort Henry. Spreading papers and maps before his commander, he began to describe his plan. Halleck wasn't listening. The senior general cut him off when he saw where the discussion was heading and summarily dismissed Grant from the room. The meeting was over. In his memoirs, Grant recalled that Halleck had showed him so little cordiality that he returned to his headquarters in Cairo "very much crestfallen." He also added, "I perhaps stated the object of my visit with less clearness than I might have done."[16] Halleck was indeed thinking of such an advance but did not want to be instructed on operational options by his subordinate.

Grant remained anxious to strike at the enemy, and Fort Henry in particular. He soon received a morale boost from a report by Gen. C. F. Smith, commanding in Paducah. Smith had seen Fort Henry with his own eyes on one of Lieutenant Phelps's gunboat patrols and believed that two vessels alone could take the fort. Smith also was a man Halleck trusted. On January 28, Grant sent Smith's report forward and continued to badger his commander: "With permission I will take Fort Henry on the Tennessee and establish and hold a large camp there."[17] Halleck received the message from his subordinate in Cairo but probably placed it on one of the piles on his desk. "Old Brains" was not yet convinced. Also, he was not the type to act alone and still wanted the cooperation of General Buell advancing from Louisville.

The next day, Halleck heard from his senior commander, whose message most certainly got his attention. General McClellan gave word of a deserter's claim that General Beauregard was on his way from Virginia with fifteen regiments to join Albert Sidney Johnston. This force, led by the hero of Manassas, could conceivably reinforce Fort Henry or even give an offensive capability to Johnston's army in Bowling Green.

Halleck believed *this* report, and the news of Beauregard on the way actually prompted the usually slow Halleck into action, at least somewhat. It appeared that the time to act was now, before this rumored force could arrive opposite his department. The general wired from St. Louis to Grant in Cairo: "Make your preparations to take and hold Fort Henry; I will send you written instructions by mail."[18]

General Halleck was still feeling the pressure from Lincoln to begin an offensive, and throughout his department, Grant alone was reporting as ready to move. Halleck was characteristically cautious, but evidently Grant's gunboat reconnoiters, backed by General Smith's assessments, finally provided him with some fortitude.[19]

Still, Halleck was not convinced to the point of actually launching an expedition. He had yet to receive approval from his old friend McClellan, and General Buell and he were as far apart as ever on developing a coordinated strategy. Also, Confederate forces in western Missouri under Gen. Sterling Price were an ever-present and growing threat. Henry Halleck was not confident that he had enough men to send away on an expedition and still keep a hold on Missouri.

For the moment, though, even if Grant was ready, he could not begin an advance up the river. Although the army was ready to go, the navy was not. Grant currently had only three wooden gunboats and one ironclad at his disposal. The ironclad *Essex* could not challenge a fort on her own, and while the timberclads were proven ideal for reconnaissance duty, they were entirely unsuited to assault an earthwork.

All of the city-class boats were commissioned by January 16, but that did not mean they were ready for combat. They were still being fitted out, and more worrisome, they were critically short of men. Foote kept the telegraph lines humming and postal offices busy with his appeals for seamen. Eventually another 500 idle navy men in the East were transferred to Cairo and placed on the receiving ship *Maria Denning*. On board, the old hands of the deep-water navy intermixed with the new recruits of rivermen, Great Lakes sailors, and the midwestern farmers and lumbermen. Quite a few foreigners were mixed in, too, mostly Germans and Irishmen. Most had never seen service or action of any type, but the few who had were the nucleus to forge the crews with naval discipline.

Efficient crews are not made overnight, and Foote needed time to organize and train his men. He quickly found that there were still only enough to fully man four of the seven new ironclads, and the skeleton crews of three of these were stripped away to complete the crews of the boats designated to take part in the coming operation. This move nearly caused a mutiny, for the men had already grown attached to their boats. So for any operation in the near future, Foote could man a total of five ironclads and the three timberclad gunboats. (The ironclad *Cairo* would remain behind as a guard ship with a composite crew, and the *Benton* was undergoing repairs and refit in St. Louis.)

Yet another challenge to overcome was a critical shortage of ammunition for the big naval cannons. Through determined efforts, Foote finally found enough for the boats to enter combat, but there was little to spare for gunnery practice and training. The crews had to hoard their small supply and try to make every shot count. Marksmanship was particularly stressed. Foote insisted that crews attain careful sighting before firing a shot to avoid wasting expensive ammunition. James Lanning, second master, in command of a battery on the *Essex,* cautioned his men, pointing a finger at them: "Every charge you fire from one of those guns costs the government eight dollars." This was just about half a month's pay for a crewman.[20]

So while Flag Officer Foote got his boats ready, General Grant gathered his forces for an offensive, a process that he had actually begun some time earlier. He directed Brig. Gen. John McClernand to assemble his best regiments for movement, planning to leave only a token force of green units to hold the fortifications and camps scattered throughout the Department of Cairo. General C. F. Smith also prepared his forces, dividing the regiments in Paducah and Smithland into a field division of two brigades. Drilling became incessant, and reviews and inspections came often for the troops. In Cairo, Grant stockpiled supplies and ammunition and arranged for the hiring of as many steamboats as there were crews available. His army would need them to carry out his plan, not only to get it to its objective, but to also sustain it deep in enemy territory.

As a final precaution, Grant sent two timberclads on what would be the final reconnaissance of Fort Henry. Under Lieutenant Phelps, the *Conestoga* and *Lexington* crept up the Tennessee to ascertain the latest developments. On board for this voyage was Brig. Gen. Lew Wallace, who would later gain fame for his novel *Ben Hur.* He took to pen to record his impression of Fort Henry as it came into view:

> We saw a fortification built squat on low ground with three bastions offered fronts to us with three heavy guns commanding all down the river. [One of these was the newly mounted Columbiad.] One bastion extended its outward angle into the river. . . . While we were looking, a man, evidently an officer stepped out on the parapet by the big gun of the lower bastion of the fort, and entertained himself returning our bravado like for like.[21]

Wallace later learned that the dashing officer in gray was Brig. Gen. Lloyd Tilghman himself. He did not realize at the time that he would soon succeed Tilghman in command of the fort. Upon his return to Paducah, Wallace reported to Smith, who sent the findings up the chain of command.

The massing and movement of such a number of Federal troops throughout Grant's department could not go unnoticed or be kept secret for long. The increased patrols on the Tennessee also indicated to the enemy that a major movement was being planned. Over in Bowling Green, Albert Sidney Johnston faced a growing dilemma. He was receiving reports from his rudimentary intelligence system that varied widely regarding enemy troop strength and intentions, but all agreed about one thing: The North was raising an army of unprecedented size backed up by ironclad gunboats. Against this horde, he had only about 43,000 troops scattered across hundreds of miles of the Western Department. Even now, many of these troops were still poorly armed, and the state of drill and training was bad as well.

Johnston soon learned that Grant was assembling a mobile army and began to shift forces to meet the threat. From Bowling Green, Brigadier Generals John B. Floyd with his brigade and Simon Buckner with the bulk of his division were sent to Russellville, the seat of the Confederate government in Kentucky. This move placed these units halfway between Bowling Green and Clarksville, and within easy reach of both. These forces were Johnston's ready reserve. No additional troops were sent as yet to Forts Henry and Donelson.[22] Johnston would await further developments before making any more major troop deployments.

As January 1862 drew to a close, Johnston learned to his dismay that Tilghman at Fort Henry was still pondering whether to actually fortify the ground across the river. "It is most extraordinary," wrote Johnston. "I ordered General Polk four months ago at once to construct those works. And now, with the enemy on us, nothing of importance has been done. It is most extraordinary." A frustrated department commander wired General Tilghman: "Occupy and entrench the heights opposite Fort Henry. Do not lose a moment. Work all night."[23] Major Gilmer then returned to Fort Henry on General Johnston's behalf and found the work there complete, but confirmed that Fort Heiman was not ready. The men in gray continued to work there but there was little time. Down the river, Grant was on the move. What Johnston did not fully understand was that Ulysses S. Grant did not plan to use the roads or railroads in his operation. He would use the approaches where the Federals held the decisive edge: the western inland rivers.

Although now virtually complete, Forts Henry and Donelson were still small affairs designed to defend against traditional wooden gunboats and to stop commercial river traffic. A comparison with the number of guns present at Columbus is staggering. There the Confederates placed 142 guns to cover both the river and landward approaches. Forts Henry and Donelson combined at this time had only 23 heavy guns, and but three light field batteries dedicated to landward defenses.

The designers of the forts truly did not fathom the large armies that would mass to attack them. Forts Henry and Donelson were about ten and fifteen acres in size, respectively, and could not hold more than a few thousand troops. The first ring of outer works at Fort Henry was built to counter the threat of an infantry assault, but the anti-infantry defenses clearly show the lack of vision regarding the type of warfare that would ensue. Most of the artillery facing the landward side was mounted in the fort proper and not in the outer rifle pits. This severely limited their range and usefulness. The fort even sported a drawbridge, which had no practical purpose in modern warfare. As the leaders and engineers began to realize the size of the armies they would confront in this war, it was far too late to build more suitable fortifications. The Confederates took what measures they could to compensate. They dug additional rifle pits at both Fort Henry and Fort Donelson to provide cover for the water batteries against assault from the land and incorporated novel underwater torpedoes and other obstructions into the defenses.

The constant changing of commanders slowed the organizing of labor and construction of the forts. Just as a sense of loyalty between a commander and his men formed, he was likely to be reassigned. Most of the commanders felt that the assignment to the forts was undesirable, or that they had been relegated to the backwater of the war. Perhaps it was true. Both Fort Henry and Fort Donelson were low in priority for units, cannons, and labor to make the defenses formidable. It is also hard to fault any soldier who did not take to the spade with vigor when his commander did not think highly of the position or of the fighting qualities of the regiments in the garrison.

It is interesting to explore the possibilities had Gen. C. F. Smith occupied Fort Heiman during the reconnaissance of western Kentucky. On the surface, this appears like a golden opportunity lost, being able to force the Confederates to abandon Fort Henry without a shot. On the other hand, the Federals were not prepared to quickly exploit this gain had it occurred. General Grant was still trying to arrange for enough supplies and transport to sustain the campaign. Units were still scattered throughout the department, and it would take time to assemble them and move them into a favorable position. Meanwhile, Smith and his men would be alone in a hostile land, where the Confederate command could conceivably counterattack and overwhelm them.

What Grant's reconnaissance through southwest Kentucky did was convince General Polk that any future Federal thrust would be aimed at Columbus. He consequently consolidated all of his forces there and was very reluctant to detach any sizable force to reinforce Tilghman on the Tennessee.

General Johnston's available forces were arrayed along an arc from Bowling Green to Forts Henry and Donelson and over to Columbus, and moving troops from one post to the other required long marches over poor roads. In military jargon, the Confederates did not have the advantage of interior lines. A strategic reserve would ideally be used to reinforce a threatened sector but Johnston failed to establish one. Instead he was forced to strip forces from one sector to reinforce another using the rickety but functional railroad system. If the Union armies did not advance simultaneously, as Lincoln called for, he conceivably still held a good chance of concentrating against a single enemy thrust, defeating it, and repositioning to meet the next one. Johnston was also counting on the winter weather to buy more time to prepare the defenses. The roads were in bad condition from the winter rains, and the movement of a large army on any of them was considered unthinkable. Armies in North America had not yet done any serious campaigning during the winter, and so far this war seemed to be no exception. Other than short-range reconnoiters from Paducah and Louisville, and the occasional visit by a gunboat below one of the river forts, the situation was fairly quiet all across the department.

It is apparent that Johnston was counting on the foul winter weather to hold back the invaders for the time being. Most Union armies, like Buell's in Louisville, were bogged down during the winter months due to the heavy rains and resultant muddy roads. It seems clear, though, that Johnston did not realize how quickly the rivers would rise and become avenues of advance into his department. Of the Union commanders, Grant was uniquely able to capitalize on this because of the Ohio, Tennessee, and Cumberland Rivers, which flowed through his jurisdiction. Using gunboats and transports, Grant could advance deep into the South during the winter in spite of the lack of paved roads or railroads. This was a lesson that the Confederates seemed to have missed at Belmont. Instead, Johnston continued to see Buell's large army as the primary threat, in spite of Grant's demonstrated ability to move quickly using the western rivers.

CHAPTER FIVE

The Battle of Fort Henry

February 2–6, 1862

IT WAS A RARITY AT THIS STAGE IN THE WAR TO FIND A GENERAL WHO WAS ready to move upon receipt of orders. During this campaign, it was Ulysses S. Grant. Receiving approval to prepare for an advance on Fort Henry, he began the process of massing his widely dispersed forces. Paducah, Kentucky, was chosen as the army's rallying point. Paducah offered a number of options because of its geographic location. From there, Grant could ascend either the Cumberland or Tennessee River, or he could march overland between the two, using them to cover his flanks from attack. The Confederates were relying heavily on shifting forces to meet any threat in the area, and Grant's intentions would be very hard to predict. They may not have known where he would strike, but Grant surely did. He fully intended to ascend the Tennessee River and take Fort Henry.

In hindsight, it is amazing that the people within Grant's district or even the Confederates did not have an idea of the size or timing of the operation. For more than three weeks, quiet but unmistakable preparations for a movement of some kind had been visible at Cairo, and other points as well. But so secretly were the preparations conducted that no intimation of the destination, size, and probable time of the expedition could be obtained from those supposed to be in on the secret, and observers could only watch and wait. They would not have to wait long.[1]

February 1 was the day of decision. In St. Louis, General Halleck pored over his maps, assessing the situation. General Beauregard was due to arrive in his sector at any time, and both Halleck and Buell were as far from cooperating as ever. On the other hand, Grant, backed up by Gen. C. F. Smith and Flag Officer Foote, urged an immediate strike on Fort Henry, which was supposedly a very weak point. Meanwhile, the president was looking for an advance, and his patience certainly had limits. Finished with his military and political calculations, General Halleck made his decision.

Without any authorization from McClellan or any cooperation from Buell, Halleck sent the detailed instructions he had promised Grant. These instructions ordered his subordinate to proceed with the operation to take Fort Henry as soon as possible. They also gave some discretion, but there were a few tasks Halleck wanted done, too. First and foremost, Grant was to leave an adequate force behind to guard Cairo and other outposts against any attack from Columbus. He was also to run a telegraph line behind him from Paducah to Fort Henry. After Fort Henry's capture, Grant was then to send his cavalry farther up the Tennessee River to cut the Memphis and Charleston Railroad line that connected the two wings of Johnston's department.[2] Halleck's micromanagement somewhat limited Grant's freedom of movement, but the effects would decrease the farther the army advanced away from the headquarters.

The Fort Henry–Fort Donelson campaign had begun.

General McClernand's division at Bird's Point and Cairo was a flurry of activity as tents came down and troops assembled to board a fleet of river steamers. The scene was replayed at Paducah and Smithland. The excitement was tremendous, since by now the vast scale and probable intent of these movements were not lost on anyone in the local area. A gunboat escort preceded the steamboat convoys.

The preparations for this movement were arduous and included a massive movement of supplies and ammunition. This phase of the operation went off without a hitch and is a tribute to the leaders up and down the chain of command. General Grant had passed the first test of his capacity to lead an army in a major campaign with flying colors.

Over in Louisville, General Buell learned of the planned advance and wired Halleck to get the details. Now that he was caught flat-footed and his rival was in motion, General Buell asked if he could be of assistance. Halleck's reply was almost a rebuke: "I plan to take Fort Henry and I don't need assistance." For the moment, the tone of Halleck's messages was confident and almost to the point of gloating. As for Don Carlos Buell, for the rest of the campaign he would play the role of the naysayer, quick to point out dangers but lending little support.[3]

As for troop strength, Grant had about 9,000 troops immediately available for an offensive. About 6,000 reinforcements were scheduled to arrive from St. Louis and elsewhere, and Grant believed that these could be sent upstream as soon as additional transports became available. If no more steamboats were forthcoming, the plan was to move the army in shifts. Grant gave the task of rounding up all available transports to Lewis B. Parsons of the army's Quartermaster Department, who also became personally responsible for efficiently routing them to where they were needed.[4]

Grant could not take every man under his command, for the bases at the rear had to be protected against any Confederate thrust up the Mississippi or from raiders. No one could guess how strong the Confederates actually were at this time or just how they would react to the invasion. Many of the forts in this department were in pro-Southern areas and would be looted or pillaged if left abandoned. A brigade under the command of Brig. Gen. Eleazer A. Paine, supported by four batteries of artillery, was given the mission of guarding the vital depot at Cairo. Another, under the command of Col. James D. Morgan, drew the assignment of guarding the outpost at Bird's Point.[5] In gathering the troops for the expedition, however, Grant had stripped these two garrisons of the best troops, leaving only the bare minimum of raw units for their defense.

Before he left his headquarters in Cairo, Grant took pen and paper and wrote General Order No. 7, which laid out some basic rules for the novice army that was assembling for the expedition. There would be no firing, except when ordered by proper authority, and the plundering and disturbing of private property were prohibited. Company officers were to see that all of their men were kept in camp except when on duty.[6] The memory of troops stopping to loot the Confederate camp at Belmont was fresh in his mind. It would not be repeated if he could help it.

Grant also laid out the brigade organizations for the coming campaign. The 1st Brigade, commanded by Col. Richard J. Oglesby, consisted of seven infantry regiments, two artillery batteries, and four companies of cavalry. The 2nd Brigade, commanded by Col. W. H. L. Wallace, had four infantry regiments, a cavalry regiment, and two artillery batteries. For the most part, these units had been scattered across the department for months, conducting reconnaissance and guard missions, although some of them had seen action together at Belmont. These two brigades formed the 1st Division, which was placed under the command of Brig. Gen. John A. McClernand.[7]

The 1st Division formed the vanguard of the expedition, and Grant used every steamer available in his district and beyond. Not only did the men need transport, but the means of sustaining and supplying them in a hostile land were needed as well. With foresight, Grant had quietly begun to ship bulk supplies forward to Paducah a few days previously, but the amount was not yet enough to sustain a protracted campaign.[8] Meanwhile, the 2nd Division was formed in Paducah under the command of Brig.

Gen. C. F. Smith. When the army was fully assembled before the walls of Fort Henry, Grant would have roughly 15,000 men.

Flag Officer Foote was also working overtime to ensure success by assembling the most powerful naval force yet to serve on the western waters of the United States. The four ironclads *Carondelet, Cincinnati, Essex,* and *St. Louis* arrived at Paducah, joining the three older wooden gunboats *Tyler, Conestoga,* and *Lexington,* under Lieutenant Phelps. The ironclad *Cairo* remained at the pier as a guard ship, while two other ironclads also remained for want of crews.

At this point, a potentially disastrous problem came to light. James B. Eads, the builder of the city-class gunboats, had not been paid to date and still technically owned the boats. Worse, it looked as though it would be weeks before the contract would be settled. But Eads allowed Grant and Foote to take the boats into combat in good faith, even though no one was sure just who would be financially responsible for a boat that was damaged or sunk before the contract was closed.[9]

The gunboat fleet had quickly assembled at Paducah, but the transports to carry Grant's army were behind schedule. Foote used the additional time to arrange signals and coordinate the activities of his boats and men in the coming battle. Most had never fired a shot in battle, and for those who had it had been little more than trading a few shots with an enemy boat or battery before withdrawing. The crews were raw, in any case, and the ones who had drilled were now only parts of composite crews, as likely to be serving on a completely new gunboat as not. The city-class boats themselves were untested, and no one was really sure just how well they would hold up in a fight.

Foote's special orders detailing the preparation of the vessels for the attack were distributed to the skippers. Hoods covering the hatch gratings were taken off to prevent damage and injury during the firing of the guns. Anchors were to be unstocked if they interfered with the firing of the bow guns. Officers were to watch the flagship for signals, and commanders were to be prepared to communicate with Foote verbally if necessary. Ammunition conservation was stressed again, the frugal Foote reminding his officers that each round was a precious commodity.

As for tactics, Foote's battle plan for the river fleet was simple. The four ironclads would advance side by side, evenly spaced, with their bow guns and heaviest armor facing directly toward the river batteries of Fort Henry. Firing quickly but accurately, they were to close with the batteries as fast as possible. The three wooden gunboats, *Tyler, Conestoga,* and *Lexington,* would follow the ironclads at a distance and lob shells into the fort at long range.

On Sunday, February 2, Grant was anxious to get under way. He had come to know Halleck, and he knew that "Old Brains" could change his mind in a moment and call off the operation. There were still not enough trained rivermen or available steamboats to move his entire army at once, but Grant would not delay the operation. Instead, he would move half his army at a time in shifts. Grant further reasoned that the Confederates were probably reinforcing Fort Henry, and the more time he gave them, the stronger they would be. He did not overestimate the danger, though. When some officers voiced their concerns about the heavy rains and their effect upon the river and roads, he was reassuring. Knowing the Confederates relied upon the local roads more than he, Grant replied: "The weather will operate worse upon the enemy, if he should come out to meet us, than upon us."[10]

When a telegram arrived from St. Louis, there likely was tension at headquarters. Would Halleck give the final order to advance, or would he try to call off the operations as he had tried in January? "Take and hold Fort Henry at all hazards," the telegram read. Grant immediately set his army into motion.

To say that Grant wasted no time in moving is an understatement. Some of the lead elements did not even have time to land in Paducah. Around 3:00 in the afternoon, General McClernand arrived in Paducah in advance of his division. While he waited for the rest of his transports to come up, Grant ordered him to advance up the Tennessee as soon as they arrived. The bulk of the cavalry, including the 4th Illinois Cavalry Regiment, was to disembark at Paducah and ride overland. They were to travel light and fast, taking no wagons and only one day's forage and rations. General Halleck had suggested this cavalry movement to Grant by telegraph.[11] This movement would provide more space on the limited number of transports for the infantry and would serve to sweep the land between the Tennessee and Cumberland Rivers of any Confederates along the way.

McClernand's transports left Paducah at 4:30 in the afternoon and made their way up the sixty miles of mud yellow Tennessee River, escorted by the *St. Louis* and *Essex*. The troops were in a festive mood in spite of the bleak weather. Many of the men of the 31st Illinois had stuffed their haversacks with sausage, cheese, and tobacco, bought on credit from a sutler, who was left on the levee watching his debtors sail up the Ohio.[12] Working around snags and other hazards to navigation, the fleet approached the Tennessee line.

Around 4:30 in the morning of February 3, McClernand rounded Panther Island at Bailey's Ferry and sighted the low lines of Fort Henry in the distance, some two miles upstream. The fleet quietly dropped back and, under the cover of the gunboats, landed the troops at Itra's Landing, a point eight miles below the fort. Staff officers were dispatched to look for a suitable encampment. McClernand took a detachment of Stewart's Illinois Cavalry Battalion forward to reconnoiter and ascertain the location and strength of the landward forces.[13]

Once ashore, General McClernand met a local farmer, who told him that there was a small band of gray-clad horsemen in the area. One of McClernand's aides then spotted some mounted men on the opposite bank. Word was sent back to the gunboats, and in short order, a naval shell dispersed these unidentified horsemen.[14]

Back in St. Louis, Gen. Henry Halleck received word of the advance up the Tennessee. Grant's telegram simply read: "Will be off up the Tennessee at six o'clock. Command twenty-three regiments in all."[15] This was Halleck's first big offensive, and he was nervous. Although he was a master of administrative details and formulating grand strategy, the forces of the unknown unnerved him. Halleck still believed that Beauregard was coming west with fifteen additional regiments, which could pounce on Grant and his little army as they besieged Fort Henry. To his credit, Halleck did everything he could to send all reinforcements up the river to Grant, but three regiments were the sum of his efforts thus far.

At this juncture, Halleck's confidence began to slip. Too late to recall the expedition, he looked beyond his department for reinforcements and assistance. He now even pleaded with his rival, General Buell in Louisville, to make a demonstration on Bowling Green to tie down the Confederates there. Buell, still stinging from Halleck's rebuke a few days earlier, refused to move. Only after much bickering and General McClellan's intercession did Buell finally transfer a single green brigade to Halleck's department. Even this token force would not move for a few days.[16]

While the Union senior commanders debated strategy and the assignment of forces, Grant was blissfully unaware of these proceedings and continued on with the business of taking Fort Henry.

While McClernand's troops landed and Halleck worried in St. Louis, the Confederates seemed completely unaware of the pending danger. In the early morning, General Tilghman and Major Gilmer of the engineers inspected Fort Henry and the new rifle pits of Fort Heiman across the river. By 10:00 in the morning, the pickets on both sides of the river had yet to spot any enemy boats or troops, which at that moment were anchored downstream.[17]

The rising waters from the winter rains had drastically changed the situation at Fort Henry. The Tennessee was rising out of its banks, nearing the flood marks left on the trees the previous year. Apparently Captain Taylor of the artillery had been right about the floods all along. The water was rising at an alarming rate and threatened the powder magazine and the heavy batteries covering the river. The guns were now only six feet above the water. Not surprisingly, some Confederates began to wonder which would defeat the fort first: a Yankee attack or the river. Men were detailed to throw earth up around the magazine to keep out the water and to build a temporary bridge across the backwater that now surrounded the fort. Equipment and provisions in danger of being washed away were moved to safer locations.[18] With no sign of enemy activity, Tilghman placed Colonel Heiman in command and left with Major Gilmer to inspect the defenses of Fort Donelson.

While in temporary command of the fort, Colonel Heiman sent a detail downstream on a special mission. This small band of men carried a number of explosive torpedoes like the ones laid in January in the main channel. With the rising river, the western channel was now navigable and needed to be blocked. Twelve of these devices were boldly sunk in the chute at the foot of Panther Island, but for want of powder and time, no additional ones were employed in the main channel.[19]

Downstream, Flag Officer Foote came up on the *Tyler*, took command of the flotilla, and transferred his flag to the *Cincinnati*. General Grant returned from Paducah shortly and found, much to his satisfaction, that McClernand had stopped short of the fort and out of range of the heavy guns. But before sending the boats back for the rest of the army, he wanted to get the troops as close as possible to the fort without being in range of the Confederate cannons. Grant's plan for the attack depended upon swift ground movement, and he knew his army had to cross Hughes and Panther Creeks. Normally insignificant ravines, they were now swollen by the winter rains. If possible, Grant wanted to get his forces south of these creeks to eliminate two more obstacles along the planned route of march.

The winter rains had come and gone repeatedly, but this day, another great storm deluged the region, causing the river to again rise suddenly. The increasingly swift current brought down great quantities of branches, fences, lumber, and even large trees. Much of the land along both banks was already underwater. Although Foote's fleet was at anchor, there was a growing danger that the gunboats would be swept downstream with the current. The ironclad *Carondelet* became tangled in a mass of driftwood and was dragged over half a mile downstream, even though she had both anchors out and was operating at full steam.[20] The crews were cold, wet, and tired.

Many of the old hands on the gunboats took the angry river as a bad omen, but the miserable conditions actually worked to their advantage. The rushing floodwaters of the Tennessee carried away not only trees and debris, but revealed the Confederate underwater torpedoes as well. With a river free of torpedoes, Foote could steam his boats just about anywhere with impunity. To make sure the underwater threat was gone, Foote ordered the wooden gunboats *Conestoga* and *Tyler* to lower their lifeboats to clear the area of all of the menacing devices. A quick sweep retrieved six more of the weapons. A subsequent inspection revealed that all but one had defective seals that allowed water to dampen the powder. In such a state, they were harmless. As a result, torpedoes played no further role in the defense of Fort Henry, although one was reported to have passed between the *Carondelet* and *St. Louis* during the battle without effect.[21]

One of the underwater mines was brought aboard the flagship *Cincinnati* for closer inspection. General Grant was aboard to confer with Foote at the time, and the device caught their attention. They both went to the fantail of the vessel to get a closer look at the item of curiosity.

It was a formidable affair, an iron cylinder about five feet long and eighteen inches in diameter, pointed at both ends, with a rod projecting upward with three prongs at the tip. The prongs were designed to catch on the hull of a passing boat and trip an ordinary musket lock to detonate the powder. Grant asked to see how the device worked. The boat's armorer went to work with a monkey wrench, hammer, and chisels. As the assembled officers watched over his shoulder, he removed one end of the device with no difficulty, exposing a threaded screw. When the screw was turned, the escaping gas produced by the wet powder made a hissing sound. Thinking the weapon was about to explode, the crew shoved the device overboard, and Grant and Foote lunged for a ladder. Grant got there first and, followed closely by Foote, scrambled to the upper deck. Collecting their wits, they smiled at each other. "What's your hurry?" asked Foote, to which Grant replied, "The Army can not afford to let the Navy get ahead of it."[22]

In conferring with Foote, Grant realized he needed to know just how far the guns of Fort Henry could shoot, and there was only one way to find out for sure. He set out on Commander Porter's *Essex* to draw fire so that he could ascertain the range of the water batteries. The foray would also serve as a reconnaissance of the Tennessee River. The *Essex,* escorted at a distance by the *Cincinnati* and *St. Louis,* proceeded without incident and lobbed a few shots into the fort without apparent effect or reply.

But evidently the Confederates did take notice after Porter turned his boat about and the *Essex* was about two and a half miles downstream, the fort fired a shot from the rifled 24-pounder. It missed but passed danger-ously close and cut down a number of saplings onshore. Another round fol-lowed a moment later with astonishing accuracy at such range. The shell hurtled over the spar deck near Grant and Porter, passed through the offi-cers' and captain's quarters and the pantry, blasted through the aft wall of the cabin, and splashed into the yellow water. Besides the holes in the bulk-heads, the only damage was to some of the captain's dishes and to a pair of his socks, the toes of which were sheared off as they hung from the back of a chair.[23] The *Essex* quickly retired out of range before another shot was fired.

Having found out firsthand just how far the Confederates could shoot, Grant now ordered McClernand, who had just returned from his own reconnaissance, to reembark his troops. They were to begin the process of landing at Bailey's Ferry, about three miles below the fort and just beyond the range of its cannons. Grant then boarded a steamer and returned to Paducah to bring up the rest of his army, which was composed chiefly of Smith's division.

The approach of the *Essex* was the first sign of the enemy seen by the Confederates, and Colonel Heiman evacuated the entire garrison except Taylor's Battery. As ordered, the Southern infantrymen melted into the woods to a distance reasoned too far for the naval guns to hit.

The reason why Fort Henry had remained silent for so long was because the *Essex* had been hovering beyond the range of the fort's guns. At this time, Fort Henry had eleven guns bearing on the river approaches; seven were moderate-range 32-pounder smoothbores, and two were 42-pounders that had neither shot nor shell available. The two most effective pieces were a massive 10-inch Columbiad and a rifled 24-pounder, but the Columbiad had technical difficulties. Even though it was mounted on an iron carriage, the gun had nearly dismounted itself due to excessive recoil when it was tested a few weeks earlier with a full charge. Makeshift clamps were installed, but one later broke loose. In this state, the big cannon was being held in reserve for use against any determined attack. This left only the rifled 24-pounder to challenge the *Essex*. To everyone's relief, the Union gunboat withdrew without pressing an attack.[24]

The Union troops began arriving at Bailey's Ferry in force around noon, with the gunboats shelling the woods to cover the operation. By now the Confederates knew that the gunboats were not alone, and that a large body of Union troops was on their doorstep. Colonel Heiman sent additional scouts to keep an eye on the Federal landing process. Meanwhile, General McClernand took another opportunity to reconnoiter the area and also sent cavalry detachments to scout the roads. One patrol reconnoitered forward from the landing and attacked an outpost some three miles north of the fort, killing three Confederates and driving the others back into the trenches. Another scouting party found and cut the telegraph line connecting Fort Henry and Fort Donelson.

Not yet having a telegraph of his own, General Grant sent off a message to General Halleck on a returning steamer: "Not having sufficient transportation for all troops, the larger portion of the steamers have to return to Paducah for the remainder of the command. . . . I expect all the troops by 10 o'clock A.M. tomorrow. Enemy is represented as having re-enforced rapidly the last few days."[25]

At the landing, McClernand's division took up positions some 400 yards inland on a range of hills overlooking the transports, with the 1st Brigade on the right and the 2nd Brigade on the left. McClernand dubbed the new encampment Camp Halleck in honor of the department commander. He also took the time to issue a field order detailing instructions to his brigade commanders. The general was particularly concerned about the placement of the artillery and detached a company of infantry to each battery for its protection. He also was greatly concerned about "depredators" within his command and enjoined his brigade commanders to mete out swift and sure punishment.[26]

Patrols soon reported on the number of Confederates at Fort Henry, with estimates ranging from 6,000 to 20,000. Also, a small Confederate steamer could be seen plying back and forth between the east and west banks, possibly indicating that more troops were on the way.[27]

By the end of the day, the bulk of McClernand's division had finished shifting upstream to Bailey's Ferry and began preparing for offensive operations. Two regiments supported by a battery were also pushed forward to cover a ford across Panther Creek. Alone in a hostile land, McClernand's division waited nervously for Grant's return in the endless mud of Camp Halleck.

The smoky campfires of McClernand's division dotted the hills and ravines along the east bank of the Tennessee that night. Being out of range of the enemy guns, the Union soldiers were permitted to build fires, which they used to brew their coffee, cook their rations, and keep warm. The campfires were easily seen from Fort Henry, as well as Fort Heiman on the opposite bank. This grand spectacle tended to exaggerate the true numbers of McClernand's men.[28] The songs played by regimental bands also echoed across the way to the ears of the Fort Henry garrison. The repertoire included "Yankee Doodle," "Hail Columbia," "The Star-Spangled Banner," and "St. Patrick's Day in the Morning." Randal McGavock of the 10th Tennessee believed the last tune was specifically played for the benefit of his Irish regiment.[29]

On the morning of February 4, the two armies began to get acquainted. Colonel Heiman entertained no serious ideas about resisting an enemy landing, but positioned the available forces as best he could and sent for General Tilghman. As the courier rode off at a gallop, Heiman sent patrols up both banks, and then directed a cavalry company from Nathan Bedford Forrest's 3rd Tennessee to occupy several trails from Bailey's Ferry to determine the enemy's strength. He then sent two companies of the 4th Mississippi and a section of Culbertson's Battery to the outer rifle pits to defend the Dover Road. Two companies from the 26th Alabama Regiment occupied the rifle pits across the road leading to Bailey's Ferry. Working their way upstream, the Confederate sentries soon spotted the gunboats and endless line of transports through the morning mist, and the black coal smoke trailed back as far as one could see. They launched signal rockets to warn Colonel Heiman.[30]

While Grant's army assembled at Camp Halleck, Gen. Lloyd Tilghman was twelve miles away on the Cumberland, inspecting the defenses at Fort Donelson. At noon, he heard the heavy artillery firing at Fort Henry for half an hour, and then gradually cease. (This firing was the gunboats covering the landing.) The telegraph line to Fort Henry was strangely silent, but at 4:00 in the afternoon, a courier arrived with the news that the enemy was landing in strong force. Tilghman ordered Colonel Head to prepare the 49th and 50th Tennessee to move at a moment's notice with two pieces of artillery in support. The troops were to carry three days' rations and to march without camp equipment. Wagons were permitted only to carry reserve ammunition. The roads between the forts were little more than narrow tracks through the hills, and the heavy rains had turned them into mud. There was a good chance that any wagon would become mired and halt or delay the entire column. Colonel Head later received orders to move his forces to the Peytoma Furnace, halfway on the Dover Road to Fort Henry. This was General Tilghman's reserve for the coming battle.[31]

With orders given, Tilghman departed Fort Donelson with Gantt's Tennessee Cavalry Battalion and accompanied by Major Gilmer, reaching Fort Henry a half hour before midnight. He received an update on the situation and became convinced that the Federals were indeed landing in strong force. The cavalry covering the approaches from Bailey's Landing confirmed this assessment. As arrayed at this time, the Confederate garrison was in position to receive reinforcements from Fort Donelson or retreat.[32]

Around midnight, Tilghman wired General Polk at Columbus to update him on the situation. He also asked for reinforcements, but more important, he asked Polk to come to Fort Henry to take command of the army there. Polk's reply is lost to history, but a later wire from Tilghman sums up his apparent response. Instead of infantry, Polk offered a detachment of cavalry. Tilghman implored Polk not to trust any reinforcement of Fort Henry to General Johnston in Bowling Green, and not to send any raw troops who were just organized, for they would only be in his way.[33] Polk apparently would show as little interest in the twin river forts on the eve of battle as he had the previous seven months.

Leonidas Polk knew that the North wanted the Mississippi open, and that Columbus was the vanguard of its defense. The attack at Belmont and the numbers of feints and reconnoiters in his direction indicated to him that a full attack on Columbus was imminent. In his mind, the forces assembling against Fort Henry were probably a feint, so any dispatch of troops to Tilghman was out of the question. What Polk did not see was that Grant was coming in the back door. If Fort Henry fell, Columbus was flanked and untenable. In the end, General Tilghman and Fort Henry were left to their own devices.

Tilghman had about 2,600 men with him at this point, but they were still mostly raw regiments armed with shotguns and hunting rifles. The best-equipped regiment in the command was the 10th Tennessee, which was uniformly armed with old flintlock muskets that had seen service in the War of 1812. Tilghman quickly organized his available forces into two brigades supported by field artillery batteries to defend the fort.[34] The 48th and 51st Tennessee were located upstream at Paris Landing, and the steamboats *Dunbar* and *Lynn Boyd* were sent to bring them to Fort Henry. The first regiment soon arrived in bulk; only two companies came from the second, under the command of Maj. Edward Clark.[35]

As events unfolded on the Tennessee, General Beauregard finally arrived in Bowling Green and reported to Albert Sidney Johnston. He received a situation briefing and learned, to his amazement, of the deplorable and vulnerable shape the defenses were in. Beauregard found that the Confederates had 14,000 men at Bowling Green and 11,000 more at points southwest of the town. In the center of the Confederate line at Forts Henry and Donelson were 5,500 men. The force at Columbus, on the extreme left, numbered 17,000. Thus a 150-mile line in length was being held by 48,000 troops. West of the Mississippi in Arkansas, but under Johnston's command, were 20,000 under Gen. Earl Van Dorn. Those forces in theory could be brought east across the Mississippi, but politically the Confederates could not abandon Arkansas to the Union forces in Missouri.[36] Opposing this extended line was an imposing array of Federal armies that was beginning to advance upon it in force.

Beauregard was also shocked by the Confederate dispositions. Bowling Green and Columbus were salients that protruded north, leaving Forts Henry and Donelson behind in the center. This array left the Confederates operating on exterior lines, thus making it more difficult to shift forces to threatened areas quickly. This military weakness was offset somewhat by the railroad connecting Columbus and Bowling Green. However, the railroad crossed the Tennessee and Cumberland Rivers and was protected there only by Forts Henry and Donelson. Beauregard also saw that Johnston had not established a strategic reserve. Any shifting of troops would weaken the front of another sector.

In view of the importance of holding the Tennessee, Beauregard proposed to pull most of the forces out of Bowling Green and heavily reinforce Forts Henry and Donelson. There the Confederates would defeat Grant's army with superior numbers while it was under the disadvantages of being isolated and without support. He also stressed that this was an essential measure toward maintaining control of the rivers, as well as placing the available forces in a better overall defensive position.

General Johnston acknowledged the weight of Beauregard's arguments but refused such moves, principally for the reason that a retreat from Bowling Green would open the direct rail line to Nashville to Buell's army. Albert Sidney Johnston was not of the mindset to risk his army in bold moves. If he failed to defeat Grant, the army could be crushed between that force and the army under Buell. If Johnston lost his army, then the entire West was lost as well.[37] What came of the meeting was nothing. Johnston ordered no other forces to the threatened sector, nor did he give General Polk in Columbus any particular guidance or advice. Instead, he would wait and see what developed over the next few days.

In the early morning darkness of February 5, Lloyd Tilghman again wired General Polk in Columbus: "The enemy is landing troops in large forces on this side of the river, within three miles of the fort." A short time later, he added: "If you can re-enforce strongly and quickly we have a glorious chance to overwhelm the enemy . . . the enemy said to be entrenching below. My plans are to concentrate in and under Henry." Tilghman ends his dispatch with these words once again: "Don't trust Johnston's re-enforcing me. We need all. I don't want raw troops who are just organized; they are in my way. Act promptly, and don't trust anyone."[38] The fact that Tilghman did not trust Johnston in matters of reinforcement was justified by the general's inaction to date, but with few exceptions, all of the troops in the department were newly organized and as novice as they came. Just where Tilghman expected Polk to get veteran troops is a matter of speculation. But unfortunately for the garrison of Fort Henry, General Polk was just as unreliable for reinforcements as General Johnston.

After sending this message, Lloyd Tilghman was getting a clearer picture of just how many enemy soldiers were at the landing, and his optimism began to slip away. He also learned that the large masses of Federal troops were growing each hour as more transports arrived. The seven gunboats with their fifty-four heavy cannons had come into view, and it didn't take much imagination to see that Grant planned to use them to pin down the fort while his army marched around and attacked from the rear. Clearly the Confederates were badly outnumbered and outgunned. The few roads were rivers of mud, and the poorly armed Confederates in Fort Henry were not up to the task of maneuvering in formations over the broken terrain. General Tilghman also watched the ever-rising waters of the Tennessee, knowing that within hours, the floodwaters would cover the powder magazines and possibly the guns themselves. Taking all of these factors together, he decided he did not stand a chance against a serious attack.

Under an iron gray sky as the morning fog hung over the hills, General Tilghman ordered the unfinished Fort Heiman abandoned, trusting that the poor roads would prevent Grant from mounting heavy guns there to fire on Fort Henry below. An Alabama cavalry battalion under Capt. David C. Hubbard and Padgett's Spy Company were left behind to harass and annoy any enemy occupation of the fort, while the 27th Alabama and 15th Arkansas were taken over to Fort Henry. The night alarm was passed by word of mouth, not by the "long roll" of the drums, so that the enemy would not be alerted of the move. This redeployment was completed in the early morning, but in the haste to leave, all of the soldiers' camp equipment and blankets were left behind. Tilghman was not yet ready to abandon Fort Henry, though, and he did not plan to leave without some sort of a fight. There were not enough units to man all of the outer works, so only the walls of the fort proper and the rifle pits immediately around the camp were occupied. Detailed instructions were given to each unit, and the garrison settled in for a siege.[39]

Neither side really knew what the other was doing, and the commanders wanted information. Both sides sent reconnaissance parties forward with orders to find out just what the other was up to. During the late morning, Capt. Henry Milner's Confederate troopers made contact with their Illinois counterparts in Capt. James J. Dollins's company. In a sharp engagement and a mounted charge, the Confederate cavalry drove off their antagonists, with a loss of one man for each side. An Illinois infantry regiment supported by even more cavalry then moved up and drove off the Confederates. Tilghman responded to this threat by personally leading five companies of the 10th Tennessee and five from the 4th Mississippi toward the sound of the firing, only to find that both sides had withdrawn to their respective lines. He left the reinforcements in position at the outer works and returned to the fort proper around 5:00 that evening.[40]

If the growing menace downstream didn't dampen the spirits of the beleaguered Confederates, the rain surely did. The night brought even more heavy showers. The already swollen Tennessee River rose even further, bringing the water ever closer to the river batteries of Fort Henry. The fort proper was in danger of being flooded and washed downstream by the annual winter floods. The parade ground was underwater, as were the first two feet of the flagpole. Fatigue parties worked steadily at building up the walls to keep the rapidly rising water out of the fort. The lower magazine was now flooded and under two feet of water. The ammunition had been removed earlier and stored in a temporary magazine above the ground. To protect this magazine, round-the-clock working parties filled sandbags and constructed a traverse.[41] It now truly appeared that it would be a race between the river and Grant to see which would be first to defeat Fort Henry.

Lloyd Tilghman clearly saw the futility of defending Fort Henry against a determined attack by Grant's army and gunboats. He now thought there were at least 25,000 Federals opposite him, and transports continued to arrive each hour bringing even more. After conferring with his senior officers, he made the decision to evacuate Fort Henry and fall back on Fort Donelson. General Tilghman recognized the difficulty of withdrawing his raw troops over the wretched roads with the danger of enemy cavalry at his heels. He needed to buy some time. Tilghman turned to his artillery chief, Capt. Jesse Taylor, and asked, "Can you hold out for one hour against a determined attack?" Receiving a reply in the affirmative, Tilghman turned to his officers and said, "Well then, gentlemen, rejoin your commands and hold them in readiness for instant motion." The force assigned to cover the withdrawal consisted of part of Company B, 1st Tennessee Artillery, commanded by Lt. W. Ornsby Watts, and fifty-four men. A handful of additional volunteers from various units also remained behind to assist the gunners. Captain Taylor was placed overall command of this detachment.[42]

At dark, the two sides broke contact for the evening. On the river, General Grant returned from Paducah with the rest of his army in his wake.

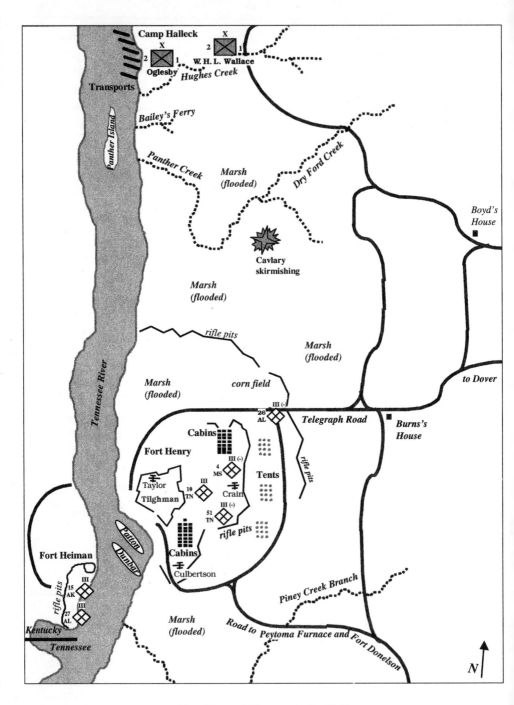

Fort Henry, February 4–5, 1862

The 4th Illinois Cavalry Regiment also rode into camp having completed its overland trek, thus doubling the amount of horsemen available for reconnaissance and security missions. The two brigades of Gen. C. F. Smith's division landed at Pine Bluff, which was about three miles north of Fort Heiman on the western bank of the Tennessee. Once ashore, they were in position to move to the rear of Fort Heiman, although the rain was falling in torrents and the water-saturated roads severely impeded any movement. At the prearranged time, General Smith was to take the small fort and place his artillery in position to shell Fort Henry. Smith was also to prepare to send a brigade back across the river to support McClernand if the need arose.

The navy had confirmed by reconnaissance that there was a channel on either side of Panther Island. For most of its length, the main channel, to the east, was in sight of the guns of Fort Henry. The western channel was covered by the heavy timber of the island, which would allow the flotilla to advance within a short distance of the fort with impunity. Grant did not know it, but this is where Colonel Heiman's detail had planted its underwater torpedoes. Most, if not all of them, however, had already been swept downstream. To employ the topography to best advantage, Flag Officer Foote's gunboats were instructed to form behind Panther Island, using it for cover against Confederate shells.[43]

General McClernand suggested to Grant that some gunboats now use the cover of darkness and rain to run past Fort Henry and take up positions to its rear. He argued that they could cut off the enemy from any further reinforcement and sink any nearby transports. Both Grant and Foote dismissed the suggestion. Instead, General Grant simply told his subordinate commanders to be ready to move in the morning. Ready or not, the army would advance.[44]

Around midnight, Tilghman sent an update of the situation to Johnston. Any reply is lost to history, but no reinforcements were sent.

The morning of February 6 saw the end of the rain and by midmorning the skies were clear and sunny. With the gunboat reconnaissance complete and the last troops arriving from Paducah, Grant made the final touches to his plan.

On this Thursday morning, Grant was ready for the assault to begin and was anxious to get under way, for in his mind, time was not on his side. He knew he had the advantage of men and firepower, but how long he could maintain it was uncertain. General McClernand's reports over the past two days indicated that Fort Henry was receiving reinforcements. No one on the Union side yet realized that Fort Heiman was abandoned and that the Confederate troops were not new reinforcements, but the fort's small garrison being ferried across the river. But given the vital importance of Fort Henry to the Confederates, General Grant naturally assumed that they would be quick to send more troops to the threatened sector. He now calculated that there were about 10,000 Confederates in the fort, with more perhaps on the way.[45] Grant also knew that his commander, Henry Halleck, could call the whole operation off on a whim, even though he was rapidly reinforcing Grant's army from Cairo.[46] Furthermore, in the haste to bring up the army from Paducah, most of the troops did not have their baggage or tents. The incessant rain and cool February temperatures would wreak havoc on the soldiers' health and morale. As a result, he could not delay the operation further.

Although Grant seemed short on time, for the Confederates it had run out. At 11:00 in the morning, Grant's army and Foote's flotilla would commence their assault. The final plan was simple. Foote's fleet would shell the fort while the army marched to the rear of the fort to cut off the escape of the garrison. Across the river, General Smith would capture Fort Heiman.

As was his custom, General Tilghman spent the night on the steamer *Dunbar,* anchored about a mile and a half upstream of Fort Henry. He returned to the fort in the early-morning darkness and planned his actions for the day with Colonel Heiman. Around 10:15 in the morning Lieutenant Colonel McGavock of the 10th Tennessee sent a report that Grant's army was breaking camp and preparing to move. By now, though, floodwaters extended back several hundred yards on the east bank, closing off all but one route of escape. It was time to decide whether to face the combined forces of Grant and the Tennessee River or to retire. Tilghman ordered Heiman to immediately move the bulk of the command to Fort Donelson, while he temporarily remained with the artillerists. His plan was to engage the fleet, inflict as much damage as possible, and buy time for the garrison to escape. Tilghman hoped to continue the fight at Fort Donelson, which, properly reinforced, could offer battle at better odds.[47] No doubt the gunners felt some trepidation as they watched their comrades march away in column toward Fort Donelson and safety.

The morning air of the valley was filled with the clear notes of bugle calls and rolling drums, as regiments in blue moved into their attack positions. The soldiers were told to leave any unit baggage, tents, and blankets at Camp Halleck in order to speed the march. The advance guard of Grant's army moved out of the camp on schedule, but there was some delay with individual regiments. The 4th Illinois Cavalry led McClernand's division on its envelopment of Fort Henry, supported by four artillery batteries. Companies were dispatched to serve as flank guards, and a cavalry company trailed the column as a rear guard. But Grant had not taken into account the poor condition of the roads, and the pace became a crawl as regiments floundered in the mud and in the deep hollows and steep ridges along the seven miles to the rear of Fort Henry.[48]

On the western bank, Smith's division began its march against Fort Heiman on schedule. Smith used an advance guard preceded by a small cavalry detail, taking the single road toward their objective. The *Conestoga* steamed alongside the column and occasionally lobbed a shell ahead of the advancing soldiers to flush out any hidden batteries or ambushes. The midwestern boys cheered at each shot. As the hours passed, the men became energized. If a sheet of backwater spread itself across the road, a bog intruded, or a fallen tree blocked the path, there was a cheer, a rush, and the obstacle lay behind. Even Wood's Illinois Battery was hauled through the mire in short order.[49]

As the army moved on land, the navy was also under way. Flag Officer Foote signaled his flotilla to build steam and clear for action, at 10:20 A.M., the ironclads moved forward in column from Bailey's Ferry to Panther Island and jockeyed into a line formation against the strong current. The three timberclads assumed a position to the rear and right of the ironclads.

Across the way, General Tilghman had returned to Fort Henry on a small boat from supervising the final disposition of forces of Fort Heiman. He watched the Federals prepare their attack from the center battery. Observing Foote's gunboats getting into battle formation, Tilghman gave orders for the crews to man their guns. Captain Taylor inspected the crews and assigned a specific gunboat to each of them. Foote's flag-officer pennant was spotted on the *Cincinnati,* and she became the primary target. Taylor himself took charge of the rifled 24-pounder, and Capt. Charles Hayden assumed command of the 10-inch Columbiad.[50]

With the army on the march, Flag Officer Foote commenced the gunboat attack—the first use of ironclads against earthen fortifications in naval history. As the flotilla rounded the bend at the head of Panther Island, the bright colors of the Confederate flag and Fort Henry came into full view. The *Cincinnati* reached the head of the island at half past noon and commenced firing. An 8-inch shell was lobbed a distance of 1,700 yards and was the signal for the other boats to fire.[51] Battling against the flood current, the fleet slowly approached the fort while attempting to keep abreast of the plodding infantry on the east bank. As ordered, the three wooden gunboats stayed to the rear of the formation, throwing heavy shells into the fort by firing them over the ironclads. The fire from the guns increased with rapidity and accuracy as the range closed.

In the fort, General Tilghman briefly held his fire to assess the effectiveness of the naval bombardment. Satisfied with his observations, he ordered Captain Taylor to fire. The heavy Columbiad fired first, followed quickly by the rifled 24-pounder. As the gunboats closed, the 32-pounders joined in, as did the 42-pounders, dangerously using makeshift ammunition designed for the 32-pounder guns. To the crews of the gunboats, the fort's response was like a sheet of flame.

If Foote had admonished his officers not to waste ammunition, Commander Porter of the *Essex* was a fanatic. Porter issued orders to his gunners not to fire immediately after the *Cincinnati* so as to judge the effect of her fire. The *Essex* gunners were told to profit from the *Cincinnati's* mistakes by adjusting their calculations. The first three rounds from the flagship fell short, and orders on board the *Essex* were to increase the elevation and commence fire. The 9-inch number two port bow gun sent her shell neatly into the breastwork, which exploded with great effect, sending clods of earth in all directions. The *Essex* fired the first shell to strike home, and it was the first of many.

As the battle raged, the wind was blowing across the bows of the gunboats, clearing the smoke and preventing any obstruction of view. As the distance closed, the shell fuses, which were set to fifteen seconds, were reduced to ten and then to five seconds. The elevation of the guns was depressed from seven degrees to six, to five, to four, and then to three.

Aboard the *Essex,* junior officers pointed out to Commander Porter that the officers on the other vessels were leaving the spar decks and going below. Porter hesitated, saying, "Oh yes, I see. We will go too, directly." At this moment, a shot struck the unarmored pilothouse, causing a spray of deadly splinters. This incident encouraged all to quickly seek the protection of the armored casemate below. Porter briefly addressed his crew and ordered those in the stern to relieve the forward gunners. Just after the rotation of the gun crews, disaster struck the *Essex*.[52]

A well-placed shot passed through the casemate just above the left-forward gun port, then penetrated on through the boat to the middle boiler. The ruptured boiler released a torrent of scalding water and steam, which swept the forward half of the vessel. Those near portholes leaped out, but those who could not escape died where they stood in horrible agony. When the steam dissipated, men from the aft section rushed forward to find the deck covered with the dead and dying. Both civilian pilots were found in the wheelhouse, one still holding a spoke of the wheel with one hand, hid other hand grasping the signal bell rope. Commander Porter had been standing by one of the boilers at the time and immediately rushed to a porthole on the starboard side. Throwing himself through, he had expected to fall into the river but was caught by a seaman about the waist and brought to the afterdeck and safety. Seriously scalded, Porter turned command of the vessel over to his executive officer, Lt. Robert K. Riley.[53]

But the *Essex* was out of the fight and the campaign. She had lost thirty-two men dead or wounded by scalding, including her commander. During her conversion from steamboat to ironclad, Porter had seen to it that virtually every system was powered by steam. Without her boilers, she was completely immobilized and was even unable to work her bilge pumps.[54] Although the *Essex* and her feisty skipper would return together in combat, for now the ironclad dropped out of line and fell back with the current until the steamboat *Alps* took her in tow.

Flag Officer Foote noted the loss of the *Essex* and continued to advance, with increasing effect. The other gunboats were taking a pounding but would fare far better than the *Essex*.

The Confederate rifled 24-pounder shifted its fire from the *Essex* to the flagship *Cincinnati*. She received a total of thirty-one hits from Fort Henry, which riddled her pilothouse, after-cabin, and boats, and disabled two of her guns. The only fatal shot was one that passed through the armor at the front of the casemate, killing one man and wounding nine. Foote remained in the pilothouse for the duration of the battle. As for the other boats, the *St. Louis* received seven hits and the *Carondelet* six. Neither had combat casualties or extensive damage.[55] During the battle, however, the *St. Louis* brushed up against the *Carondelet* and became snagged. The two ironclads fought the better part of the battle in this condition before finally separating. In all, the men served their boats with a cool determination.

Meanwhile, the land phase of the operation was not going well at all. General McClernand's division was making very slow progress and actually halted at the fork of the Dover and Telegraph Road. Although it was vital to close this escape route to the Confederates, the southern road to Fort Donelson was still open. The cannonade between the fort and the gunboats did have the effect of increasing the Federal rate of march, though. The men cheered as they picked up the pace, no one wanting to miss out on the fight.[56] Grant had positioned himself according to the textbook with his reserve, which was at the tail of the column. In this position, he was unable to influence the pace of the march and was forced to rely solely on McClernand's aggressiveness and judgment. What McClernand displayed of either is open to question.

The battle was not going well for the Confederates, either. The fort appeared to hold the advantage during the first thirty minutes of the river duel, but Fort Henry was taking a pounding. After the disabling of the *Essex,* a series of disasters struck the fort in rapid succession, tilting all advantages to the side of the gunboats. At half past noon, the 24-pounder rifled gun exploded, killing Sgt. W. J. B. Cubine and disabling every other man at this very effective piece. A naval shell from the *Carondelet* exploded at the mouth of one of the 32-pounders, disabling the gun and killing or wounding all of its crew. A premature explosion at a 42-pounder killed three men and wounded others. A broken priming wire in the gun vent accidentally spiked the 10-inch Columbiad, rendering this gun useless and leaving the fort with no effective heavy guns. Only four 32-pounder smoothbores were still in action.

The remaining Confederate gunners became discouraged, and some left their guns in the mistaken belief that the 32-pounders were ineffective. General Tilghman noticed that some of the guns were not firing and was told that it was because the other crews were dead, wounded, or exhausted. With no other men to relieve them, Tilghman tore off his coat and manned a 32-pounder himself, directing two shots at the *Cincinnati,* which was moving to a position to rake the remaining guns. The ironclad altered course, but all of them had closed to within 600 yards of the fort. General Tilghman could no longer inspire his men. The Confederate fire noticeably slackened.

Colonel Heiman, who had led the garrison out a short distance, returned to the fort at this time for further instructions. There he found the general with the gun crews. Heiman and Major Gilmer of the engineers suggested to Tilghman that he should consider surrender. The embattled commander would not entertain the notion as long as he had any means to resist. But inside the fort was chaos. The guns were disabled or being dismounted, and the dead and dying lay about in the calf-deep water. Many of the cabins and tents had been set afire by the gunboats' shells, sending dense wreaths of smoke.

Meanwhile, onward the three black ironclads came, blasting large chunks from the remaining earthworks. Grant's troops were also continuing to move around the fort, hoping to cut off all escape routes. Time was running out, and Tilghman faced a personal dilemma. It was clearly time for him to rejoin his forces, which were on their way to Fort Donelson. Yet he felt that his place was with the gallant men serving the cannons that were holding off the gunboats. Tilghman ordered Heiman to have fifty more men brought up to assist the exhausted and demoralized gunners. Having no orderly with him, Heiman returned to the retreating column to carry out this order personally.[57]

Just before 2:00 P.M., even Tilghman saw the futility of resisting further, saying: "It is vain to fight longer; our gunners are disabled; our guns dismounted; we can't hold out five minutes longer."[58] He took up a white flag and waved it from the parapet. The dense smoke apparently obscured the gesture, for the fire from the gunboats did not cease. Tilghman ordered Captain Taylor and Orderly Sergeant Jones to haul down the flag from the fort's flagpole. They had to wade through waist-deep water to perform their mission. Lieutenant Colonel Haynes was further down the gun line when the order to cease-fire was given. He had not heard of Tilghman's decision and immediately countermanded the order. An artilleryman grabbed Haynes by the sleeve and pointed at the white flag waving over the fort. Indignant, Haynes replied, "Go tear it down and shoot the man who raised it." The soldier quickly returned with the official news. The crews finally stood down from their guns. As the colors were struck and the cannonade stopped, a silence settled over the valley—a silence that was quickly pierced by the cheers of over 17,000 Union soldiers and sailors.[59]

Colonel Heiman was just returning with fifty men to relieve the exhausted gunners. Since he was not technically present when the surrender occurred, Heiman was ordered to quickly turn around and rejoin the retreating column. Haynes and Major Gilmer also took the opportunity to escape capture. Haynes did so on the claim that he was there only on detached service and was not a member of the garrison. Gilmer apparently took a similar stance, being the department engineer.[60]

Flag Officer Foote initially thought the white flag was a ruse, but he was finally convinced when a small boat came out from the fort to parley. The boat contained the fort's adjutant general and captain of engineers and came alongside the *Cincinnati*. The officers reported that General Tilghman wished to communicate with the flag officer. Foote dispatched officers to hoist the American flag over the fort and to inform Tilghman that he was to be taken on board the *Cincinnati*. By now the waters of the Tennessee had flooded the lower fort proper, covering the infantry support positions along the river reaching the guns. The boat carrying the Union officers pulled in through one of the embrasures.[61] Lloyd Tilghman, with two or three of his staff, then boarded the *Cincinnati* and formally surrendered Fort Henry to Foote. In surrendering to the flag officer, Tilghman remarked, "I am glad to surrender to so gallant an officer." The old salt replied, "You do perfectly right sir, in surrendering, but you should have blown my gunboats out of the water before I would have surrendered to you."[62] Commander Henry Walke was then sent for and told to take command of the fort until the arrival of General Grant. This time, the navy did indeed get ahead of the army.

General Lloyd Tilghman is remembered now for his gallantry and chivalry, but at the time, the strain was telling. After his capture, a newspaper reporter asked, "General, will you be kind enough to give me the correct spelling of your name?" The captive office replied haughtily, "Sir, I do not desire that my name should be made use of at all, in connection with this affair, except as it may appear in the reports of General Grant." When told his name was needed only for the list of prisoners, Tilghman shot back, "You will oblige me sir, by not giving my name in any newspaper connection whatever."[63]

With victory came a euphoria that pushed the discipline of some of the new crewmen beyond their limits. In approaching to take possession of Fort Henry, the *St. Louis* ran ahead of the fleet, and with frantic cheers, some of her crew landed at the fort, contrary to the express orders of the flag officer. Adding to Foote's ire, when the *Cincinnati* and *Carondelet* steamed up together, the latter ran aground near the batteries. The *Cincinnati* did not push onto land, and when she cut her engines, she drifted down with the current. At first glance, it appeared that the *Carondelet* was pulling ahead of the flagship, when in fact she was stuck fast while the flagship drifted downstream. With emotions running high, Foote grabbed a voice trumpet and shouted to the "insubordinate" Commander Walke to maintain his place in the line. In frustration, Foote passed the voice trumpet to a junior officer, who had as little effect on the situation. The misunderstanding was soon realized, and tempers subsided as the *Carondelet* pulled off the bank.[64]

The gallant Fort Henry garrison surrendered after fighting for one hour and fifteen minutes. Twelve officers and sixty-six men in the fort, as well as sixteen men in the hospital boat *Patton,* surrendered. Fort Henry had no wagons, so the retreating garrison had left virtually everything behind, including all of the camp equipage and stores. Accounts conflict, but casualties may have been as high as fifteen men killed and twenty wounded. Also captured were about twenty cannons of various sizes. Foote planned to turn all of this over to General Grant as soon as his army cleared the mud. Tilghman's headquarters ship, *Dunbar,* escaped capture for the moment by beating a hasty retreat upstream.[65]

Fort Henry itself was a shambles. Some of the small log cabins in the rear of the fort were still on fire, and sailors were dispatched to put out the flames. Several 9-inch shells from the *Essex* were found beyond the cabins unexploded. The rest of the fort was equally devastated. Some shells had passed through or detonated in the breastworks, throwing tons of dirt and debris in every direction. After the wounded had been cared for and the

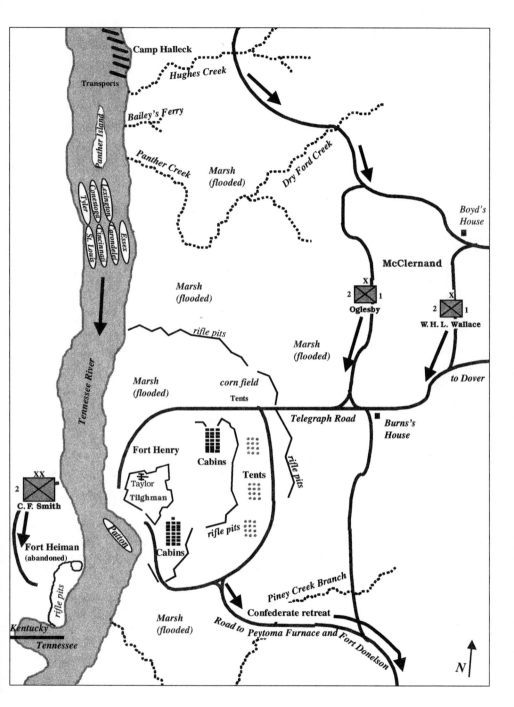

Fort Henry, February 6, 1862

excitement subsided, the men began the gruesome task of collecting the dead from the land and water and giving them a decent burial.[66]

Still short of his objective, General McClernand noticed the quiet along the river and learned that the Confederates were evacuating the fort. He ordered his cavalry to advance to find out if the report was true. About three miles southeast of the fort, the blue cavalry came upon the rear of the retreating Confederate column. The infantry, led by Colonel Oglesby and the 18th Illinois, pushed on through the mud, and the head of the column entered Fort Henry at 3:30 in the afternoon.[67]

On the western bank, the operation there was coming to a close. After an hour and a half of slogging through the mud, Gen. C. F. Smith's men were nearing Fort Heiman. Apparently the Alabama cavalry battalion and Padgett's Spy Company did little or nothing to hinder their progress, for there is no mention of resistance in any subsequent reports. The longest delay occurred when the column was required to make a temporary bridge to carry the field guns over a bog. As the column finally approached Fort Heiman, Smith noticed that the cannon duel on the river had stopped. Shortly after, a scout rode up and reported that Fort Heiman was abandoned. Smith asked the trooper how he knew this and was told that the man had already been inside the works. The general exclaimed, "The devil!" and ordered his lead brigade to move forward quickly and occupy the little fort.[68]

Brigadier General Lew Wallace rode at the head of his brigade as it filed into Fort Heiman. Stopping at a double Sibley tent, he entered to find papers scattered about in careless heaps. A glance showed that this had been Colonel Heiman's headquarters. Detailing an aide to collect the papers, Wallace went onto an adjoining tent to find an agreeable surprise. Dinner was ready. On the fire simmered a pot with a block of pork "done to a turn." Fresh corn bread was nearby, and upon invitation, General Smith joined in the meal. Down below, Wallace could see the Stars and Stripes flying from the flagpole over Fort Henry. From his perch, he noted that the fort was nearly submerged. Meanwhile, men in blue swarmed through the cabins, tents, and rifle pits.[69]

Back in St. Louis, General Halleck, as yet unaware of the victory, wired Washington: "Fort Henry is largely re-enforced. . . . They intend to make a stand there. Unless I get more forces I may fail to take it. . . . The gunboats are bombarding it. I am sending every available man from Missouri."[70] It probably did not embarrass him in the least when he found out the results of the attack a short time later, for he did not miss a beat in his telegrams. The euphoria of victory quickly washed the memory of the message from everyone's mind. Any reinforcements sent under this plea would only add to the strength of Grant's army for the expected move on Fort Donelson.

As Grant's army occupied Fort Henry, the Confederates tried their best to reach the relative safety of Fort Donelson to the east over the wretched roads. Colonel Heiman's column had to ford the flooded Standing Rock Creek five times while being harassed by McClernand's cavalry. The stream was a violent torrent that required the men to lock arms together to form a chain. They would ease in the first men, who would then pull the others out when they reached the opposite side. The Confederates soon found out that they could not drag the field artillery through the muddy bottoms and swift waters of Standing Rock Creek and abandoned six field guns and a caisson. During the march, a number of Confederates also discarded weapons and accoutrements in order to speed their pace. The pursuing Federal cavalry scooped up much of this equipment.[71]

Elements of the 4th Illinois Cavalry and some of the independent cavalry companies caught up with and attacked the rear of the gray column. Lieutenant Colonel McGavock bitterly noted in his diary that the 9th Tennessee Cavalry Battalion under Lieutenant Colonel Gantt did not screen the retreat as planned. Instead, the gray troopers nearly stampeded over the infantry in their haste to retreat. Gantt's men continued to ride to the east at a gallop until they were out of sight. To meet the threat to the rear, the 15th Arkansas and the two companies of the 26th Alabama halted, turned about, and formed a line of battle. The Southern infantry returned the fire of the pursuing enemy troopers, and in the melee, Major Lee of the Arkansas regiment, Capt. Elbert C. Leach of the Alabama battalion, and thirty-six men were separated from their units and captured.[72] The Federal cavalry continued its pursuit for a time, but at a much more discreet distance. The column of exhausted Confederates reached the safety of Fort Donelson at 2:00 that morning. Some of the men had been without food for over thirty-six hours, and the hellish march was a great ordeal for the raw soldiers who had never seen active service. Their ordeal was far from over.

In summary, the battle of Fort Henry was the first step in the dismemberment of the Confederacy and was a great success. Unlike the battles at Belmont and Mill Springs, here was a clear and decisive Union victory. General Grant had seized the initiative and for the rest of the campaign, both the Federal high command and the Confederates would try to catch up with him.

The success on the Tennessee was a purely naval victory and catapulted Flag Officer Foote to national acclaim. However, it was General Grant's show. Any failure on the part of the army to capture the garrison was blamed on the poor, muddy roads and the fact that the Confederates chose to flee instead of putting up a fight. Grant needed all of the credibility in order to obtain support from senior officials in the Lincoln administration and Congress in the weeks to come, and this battle cemented their confidence in him.

The operation against Fort Henry was also important in that it further trained the officers and men in the art of war. In fact, at this battle, an army was born. Until this time, the forces under Grant consisted of individual regiments that were scattered throughout his department, guarding river forts, railroad bridges, and flushing out guerrilla bands. They were mostly novice recruits led primarily by amateurs just learning the trade of war. Almost unique in the western theater at that time, these regiments were being forged into an army in the furnace of war, not on the parade field. Battles such as Belmont and Fort Henry, and the reconnoitering in between, were teaching the skills of moving large numbers of men in coordination and keeping them supplied. Small-unit leaders were gaining self-confidence, and their men's faith in them grew as well. Although Grant's army at Fort Henry fired few shots, the experience gained would be invaluable in the coming days. To say that the men who fought in the campaign would become the nucleus of the battle-hardened and victorious Army of the Tennessee is no understatement.

Grant did well at Fort Henry in spite of some serious shortcomings. He had not yet developed a staff to assist him on minute or generally routine actions, which consumed a great amount of the general's time and energy. The organization of his army was *ad hoc* at best, essentially put together of units scattered across his department and organized as they loaded the transports. But many of these regiments consisted of veterans of Belmont and smaller skirmishes and were led by capable officers such as C. F. Smith and Lew Wallace.

Ulysses S. Grant was clearly learning his trade as a general officer. He had learned from his experience at Belmont, and this time he maintained a reserve force. Yet the poor roads would not have allowed him to employ it quickly had he needed to. By staying with the reserve toward the rear of the column, he was not in a position from which he could influence the battle. Had he been at the front of the column, he could have spurred the men into a faster pace and countermanded any delaying orders by McClernand.[73]

An element of running an army that was not tested in this operation or any other up to this point was the resupply of ammunition during a protracted battle. Belmont and the other skirmishes in the previous months did not call for a massive movement of additional ammunition to the front.

When he made mistakes, Grant took note and made efforts to correct them. But this is one area he failed to adequately note at this time.

Conversely, the Confederates had shown that they were learning little or were learning the wrong lessons. At Belmont, Grant demonstrated that he was a man of action and that he could and would use the rivers to carry his army. This method of river-borne operations was ideal for use on the Tennessee and Cumberland Rivers, but still the Confederates gave the forts guarding them a low priority for men and materiel.

Tactically, the Confederates had of necessity spent most of their time digging ramparts and trenches and had no real training in fighting a battle of maneuver. The men under Tilghman's command at Fort Henry not only were too few in number to effectively oppose McClernand at Camp Halleck, but also lacked the skills of fighting and maneuvering in formation to even harass the invaders. General Tilghman could only send token forces to skirmish with the Federal patrols. Acknowledging that he was greatly outnumbered, when it came time for a real fight, he sent his men scurrying to Fort Donelson without even a pretense of resistance from the infantry.

One of the poorest lessons the Confederate troops learned from their officers was that surrender or fleeing the battlefield was somehow tolerable. Colonel Heiman, Lieutenant Colonel Haynes, and Major Gilmer fled from the scene even though they were inside the fort at the time of surrender. And the Confederate officers learned that when they surrendered to General Grant, they would be well treated and shown a measure of respect. The captured soldiers were treated well, too, receiving medical treatment and food, and the dead were buried with some measure of dignity. This was relayed to the Confederates through Tilghman's after-action report, which was allowed to pass through the lines a day after the battle. The press also wrote of how well the prisoners were treated and it is most probable that the defenders of Fort Donelson suspected they would receive good treatment if captured. The net effect of this may have been to lessen the resolve of the commanders and soldiers in the weeks to come. And the precedent had been set that a fortified position was not necessarily defended to the bitter end. At the brink of defeat, it was acceptable to simply leave and escape capture.[74]

As for the Confederate command, Lloyd Tilghman never planned on surrendering himself at Fort Henry. It was purely an emotional decision made in the heat of battle. Tilghman's original plan was to fight briefly with the batteries, rejoin his column marching toward Fort Donelson, and renew the fight there. He was in command of both forts and thus responsible for each one equally. By surrendering himself at Fort Henry, he was derelict in his duty to defend Fort Donelson. History has been kind to Lloyd Tilghman, mainly because of his gallant defense of the doomed bastion and his gentlemanly demeanor afterward.

Generals Johnston and Polk also deserve some scrutiny. They each had more than two days in which to shift forces to the threatened sector but refused. Instead, each was convinced that an attack was imminent to his front, and they both left Tilghman to defend Fort Henry with a fraction of the men and firepower to successfully do so. If the plan was to abandon Fort Henry, they had several days during which they could have deployed units to contain the disaster or gathered enough combat power to defeat Grant in his isolated position. What occurred instead was a paralysis in the senior levels of the Confederate command and a loss of an opportunity to restore the line.

The day after the battle, Flag Officer Foote was able to assess the effectiveness of the new ironclads. In his report to the secretary of the navy, he wrote: "The armored gunboats resisted the shot of the enemy when striking the casemate. The *Cincinnati,* flagship, received thirty-one shots; the *Essex* fifteen. The *St. Louis* received seven; and the *Carondelet,* six; killing one and wounding nine in the *Cincinnati,* killing one in the *Essex,* while the casualties in the latter from steam amounted to twenty-eight in number. The *Carondelet* and *St. Louis* met with no casualties."[75]

In all, Foote was very pleased with the performance of his commanders and crew. Few of them had worked together before, and for those that had, it had not been long enough to really feel like a well-drilled team. Yet he heaped a good deal of praise on his deserving men. In their first determined fight, they stood to their posts with exceptional gallantry. It was certainly more than the old salt Foote would have expected from a menagerie of raw recruits from the Midwest.

But the reports were a bit misleading. Although the casualties due to direct fire were fairly light, it was clear that the boilers and machinery were vulnerable. A gunboat commander could not count on even the frontal armor to protect his ship against the heavier artillery projectiles, particularly at close range. The level of the river negated any advantage of height the fort had when first constructed. This meant that the Confederates were firing on a flat arch, which was the kind of shot the ironclads' armor was designed to protect against. The enemy gunners were never in any position to deliver fire onto the unarmored topsides. It was later found that the Confederates also knew the boats' weaknesses. In fact, one of the prisoners had the written specifications of the gunboats, and the gunners all knew where to strike them in the most vital parts.[76] Yet all in all, the boats were effective. Andrew Hull Foote and his officers realized, however, that they were relatively lucky and may not be so again.

One can question Flag Officer Foote's judgment in leaving any ironclad gunboat behind at Cairo when the crews of the older wooden gunboats could have been used to man them. As used in battle, the timberclads remained behind their armored sisters and lobbed shells into the fort at long range. Although they had some effect on the battle, the decisive means to deal with the fort's guns was to dismount them with solid shot. Never designed to withstand direct hits by cannons, the older boats were completely ill suited for a direct attack on any fort. So why didn't Foote take their crews and use them to operate the more effective ironclads?

One reason was Foote's concern over the effect on crew morale if they were transferred to another boat. In forming the ironclad crews, many sailors were on the brink of mutiny when told of their last-minute transfer to other boats. The crews of the timberclads as a whole had operated as a team for several months. So although the vessels were not armored, the wooden gunboats were probably the most efficient vessels in the flotilla.[77] Another reason was that the timberclads were ideally suited for their subsequent mission, a raid up the Tennessee River.

The location of Fort Henry obviously doomed it from the onset against an attack during the winter months. In fact, the fort would be completely underwater within two days.[78] In hindsight, had Grant delayed his attack, there would have been no battle at all. In spite of the survey team's and Captain Taylor's warnings the previous summer, work continued on the fort up to the time of the battle.

Reports of Fort Henry's strength had varied widely from very strong to very poor, but many times there was a personal agenda behind the opinion. Major Gilmer of the engineers wrote: "The main fort (a strong field work of fine bastion front) had been put in good condition for defense, and seventeen guns mounted on substantial platforms, twelve of which were so placed as to bear upon the river."[79] On the other hand, General Tilghman, commander of Fort Henry, had another view: "The work itself was well built; it was completed long before I took command, but strengthened greatly by myself and in building embrasures and epaulements of sand bags. An enemy had but use their most common sense in obtaining the advantage of high water, as was the case, to have complete and entire control of the position." Tilghman further states in his report that Fort Henry was in a "wretched military position. . . . The history of military engineering records no parallel to this case." Tilghman was never slow to find fault or to voice his displeasure, as shown in his correspondence with the various departments that were to send him men, supplies, and ordnance. He had also been at odds with the engineers supervising work on Fort Henry. Yet it was not until after the surrender that he objected to the *location* of the fort.[80]

There certainly had been other options for the location of Fort Henry. One was at the mouth of Standing Rock Creek, where the original survey team recommended construction. Walking around the area today, one can see a number of other sites that would have served well, or certainly better. The present-day Boswell Landing is just a mile downstream from the original site. Even with the damming of the Tennessee, it is more than ten feet clear of the water. In February 1862, a fort at this location would have been more than thirty feet above the floodwaters. Certainly the choosing of Kirkman's Landing over the objections of the engineers ranks among the most egregious military follies.

CHAPTER SIX

The Tennessee River Raid

February 6–12, 1862

WHEN GENERAL GRANT ENTERED FORT HENRY, HE GAVE THE GO-AHEAD to the next phase of the operation. Hardly had the smoke of battle cleared when Flag Officer Foote dispatched the three timberclads, the *Tyler*, *Conestoga*, and *Lexington*, under the command of Lt. Seth Ledyard Phelps, on a special mission. This little gunboat division was to steam up the Tennessee to destroy or disable all installations that were supporting the enemy war effort. All ferries, steamboats, and bridges were likewise to be destroyed or captured to disrupt the Confederate transportation network. Captured materials and boats were to be brought back intact or destroyed in place if that proved unfeasible. Phelps eagerly ordered his boats to build up steam and proceeded upriver.

This operation would underscore the importance of Fort Henry and just how vulnerable the Confederacy was now.

A mile upstream from Fort Henry, the *Dunbar* lay at anchor while her crew waited for the outcome of the battle. When the three enemy gunboats began to move in his direction, Capt. Gus Fowler ordered his boat upstream at best speed. The *Dunbar* arrived at the Memphis & Charleston Railroad Bridge, twenty-five miles above Fort Henry, in the late afternoon with word of the disaster. Here were the old camps of the 48th and 51st Tennessee, as well as the alarmed city of Danville. Hurried plans to evacuate military supplies and other property were made, and the steamers *Appleton Belle*, *Lynn Boyd*, *Samuel Orr*, and *Time* arrived to load up what they could and flee upriver.[1]

The gunboat flotilla arrived at the railroad bridge after dark. Lieutenant Phelps knew that cutting this line would disrupt communications between Johnston's army in Bowling Green and Polk's in Columbus. It was in fact his primary target for the raid. The bridge was an imposing structure 1,200 feet long, with several hundred feet of trestlework at either end and a swinging draw in the middle. The draw of the bridge was found closed and blocking the river, the machinery to turn it disabled by the retreating Confederates. About a mile and a half farther from the bridge were five or six enemy transports escaping upstream to spread the alarm. The way barred for the moment, the frustrated Phelps halted and landed a party to open the draw. The engineers completed this task in about an hour, with much swearing and backbreaking labor.

The *Tyler* was the slowest of the gunboats, so Phelps ordered her commander, Lt. William Gwin, to land another party to destroy a length of the track on the eastern approaches and to secure any military stores that might be in the area. He was not to destroy the bridge, however. General Halleck at this time wanted only the railroad denied to the Confederates. Halleck saw that the bridge could be used in future campaigns after the Federals repaired the railroad at their leisure. Gwin's crew made quick work of it. The men tore up some of the trestlework at the end of the bridge and burned it as well as a quantity of camp equipage found nearby. The railroad linking Columbus to Bowling Green was now cut, and Albert Sidney Johnston's army was divided.[2]

While pillaging the deserted Confederate camp, the men found some official-looking documents, which they brought back to Gwin. The documents detailed the Confederate naval defense plans of the Mississippi, Tennessee, and Cumberland Rivers and were of significant intelligence value. They were signed by Lt. I. N. Brown, formerly of the U.S. Navy, who now held a commission in its Southern counterpart. Three letters were from Matthew F. Maury, the inventor of the torpedoes laid at Fort Henry. More papers told of a steamer being converted upstream to an ironclad called the *Eastport.* Gwin was probably quite relieved to read that she was not yet ready for action.[3] Once his work was done, Gwin ordered his boat to catch up with the others at best speed.

As the crew of the *Tyler* had been going about their work on shore, the *Conestoga* and *Lexington* were pursuing the fleeing steamboats. Within five hours, the two gunboats caught sight of the Confederate vessels. The *Conestoga* surged ahead, leaving the *Lexington* in her wake. The Confederates soon realized they could not outrun the gunboat and scuttled the three vessels to avoid capture. Nudging up to the bank, the first to go was the *Samuel Orr.* She had lately been used as a hospital ship by the Fort Henry garrison, but her cargo this day was a quantity of munitions and torpedoes, which exploded soon after the crew applied the torch. A second boat also carried ordnance, which exploded in quick succession. Phelps had the foresight to halt his boat 1,000 yards downstream. Yet even at this distance, the *Conestoga* was affected by the concussion. Skylights were shattered, the upper deck was raised, doors were forced open, and locks and fastenings were broken. Falling debris fell over a half-mile radius. The explosions flattened the nearby house of Judge Creavatt, a Union man. Phelps suspected the Confederates chose this spot to scuttle their boats for that reason.[4]

Alone on a hostile river, Lieutenant Phelps decided to wait for the other two gunboats to catch up. Besides, the trailing *Lexington* did not have a pilot on board and did not know where the hazards to navigation lay.

Reunited, the three Union boats proceeded upriver. As they approached the half dozen or so ferryboats active along the way, their owners scuttled them to avoid their capture. There was still enough evidence floating on the water to indicate that they had all been carrying military supplies. At Hawesport and Perryville, the *Conestoga* stopped to lower Confederate flags flying defiantly. The Union boats received musket fire from the east bank on occasion, which they halted by lobbing a naval shell in the general direction of the shots.

During the night of February 7, the little flotilla arrived at the landing at Cerro Gordo in Harding County. There in the darkness was the hull of the *Eastport,* still far from complete. Armed details were immediately sent on board to look for any means the Confederates had placed to destroy the vessel. The men found that the suction pipes were broken, with the aim of flooding and sinking the boat. The leaks were soon stopped. Confederate sharpshooters tried their aim at the navy men, but again a few shells from the heavy naval cannons dispersed them.

Lieutenant Phelps surveyed the *Eastport* and found that she was 280 feet long and about half completed. Piled around the vessel was 250,000 feet of prime lumber, iron plating, machinery, nails, spikes, and fittings. Phelps saw immediately what a valuable prize he had captured and directed that all of the building materials and fittings be loaded aboard her. The crew of the *Tyler* was left behind to complete the preparations of removing the *Eastport.*[5]

Meanwhile, the *Conestoga* and *Lexington* proceeded farther up the yellow waters of the Tennessee. The two gunboats passed Eastport, Mississippi, shortly after daylight on February 8. Farther on, at Chickasaw, they came upon two more enemy steamers. The first boat was the *Sallie Wood,* which was laid up. The second was the *Muscle,* loaded with iron destined for Richmond's Tredegar Iron Works. These boats were promptly seized and prize crews put on board. The *Muscle* was damaged during her capture, but makeshift repairs stopped the leaks.

Proceeding into Alabama, the two gunboats reached the city of Florence, where shoals just upstream of town prevented them from continuing farther. Three more Southern steamboats were set afire by their crews when the gunboats came into view. One drifted in the current toward the gunboats, which maneuvered away from the flaming wreck. A few sharpshooters fired, without effect.

Here again an armed party was put ashore. The men found considerable quantities of supplies marked "Fort Henry." They brought these off the burning boats, which they then cut loose to clear the wharves. These supplies and others on the wharf were promptly seized and loaded on the gunboats and captured vessels. More iron plating for the *Eastport* was found. What could not be carried off was destroyed, with the exception of property that citizens came forward to claim with proof of private ownership.[6]

An armed party also went to the telegraph office. Using their own equipment, the navy operators tapped into the system and were soon listening to the messages that passed through Florence. It took time, but the Confederates found out what was going on and rerouted the telegraph traffic through Montgomery.[7]

As Phelps's men took to their tasks, a delegation from the city of Florence arrived on the scene. Fearing their fair city would be looted and destroyed, the citizens questioned Lieutenant Phelps as to his intent. They wished to quiet the fears of their wives and daughters, and wanted the naval commander's assurance that the womenfolk would not be molested. They also asked him to spare the railroad bridge. Phelps assured the delegation that the women would not be harmed. He was there to protect the Union of the United States and to enforce its laws. He also told them he would spare the bridge, seeing no military importance to it.[8]

The *Conestoga* and *Lexington* departed Florence when their work was done. By the evening of February 8, the two gunboats returned to Cerro Gordo, where the *Tyler* and *Eastport* lay. The crew of the *Tyler* had gotten a large quantity of the lumber on board the *Eastport,* and the crews of the other two gunboats pitched in to complete the job. As a finishing touch, Lieutenant Phelps ordered the lumbermill owned by a Jesse Hobbs destroyed.

Riding on a wave of success on the river, Phelps considered an opportunity for an unorthodox land operation. In his absence, Lieutenant Gwin of the *Tyler* had enlisted twenty-five loyal Tennessee men, who provided information on a Confederate unit at nearby Savannah, Tennessee. There, an infantry battalion commanded by Lt. Col. James M. Crew was reportedly made up of 600 to 700 men who were poorly armed and disciplined.[9] Some of these men were apparently conscripts ready to desert. After consulting with Gwin and Lieutenant Shirk, Phelps decided to attack the enemy encampment.

Thirty infantrymen transferred over from the *Lexington,* which was left behind to guard the *Eastport* and other captured boats. Reinforced, the *Conestoga* and *Tyler* steamed back upstream to Savannah. Before dawn, the gunboats made the landing without incident and put ashore 130 infantrymen and a 12-pounder rifled howitzer under the overall command of Lieutenant Gwin. Marching inland, he soon discovered that the camp was deserted. Warned of the gunboats' return, the Confederates had departed in haste, leaving all of their camp equipage, clothing, tents, and provisions. The unit eventually made its way to Murfreesboro, but most of the unwilling conscripts returned to their homes. Disappointed, Gwin had his men collect all of the Confederate property. What could not be carried off was destroyed. A large mailbag was also seized, and any letters with military information were kept.

The men reboarded the gunboats in short order and dropped down to Coffee Landing. Here the Confederates had stored a number of arms collected under the "press law." An armed party led by Second Master Jason Goudy from the *Tyler* secured about seventy rifles and fowling pieces.[10]

Back at Fort Henry, the ironclad *Carondelet* along with two companies of infantrymen on the steamer *Illinois* were sent to the Memphis & Charleston Railroad Bridge to complete the sabotage done by the crew of the *Tyler.* No longer content to leave the key bridge only damaged, the high command wanted it destroyed. Colonel James Riggins, Jr., of Grant's staff commanded the expedition, which siezed over 200 hogsheads of tobacco, 2,500 bushels of wheat, and large quantities of corn and plug tobacco in addition to destroying the bridge.

Upstream, Lieutenant Phelps seemed satisfied with the damage inflicted upon the Confederacy during his raid. He took the *Conestoga* and *Tyler* back to Cerro Gordo, where the rest of his flotilla lay. There the *Eastport, Sallie Wood,* and *Muscle* were taken in tow for the journey downstream. At the railroad bridge, the *Muscle* sprang a leak that defied all attempts to stop it. She sank with a large quantity of lumber meant for the *Eastport.* The remaining vessels passed through the draw of the bridge, but with difficulty. A long delay was caused when the *Eastport* caught the pier and swung against the bridge. It took nearly ten hours to clear her and allow the rest of the boats to pass the obstruction.[11]

In the afternoon of February 12, the timberclad division under Lieutenant Phelps returned triumphantly to Fort Henry. The final count for the raid was three enemy steamboats and the *Eastport* captured. The Con-

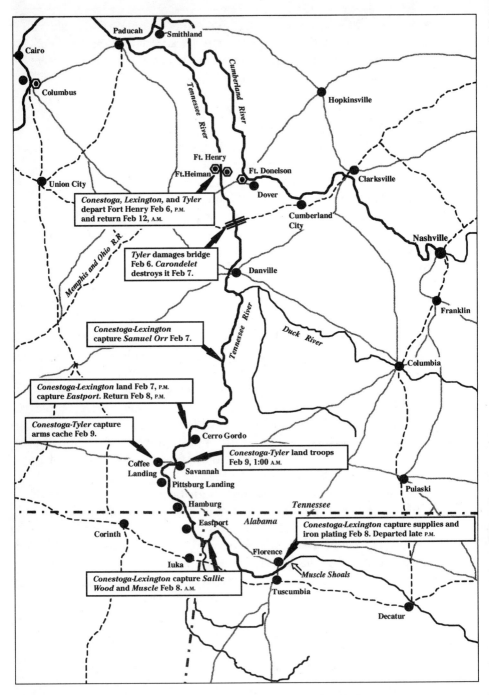

Paducah
Smithland
Cairo
Columbus
Hopkinsville
Tennessee River
Cumberland River
Ft. Henry
Ft.Heiman
Ft. Donelson
Clarksville
Union City
Dover
Conestoga, Lexington, and Tyler
depart Fort Henry Feb 6, P.M.
and return Feb 12, A.M.
Cumberland
City
Nashville
Memphis and Ohio R.R.
Tyler damages bridge
Feb 6. **Carondelet**
destroys it Feb 7.
Danville
Franklin
Tennessee River
Duck River
Conestoga-Lexington
capture **Samuel Orr** Feb 7.
Columbia
Conestoga-Lexington land Feb 7, P.M.
capture **Eastport**. Return Feb 8, P.M.
Conestoga-Tyler capture
arms cache Feb 9.
Cerro Gordo
Coffee
Landing
Savannah
Conestoga-Tyler land troops
Feb 9, 1:00 A.M.
Pittsburg Landing
Pulaski
Hamburg
Tennessee
Eastport
Alabama
Corinth
Conestoga-Lexington capture supplies and
iron plating Feb 8. Departed late P.M.
Florence
Iuka
Muscle Shoals
Conestoga-Lexington capture **Sallie**
Wood and **Muscle** Feb 8. A.M.
Tuscumbia
Decatur

Tennessee River Raid, February 6–12, 1862

federates had been forced to burn six boats loaded with supplies to prevent their capture. Two boats were known to be still operating on the river but were probably hidden up one of the tributaries of the Tennessee.[12] The raiders also had captured a great deal of materiel and broken up the organization of an enemy regiment.

Phelps was rightfully proud of his accomplishments and detailed them in his official report to Flag Officer Foote. He described a situation along the river, however, that few had considered possible. While his flotilla was striking deep into the Confederacy, the crews saw signs of loyalty to the United States all along the river. Men, women, and children often gathered in the hundreds shouting their welcome and cheering the flag of the Union. Phelps pointed out that these people did so in spite of the threat of reprisals after the gunboats' departure. He even had some physical evidence for his claims of patriotism in the form of almost 300 new recruits on board the *Tyler*.[13] Newspaper reporters traveling with the expedition seconded these observations, writing of Union families all along the Tennessee displaying the American flag and hailing the fleet with shouts of joy. Not mentioned by Phelps in his report, the people of Florence even invited the boats' officers to a grand ball in their honor, which was politely declined.[14]

Even if these incidents were true, the next invading force would not receive such a friendly welcome in April.

Sending the three timberclads upriver was a bold move on Foote's part. They had no armor and would be easy prey for any hidden battery or fort along the river. But sending the armored boats upstream was not an option. Most of the ironclads had sustained damage during the attack on Fort Henry and needed to return to Cairo for repairs. The *Carondelet* was relatively intact, but her coal bunkers were nearly empty and she could not steam all the way to Florence.[15] Also, the ironclads' slower speeds would not allow them to chase down the nimble steamboats on the river.

Although they were no match against heavy cannons, the wooden gunboats proved ideally suited for ascending the Tennessee River. With their lighter draft, higher speed, and maneuverability, they were able to proceed upriver to destroy bridges, capture steamboats, and raise havoc. Since no one knew what Confederate defenses lay beyond Fort Henry or the condition of the river, there was reason to believe that a boat or two would be damaged or lost on the raid. Although the loss of any gunboat would be grave, the loss or capture of one of the new ironclads would be disastrous. By comparison, the timberclads were somewhat expendable.

Fortunately for Phelps and his boats, there were no other defenses along the Tennessee River. The loss of Fort Henry had truly opened the river all the way into northern Alabama. The Confederates had made a grave error in not properly building Fort Henry, as well as constructing a secondary fort to buy time if the first one fell. With the river controlled by Union gunboats, the Confederates were unable to build an ironclad to challenge them. Any ship capable of conversion to one was captured or destroyed.

The defeat of Fort Henry by the gunboats and the Tennessee River raid also had a tremendous psychological effect upon the Confederates. "Gunboat fever" gripped the hearts and minds of the civilian populace, who fled at the approach of the vessels. These two events also had a dramatic effect on a number of senior military leaders, particularly Albert Sidney Johnston.

The sparing of the bridge at Florence by Lieutenant Phelps was a tremendous blunder. It did indeed have significant military value. Destroying the bridge would have virtually cut the few rail connections within the western Confederacy in two. And it was over this bridge that Johnston would move his forces to Corinth and on to the battle at Shiloh six weeks later.

News of the number of loyalists on the Tennessee surely must have been heartening news to President Lincoln and probably influenced future plans. In April, the Union army penetrated deep into the South on the Tennessee River, not the Cumberland or Mississippi. This advance was aimed to turn the flank of the Mississippi defenses and take the rail center at Corinth. Perhaps the decision to strike here was strengthened by the belief that there would be strong Union sentiment in the area. This support theoretically would manifest itself through intelligence on enemy movements and the acquisition of supplies and recruits. Liberating loyal areas would also help Lincoln politically.

The unorthodox practice of landing navy crewmen for raids ended on March 1, 1862, by order of Flag Officer Foote. Although a potentially effective tactic, Foote felt he could not afford to lose any of his understrength crews on what he felt was an army mission.[16]

CHAPTER SEVEN

The Gathering of the Hosts

February 7–11, 1862

As Commander Phelps's gunboats ascended the Tennessee, General Grant deployed his forces on what little dry ground there was around Fort Henry to organize for the next advance. Cavalry was sent to reconnoiter eastward toward the next objective, Fort Donelson. The patrols found that there were two main roads to that bastion, the direct route being about twelve miles. Another route swung to the southeast for some length, then turned due east, for a total distance of fourteen miles. They learned, too, that the worst of the mud and timbered ravines was along the first two or three miles from the Tennessee River. The terrain between Forts Henry and Donelson was very rolling, thickly covered with timber, and sparsely populated.[1] It was ideal for ambushing columns strung out along the narrow little roads.

So far, the scouts reported that the Confederates had not made any attempts to obstruct the roads by felling trees or destroying bridges. Grant sent strong detachments of cavalry to scour the area continuously to prevent any enemy details from doing just that. On the other hand, the Confederate picket screen was strong enough that none of the cavalry patrols were able to get close enough to Fort Donelson to assess its strength or ascertain how many troops were there. A composite battalion of cavalry under Col. John Noble pushed back a Confederate patrol until shots were heard to the rear. Noble then found his band nearly surrounded, and after a few volleys and some hard riding, the men made good their escape. As long as the Confederate picket screen was this strong, Grant would have to approach Fort Donelson not fully knowing what he was up against. He was guessing that in their present state, the Confederates were demoralized, confused, and weak. At this time, he was right, but the situation would change rapidly.

After organizing the camp and sending out the cavalry, Grant sent a report back to General Halleck to let him know of the particulars of the battle. His brief statement read: "Fort Henry is ours. The gunboats silenced the batteries before the investment was completed. I think the garrison must have commenced the retreat last night. Our cavalry followed, finding two guns abandoned in the retreat. I shall take and destroy Fort Donelson on the 8th and return to Fort Henry."[2] He sent a longer report and copies of his orders through channels. Grant was unhappy about the escape of the garrison, but he spoke of the coming operation against Fort Donelson with confidence, continuing to think that it was even weaker than Fort Henry. Concerning the intervening terrain, Grant apparently was aware of the difficulties. "Owing to the intolerable state of the roads no transportation will be taken to Fort Donelson and but little artillery, and that with double teams."[3]

Grant then gathered up his staff and, with part of a cavalry regiment, rode to within a mile or two of the outer defenses of Fort Donelson on a personal reconnaissance. He recalled years later that he knew his advance would be a safe journey:

> I had known General Pillow in Mexico, and judged that with any force, no matter how small, I could march up to within gunshot of the entrenchments he was given to hold. I said this to the officers and staff at the time. I knew that Floyd was in command, but that he was no soldier, and I judged that he would yield to Pillow's pretensions. I met, as I expected, no opposition in making the reconnaissance and, besides learning the topography of the country on the way, and around Fort Donelson, found that there were two roads available for marching; one leading to the village of Dover, the other to Fort Donelson.[4]

In hindsight, Grant's confidence was validated, but neither Pillow nor Floyd was at Fort Donelson yet and Colonel Heiman was still technically in command there. That he thought little of the senior Confederate commanders there is no question.

At this time, Gen. Gideon Pillow was several miles upstream on the Cumberland. Coming out of his self-imposed retirement, Pillow had taken command of the depot in Clarksville the day before the fall of Fort Henry. He made a brief tour of the defenses around the city, and what he found was not encouraging. Not one of the fortifications was as yet complete, and the four heavy guns there were not mounted. Perhaps it did not matter too much, since there was no ammunition for them anyway. Pillow quickly wired General Johnston in Bowling Green, asking for more troops. He specifically wanted a field artillery battery and a segment of his old division at Columbus. Troops were already on the way, though, as the men of Brig. Gen. Charles Clark's brigade were marching toward Clarksville, but they were expected to arrive exhausted from the arduous march. The most ominous point of Pillow's telegram to headquarters was clear, however: "If Donelson should be overcome, we can make no successful stand without a larger force."[5] Pillow saw that there were no subsequent positions to fall back upon, and that the key to defending the Cumberland and Nashville with the best economy of force was Fort Donelson.

When Fort Henry fell, Pillow immediately sensed an opportunity to attack. He wired Johnston that he wanted to take the offensive once Clark's Brigade arrived from Hopkinsville. Reinforced, he would fall on Grant's army while it was alone and isolated. The delay of Clark's arrival, though, removed all thought of Pillow's grand advance. When the two generals did meet, they immediately quarreled, as Clark refused to recognize Pillow's authority. But Johnston sided with Pillow, and Clark soon resigned in protest. Colonel John Davidson then assumed command of the brigade.[6] After a brief rest, the brigade was sent by steamboat to reinforce Fort Donelson. In fact, General Pillow signed a local directive that would apply to all units passing through Clarksville. All arriving units would be sent downstream, whether earmarked specifically for the Cumberland defenses or not. Supplies were sent to Fort Donelson in the same manner.

On the morning of Friday, February 7, the gunboats *Cincinnati, St. Louis,* and *Essex* arrived at Cairo with whistles blowing. When the people on the waterfront saw the Confederate flag flying upside down on the flagship, there was cheering and rejoicing. The *Chicago Tribune* correspondent wrote that the expedition had accomplished "one of the most complete and signal victories in the annals of the world's warfare."

Flag Officer Foote nudged his boats up to the piers and prodded the mechanics to hammer his battered squadron back into shape. The *Essex* needed extensive repairs far beyond the capability of the facilities at Cairo and was towed to St. Louis for extensive rebuilding.[7] When told it would take several days or even weeks to repair the *Cincinnati* and *Essex,* Foote ordered the crews dispersed among the remaining boats. With this measure, the *Louisville* and *Pittsburg* were now fully manned, but it again nearly caused a mutiny among the men.

News of the fall of Fort Henry swept like wildfire throughout the North, keeping the telegraph operators working at a feverish pace. Upon hearing the news, Halleck wired his senior, General McClellan: "Fort Henry is ours. The flag is re-established on the soil of Tennessee. It will never be removed." McClellan ordered General Halleck to hold Fort Henry at all costs and told him to stand by to receive instructions for further movements.[8]

Halleck then began to receive strength reports of the Confederates at Bowling Green, numbering them at sixty regiments. It was an inflated number that did not take into account the miserable state of the Southern small arms, but if it was true, it was a sizable force. It was also rumored that some 10,000 of this force were already moving toward Fort Donelson. To Halleck, a concentration at Fort Donelson seemed the Confederates' best hope of defeating Grant and restoring the line.

Completely gone now was the confident demeanor of General Halleck when he authorized the expedition just a few short days earlier. Now, filled with trepidation and in near panic, he was sending every available regiment to General Grant, which had brought the army around Fort Henry up to about 17,000 men. If General Johnston concentrated his troops at Fort Donelson, Grant would be greatly outnumbered and in a very perilous position. Johnston was regarded as a fighting man of high ability, and Halleck naturally assumed he would strike back quickly and hard in order to restore the line.

In light of the situation, Halleck also changed his attitude toward his rival in Louisville, now pleading for assistance. Halleck requested that General Buell make a demonstration on Bowling Green to tie down the Confederates and keep them from attacking Grant. George B. McClellan echoed this idea, but the commander of the Department of the Ohio repeatedly cited the poor roads, obstructions, and the strong fortifications of the city, saying the idea was impracticable. The cautious Buell wrote to his friend McClellan, "This whole move, right in its strategic bearing, but commenced by Halleck without proper appreciation—preparation—or concert—has now become of vast magnitude." He went on to describe the consequences of any reinforcement on the Tennessee: "It will have to be made in the face of 50,000 if not 60,000 men and is hazardous."[9]

Don Carlos Buell had spent the winter overestimating the strength of the Confederate forces in his department, thought Grant was in great peril of annihilation, and wanted no part in a disaster of Halleck's making. McClellan suggested to his friend that he push forward anyway. General Buell replied: "I cannot on reflection, think a change in my line would be advisable. I shall want eighteen rifled siege guns and four companies of experienced gunners to man them."[10] Rifled siege guns were in extremely short supply, and experienced gunners at this stage of the war were rare indeed. They simply gave Buell another excuse not to move. A few days later, Buell added another reason for inactivity. Evidently 10,000 small arms were needed to replace defective ones scattered throughout his command. Although probably true, even McClellan was surprised by this excuse, which was the first he had heard of the matter. He gave his old friend an alibi by replying, "Reports to bureaus are apt to be buried."[11]

Getting no help from his rival in Louisville, Halleck wired McClellan, asking him to send him any additional troops that could be spared from Buell's command or elsewhere. In response, orders went out from the War Department to gather fragments of companies that were being recruited in the western states and quickly consolidate them into regiments for Grant's army. These forces would eventually number some 8,000 men.

The nervous Halleck also began a campaign for Buell to come to the Cumberland to take charge of the operation using this as an enticement to encourage his rival to advance. McClellan agreed: "Either Buell or yourself [Halleck] should soon go to the area of operations. Why not have Buell take the line of the Tennessee and operate on Nashville, while your troops turn on Columbus?"[12] A series of messages and telegrams on this subject began here and continued for the next several days. Unbeknownst to the victor of Fort Henry, Grant was in grave danger of being replaced.

The messages these three Union generals sent back and fort in early February clearly show the friction between them. Halleck had launched a major offensive without first obtaining the support of the commander on his flank. Buell appeared ready to allow the enemy to swallow up the men of Grant's army to prove a point. McClellan was unwilling to settle the matter decisively. One thing was clear, though: Halleck was eclipsing Buell, and even the latter's close relationship with McClellan could not stop that. With Fort Henry's fall, military effort and national attention were shifted to Halleck and Grant's offensive. The army in the mud at Fort Henry took priority for reinforcements and supplies.

By evening, Henry Halleck received instructions from General McClellan. Buell would indeed begin a slow movement on Bowling Green. For the next few days, Halleck was advised, he should not advance directly on Columbus, but proceed with turning it by operating on its eastern flank. This did not mean an advance on Fort Donelson, but a series of marches and demonstrations along the Tennessee.

General Halleck continued to ponder the replacement of Grant even if Buell did not come to the Cumberland. He knew Ulysses S. Grant was a brave soldier, but his boldness was seen as recklessness, and ill feelings still existed over the fact that the venerable C. F. Smith was serving as Grant's subordinate. Also, Grant's messages continually expressed the notion of advancing on Fort Donelson, which did not seem to fit McClellan's plan. It was also unnerving to Halleck for a subordinate to be so confident of advancing while Albert Sidney Johnston surely must be massing an overwhelming force to strike at this isolated army on the Tennessee.

A confirmation of General Halleck's feelings toward Grant occurred just after the fall of Fort Henry. The department commander relayed the thanks and praise of the nation to Flag Officer Foote, but hardly a word of congratulations or recognition was sent Grant's way. At this time, too, Halleck was maneuvering for command of the West, and this subordinate who had just won a victory was a threat. Since he was contemplating replacing him, it would be very awkward if he heaped praise upon Grant just prior to his removal.

Although Foote and his gunboats won the battle, fortunately for Grant most people saw that it was his operation. General Grant's name appeared prominently in the newspapers, and Congressman Washburne hailed his general enthusiastically. Grant also got the attention of the man who would ultimately decide his fate and that of the nation—Abraham Lincoln. Here was a general who was ready to fight and who won battles. There were no pleas for reinforcements, no excuses, no delays. This was a rare combination in a general officer at this stage of the war.

The Confederates also prepared for the next phase of the campaign. The former occupants of Fort Henry arrived at Fort Donelson during the night of February 6, numbering about 3,000 men. Nothing was saved but the small arms; apparently all of the field artillery was lost along the way in the mud. Few of the soldiers had tents, camp gear, or their personal belongings due to the haste of the retreat. Colonel Heiman was the senior officer at Fort Donelson, but there was word to expect a new general officer to take command. With that in mind, Heiman arranged the haggard and demoralized regiments within and around the walls of the bastion to recover from their ordeal and sent out a few cavalry patrols. Besides this and sending a situation update to Bowling Green, he did little else. His report included the news that the telegraph line from Cumberland City was down, and that he expected no fighting until the next day at the earliest.[13]

Major Jeremy Gilmer, chief engineer of the Western Department, was at Fort Donelson, having made his escape from Fort Henry. Assessing the size of Grant's army, he knew the small fort was no match against it. To hold it, the ridges beyond had to be fortified to protect the vital water batteries and the little fort shielding them. Here, too, the Confederates had their backs to the Cumberland River and had to consider an attack from three directions. To the northwest of the fort was Hickman Creek, and even during low water, this formed a deep marsh. Now, with the winter floods, it was completely impassable. Gilmer anchored the right of the new defensive line on a hill overlooking this swollen stream. Hickman Creek offered an extreme advantage to the defenders by relieving them of having to fortify a few hundred yards of trenches, thus shortening the line. But it made it impossible for the Confederates to interdict any landing of troops and supplies immediately downstream.

Major Gilmer then traced the defensive line following the fifty- to eighty-foot-high ridges, crossing Indian Creek, and finally anchored it on the flooded Lick Creek on the other side of Dover. This line ran generally parallel to the river, which was about 1400 yards distant. A potential weakness was the valley of Indian Creek, which made a break in the center of the line. This flooded stream also made lateral movement between the two wings of the defense difficult, but there was a single fording site. The surrounding terrain was heavily wooded, with thick underbrush, and only a few cleared fields scattered about. The thick vegetation, steep hills, and ravines offered little opportunity for long-range fire. The terrain and vegetation hindered movement of large formations as well. The advantages appeared to favor the defenders.

Spurred by Major Gilmer, the regiments began to entrench in their assigned sectors. With the original garrison, the Fort Henry survivors, and new reinforcements, there were about 6,000 men at Fort Donelson by midday of February 7. The fatigue parties began to work day and night at a frantic pace felling trees and digging rifle pits. Presumably any slave work parties that were present prior to the fall of Fort Henry were employed to dig trenches. As more reinforcements arrived, the defenses were extended along Gilmer's line to enclose the town of Dover, where the only available steamboat landing was located.

As the separate regiments entrenched around Fort Donelson, Albert Sidney Johnston met with his senior officers at the Covington Hotel in Bowling Green. There they were to decide the next move. General William J. Hardee was present, along with Gen. P. G. T. Beauregard, who had been in town for three days. Again, Beauregard had with him but a few staff officers, and not one soldier of the fifteen regiments Henry Halleck thought were en route from Virginia.

Johnston as yet did not know the particulars about the battle at Fort Henry, but he did know that the gunboats took the fort without the direct help of Grant's army. That the fort was subdued by the ironclads alone seemed to show that the North had an irrepressible weapon of great power. Johnston had never been to Fort Henry to appreciate its weakness, and like many others, he began to overestimate the power of the ironclads. Also, the guile and bluff that had held the Federals in check and the Southern hopes high for so long worked against him. If a handful of gunboats were sufficient by themselves to reduce the "powerful" Fort Henry, how could any fort stand up to them?

Johnston was now in a desperate situation. The Confederates, with numerically inferior forces, were already operating on the line outside of a circle created by the Columbus and Bowling Green salients. The disadvantage of this exterior line was partially offset by control of the railway from Bowling Green to Columbus. But what was feared came to pass. The railroad to Memphis was now cut, Columbus had been flanked, and General Grant was between the major Confederate forces. There was also no strategic reserve to plug the gap. Adding to his despair was a report submitted by Gen. Simon B. Buckner, who had just received a message from an operative in Louisville. Evidently someone on Buell's staff was overheard saying the expedition up the Tennessee and Cumberland was chiefly a diversion, and Bowling Green was the main objective of the enemy.[14]

Johnston knew he had to act quickly, and there were few options. The Confederates could concentrate at Fort Donelson immediately and try to destroy Grant before he was reinforced. This choice was a gamble: If Johnston's army was destroyed there, the Confederate defense in the West would be irreparably shattered. It would also leave Buell free to occupy Bowling Green and make a drive on Nashville. A second option, dividing the army to keep part of it at Bowling Green, might not leave enough troops to get the job done in either sector. The third choice was not promising either: abandoning Fort Donelson and Bowling Green to strike at some future date would mean the immediate loss of Nashville and most of Tennessee.[15]

Needing advice and assurance, Johnston asked for the opinions of his two trusted subordinates. Beauregard, with Hardee's unenthusiastic concurrence, urged an immediate concentration at Fort Donelson to defeat Grant. He thought they could bring up 27,000 men against Grant's army by February 19 at the latest. Although Beauregard's timeline was optimistic, the Confederates had an operational rail system that could have brought such a number into position. This plan was bold, and boldness was needed at this juncture.[16]

Beauregard's view to defeat Grant before the cautious Buell moved out of Louisville had the merit of regaining the initiative. It also fit Jefferson Davis's strategic concept of defending all territory by counterthrusting against any Union offensive. The rail line at Johnston's disposal could speed the army at Bowling Green to Fort Donelson, where it could crush Grant before he was reinforced into an overwhelming army. None of the three generals mentioned it here, but possibly, in spite of the swampy landward approaches, the recapture of Fort Henry was possible. The most apparent and unimaginative course was to abandon the line of the Cumberland and Nashville with its precious storehouses, factories, and arsenals. But Beauregard was more talk than action. When offered command of the forces assembling at Fort Donelson, he declined, citing the severe throat ailment for which he had recently undergone surgery.[17]

Johnston's final plan of action, born of the council of war, was anything but bold, and its ultimate aim is hard to determine. One might even argue that the disaster at Fort Henry upset his balance and reasoning abilities. Fearing an advance by General Buell, who still showed no signs of movement, he felt limited in his options. Instead of concentrating and striking a decisive blow, Johnston decided to take the middle ground, with the aim of taking no chances. Johnston drew up a memorandum outlining his plan and had Beauregard and Hardee cosign the document in concurrence.[18]

The memorandum ordered the immediate abandonment of Bowling Green and, with it, the Confederate defenses in the West. Where the army was to go was unclear, but it was to cross the Cumberland at Nashville with all haste to "a strong point some miles below that city being fortified forthwith, to defend the river from the passage of the gunboats." Units were directed to prepare to fall back to Stevenson, and even farther if circumstances dictated.[19] The troops at Clarksville were ordered to cross to the south side of the river, leaving only enough troops in the city to protect the manufacturing facilities and government property.

For the defense of the Mississippi, Johnston ordered Beauregard to take charge of the western half of the army in Columbus. Beauregard accepted in spite of the throat ailment he claimed was too severe to allow him to exercise command at Fort Donelson. He was to evacuate Columbus, leaving only a token force assisted by the small Confederate river fleet. Johnston wanted this guard to make a desperate defense, but he also ordered that transports be kept there to remove the garrison when the position became untenable.[20] Meanwhile, the rest of the army at Columbus was to fall back for an eventual reunion. The total abandonment of Columbus was ordered a few days later and was a bitter irony. The city had been occupied back in September—in violation of Kentucky's neutrality—because it was considered vital to the defense of the Mississippi valley. Now the city was abandoned without a fight.

On the status of Fort Donelson, Johnston's memorandum is subject to question. Whether additional troops were to be sent there and the fort's mission and role were unclear. What was evident, though, was the need to hold the fort for at least a short time. If the Federal gunboats reached Nashville unchecked and destroyed the bridges, Johnston's army would be trapped north of the Cumberland and destroyed. So Fort Donelson had to hold at least until the army was safely south of the river. Apparently Johnston then hoped that the garrison could extract itself from the position and rejoin him at Nashville or elsewhere. Since he had never visited the site, he had no idea just how it was to do that.

The memorandum left different impressions in the minds of the subordinate commanders. Many of them saw the operation as a massive retrograde. Others read that they were to fight. A full month after the campaign, Johnston wrote, "I determined to fight for Nashville at Donelson, and gave the best part of my army to do it, retaining only 14,000 men to cover my front, and giving 16,000 to defend Donelson."[21] Had he spoken so decisively before this time, the Confederate command would not have experienced many of the problems that were about to occur.

Units in Bowling Green were soon on the march to reach the south bank of the Cumberland River before the enemy gunboats could cut them off. General Buckner was ordered to take his division from Russellville to Clarksville, and General Floyd was to move his Virginia brigade there as well. Unbeknownst to these gentlemen, as the lead regiments arrived in Gideon Pillow's domain, they were immediately forwarded downriver to Fort Donelson under the established directive and without their knowledge.

Meanwhile, Fort Donelson indeed received a new general officer this day, and that man was none other than Bushrod Johnson. En route to his new post, the new brigadier stopped in Clarksville and met with General Pillow, and by late afternoon, his steamer was off again. The boat had the 2nd Kentucky from General Buckner's division on board. Long after dark, the vessel nudged up to the bustling landing at Dover. Johnson led his horse down the gangplank, mounted, and rode up the slope to the Dover Hotel, currently used as the fort's headquarters. Besides the 2nd Kentucky, Bushrod Johnson now had four infantry regiments and the two demoralized brigades that had escaped from Fort Henry, making a total of eleven regiments, or about 7,000 men. This included three artillery batteries and enough horsemen to form the rough equivalent of a cavalry regiment. Johnson began to organize the defenses by supervising the unloading of rations and ammunition from Nashville, evacuating the sick to Clarksville, and moving the troops he had to defensive positions. He did not yet have any idea how many more units were earmarked for Fort Donelson.[22]

Huge mounds of supplies and ammunition ringed the steamboat landing in Dover and accumulated as each steamboat arrived. Major J. W. Jones was appointed post quartermaster, and Major Dollam was the commissary. They were quickly overwhelmed by the sheer amount of war goods. Most of the crates and boxes were haphazardly piled, and no system was in place for inventory or accountability. There were no warehouses, so unless someone was thoughtful enough to throw a piece of canvas over them, the supplies were essentially exposed to the elements. The few available wagons served the logistical needs of the fort proper but could not hope to supply the entire force assembling there. Most of the new infantry regiments relied on borrowing wagons from citizens or sending details of men on foot to the landing to draw what they needed. The amount of supplies is open to speculation today, but contemporary accounts suggest that they could have sustained an army several days or even weeks by the time of the battle.

Bushrod Johnson commanded only a matter of hours, for later that day, Gideon Pillow also received orders to assume command of Fort Donelson. Although he held the same rank, Pillow was the senior officer by date of commission. Pillow was obviously pleased at this sudden development, seeing Fort Donelson as an independent field command, which was much preferable to a supply depot in the rear. He wired Bushrod Johnson of the news, as well as his intentions to send more reinforcements quickly, using the three operational boats left on the Cumberland.

To Gideon Pillow, there was no doubt that the key to defending the Cumberland River was Fort Donelson. While he had not yet personally inspected the fort at Dover, his nature dictated that the enemy must be stopped at the front line. Tennessee was his home state, and he was doing all he could to prepare for its defense. Pillow was chiefly responsible for the vast amount of supplies sent to the fort, and for its reinforcement. Offensive in spirit, Pillow probably was not intending only to hold the fort, but was looking for means to exploit any possibility of launching an attack.

On February 8, General Grant was impatient to advance on Fort Donelson, but he did not order such a movement this morning. At present, the army encamped around Fort Henry had an immediate concern for its welfare. The new enemy at hand was a former ally, namely the Tennessee River. The rain had stopped, but the floodwaters had not. The rising water was now several feet over Fort Henry and threatened to sweep the piles of supplies and equipment amassed at the landings downriver. These stockpiles were vital for the coming campaign, and soldiers spent the next few days moving them inland to drier ground.

In the rain and mud, the little army on the Tennessee was doing all it could to prepare for an advance on Fort Donelson, but Halleck began to add more tasks. He sent a telegram ordering Grant: "If possible, destroy the bridge at Clarksville. It is of vital importance, and should be attempted at all hazards." Just how Grant was to do this without first capturing Fort Donelson is hard to imagine, for it was located even farther upstream. Halleck added a note ordering the use of slaves and secessionists in the area of Fort Henry to strengthen it against land attack. It is clear that from faraway St. Louis, Halleck had no idea of the situation on the Tennessee. Fort Henry by this time was completely under water and the soldiers of Grant's army were busy clambering to higher ground and saving what they could from the rapidly rising waters. And as Fort Henry was in a fairly remote location, there were no large groups of slaves or local white people to be pressed into digging rifle pits.

General Halleck also pondered the telegram from McClellan suggesting that he proceed to Fort Henry and take command of the expedition. Halleck was not prepared to assume a field command with so much unfinished work to do at his headquarters. He did come up with a replacement for Grant, though. Ethan Allen Hitchcock was a high-minded, scholarly soldier who seemed ideal for the job. Hitchcock had resigned from the army in 1855 as a brigadier general and had taken residence in St. Louis. Both Gen. Winfield Scott and General McClellan, however, were considering the sixty-three-year-old's recall to active duty. Fortunately for the commander on the Tennessee, Hitchcock declined Halleck's offer, citing in his diary that the move was unnecessary since Grant was doing all he could.[23]

Unaware of the maneuverings against him, Grant wired Halleck to update him on the situation and inform him of his plans. "At present we are perfectly locked in by high water and bad roads, and prevented from acting offensively, as I should like to do. The banks are higher at the waters edge than farther back, leaving a wide margin of low land to bridge over before anything can be done inland. The bad state of the roads will then prevent the transportation of baggage or artillery." In his desire to advance before Fort Donelson was reinforced, Grant had actually contemplated taking Fort Donelson on this day with just infantry and cavalry alone, but almost all the troops were needed just to save the supplies from the rising waters of the Tennessee.

In the afternoon, Albert Sidney Johnston wired the secretary of war in Richmond. Acknowledging that he had few details of the battle at Fort

Henry, Johnston made a remarkable assessment: "The slight resistance at Fort Henry indicates that the best open earth-works are not reliable to meet successfully a vigorous attack of iron-clad gunboats, and although now supported by a considerable force, I think the gunboats of the enemy will probably take Fort Donelson without the necessity of employing their land force in co-operation, as seems to have been done at Fort Henry." He then added that should Fort Donelson fall, the route to Nashville would be open and give the Federals the means to destroy the bridges and ferryboats to the head of navigation. With such a possibility at hand, he announced the need for speed in making the movement to Nashville and the safety of the south bank of the Cumberland.[24]

Knowing a disaster when he saw one, the secretary of war finally ordered reinforcements to Johnston's department. These consisted of twelve infantry regiments, one of cavalry, and a number of independent companies, which were en route to eastern Tennessee. The orders from Richmond explained that with these new regiments coming into the department, the regiments already near Knoxville were available for immediate service wherever Johnston saw fit. Orders were also sent to Gen. Mansfield Lovell in New Orleans to send five or six of his best regiments north toward Memphis. In addition, Richmond ordered about 3,000 muskets shipped to Nashville and called on the states for a new levy of recruits.[25] These last two measures had no hope of influencing the campaign at this late juncture. The additional weapons would take several days in transport, and raising troops was measured in weeks and months.

Apparently realizing there were at least four general officers of the same rank on the Cumberland, Johnston designated former secretary of war John B. Floyd to take formal command of the river defenses, including the garrison of Fort Donelson. As the senior brigadier general, he was the commander by default. In the command culture of the day, Johnston gave Floyd wide latitude as to how he would deploy his forces, except that Johnston wanted units south of the Cumberland. But Floyd needed specific instructions on just what was expected of him. A review of Johnston's dispatches shows a presumption of a determined defense at Fort Donelson but nothing more. The novice Floyd needed far more guidance than that.

By late evening, General Floyd arrived in Clarksville. He informed General Johnston of the state of affairs there. Most of the troops were already at Fort Donelson or en route there by steamboat. Noting a lack of intelligence on enemy movements, he echoed Johnston's assessment of the gunboats' invulnerability. Floyd reported that the defenses at Clarksville amounted to nothing but a work upon the river hill about 200 yards from the water and another on the bank that was nearly submerged. He felt the place was capable of being made very strong indeed, however, and requested a good engineer officer and a supply of entrenching tools. More telling of the Confederate command posture was Floyd's closing lines: "I wish, if possible, you would come down here, if it were only for a single day. I think in that time you might determine the policy and lines of defense. I will, however, do the best I can and all I can with the means at hand."[26]

At this time, Johnston was far too busy personally directing an unopposed retreat from Bowling Green to give more specific guidance to General Floyd.

On Sunday, February 9, the telegraph wires between St. Louis, Louisville, and Washington hummed as the Union high command discussed strategy and continued to react to the victory at Fort Henry. General Halleck announced his further reinforcement of Grant on the Tennessee, and Buell cynically wired that he was planning to come to the rescue of the column should the need arise.

Still fixated on the bridges at Clarksville, Halleck wired Flag Officer Foote, asking him to run his gunboats past the batteries of Fort Donelson in order to destroy them. Not knowing the strength of Fort Donelson or of any obstacles on the river, Foote declined to make the attempt. Instead, he used what little time he had in preparing to support Grant's next move.

Upriver, Grant was not privy to these exchanges and went forward with a cavalry patrol to take another look at Fort Donelson and the surrounding area. He again got within a short distance of it and was able to ascertain the condition of the roads. He could not yet tell, though, how many Confederates were in the trenches being dug around the fort and the town of Dover.

Upon his return to Fort Henry, Grant had some housecleaning to do. Apparently some of the officers were inclined to avoid the muddy camps surrounding the submerged Fort Henry. He issued an order to all of his regimental officers that they were to remain in camp with their troops and stay off the more comfortable steamboats. Grant also issued another field order aimed at halting the pilfering and marauding by some of the troops. He informed his army that commanders at all levels would be held responsible for their subordinates and pledged to have any infraction traced back to a guilty party, who would receive punishment.[27] Grant not only was trying to maintain some level of accountability over his soldiers, but also saw that a ruthless and plundering army would stiffen Confederate resolve. The growing restlessness in the camps also explains his anxiousness to advance. A time-tested observation is that idle soldiers cause trouble.

In a letter written this day to his sister Grant said, "I intend to keep the ball moving as lively as possible, and been detained here [at Fort Henry] from the fact that the Tennessee is very high and has been rising ever since they had been there, overflowing the back land and making it necessary to bridge it before we could move." He added: "G. J. Pillow commands Fort Donelson. I hope to give him a tug before you receive this."[28]

Gideon Pillow had indeed assumed command at Fort Donelson, arriving at Dover by steamer and setting up his headquarters in the Rice house, which was owned by one of his staff officers, Maj. Frank Rice. He found the morale of the troops very low, "a deep gloom." He issued an assumption of command memorandum that was designed give heart to the Southern soldiers. It was typical of Pillow's style, full of bravado and pomp. "Drive back the ruthless invader from our soil and again raise the Confederate flag over Fort Henry. . . . I expect every man to do his duty. . . . With God's help we will accomplish our purpose. Our battle cry, 'Liberty or Death.'"[29]

Accompanied by Major Gilmer of the engineers, General Pillow then inspected the defenses. Pillow was impressed with the location of the water batteries, noting that they were about thirty feet above the water at this stage of the river. He thought the narrowness of the river at this point would probably allow no more than three (actually four) gunboats to bring their guns to bear at a time. Although the location was good, he found the work on the river batteries unfinished and wholly too weak to resist the force of heavy naval cannons. Pillow also noted that although the lighter guns were mounted, the heavy 10-inch Columbiad and a rifled 6.5-inch gun were not. His orders set the work in motion to correct these deficiencies and established around-the-clock work parties to begin the task of improving the fortifications. Those men not digging trenches were busy preparing ammunition brought down from Nashville or learning the routine of firing the heavy guns. Lieutenant Colonel Haynes again took personal charge of this task, as he had a few weeks earlier.

Pillow also noted that there was a shortage of men detailed to the heavy guns on the river. He first assigned a company from the 10th Tennessee Infantry, which balked at the task. Pillow then asked for volunteers from the field artillery, and Capt. Reuben Ross and his men reported for duty. They were assigned the guns of the upper river battery and the 10-inch Columbiad. Their light field guns were turned over to a Captain Parker of Pillow's staff, manned by a composite detachment from different units, and positioned in reserve near the Dover cemetery.[30]

The inspection continued as Pillow and Major Gilmer rode across the landward side of Fort Donelson. As laid out by the young engineer, the line of outer defenses ran along the ridges from Hickman Creek on the right to Lick Creek on the left. This made an extremely long defensive line of about two miles in length, but it protected the town of Dover and the vital steamboat landing. The gap in the line created by Indian Creek was covered by placing artillery batteries on the hills on each side of the valley. Pillow positioned other artillery batteries at key points dominating the other likely approaches to the defenses.

The construction of the outer defenses was entirely inadequate, and the new commander placed the priority on the digging of rifle pits. Felled trees were piled and covered with dirt to form the outer defense line, which proved a very strong fortification. Teams were also sent forward to cut trees off at about chest height, the fallen trunks and branches making a crude but effective infantry obstacle. Thick underbrush that made movement difficult covered most of the ground; branches on these shrubs, along with the felled trees, were cut and sharpened to further hamper an infantry assault.[31]

Pillow then took time to sort out the massive amount of stores at the landing, bringing a semblance of organization as he had done at the depot at Clarksville. As the long day drew to a close, he was still hard at work on the defenses. He ordered more ammunition for the heavy guns from Nashville, and with Gen. Bushrod Johnson's assistance, Pillow organized his infantry forces, actually taking into account the sensitivities of Buckner and Floyd. Although General Buckner was not yet present, he was designated commander of the right wing, which was anchored on Hickman Creek and extended in a broad arc to Indian Creek. This wing consisted mostly of Buckner's troops arriving from Bowling Green. Bushrod Johnson was given command of the left wing, which ran from Indian Creek to Lick Creek. These troops included the Fort Henry evacuees, the original garrison, and various units arriving from Hopkinsville. The Virginians of Floyd's brigade were arriving, but Pillow did not yet assign them to either wing. They camped just outside of Dover, awaiting word of their position in the line.

By the end of the day, Pillow was beginning to feel better about the state of affairs at Fort Donelson, and perhaps for good reason. By nightfall, the defenses were at least organized, if not yet fully prepared. But that was changing too, as the men continued to dig earthworks and construct obstacles.[32] Morale was improving, the supply system was function fairly well, and the reinforcements from Buckner's and Floyd's commands were pouring in. Fort Donelson and the surrounding trenches were becoming a formidable defensive work and getting stronger. Pillow showed much of his optimism in a wire to General Floyd: "I feel very confident of holding it against assault by the infantry and if I am allowed time to complete the works and mount all the guns I have confidence in being able to resist the attack of their gun-boats if they are vulnerable to all metal." Pillow also sent a wire to Governor Harris: "Upon one thing you must be rest assured. I will never surrender the position, and with God's help I mean to maintain it."[33]

Not everyone shared Pillow's upbeat attitude. Upstream at Clarksville, Gen. Simon B. Buckner arrived and learned to his surprise that most of his division was not there, but downstream at Fort Donelson digging rifle pits and under the command of his old nemesis, General Pillow. He was infuri-ated, to say the least.

Events over the past few months had not gone altogether well for Gen-eral Buckner. When he left the Kentucky State Guard and joined the Con-federacy, he came under bitter attacks in the press of the North. Worse, heavy taxes were levied on property behind the Union lines, and blue cav-alry went to his farm near Mundfordville to seize his stock and a large quantity of produce. The Nashville Railroad Company sued him for damages caused by his troops, and his Louisville home and the farm were sold off by court order for a fraction of their worth. Family calamities occurred as well, the first being the death of his son in December. The funeral procession was not allowed to pass through the Federal lines, which added bitterness to the grief. On January 6, his mother passed away. So after this string of heartbreaking events, Buckner arrived to find his division under the immediate command of Gideon Pillow, a man he despised.[34] This animosity would have a significant impact on the events of the next several days.

As the sun rose on Monday morning over St. Louis, Halleck sent a telegram to McClellan warning that Beauregard was preparing to move from Columbus either on Paducah or Fort Henry. He added a call for more reinforcements to meet the expected Confederate counterattack: "An immense collection of boats have been collected, and the whole Bowling Green force can come down in a day, attack Grant in the rear, and return to Nashville before Buell can get there. . . . I can do no more for Grant at present. I must stop the transports at Cairo to observe Beauregard. We are certainly in peril."[35]

Three hours later, a more coherent but not entirely accurate Halleck acknowledged that the Kentucky roads were appraised to be impassable until well into April, which would stymie any major move on Buell's part. Halleck then became bold for the moment and again wired McClellan, saying, "Give us the means and we are certain to give the enemy a telling blow." The city of Clarksville was again on Halleck's mind as he wired Grant at Fort Henry: "If possible destroy the bridge at Clarksville. Run any risk to accomplish this." It is clear that General Halleck was under enormous pressure and perhaps was about to break under the strain.[36]

In contrast, General Grant was calm but anxious in his desire to pull out of the swampy encampments along the Tennessee and get the operation in motion. By now the three wooden gunboats had returned from their raid upriver, with the unfinished *Eastport* in tow. Grant immediately gave orders to Phelps to proceed down the Tennessee and steam up the Cumberland. He was hoping to launch a joint naval-land attack in the next few days, but he knew the three timberclads would not be enough. He wrote a message to his ally Flag Officer Foote in Cairo: "Can you not send two [ironclad] boats from Cairo immediately up the Cumberland? To expedite matters, any steamers from Cairo may be taken to tow them. Should you be deficient in men, an artillery company can be detached to serve on the gunboats temporarily."[37] Not waiting for a reply, Grant also directed Commander Walke of the *Carondelet* to proceed down the Tennessee and ascend the Cumberland to Fort Donelson.

Having arranged for his naval support, Grant gave a warning order to his own troops to be in readiness to march: "The troops from Forts Henry and Heiman will hold themselves in readiness to move on Wednesday, the 12th instant, at as early an hour as practical. Neither tents nor baggage will be taken, except such as troops can carry. Brigade and regimental commanders will see that all their men are supplied with forty rounds of ammunition in their cartridge boxes and two days' rations in their haversacks. Three days' additional rations may be put into wagons to follow the expedition, but will not impede the progress of the main column."[38] Grant wanted to travel light and fast.

The general also reorganized his army. From the reinforcements received in the past few days, he formed two new brigades, giving one to each existing division. This meant that the two divisions of Grant's little army now had three brigades each. Two infantry regiments were chosen to remain behind to guard Fort Henry, and Gen. Lew Wallace and his brigade, much to Wallace's disappointment, was to remain at Fort Heiman.

Some twelve miles away, the Confederates continued to dig trenches around Fort Donelson. Although he was confident of holding the post, General Pillow's daily dispatch to Floyd showed that he had given up the notion, at least for the time being, of a drive to retake Fort Henry, and that he had begun to realize that a hostile force could cut off his land escape route by moving astride the Wynn's Ferry and Forge Roads leading south out of Dover. But there was good news this day, too. A most welcome addition to the garrison was the 3rd Tennessee Cavalry, under the command of Lt. Col. Nathan Bedford Forrest. There had been too few cavalrymen available up to this point, and Forrest's men were deployed to acquire additional information on Grant's movements. Pillow also established a line of observation posts along the east bank of the Cumberland to within eight miles of Smithland to warn of any movement from that direction.[39]

In Bowling Green, Gen. Albert Sidney Johnston was already convinced that the enemy gunboats were invincible, and the report from his chief engineer now lying on his desk confirmed his worst fears. Major Gilmer, the man who had surveyed Fort Donelson's outer defenses, described the attack on Forty Henry, as well as the current defensive potential of Fort Donelson. Gilmer relayed his fears that the expected attack was to be a combined one, using the ironclad gunboats in support of a land attack. He added: "The effect of our shot at Fort Henry was not sufficient to disable them [the gunboats], or any one of them, so far as I have been able to ascertain. This was due, I think, in a great measure, to the want of skill in the men who served the guns, and not to the invulnerability of the boats themselves." He also pointed out that it was impractical to establish a boom across the Cumberland in its flooded state, which left only the guns of Fort Donelson to halt the gunboats. If there was any shred of encouragement, it was Gilmer's confidence that Fort Donelson could be held against a ground attack. He reported that the men were working hard to fortify the place, and given ten days, they would provide overhead cover to the heavy guns. As events turned out, they would not have those ten days.[40]

If everyone around him was filled with doom and despair, General Johnston began hearing from a man who was full of fight and positive in his outlook for the successful defense of Fort Donelson. That man was Gideon Pillow. His telegrams echoed his earlier observations, that the narrowness of the river would hamper the gunboats, and assured the nervous commander that the place was defendable. Another such message went to General Floyd's headquarters at Clarksville saying much the same. In this note, Pillow added more detail of the defensive preparations. The men were working at a feverish pace and mounting the rifled 6.5-inch gun in the upper river battery and the heavy 10-inch Columbiad in the lower.[41]

In Clarksville, General Floyd met with the infuriated Simon Bolivar Buckner to discuss strategy. General Buckner proposed that the remaining troops at Clarksville and his original command, which was already at Fort Donelson, be brought upstream to Cumberland City, which was about halfway between the fort and Clarksville. Buckner argued that Cumberland

City, not Fort Donelson, was where they should make a determined stand. Pillow's mission would be to fix Grant at Fort Donelson as long as possible with only the original garrison and a few additional units. Buckner reasoned that a force in Cumberland City could then operate against Grant's line of logistics without fear of being cut off by the gunboats or by land forces, as it might be at Fort Donelson. In Buckner's plan, Pillow and Fort Donelson would become expendable.

The two generals then went downstream and visited Cumberland City to assess the terrain. Afterward, Floyd approved the plan. At this late date, however, no defensive preparations were made there, and the small force Buckner intended to leave at Fort Donelson would be completely inadequate for its task of fixing Grant. Yet orders were sent to Pillow to remove Floyd's and Buckner's troops from Fort Donelson and transfer them to Cumberland City. Buckner went to Fort Donelson to deliver the orders in person and to supervise the removal of the units.

Buckner arrived in Dover late in the night and met with Pillow at his headquarters. Not surprisingly, Pillow wanted no part in the scheme, since it meant retreating. He saw this plan as another Fort Henry scenario and urged a delay in implementing it until he could discuss the matter with Floyd in person. Buckner was unyielding. Pillow then pulled rank and forbade the removal of any troops until he could meet with General Floyd. At first light, Pillow boarded a steamboat and traveled the fifteen miles to Cumberland City to persuade his senior to change his mind.[42]

John B. Floyd was also under enormous strain and was unsure of the strategy Albert Sidney Johnston wanted to employ. He had telegraphed his commander earlier asking for guidance and for Johnston to pay a visit to the threatened sector of his command. Besides, it would be a natural expectation of the commander in chief to oversee the frontline situation at the fort himself. But Johnston felt that with the possibility of Buell advancing from far-off Louisville, Bowling Green needed his attention more than the immediately threatened Fort Donelson. He held this view in spite of a growing garrison of over 18,000 Confederates around Clarksville and Dover, whose assorted elements were commanded by separate brigadier generals of conflicting personalities. Johnston had at his disposal Major General Hardee, who was more than competent to withdraw the army from Bowling Green without his personal direction. But Floyd's repeated telegrams irritated Johnston, who saw them as simple vacillations. The fact was that Floyd was not confident in his own abilities and apparently put his faith and trust in Johnston, with his superior authority and experience, to decide what should be done.[43]

Floyd later telegraphed Johnston about his concerns over sending all of the forces into Fort Donelson:

I have thought the best disposition to make of the troops on this line was to concentrate the main force at Cumberland City, leaving at Fort Donelson enough to make all possible resistance to any attack which may be made upon the fort but no more. The character of the country in the rear and to the left of the fort is such as to make it dangerous to concentrate our whole force there; for if the gunboats should pass the fort and command the river, our forces would be in danger of being cut off by a force from the Tennessee.[44]

Floyd may have been right, but for the wrong reasons. He also weakened his argument a few sentences later by in fact pointing out the need to concentrate all available forces for a decisive strike.

On Tuesday morning, February 11, General Halleck awoke and soon had the telegraph operators busy again. He urged Flag Officer Foote in Cairo to push forward with whatever he had on hand. What Foote had was three ironclad gunboats ready to catch up with the *Carondelet* and two wooden gunboats. The other boats were mechanically unfit, lacked crews, or had been assigned to guard the Mississippi. Foote assembled what he had, though, and left Cairo with the ironclads *St. Louis, Louisville,* and *Pittsburg.* Along the way, these gunboats met up with a number of transports and support vessels and escorted them up the Ohio. The transports were loaded with reinforcements, six regiments in all, including the brigade previously sent from Buell's department. Some of these units had made it all the way to Fort Henry before being turned around and told to ascend the Cumberland.

Halleck's messages to Grant this day again urged him to destroy the railroad bridge at Clarksville. This was obviously impossible to do without first reducing Fort Donelson, but the general on the Tennessee did not want to antagonize his commander with a flippant reply. Instead, he wrote, "Every effort will be put forth to have Clarksville in a few days."[45]

Although General Halleck's behavior and attitudes may seem somewhat bizarre, he earnestly was working to gather and forward troops and supplies to Grant. He even sent his own chief of staff, Gen. G. W. Cullum, to Cairo to oversee their movements. Seasoned troops from Missouri and regiments from the training camps in Illinois, Indiana, and Ohio were hurried to the front. Many of these units were so newly organized that they had just received their uniforms and weapons and had not yet learned the manual of arms.[46]

Meanwhile, Grant assembled his senior officers together for a conference aboard the steamer *New Uncle Sam* to discuss future movements. The mood was purely business, and there was little or no sociable talk. After a while, Grant stepped up to a table and said quietly and calmly: "The question of consideration gentlemen, is whether we shall march against Fort Donelson or await reinforcements. I should like to have your views." The generals spoke in turn of seniority. Charles F. Smith simply said that he was ready to march at once. In stark contrast, John McClernand produced a paper from his pocket and began to read it. The former congressman laid out his views in minute and patronizing detail, and some officers became restive. Before the paper was finished, Grant interrupted him by turning to Lew Wallace, who nodded and said, "Let's go, by all means; the sooner the better." As fast as called upon, the other officers responded in the affirmative. Grant finally ended the meeting by saying: "Very well gentlemen, we will set out immediately. Orders will be sent you. Get your commands ready." It occurred to Wallace that Grant had made up his mind well before he summoned the meeting. Grant apparently never called another such a council of war again during the war.[47]

Lieutenant Colonel James B. McPherson, Grant's chief engineer, had been occupied over the previous few days assessing the land between the two forts. The reconnaissance patrols toward Dover ascertained that there were only the two roads found earlier. The northern route, the Telegraph Road, was more direct, at twelve miles; the southern route, the Ridge Road, was two miles longer. The most difficult part of each road was the first two or three miles from Fort Henry, where the deep ravines were still flooded by the spring rains. The roads were clear of obstructions, the Federal cavalry having prevented the Confederates from felling trees or destroying bridges along them. McPherson also noted that the terrain was very rolling, covered by thick timber, and sparsely populated. There were many ideal places from which to ambush an advancing column.[48]

To overcome the rough, muddy terrain of the first leg of the march, the artillery and a good portion of the infantry were moved forward in the late afternoon. As ordered, General McClernand moved his 1st Brigade from Fort Henry to a bivouac on the Ridge Road about five miles in advance, and his 2nd Brigade up the Telegraph Road about five and a half miles, where the men stopped and encamped for the night. The 3rd Brigade came up to about half a mile to the rear of the lead brigades. Cavalry was deployed forward of the infantry to again reconnoiter to within two miles of Fort Donelson and to provide a security screen.[49]

The 2nd Division, under Gen. C. F. Smith, was to follow along the Dover Road. Grant's orders for the advance gave little direction other than the contingency of sending a brigade from the 2nd Division into Dover to cut off an enemy retreat if the opportunity arose.[50] Although these written orders did not give a specific time of departure, every officer present at the council knew without a doubt that tomorrow they would finally leave their muddy camps and advance on Fort Donelson.

Grant's determination to move next on Fort Donelson is interesting. Halleck's original order authorized no such move, only the capturing of Fort Henry and the cutting of the railroad. Had Grant moved immediately upon Fort Donelson on February 8, he might have fairly easily captured the bastion. At that time, there were only about 6,000 badly shaken Confederates within the walls.[51] But poor roads had prohibited Grant from taking artillery, and the gunboats were still at Cairo. Crossing hostile territory to reduce a fortification without heavy fire support was a gamble that even Grant was not willing to take. If he had captured Fort Donelson at this time, the Federals would have taken far fewer prisoners, and the gunboats would not have been available to exploit the success with a run up to Nashville.

General Grant also was still learning his trade of commanding an army of such magnitude. The army Grant was managing was larger than he had ever seen, let alone commanded. In fact, it was larger than either Winfield Scott's or Zachary Taylor's had been in the Mexican War. His staff was small, and all of his officers and men were still learning the art of war. Supplies and ammunition had to be sorted out and distributed through the endless mud and swamps around Fort Henry, and reinforcements were arriving from Paducah daily and had to be absorbed into the brigades and divisions. In retrospect, it is amazing that he was able to march on to Fort Donelson when he did. It is also apparent too that the officers and men of the command had a clear understanding of the mission and intent of the army commander at this juncture.

Ulysses S. Grant was showing how different he was from most of his contemporaries. Whereas General Buell and others were calling for reinforcements before engaging in any offensive, Grant was deep in enemy territory and had to this point asked for none. He was also about to advance upon a force he knew little about. Reports over the past several months as to the strength of Fort Donelson varied widely. It was natural to assume that the fort was being reinforced, but even at this time, the reports were inconclusive. Few commanders now or then would make such an advance, in two columns moving over rough terrain against an enemy in unknown numbers in a fortified position. Grant did know that Gideon Pillow was in command of the garrison, and he was banking on Pillow's ineptitude and failure to launch an attack against the blue columns as they were strung out along the miserable roads.

Grant realized, too, that the fickle Henry Halleck could lose his nerve at any time. The dispatches from St. Louis did not show a man who was calmly directing an operation. The army was in readiness, and it was time to make a move before anything went astray or the operation was canceled.

In Halleck's perspective, Grant was being bold almost to the point of recklessness, and perhaps Grant sensed this. To placate Halleck's fears of a Confederate counterattack, Grant left a fairly sizable force behind on his initial march on Fort Donelson. Brigadier General Lew Wallace and about 2,500 men were far more than needed to prevent the recapture of the flooded bastion. No one in a blue uniform knew it at the time, but there was no serious talk from anyone in gray of retaking Fort Henry. By the evening of February 11, Johnston's single focus was on saving the army at Bowling Green. Polk was preparing to evacuate Columbus. No one clamored for any attempt to recapture a flooded fort that had been blasted into submission by the ironclads. Halleck did not know this, though, and was nervous of the precariousness of Grant's position. Had he learned that Grant abandoned Fort Henry outright, he probably would have relieved him of command.

As for the navy, it was supporting the operation as best it could with the few boats it had available. Flag Officer Foote is well known to history for his cooperative spirit with the army commanders, but he refused to run the batteries of Fort Donelson when asked to by General Halleck. This was asking a great deal, since no one really knew how powerful the water batteries were. What Foote did know was that his ironclads had armor protection only on the front two-thirds of the vessels. By running past the batteries, the boats might be subjected to fire against their unprotected sterns. Also, their slow speeds against the floodwaters of the Cumberland would place them under fire for a long period of time. Foote had seen firsthand how deadly cannon fire was from the front; he was in no mood to take it from the rear. On the other hand, had the fleet actually made it past the fort, the garrison would have been effectively cut off. It is likely that the Confederates would have evacuated the fort without a fight at that time.

At the end of January, Johnston reported to Richmond that he had 28,000 men around Bowling Green, organized into fifty regiments of infantry and cavalry and twelve artillery batteries. In Columbus, Polk had some twenty-five regiments in addition to some 2,000 garrison troops, for a total of 17,000 men. At Paris, there were about 1,100 cavalrymen, and Forts Henry and Donelson had about 6,000 men total. Railroads were available for rapid movement of troops, as were the steamers on the rivers. This transportation network gave the Confederates an ability to shift forces and concentrate on a threatened sector, which was now at Fort Donelson.

General Johnston, however, had not formed a strategic reserve for his department, which now forced him to make some difficult decisions. What army should he strip troops from to send to the threatened Fort Donelson? How many troops, and who would command them? Johnston had thought for months that Buell was the primary threat, but the Federal general was still in Louisville and faced a long overland march. No Federal movements were detected toward Columbus either. It should have been clear that Grant's army was alone, with support far away. If General Polk had made a feint toward Cairo, or even a token force had moved north from Bowling Green, such an advance surely would have panicked the Union high command and cut off any further reinforcement of Grant until the threat was neutralized. In the ensuing panic, Grant's army may have been withdrawn or at least left on its own and vulnerable.

The western commander was now fully aware of the stakes involved if Fort Donelson was lost. Johnston knew of the Union fleet's ability to ascend the rivers and bring invading armies deep into the interior of the Confederacy. He also realized that if Fort Donelson fell, Nashville and its manufacturing facilities would be lost as well. But at a time when boldness and daring was needed, his plan was neither. Johnston was simply reinforcing Fort Donelson in the hope of buying time for his army at Bowling Green to withdraw over the Cumberland. In spite of a later claim, "I determined to fight for Nashville at Donelson," he also told General Floyd, "If you lose the fort bring your troops to Nashville if possible." Obviously he had no consistent plan to defend the fort or to defeat Grant and restore the line.[52]

The primary reason for Johnston's instability was the presence of Flag Officer Foote's ironclad gunboats. Johnston knew they had blasted Fort Henry into submission, but he received most of the details of the fight from his engineer. Major Gilmer submitted a report of the battle on February 10, which certainly had an impact on the decisions of the day. Gilmer was well known to Johnston, and being a West Point officer, he had a fair degree of credibility. His report was full of errors, however, stating that the gunboats were invulnerable to even the heaviest shot, and that the marksmanship of the Confederate gunners was wanting. Major Gilmer witnessed the gunboat attack at Fort Henry but must not have seen the fateful hit on the *Essex*. This is curious, since the secondary explosion of the boiler and the great clouds of escaping steam could not have been missed by anyone with a clear view of the river. By all other accounts from both sides, the gunners at Fort Henry had made a good account of themselves, too. But this report caused General Johnston to lose all faith in stopping the new ironclads, and he made most of his decisions accordingly.

Thus Johnston ordered the withdrawal from Bowling Green to Nashville to a "strong point some miles below the city being fortified forthwith, to defend the river from the passage of gunboats and transports." Whether this strong point was Fort Donelson is unclear, but it probably was not. Johnston had also ordered Nashville fortified, but lack of manpower, materials, and time prevented this. Again, he had not taken the time to leave his headquarters to inspect the river defenses himself and so was making critical decisions without accurate information.

General Johnston's judgment comes into question. If he truly believed in the invulnerability of the ironclad gunboats, his decision to send "the best part" of his army to Fort Donelson was irrational. If the ironclads were so powerful, then the garrison was doomed from the onset. Even if a hostile land force had not yet invested the fort, the running of the gunboats past the water batteries would cut the only convenient line of withdrawal. The retreating Confederates would be forced to march over roads more miserable than the two Grant had to plod along from Fort Henry. Not only would such a retreat still run the risk of being intercepted or overrun by the Union army, but the roads led only farther into the backcountry and away from any strategic point of interest.[53]

Historian Bruce Catton points out that Johnston really had no good option. Catton maintains that by dividing his forces, Johnston was risking more of his army than he could afford to lose and was leaving himself too few men to hold off General Buell. But whether Johnston then had enough time to get all of the Bowling Green troops to Fort Donelson ahead of Grant is open to question, and in any case, Johnston was badly outnumbered and dreadfully pressed, and anything he did was likely to turn out badly.[54] Actually, the Confederates were not that hard-pressed in any other sector. There was no enemy movement detected in the department except for Grant. Days would lapse before that would change. If Johnston thought he was on the brink of disaster, he met it with half-hearted measures. He sent half of his men posted in Kentucky to Fort Donelson in the hope they could hold Grant. By doing so, Johnston ended up sending too few men to hold Grant and more than he could afford to lose. The blunder was compounded by not choosing a strong commander.

General Pillow's messages to headquarters must have been received with a mix of optimism and skepticism. He was not well respected for his military abilities in most circles, yet it would be hard to completely ignore a commander on the scene who displayed such spirit and confidence. Pillow was, after all, from Tennessee, and he was defending his native state. With the exception of Bushrod Johnson, who was actually from Ohio but lived in Tennessee, all the other generals involved in the campaign were from other parts of the South. Probably the one man who began to trust Pillow at this stage was Albert Sidney Johnston. Johnston was a desperate man who was watching the defenses of his department crumble around him. The sole voice not speaking of defeat and despair was Gideon Pillow. For all of his shortcomings, Pillow saw that if the invader was to be defeated and the defensive line restored, the way to do that was to defeat Grant at Fort Donelson.[55]

Pillow's plan to assemble Clark's (Davidson's), Floyd's, and Buckner's commands to strike at Grant was not one of his half-baked schemes. He saw that this was the crucial time to strike a blow to Grant's army, while it was isolated and before it was reinforced. Had Pillow moved quickly enough, there was a chance that the Confederates would have caught Grant's army in column as it advanced on Fort Donelson or pinned it down in the swamps around Fort Henry as it prepared to advance. In the latter scenario, Grant's army would have had little defensible terrain on the landward side, and only the heavy guns of the gunboats could have kept disaster from befalling the Federals.

In the plan devised by General Buckner, Cumberland City offered no terrain significantly better than Fort Donelson on which to mount heavy guns. No preparations had been made whatsoever to fortify the area, provision the troops, or mount cannons. General Floyd was considering a scheme to secure a raft against the piers of the railroad bridge to create an obstacle for the gunboats, but the high water made this impossible. The only apparent advantage Cumberland City had was that an army could easily retreat from it. This is hardly the criterion a bold and determined commander uses to select a battlefield. Also, with the force ratio Grant could eventually muster, the garrison at Cumberland City was just as vulnerable to being cut off as that at Fort Donelson.

This plan also left far too few men to hold Fort Donelson against the forces Grant had on hand to mass against it. To conduct a protracted defense, both the fort and the town of Dover, where the only available steamboat landing was located, had to be held. It was at this steamboat landing that the necessary supplies were massed, not in the fort itself. Had the Confederates concentrated only between Hickman and Indian Creeks, fewer troops would have been needed to defend the site. However, the garrison could not have hoped to last long with few supplies and the surrounding hills dominated by the enemy. The men there would have truly been sacrificed to buy very little time for whatever plan Floyd and Buckner came up with.

Johnston, Pillow, and Floyd all missed the best opportunity at this time to defeat Grant, by concentrating at Fort Donelson. Every other option surrendered the initiative to the attacker, and the Confederates were ill equipped to react.

CHAPTER EIGHT

First Contact

Tuesday, February 12, 1862

THE FIRST MOVEMENT OF THE DAY CAME NOT FROM GRANT'S ARMY encamped around Fort Henry, but from Flag Officer Foote's fleet then assembled at Paducah. At 4:30 in the morning, the fleet brought up steam and begun its slow ascent up the Ohio and Cumberland rivers. The pace was slow as the ironclads *St. Louis, Pittsburg,* and *Louisville* battled the flood currents. The *Conestoga* was normally a swift boat for these waters, but today she was towing a large coal barge to refuel the fleet. Eleven river steamers packed with about 6,000 troops from Indiana and Ohio trailed behind the warships. These were the regiments promised to General Halleck by General Buell some days earlier.[1]

The fleet passed many deserted farms and settlements on its long way up the Cumberland River. Whole fields of corn and tobacco were left unharvested, weed-choked, and abandoned. Not all signs of human habitation were missing, however. Much as with the timberclads on the Tennessee a week earlier, signs of loyalty to the Union met this fleet. At Eddyville, a crowd waved handkerchiefs and miniature Union flags from shore and from the windows and housetops. A reporter on board the *Louisville* noted a solitary act of defiance as a man waved a Confederate flag from his window. It was a brief affair, for a mob formed, stormed the house, and hauled down the banner. The scene of a welcoming crowd was repeated at Canton, just sixteen miles from Dover. There the band of the 57th Illinois struck up a number of patriotic tunes in reply. During the strains of "Yankee Doodle," an old gentleman rose with difficulty, held aloft his hat, and gave three hearty cheers for the Union.[2] Few on the boats believed this was a true reflection of the region's attitude as a whole. The reporter on the *Louisville* added, "Can it be possible that these people are at heart Unionists, or do they affect to welcome us merely in fear of personal violence?" The answer lies in the fact that there were no men of military age seen. They had joined the Confederate Army and may well have been awaiting the advancing flotilla at Fort Donelson."[3]

Meanwhile, General Grant's army had departed Fort Henry by 8:00 in the morning, following the prescribed plan. The army at this time had grown to about 15,000 men. During this march, Grant rode at the head of the column in order to control the pace and be in position to make critical decisions. Dr. John H. Brinton, who had come up from Cairo a few days earlier, rode beside him. The doctor's horse was a headstrong animal and insisted on moving ahead. One of Grant's quirks was a strong distaste for anyone riding in front of him, and at some length, he at last turned to the surgeon and said, "Doctor, I believe I command this army, and I think I'll go first."[4]

Screened by cavalry, General McClernand's division covered the distance between the forts rapidly and in good order, despite the narrow roads and hilly terrain. By 11:00 A.M., the lead elements were within three miles of Fort Donelson's outer trenches.

It was here that first contact was made. In command of a scouting party from the 2nd Illinois Cavalry, Maj. John J. Mudd encountered a strong detachment of Confederate horsemen, intending to resist any further progress.

The gray troopers were under the command of Nathan Bedford Forrest, who ventured forward of the trenches to observe any enemy movements. Sighting the blue infantry column and its cavalry, Forrest promptly dismounted his men. They then formed a line of battle along the crest of a ridge that ran obliquely across the road. In this commanding position, Forrest placed Charles May's and J. M. Hambrick's companies, which were armed with breech-loading Maynard rifles. To the front of this position was a narrow field of cleared land, through which McClernand's division had to pass.

For the next few hours, each side fired, charged, and withdrew without significant advantage gained. Major Mudd then held his cavalrymen in position until the arrival of infantry support from the 30th Illinois. General McClernand subsequently ordered a column to move to the right of the Ridge Road, through some old fields toward Dover, in an attempt to get behind the troublesome gray troopers.[5]

Forrest quickly noticed this attempt to flank his position and shifted his men to meet the new threat. Meanwhile, May's and Hambrick's companies remounted and made a gallant charge down the road against the Union cavalry. It was met by the timely arrival of Federal reinforcements. The 8th

Illinois formed in column of companies at the foot of the hill, and the rest of the blue column held its position in the line of march. When the attack began, it was steadily resisted by Mudd's cavalry detachment for ten minutes, when the Southern horsemen again fell back. Finding no chance to break this line, Forrest's cavalry, now in large force, attempted to gain the rear of it. The blue cavalry was ordered to retire through the 8th Illinois, which wheeled into line and checked Forrest's maneuver by a vigorous fire. McAllister's Illinois battery arrived on the scene, unlimbered, and sent a shell into the gray ranks, compelling them to withdraw. The Confederate cavalrymen kept up a constant fire, however, with the overall effect of delaying the Federals until about 3:00 P.M. At this time, orders were given for all Confederate forces to withdraw back into the outer works.[6]

Grant was advancing on an enemy he knew very little about, but he was learning more. Engineers had told him that the earthworks around Fort Donelson were poorly built, but still no one knew just how many Confederates were in them. After this skirmish with Forrest's cavalry, a few prisoners were taken who claimed that the garrison had 20,000 to 25,000 men, commanded by Generals Floyd, Pillow, Buckner, and Johnson.[7] Grant had no regard for the martial qualities of either Floyd or Pillow, but he may have acted differently had he known his old friend Simon Buckner was technically in command. Gideon Pillow at this time was still upriver trying to confer with John Floyd on the subject of withdrawing troops from Fort Donelson. Grant still had no need to fear, though. General Buckner was under orders not to bring on an engagement and was really only interested in getting his division back to Clarksville anyway.

A few miles away on the river, the ironclad *Carondelet* arrived around 11:20 A.M., under the tow of the transport *Alps* in order to save fuel. After pausing at a makeshift landing, the *Carondelet* then proceeded upstream to get a look at Fort Donelson. Coming within extreme range, the crew did not see a living creature. The hills and woods on the western side of the river partially hid the Confederate defenses, but the two positions of deadly guns of the river batteries were clearly visible. Commander Walke recorded that they "reminded [him] of the dismal-looking sculptures cut into the rocky cliffs near Jerusalem, but far more repulsive." Receiving no response to his presence from the Confederates, Walke ordered the bow guns fired in an effort to provoke them, as well as announce to General Grant that his boat was on station. The dull booming of ten naval shells echoed up the valley. Receiving no reply, and noting that the fort appeared evacuated, Walke drifted the *Carondelet* downriver, dropped anchor, and waited for Grant's arrival with further instructions.[8]

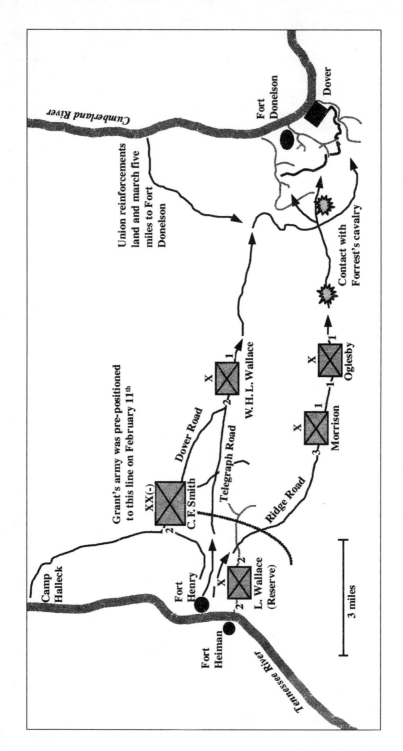

Grant's Advance on Fort Donelson, February 12, 1862

The guns of the *Carondelet* were heard not only by General Grant, but also by the men of his army. The men cheered heartily but were determined not to let the gunboats get ahead of them as they had back at Fort Henry. Commanders at all levels urged their men onward, and the troops were quite eager to comply. As the men quickened their pace, the February drizzle slackened, the sun shone, and the temperatures rose. Spring appeared to have come early, and according to one of the enduring legends of the campaign, the line of march was soon strewn with discarded overcoats, blankets, and equipment as some men threw them away to lighten their loads.

Although some of the raw troops likely did thoughtlessly discard some of their equipment, the actual occurrence of this was probably low. The supply system was not known for its reliability, and even the raw recruits knew that they would be lucky just to get food and ammunition deep in enemy territory as they were, let alone a new issue of camp equipment. Most had just spent over a week in the rain and mud and had a deep appreciation of the value of a tent, blanket, or overcoat. There was a far more common occurrence that accounted for the amount of gear found along the route of march. Commanders were expecting to encounter an enemy sortie at any time and were also trying to make the best time to Fort Donelson. In order to quicken the pace and also be ready for instant action, many regiments placed knapsacks, tents, and other heavy gear into piles and assigned an invalid or two to guard them. These units planned to send small groups of men back to retrieve them later.

Coming up shortly after 2:00 in the afternoon, General Grant occupied a house owned by the Widow Crisp for use as his headquarters. It was described at the time as a "poor, little, unpainted clap-boarded affair of the 'white trash' variety, of logs and a story and a half, with a lean-to on the side, half-room and half-porch." There Grant directed Gen. C. F. Smith's 2nd Division to take a position on the left of the line. McClernand was directed to continue his advance to the right so as to cover the enemy trenches in the direction of the town of Dover.

In preparation for this movement, McClernand ordered a hasty reconnaissance up to the Indian Creek Road, which was found to be clear of the enemy. He then sent his three brigades in column to ascend the range of steep hills opposite the center and right of Fort Donelson's outer defenses. Once into position to cover the length of the Confederate line, the Federal brigades were to form a line of battle and await further instructions. This arrangement not only covered the likely avenues of escape for the garrison, but also brought both McClernand's and C. F. Smith's divisions within supporting distance of each other. The artillery batteries were dispersed along the crests of the hills to provide support to the infantry formations.

The 1st Brigade, under Col. Richard Oglesby, formed the vanguard of the blue column. When it reached the point where the road descended into the valley of Indian Creek, it came in full view of the enemy camps on the wooded hills enclosing the open valley. The Confederates were in strong force, and Oglesby ordered up a howitzer from Schwartz's battery to the brow of the hill to cover the movement across the danger zone. A spirited fire was opened, but the distance proved too great for the short-range piece. To correct this deficiency, Capt. Jasper M. Dressor was ordered to bring forward one of his James rifled pieces, which opened a well-directed fire.[9] The gun fired twenty-one shells upon the enemy's camp at a distance of three-quarters of a mile, resulting in the dispersion of a body of infantry that had drawn up in line of battle. With the Confederates temporarily in disarray, the 1st Brigade resumed its march, cleared the open ground, and ascended into the safety of the woods on the opposite side of the valley. Once safely across, General McClernand halted the lead brigade and ordered another reconnoiter to the front.

So near to the enemy and with so many open fields to cross, speed was needed to minimize exposure of the men to hostile fire. Units received orders to draw up quickly into a line of battle and marched toward a row of hills in the general direction of Dover, which reconnaissance indicated the enemy occupied. McClernand's division swept up the slope, prepared to engage whatever force might oppose it. But when the troops reached the high ground, a few smoldering campfires were all that remained. The advance then continued directly to the front, passing from one to another of the many ridges, encountering none of the enemy's forces, until the division reached the ridge overlooking the outer trenches of Fort Donelson. Withdrawing just beyond the crest of the hill to avoid enemy fire, the men rested upon their arms in front of the Confederate works and within range of their guns.[10] By now most of the soldiers' overcoats, blankets, knapsacks, and rations were some two miles to the rear.

As General McClernand edged his division farther and farther to the right, it became clear that he did not have enough men to fully enclose the Confederate garrison and maintain contact with Smith's division to his left. General Grant was notified of the development. Grant was also getting an idea of what he was up against, and it startled him. Estimates showed that the Confederates outnumbered him by at least 5,000, and deploying his men on a wide arc to surround the fort had spread his forces dangerously thin. Grant needed more troops this instant and could not wait for reinforcements from St. Louis. Against such odds, even if Floyd or Pillow commanded the garrison, Grant's recklessness came to an end.[11] The Confederates had missed another opportunity to attack under favorable numerical odds.

Back on the Tennessee, Gen. Lew Wallace was not pleased that his brigade had been left behind to guard Forts Henry and Heiman. While stuck in the role of reserve, he transferred his headquarters to a steamboat to await further orders. On board, his staff discussed the odds of success for the army that was now surrounding Fort Donelson. A young staff officer pointed out that General Grant had only 15,000 men with him, and that the poor roads prevented the movement of heavy artillery. He also noted that their comrades were going up against fortifications manned by at least as many men, which were probably being reinforced. Grant needed more men, he surmised. At this flash of insight, General Wallace dictated a note for his regiments to prepare to march at a moment's notice, and then ordered four transports to maintain steam in order to bring the troops over from Fort Heiman quickly. Wallace also had a tent and boxes of ammunition loaded on two captured wagons as a final precaution. If new orders came, the men were ready.[12]

Meanwhile, General McClernand could have used this brigade at the moment, for his ultimate object was to extend still farther to the right and, if possible, get some artillery to bear upon the river above Dover. As he extended his line to the right throughout the day, it became more and more detached from the rest of Grant's army. The advance in that direction was also hindered by the terrain, which was very much broken, had no roads, and was covered with an almost impenetrable growth of small oaks. Command and control was difficult. Against his division, reconnaissance patrols confirmed that the Confederates were strongly posted on a range of hills varying from fifty to eighty feet in height, with artillery batteries placed on the commanding points. In front of these defenses, the patrols noted the immense quantity of timber that had been felled to create an abatis, a defensive obstacle to any infantry assault.[13]

Having shifted about a half mile farther to the right, McClernand's 1st Brigade again deployed into line of battle and moved forward to within sight of the enemy's works. This movement, which was boldly and rapidly executed by Colonel Lawler, actually brought his regiment within hearing distance of enemy officers directing an artillery battery to open fire upon him in the morning. In the fading light, a timely change of position of his regiment avoided this unhappy result. But while attempting to draw the regiment back under reduced visibility, an unfortunate discharge of musketry into the ranks of the 29th Illinois killed and wounded several men. Skirmishers were then deployed, who approached the enemy's pickets in the evening and fired upon them, killing two Confederates and wounding four. The rest were driven back to the trenches. Dresser's battery was positioned behind the main line with the horse teams hitched up and ready for instant movement. Permission was given to Col. James S. Reardon to move the 29th Illinois to the left of the brigade for the night to care for his wounded men. The 29th Illinois would return to its position in line early the next morning, and was stationed in rear of the 8th Illinois as a reserve for the day.[14]

Following the 1st Brigade as it shifted to the right, the 2nd Brigade, under Col. W. H. L. Wallace, occupied a ridge south of the center of the enemy's fortifications. Some slight skirmishing with the Confederates occurred here, and after resting and further reconnaissance, Wallace moved his brigade by the right flank.[15] Near sunset, the 2nd Brigade had followed Colonel Oglesby's brigade across Indian Creek, but after dark and the incident of fratricide, General McClernand ordered the brigade to retrace its steps across the valley. Meanwhile, the 3rd Brigade formed into line on the left, using a flanking movement. By nightfall, all of the main roads out of Fort Donelson and the town of Dover were blocked. In these positions, the men rested for the night.[16] Being so close to each other, the soldiers of both armies slept upon their arms and without fires.

General Grant returned to the Widow Crisp's house after inspecting the lines. Here he mulled over the events of the day and formulated his strategy. The resulting plan was simple and essentially a replay of Fort Henry. The army would cut off any possible escape of the enemy garrison; the gunboats on the river would destroy the water batteries; and the field artillery would bombard the fort from the landward side. Surrender should follow quickly, just as at Fort Henry. But this time Grant's army was astride all avenues of escape for the Confederates prior to the naval attack.

Contrary to his West Point instruction and the established practice in sieges for thousands of years, the inexperienced Grant did not entrench his army.[17] He apparently decided there was no need to build earthworks because his army would move on to the fort before they were completed. Also, the soldiers did not have the necessary tools, which would have to have been brought forward from Fort Henry or from the makeshift landing on the Cumberland.

As Grant's army marched upon Fort Donelson, General Halleck continued to try to goad his counterpart in Louisville into advancing. He wired: "Gunboats destroyed everything on the Tennessee. . . . Expedition

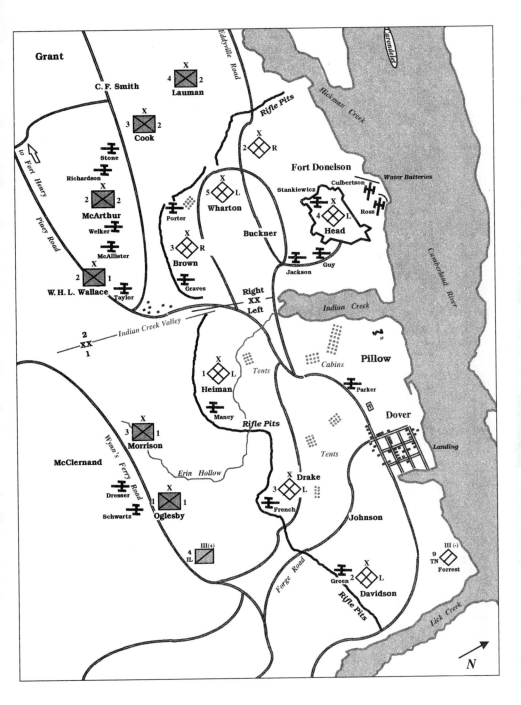

Fort Donelson, February 12, 1862

started up the Cumberland last night led by three gunboats. It is reported that 40,000 rebels are at Dover and Clarksville. If so, they have all come from Bowling Green. If you conclude to land the column on the Cumberland, come at once, with your spare forces."[18] Halleck was again overstating the numbers but shrewdly concluded that Albert Sidney Johnston was stripping Bowling Green for reinforcements for Fort Donelson.

On this day, Don Carlos Buell suddenly realized that the war was proceeding without him, and that he was in danger of being eclipsed by Halleck for good. With General Grant closing in on Fort Donelson and the Confederate evacuation of Bowling Green apparently under way, Buell was beginning to look a bit foolish for his past caution. He now acted with uncharacteristic speed by dispatching Brig. Gen. William Nelson's division to the Cumberland operation. With most of the available river transports now diverted to the mission of supplying Grant's army, however, this movement was destined to take some time.

General Buell wired Halleck to inform him of this change of heart: "Will move on the line of the Cumberland River or Tennessee River, but it will take ten days at least to effect the transfer of my troops. They are moving as fast as possible to the railroad." The rest of his message gives a clear picture of how little he had ever seriously contemplated moving out of Louisville in the past few weeks: "Why is it necessary to use the Cumberland? Where are the reinforcements to land, where to form a junction, and by whom are they commanded? Have you a map of the ground? If so, please send it to me."[19] At this late date, Buell had no appreciation of the terrain, nor a clear view of the situation. As a result of high-level politics, poor intelligence regarding the enemy forces, and procrastination, he would not play any further part in the campaign. His reputation for slowness now secure, Buell's months left in command of a field army were numbered.

General Pillow returned to Fort Donelson by midday from his fruitless attempt to find General Floyd. Hearing the boom of cannons from Clarksville, he boarded a steamboat and arrived to find Grant's army moving through the hills surrounding the fort in force and the Confederate pickets driven into the protective outer trenches. Pillow tersely informed Buckner that his orders for evacuation were canceled, and that he should join his division on the line. General Buckner and his men were now stuck at Fort Donelson.

The men in the defensive works continued to labor on the trenches, unaware of the friction between the general officers. The smoke of the gunboats and transports downstream and the encroaching Federal regiments brought a renewed vigor to their digging efforts.

As scattered skirmishing erupted along the line, no one wanted to miss out on the fight. John S. Wilkes of the 48th Tennessee had earlier been detailed to take the regimental wagons to Dover for supplies. As the little train passed up the road to town, an enemy shell screamed overhead and exploded on the opposite hill. It was the first hostile shot any of the men had ever seen, and in less than a minute, every mule had been unhitched and the squad of men flew at full speed back to the fort. There the men clamored around Col. John C. Brown, explaining to him that they were not willing to be loading wagons while there was a fight on. Brown assured them that the real fight had not yet begun, but they must hurry to Dover to get the supplies before it did. They went back, and John Wilkes never saw such rapid work in loading wagons.[20]

Back at his headquarters, Pillow telegraphed Cumberland City and ordered any remaining troops to come to Fort Donelson. He then telegraphed an optimistic situation report to his immediate superior, General Floyd: "If I can retain my present force, I can hold my position. Let me retain Buckner for the present. If now withdrawn, will invite an attack. . . . With Buckner's force, I can hold my position. Without it cannot long."[21]

Having no confidence in Floyd's judgment, General Pillow also sent this report directly to department headquarters in Bowling Green. There Albert Sidney Johnston saw that Pillow was the man actually on the scene, and his assurances that Fort Donelson was defensible contradicted Floyd's assertions and plans. It also eliminated all faith Johnston had in Floyd's ability to orchestrate the defenses of the Cumberland from far away in Clarksville. Johnston immediately telegraphed Floyd and ordered the Virginian to go with all available forces to the beleaguered fort. Acknowledging the orders by telegraph, Floyd packed his trunk and left by steamboat. He would arrive at Dover the next morning before daybreak.

John B. Floyd was faced with a personal dilemma. He had never received the visit from General Johnston he repeatedly asked for, nor detailed instructions for defending the Cumberland River. Without specific guidance, Floyd was forced to guess at what his mission was. He wrote after the battle: "I thought the force already there [Fort Donelson] sufficient for sacrifice, as well as enough to hold the place until Bowling Green could be evacuated, with its supplies and munitions of war. This I supposed to be the main objective of the movement to Donelson, and the only good that could be effected by desperately holding that post with the entirely inadequate means at hand for defense of the Cumberland and Tennessee Rivers."[22] So was Floyd to "make the fight for Nashville at Fort Donelson" or only hold it until the army at Bowling Green could escape across the Cumberland?

Those were two very different missions, and Johnston and Floyd were not acting in concert.

As night fell across the landscape, the Confederate soldiers were not idle. They continued to work in shifts, digging the trenches of the outer defenses ever deeper, and a few men ventured forth to fell more trees to further hamper any infantry assault. General Bushrod Johnson on the left wing and Nathan Bedford Forrest provided sterling examples and encouragement by sharing the work with their men. As the men toiled, they would get little rest for the arduous days to come.

In summary, in the movement to Fort Donelson, General Grant had applied the experience gained at Belmont and Fort Henry. He formed right and left columns to give flexibility if one became engaged or stalled. He also organized a ready reserve, which followed on the best road. Another reserve force was held at Fort Henry. This time Grant positioned himself at the head of the main column, where he could see and influence events.

Grant's plan for the reduction of Fort Donelson was basically a replay of Fort Henry. As at Fort Henry, the plan and the movements involved were kept simple and straightforward. This army was still novice and not tested in complicated maneuvers under fire. Also, Grant wanted to keep casualties to a minimum. His plan was based on a few misconceptions, however. Fort Donelson was physically in a stronger position than Fort Henry had been. The water batteries were well above the waterline and capable of delivering plunging fire against the unarmored topsides of the ironclad gunboats. The outer defenses were relatively well built, well manned, and protected by an abatis of felled trees. And the garrison was heavily reinforced, its troops outnumbering Grant's army as he initially approached it.

As events unfolded, Grant was probably very lucky. On this day, Federal losses were generally believed to be about 30 men killed and approximately 170 men wounded or missing. This somewhat large number of casualties resulted, to a great extent, from recklessness on the part of the men, many of whom were so anxious to fight that they exposed themselves to fire at the enemy. A large number of wounds were also caused by limbs and branches that were felled by Confederate artillery fire.[23] As the men grew more accustomed to the realities of combat, these incidents would become more rare.

Grant's army did not prepare hasty defensive positions for several reasons. First, Grant did not think it was necessary, believing that the gunboats and artillery would make quick work of the fort. Second, the positions his men held were generally along ridgelines with steep gullies to the front, which were considered favorable for defense. Third, even if he had ordered entrenching, the men had stripped themselves of their equipment in order to hasten the march. There were few, if any, shovels in the ranks, necessitating the transport of these implements either from Fort Henry or all the way back from Cairo or Paducah. Also, at this stage of the war, many leaders and soldiers felt that it was unmanly to entrench, or that troops in trenches grew complacent. Few generals routinely had their men dig in at this time, and those who did were often ridiculed. Even the esteemed Robert E. Lee was derisively dubbed "the Queen of Spades" during the early months of his command for requiring his men to entrench.[24]

The Confederates made but a half-hearted attempt to slow Grant's advance from Fort Henry, mainly by sending Forrest's reinforced cavalry battalion out to harass the Federals. But Forrest's battalion was not supported by either infantry or artillery and could only annoy the approaching Federal divisions. It is difficult to conjecture whether the Confederates would have been more aggressive if General Pillow had been present, rather than being upstream looking for Floyd. Pillow demonstrated at Belmont that he was recklessly aggressive, but he did not have an opportunity this day to show it. Most historians acclaim Simon Bolivar Buckner as the most proficient warrior of the Confederate generals present, and he was technically in command during Pillow's absence. He had no interest in making a fight at Fort Donelson, however. He was there only to put his and Floyd's troops onto the first available steamboat and transfer them to Cumberland City. He was not about to risk becoming decisively engaged and tied down to the fort. With such a state of affairs within the Confederate command, Grant's army was able to envelop Fort Donelson virtually unmolested.

Finally, Albert Sidney Johnston again demonstrated how badly he had lost control of the situation. An enemy army was on his flank, preparing to cut off his army. Grant was alone and unsupported, however, and any threat from Buell was miles away and showed little sign of movement. Meanwhile, Floyd was pleading for assistance and guidance but received neither.

Fort Donelson was on its own.

CHAPTER NINE

Opening Round

Wednesday, February 13, 1862

BEFORE DAWN, A STEAMBOAT NOSED INTO DOVER WITH THE COMMANDER of the Confederate forces on the Cumberland on board. The reluctant John B. Floyd had arrived to assume personal command at Fort Donelson. This development left General Pillow somewhat out of a job, for when he organized the defenses, he had designated Simon Buckner and Bushrod Johnson to command the right and left wings, respectively. On paper, Gideon Pillow bumped Bushrod Johnson from wing command to that of second in command of that sector. In reality, the aggressive Pillow continued to exercise far more overall command than Floyd, who would remain oddly detached and indifferent.[1]

After his arrival, Floyd checked into a room at the Dover Hotel which became his headquarters. After breakfast, he inspected the works and apparently showed some concern over the outer line of trenches, but no sooner had he completed his tour than firing broke out along the line. Grant's army was tightening its grip around Fort Donelson.

In the early-morning hours, the bulk of McClernand's and Smith's divisions shifted their positions along the ridges surrounding the outer trenches of Fort Donelson. Artillery batteries were also repositioned without opposition during the night. These gun positions were well selected to annoy the Confederates as they labored to strengthen their works. However, no Federal batteries had yet found a firing position to bring guns to bear on Fort Donelson itself or the water batteries. What prevented this were not only the Confederate defenses, but also the nature of the terrain. The range was extremely long, and the thick woods prevented clear sighting.

Not yet in open battle, the opposing armies turned to the practice of sharpshooting, or deploying snipers. This was a common practice during the war, and this campaign was no exception. Usually regiments deployed expert marksmen with the skirmishers to shoot at anyone who dared expose himself. Favorite targets were officers, artillerymen, and other sharpshooters.

Unique in Grant's army was a regiment organized, trained, and equipped for this specific purpose. The 14th Missouri Infantry, or Birge's Sharpshooters, performed this service very effectively. Each member was dressed in gray with a felt hat adorned with a blackened squirrel tail. Armed with heavy Dimmick hunting rifles, these men were trained to hit a man at a 1,000 yards. As sharpshooters, they fought generally in the places and manner that happened to suit individual fancies, such as lying flat behind a stump and watching for a target, as would a game hunter. The sharpshooter would fire at the unfortunate Confederate who showed himself, then roll onto his back, reload, and twist back ready to fire. During the whole operation, he would not expose so much as the tip of an elbow to the enemy.[2]

These men of Birge's Sharpshooters spread out in small groups and took up advanced positions. Their fire was accurate and deadly, virtually halting any daylight work by the Confederates. Birge's men particularly found Porter's Tennessee Battery an inviting target. This battery was sited on a prominent hill toward the center of the line, and had no protective works around it. The exposed gun crews maintained their position as long as they could, but the wounding of several men led the others to seek shelter. Learning of this development, General Pillow ordered Forrest and his cavalry to drive off the enemy sharpshooters. Once again, May's and Hambrick's companies, with their Maynard rifles, were led to the trenches, and they skirmished with the Federal marksmen for over an hour. Forrest himself observed a small portion of a sharpshooter exposed in the top of a tree some 600 yards distant. He took a rifle from one of his men and in an instant brought the man tumbling headlong to the ground.[3] The sharpshooters eventually withdrew from this area for the time being, but they would remain a constant unseen threat to any unwary Confederate in the trenches.

Ulysses S. Grant by nature hated to be idle, and he knew that further delay allowed more time for the Confederates to strengthen their defenses or for General Halleck to cancel the operation. To pass the time, he took his staff to reconnoiter along the line for most of the morning. During one halt, about six shots struck around him, one bullet hitting a horse of his escort troop.

Having seen enough, General Grant altered his plan for the day. He would not simply adjust the lines and await reinforcements. Instead, the

Brig. Gen. Ulysses S. Grant:
Commanded the Union forces during the campaign. This photograph was taken a few weeks after his victory at Fort Donelson. NATIONAL ARCHIVES AND RECORDS ADMINISTRATION

Maj. Gen. Henry Halleck:
Grant's superior in St. Louis, later became chief of staff for the Union Army. NATIONAL ARCHIVES AND RECORDS ADMINISTRATION

Flag-Officer Andrew Hull Foote:
Commanded the Western Gunboat
Flotilla and months later died of
complications to his wounds received
at Fort Donelson. NATIONAL ARCHIVES AND
RECORDS ADMINISTRATION

Brig. Gen. John C. McClernand:
The Illinois Democrat who
commanded the 1st Division on
the right flank of Grant's army.
U.S. ARMY MILITARY HISTORY INSTITUTE

Brig. Gen. Charles F. Smith: Commanded the 2nd Division, which took and held a length of trenches and threatened the water batteries. NATIONAL ARCHIVES AND RECORDS ADMINISTRATION

Brig. Gen. Lew Wallace:
Commander of the 3rd Division and
sent reenforcements to McClernand in
time to prevent a rout. U.S. ARMY MILITARY
HISTORY INSTITUTE

Gen. Albert Sidney Johnston:
Confederate commander of the
Western Department. TENNESSEE STATE
LIBRARY AND ARCHIVES

Brig. Gen. Lloyd Tilghman: Commanded the river forts and allowed himself to be captured at Fort Henry. TENNESSEE STATE LIBRARY AND ARCHIVES

Brig. Gen. John Floyd:
The former secretary of war turned
soldier. Floyd's inexperience and
indecisiveness lost Fort Donelson.

Brig. Gen. Simon B. Buckner:
The reluctant brigadier at Fort
Donelson. His bitter feud with Pillow
weakened his resolve and clouded his
judgment.

Brig. Gen. Gideon Pillow: Arrogant and brash, Pillow led the attack on the left but made a critical error which contributed to the Confederate defeat. NATIONAL ARCHIVES AND RECORDS ADMINISTRATION

Brig. Gen. Bushrod R. Johnson:
The forgotten brigadier at Fort
Donelson. Ironically, he had approved
the sites for the forts during the
previous summer. TENNESSEE STATE
LIBRARY AND ARCHIVES

The USS *Lexington*: One of three "timberclads" used in the campaign. They were
ideal for reconaissance and shelling positions from long range. NAVAL HISTORICAL CENTER

Building of the "City-Class" ironclads in St. Louis: Shown here are four of the new ironclads a few weeks before their launch. NAVAL HISTORICAL CENTER

The USS *Carondelet*: This "City-Class" ironclad saw action at Fort Henry and Fort Donelson, where she was heavily damaged. NAVAL HISTORICAL CENTER

The USS *Louisville*: This typical "City-Class" ironclad saw action at Fort Donelson and was heavily damaged. NAVAL HISTORICAL CENTER

The USS *Essex*: Unique in design, this ironclad was converted from a ferryboat. She was disabled at Fort Henry when her boilers were ruptured. NAVAL HISTORICAL CENTER

Fort Henry: The artist took some liberty in this depiction. At the time of this drawing, the fort was virtually under water. TENNESSEE STATE LIBRARY AND ARCHIVES

The Battle of Fort Henry: A sensationalized view of Fort Henry during the attack. Many gun crews actually worked standing in water. TENNESSEE STATE LIBRARY AND ARCHIVES

Morrison's Attack: The ill-fated attack of Morrison's reinforced brigade on February 12. TENNESSEE STATE LIBRARY AND ARCHIVES

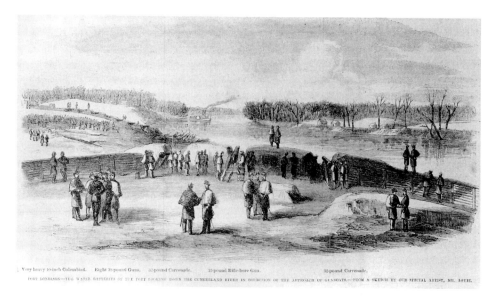

Fort Donelson Water Batteries: A post-battle view of the Confederate water batteries. The upper river with the 6.5 in rifle battery is in the foreground. The lower river battery in the background held the 32-pounders and the massive Columbiad. TENNESSEE STATE LIBRARY AND ARCHIVES

Interior of Fort Donelson: A view of the interior of Fort Donelson showing the garrison's cabins and tents. TENNESSEE STATE LIBRARY AND ARCHIVES

Prisoners at Fort Donelson: The ragged and exhausted Confederates of the Fort Donelson garrison were quickly rounded up and sent to prison camps in the North. TENNESSEE STATE LIBRARY AND ARCHIVES

Interior of Fort Donelson [modern]: The interior of Fort Donelson today. AUTHOR

32-pounder Cannon [modern]: A 32-pounder of the lower battery. The water level is approximately the same as during the campaign. AUTHOR

View of the battlefield [modern]: During the campaign most of the terrain was covered by thick underbrush and bramble as seen here. AUTHOR

The Dover Hotel [modern]: The Dover Hotel served as headquarters for generals Floyd and Buckner and it was here where the formal surrender took place. AUTHOR

The Attack on Fort Donelson: A contemporary sketch of Smith's attack in the afternoon of February 15, 1862. U.S. ARMY MILITARY HISTORY INSTITUTE

The Attack on Fort Donelson: Another contemporary sketch of Smith's attack in the afternoon of February 15, 1862. U.S. ARMY MILITARY HISTORY INSTITUTE

army would probe the defenses to ascertain whether there were any weak points in the lines. He also sent the lone gunboat present, the *Carondelet,* to challenge the water batteries.

About 9:00 A.M., the ironclad received its orders. Grant's dispatch informed Commander Walke that most of the army's artillery batteries were in position and the rest soon would be. Grant's message then asked Walke to take the *Carondelet* upstream within the hour to shell the enemy water batteries. Although no one was to bring on a general engagement, the army would "be ready to take advantage of any diversion."[4]

Much had changed over the previous week at the water batteries, and they were not as weak as before. Indeed, the Confederates had been busy under the guiding eyes of Lt. Col. Milton Haynes, chief of the Tennessee Corps of Artillery, and Capt. Joseph Dixon of the engineers. In addition to the bombproof magazines constructed in January, the armament had been greatly improved. There were now eight 32-pounder smoothbore guns in the lower battery, as well as the massive 10-inch Columbiad. This heavy gun had been mounted a few weeks earlier, but as with the one at Fort Henry, a test fire had nearly destroyed its carriage. Haynes ordered the big gun dismounted and sent an officer to the rolling mill in Clarksville to have two new traverse wheels made. These wheels were four inches larger than the old ones to increase the angle of recoil. They had arrived on one of the steamboats just the day before. Another test fire this morning showed that they worked like a charm.[5]

The rifled 6.5-inch gun also had been delivered to Fort Donelson at the end of January, but the pintle and its plate were missing. Without these critical parts, the gun was useless. Another officer was sent to Nashville to procure these and other components. He returned just in time to have this gun mounted in the upper battery and in working order as the *Carondelet* headed up the river.

At the appointed time, the *Carondelet* steamed upstream and took a position behind a jutting promontory of the riverbank. From extreme long range, about a mile and a quarter, she began to lob 8-inch shells at the fort.

In the water batteries, the novice crews were in the midst of their drills when lookouts spotted the black ironclad pressing its nose up the river. In command, Captain Dixon requested permission to return fire to drive off the gunboat and its increasingly accurate fire. General Pillow allowed him to fire the 10-inch Columbiad and the rifled 6.5-inch gun, but Dixon protested, wanting to fire all of the guns in order not to expose the locations of the heavy guns to the enemy. Pillow maintained that firing the smooth-bore 32-pounders at extended range was simply wasting ammunition. The supply of ammunition was limited, and resupply was uncertain even under the best of circumstances. Irritated at his superior, Dixon instructed the two heavy guns to fire. The first round of the Columbiad passed just over the *Carondelet,* and the second fell short. The third, however, was heard to strike with a sharp crack. After an hour and a half, Dixon either received Pillow's permission or took matters into his own hands and ordered all of the 32-pounders to fire. Even at maximum elevation, all of these shells fell short of the target.

The effects of the Confederate fire began to tell, though. After a morning of trading shots, the *Carondelet* had taken two hits. One came from the Columbiad, which passed through the port casemate forward, glancing over the barricade at the boilers, and again over the steam drum. It then struck and burst the steam heater and fell into the engine room without striking anyone, but the splinters injured twelve crewmen. When it penetrated through the side of the *Carondelet,* this shot also blew an immense quantity of splinters and shrapnel throughout the boat. Some of the men were so taken aback by the suddenness of the mishap that they were not aware of their own wounds until told of them. Damaged, but not severely, the gunboat withdrew to its old anchorage to feed the crew, make repairs, and transfer the wounded to the transport *Alps.* Hearing the sound of distant firing in the hills surrounding the fort, Commander Walke again steamed upriver to fire forty-five more shells at the water batteries. The duel continued through most of the afternoon. For the results of firing 184 shells, Walke was convinced that three of the Confederate guns were disabled, but he was in error.[6]

There actually was little or no damage inflicted on the water batteries and as yet no casualties to the gunners. Around 4:00 in the afternoon, the *Carondelet* began her final withdrawal to the anchorage three miles below the fort. Her last shot of the day, though, struck the muzzle of Number 2 gun of Bidwell's Battery. The large naval projectile dismounted the 32-pounder and scattered the crew. A retaining bolt was sheared off the carriage and struck Captain Dixon in the head, killing him instantly. Dixon was the only reported casualty at the water batteries, and afterward Capt. Jacob Culbertson took command.

Though not hit by naval fire, the Columbiad was damaged during the duel. The gunners found that with the larger wheels and the depressing of the traverse circle in front, the angle was so great that it produced a rut out of which the front wheels could not be rolled. Also, one of the forward traverse wheels of the heavy gun had been crushed, and a section of the traverse circle damaged, during the engagement. The result was that the

Columbiad now had serious limitations. In this condition, the gun could still fire, but as it was unable to traverse, it had a very limited field of fire. During an engagement, the unlucky boat toward the eastern bank would receive its fire.[7]

In his sector on the left, Gen. C. F. Smith used Lauman's brigade to probe to the front, hoping to discern any weakness in the line. While the *Carondelet* traded shots with the water batteries, the regiments moved forward.

Lauman's brigade had bivouacked during the night about a mile from the Confederate defenses. On this morning, the men moved over the intervening ridges until they came opposite of the trenches held by the 2nd Kentucky under Col. Roger W. Hanson. There a deep hollow with felled trees filled the space between the two parties.

The 25th Indiana led the advance across this space and forced its way partially up the opposite slope. There the regiment remained exposed for two hours under heavy fire, until it was recalled. To divert enemy fire during the withdrawal operation, the 7th and 14th Iowa moved up to the left of this position, as did a detachment of sharpshooters from the 14th Missouri.

To the right of Lauman's brigade, Col. John Cook moved his brigade in support to the edge of the ravine. Studying the felled trees, and noting the heavy fire of the artillery, he decided not to attempt to cross. Instead, he deployed his regiments and kept up a desultory fire at skirmishers and sharpshooters. The 7th Illinois, on the far right, advanced too far and was suddenly taken under heavy fire. It promptly withdrew out of range, as did the rest of Smith's command.

The opposing sides in General Smith's sector remained about 600 yards apart for the remainder of the day. The effect of this probing was a handful of casualties and a fairly accurate assessment of the enemy defenses. Smith had no way of knowing, but the movements of the day appeared threatening enough that General Buckner felt compelled to send the 18th Tennessee to reinforce the 2nd Kentucky.[8]

On the far right of the Federal line, General McClernand continued to shift his division to the right, with the object of anchoring it on Lick Creek. In the early morning, Oglesby's brigade marched about one-half mile in the direction of Dover, under cover of the woods paralleling Wynn's Ferry Road. As this brigade shifted to the right, the artillery batteries of both sides engaged in a vicious duel.

Dressor's battery opened this contest and initially succeeded in silencing the Confederate guns of Maney's Battery to its front. The guns then shifted their aim and poured a destructive fire into a mass of infantry, which was driven back into the shelter of the trenches. Eventually the cannon ran short of ammunition and was withdrawn to replenish its supply. Meanwhile, two of McAllister's 24-pounder howitzers were brought up and took its place. Graves's battery joined in the duel, and a well-placed shot carried away the wheel from one of McAllister's howitzers. While the wheel was quickly replaced by cannibalizing one off a limber, the balance of the McAllister's battery was reinforced by the return of Dressor's battery, and together with a section of Taylor's battery, they brought the enemy guns under fire. The combined fires apparently silenced the gray artillerymen for a short time. Throughout the day, however, the guns of both sides kept up an almost continuous fire, which cost a number of casualties among the crews and supporting infantry.

Under cover of the artillery duel, General McClernand brought the brigades of his division ever closer to the Confederate outer works for the purpose of finding a weak point in the line. Oglesby's brigade on the right advanced so far as to come under scattered musket fire from the trenches. Unfortunately for the men of the 1st Brigade, this persistent musket fire and the occasional shell from artillery never slackened. Tiring of this nuisance and mounting casualties, McClernand decided to seize a salient in the Confederate line, which dominated the terrain around him. While the artillery fired, few Confederates were seen on this hill, but McClernand reasoned that the enemy could later reoccupy this dominant point of the line in force and further threaten his own troops. Accordingly, and without approval of General Grant, McClernand ordered an assault on this position. It is unclear how McClernand could not have realized this would likely bring on a general engagement, which he had been specifically ordered not to do.[9]

Just before noon, orders went out to the respective commands. Colonel William R. Morrison led the 3rd Brigade, consisting of the 17th and 49th Illinois infantry regiments. This unit was the nucleus of the assault force. The brigade quickly maneuvered into position on a ridge opposite Maney's Battery. It prepared to advance across the steep ravine and through the dense underbrush and felled trees.

To support the assault, General McClernand then attached the 48th Illinois, commanded by Col. Isham Haynie, to Morrison's brigade. As the men made final preparations to charge, Colonel Haynie realized that he was the ranking officer and should lead the charge. Morrison felt that "this was no time to dispute about a question of rank" and offered to conduct the reinforced brigade to the assault point and then turn over command. Haynie replied, "Colonel, let's take it together." That said, the men in blue

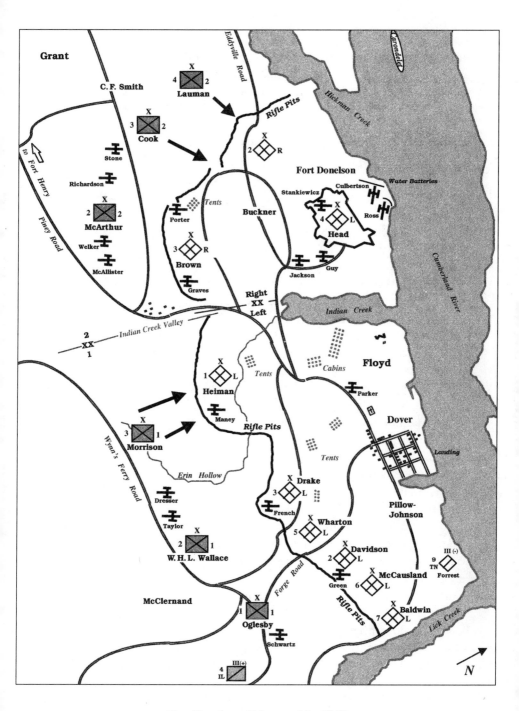

Fort Donelson, February 13, 1862

surged forward, led by the skirmishers, and struggled up a steep rise through the tangle of underbrush and obstacles. At this juncture, the brigade came under heavy fire. A bullet struck Morrison in the hip, knocking him off his horse and settling the issue of who commanded the assault force. The men pressed on, though, and only came to a halt at the abatis under a hail of deadly fire.[10]

The attackers made their way under increasing fire to a cleared space beyond the tangle of obstacles. At this point, a heavy crossfire of artillery and small arms was also poured into the assailants, yet for an hour they maintained the unequal contest, advancing to within forty paces of the trenches and firing with deliberation, but eventually falling back.

As the attack stalled, McClernand committed his reserve, the 45th Illinois, to the assault force. As it took its place in the line, the brigade moved up the hill again under heavy fire and renewed the assault. Geneal McClernand later wrote that at this critical moment, if the enemy had been diverted by an attack on the left and also from an attack on the river by the gunboats, it is probable the position would have been taken. Instead, the Confederates were reinforced, and more artillery was positioned to fire in enfilade upon the attackers. Caught in the heavy crossfire, the Federals fell back a final time.[11]

The lines separated, but they were still within small-arms range. Between the lines were the scattered dead and wounded from Morrison's brigade, numbering over 200 men. The Confederates had lost but 10 killed and 30 wounded. Tragically for those trapped between the lines, the sparks and flames from the guns of Maney's Battery ignited the leaves and brush to its front. The ensuing conflagration swept across the face of the hill, burning the bodies of the dead and those wounded men who could not escape the blaze on their own. Their cries of agony and pleas for help elicited no response from their comrades, who were afraid the Confederates would shoot at any man who exposed himself. But the Confederates on the line called to their enemy, pledging to hold their fire. Unable to bear the sight any longer, a few Confederates leaped over their entrenchments and pulled some of the wounded men from the flames.

So ended the attack on "Redan #2," as McClernand called it. Both he and Grant downplayed this event in the official reports. This was for good reason. After a stiff repulse and bloody loss, no military advantage was gained. Both generals probably just wanted to forget the whole incident.

After this attack, McClernand pulled his line back slightly. Toward evening, Oglesby's brigade withdrew about 200 yards to the higher ridge, along the Wynn's Ferry Road, and constructed a fortified position for

McAllister's battery. At nightfall, W. H. L. Wallace's brigade occupied a position along the Wynn's Ferry Road facing Heiman's and Drake's brigades. The whole front of the division was covered with a line of skirmishers during the night for security.

Meanwhile, thirty-five miles downstream, Foote's fleet of gunboats and transports continued its battle against the current of the Cumberland. Impatient, Grant sent the steamboat *Alps* to meet the column and tow a steamer or two to expedite their arrival. Meeting the flotilla, the *Alps* passed the news of the fight between the *Carondelet* and the water batteries that had occurred some hours earlier. Andrew Hull Foote was troubled by these developments and was anxious to get to Fort Donelson as quickly as possible. His understanding with General Grant had been that no attack would be made until after the arrival of the flotilla. Sensing that the situation had changed for the worse, Foote countermanded Grant's order and instructed the *Alps* to take the *St. Louis* and *Louisville* in tow. If Grant was anxious to get the reinforcements up more quickly than planned, Foote reasoned that the firepower of his naval guns was more valuable.[12] What the old salt did not know was that Grant needed men, not cannons, at this time. The Federal line was greatly extended in trying to enclose the Confederate trenches, and only more infantry could close the gaps in the line. But as the *St. Louis* and *Louisville* pulled ahead of the fleet under the tow of the *Alps,* the steamers carrying fourteen Indiana and Ohio regiments from General Buell's army followed along behind at their best speed.[13]

As the fleet made its way up the Cumberland toward Fort Donelson, two incidents occurred that almost resulted in the loss of an ironclad. First a bolt came out of the *Pittsburg's* boiler, which the chief engineer quickly repaired before disaster occurred from the high-pressure steam system. While repairs were under way, the starboard bulkhead caught fire, and the flames were dangerously close to the powder magazines. Prompt action extinguished the blaze, which had been caused by a flaw in the design of the boat: the wooden bulkheads had been placed too close to the boilers.[14]

As the sun fell on the western horizon, all of the Union troops began to realize that Fort Donelson was going to be far tougher than Fort Henry. The mild, pleasant temperatures disappeared as a driving north wind brought rain, sleet, and finally a blizzard that would deposit three inches of snow by morning. The men suffered severely as the temperatures plunged. Most of Grant's army was still without tents, blankets, and coats, which they had left in piles along the route of march. The troops were too near the enemy lines to risk warming fires, and the only food available was whatever the soldiers had left in their haversacks, primarily hardtack. They probably had coffee, but without fires, there was no way to boil water for it. In many regiments, the men stood to arms all night because there was no place to lie down. Colonel Oglesby later wrote that the men were subjected to "one of the most persecuting snow storms ever known to this country." He added that by morning, most of the men were "nearly torpid from the intense cold."[15] Adding to the misery was the occasional shot from a picket or sharpshooter.

The Confederates of Fort Donelson suffered throughout the night as well. Many of the units had also arrived without their baggage and did not have their tents or blankets either. They could not have fires, but with the sharpshooters neutralized due to the darkness, the Confederates worked throughout the night, digging the defensive trenches even deeper. They also hastily constructed fieldworks to protect Maney's beleaguered battery.

The evening of February 13 also saw the arrival of Guy's battery to the steamboat landing in Dover. Although this was not a singularly significant event, it is an illustration of the Confederate command climate that would greatly affect the events over the next few days. After his guns and limbers were unloaded, Captain Guy sought out a senior officer to place the battery in the line. He eventually met up with Gen. Bushrod Johnson, who took him to reconnoiter before deciding upon a position. When Guy returned to the landing to retrieve his command, he was met by General Pillow, who asked the young officer who he was and what unit he came from. Learning of what had transpired, Pillow became indignant that General Johnson would presume to give such orders. The movement was halted, and Guy's battery was reassigned to another sector of the line.[16] No doubt Bushrod Johnson heard from Pillow on this matter, and he would hesitate to make decisions to avoid incurring the Tennessean's wrath again. From now on, Johnson would do as he was told, and little more.

It was close to midnight when Flag Officer Foote's fleet reached the landing some two miles below Fort Donelson. There, a savage wind was driving hail, sleet, and snow. The disembarking of Col. John Thayer's brigade and other reinforcements was commenced in short order, which, under the circumstances, was a tremendously disagreeable job. When the worst of the storm finally passed, the ground here was frozen hard and covered by at least an inch of snow, which further slowed the unloading process.[17]

During the night and into the morning, the gunboat crews labored to make their vessels more battleworthy. Those short on coal filled up their bunkers from the barge towed by the *Conestoga*.[18] Chains, lumber, bags of coal, and anything else thought to be able to stop a cannonball were laid out across the unarmored upper decks to protect against plunging fire from the Confederate guns on the hill. Makeshift barricades were fashioned in the interior of the boats to protect the vulnerable boilers and machinery. The *Pittsburg,* for example, had 100 bread bags filled with coal stowed around the boilers. As a second thought, the men's hammocks were added later in the morning.[19] All hands knew the fate of the *Essex* at Fort Henry and they did not want the same to happen to them.

The *Carondelet's* crew also took time to replenish her ammunition and partly repair the damages sustained the day before. At this critical period, an inebriated gunner at the powder magazine threatened to the blow up the *Carondelet,* to send her and all hands to hell. He was immediately ironed and confined to his room under guard. The intoxicated gunner was placed under the charge of the third master but later succeeded in eluding him and made it back to the magazine hatch, where he was stopped by the surgeon, Dr. James McNeely, and again secured. The delinquent third master, who was also intoxicated and disaffected, joined the gunner in returning to civilian life about a week later.[20]

Ashore, General Grant conducted the affairs of an army commander in the field. His farmhouse headquarters was located just left of the center of the lines. It not only was a fairly comfortable dwelling, but also was in a position from which he could control his army and close enough to the river that he could confer with Flag Officer Foote. Once there, he studied the situation. The first phase of the plan had gone reasonably well. The army had marched in good order from Fort Henry and surrounded Fort Donelson without too much resistance from the Confederates. The defensive perimeter proved stronger than expected, but it was not impregnable. The next phase would begin when Foote's gunboats were ready. According to the plan, the ironclads would knock out the water batteries as they had at Fort Henry just a week earlier. Surrounded and bombarded by land troops, the Confederates would see the hopelessness of their situation and surrender quickly, or so Grant hoped.

Grant's men were strung out along at least two miles in the hills and hollows opposite the trenches of Fort Donelson. The line was pretty thin on the extreme right in McClernand's sector, and there was a large gap between the two divisions of the army. Supplies were on hand but were haphazardly placed at intervals along the line. Yet all in all, everything was going remarkably well for this untrained army.

But these new soldiers of the army were at that moment near freezing in the driving snow, and there was no way to tell when it would let up. Grant surmised that although his army was miserable, the lot of the Confederates in the trenches beyond could not be any better. He knew that most of the regiments had recently arrived without baggage, and though the rifle pits may protect them from bullets, they would not provide shelter from the howling winds and falling snow.

With Foote's flotilla now on station, General Grant was ready to put his plan into motion. Any further delay he felt would give the Confederates additional time to dig trenches or receive reinforcements. His cold men would need to be active to overcome the miseries of this evening, too. When Flag Officer Foote passed a message that the boats were ready, Grant would then give the word for them to advance and shell the fort into submission. When the water batteries were silenced, the troops would begin a general advance. With his army blocking the routes of escape, there would be no repeat of Fort Henry.

For the Confederates, February 13 provided another opportunity to attack Grant's army before it could position itself on defensible terrain or get adequate supplies in place. But by staying in the trenches, they allowed McClernand's division to deploy across the Wynn's Ferry and Forge Roads, thus blocking the main avenues of escape or reinforcement to the garrison. With each passing hour, Grant's army was becoming stronger, meaning that any offensive action by the Confederates would require a growing commitment of limited forces to do the job adequately.

The exchange between the water batteries and the *Carondelet* showed more promise. It was, in fact, a morale boost to the beleaguered garrison, with one of the vaunted ironclads making a timid appearance and eventually pulling back out of range.

On the other hand, the conduct of the firing singled out the two most effective guns to the gunboats, which could take advantage of this information during a full-scale attack. This blunder was compounded when the 32-pounders did fire, revealing their maximum range as well. Dixon made an error of judgment in firing these guns, particularly after the locations of the heavy cannons were already compromised. The Federals could not have asked for a better assessment of the capabilities of the water batteries' guns.

The general ineffectiveness of the Confederate guns would set the stage for the river battle the next day. Commander Walke of the *Carondelet* was convinced that he had silenced three guns, though in fact only one was dismounted. So if one gunboat could knock out three guns in one day, was it not logical to think that four ironclads and two more wooden gunboats firing at long range could silence the batteries without a large risk of effective return fire? If three guns were indeed disabled, there were that many less to oppose the entire flotilla. Some basic calculations show that four ironclad gunboats assaulting only seven operational cannons would receive only a limited number of hits. Using the experience at Fort Henry as a guide, Foote could see statistically that he had a good chance of closing with the batteries without receiving too much damage. Additionally, he did not have to try to maintain a position abreast of a plodding infantry column. This overall plan had worked at Fort Henry, and Foote would try it again here. Besides, this tactic had also worked some years earlier in China, where Foote had become famous. He was a fighter, and it really was not his style to loiter and lob shells at extreme range.

Andrew Hull Foote was also extremely frugal and was probably aghast at how many rounds the *Carondelet* had fired. Planning to close the range would, in theory, increase the probability of a hit from his novice gun crews. True, the boats might take a few hits themselves, but an assault might just do the job more quickly than long-range firing.

On the landward side, the day was even bloodier and less productive for the Federals. On the left, Gen. C. F. Smith's probe was halted by the irregular terrain and felled trees covered by the guns of the defending Confederates. After standing up under extreme pressure for over an hour, the attacking forces were withdrawn.

In General McClernand's sector, the brigades were stretched thinly along an extended line. But additional regiments were arriving, freeing more of McClernand's men to shift to the right and fill in the lines. The unauthorized attack on Maney's Battery, though heroic, was futile. In his report after the battle, McClernand tried to deflect some of the criticism, but since he did not coordinate this attack with anyone, this was impossible. The Confederates only had to shift very few forces to meet this threat, and any diversion in another sector would have made little difference anyway.

Many of the men on both sides suffered from the lack of blankets or overcoats. The Federal regiments had left them behind along the march from Fort Henry, and many Confederate units had arrived at Fort Donelson without their baggage. The lesson learned was severe, and no one forgot it. From this time until the end of the war, men took care of their blankets and kept them on hand.[21] They learned how to travel light and fast without leaving vital equipment and supplies behind.

CHAPTER TEN

The Vise Tightens

Thursday, February 14, 1862

AROUND 1:00 A.M., THE FOUR CONFEDERATE BRIGADIERS OF FORT Donelson met in Dover to decide what to do. This was their first meeting together, and they were a diverse assortment. Floyd was essentially a politician in uniform. Pillow was arrogant, egocentric, insubordinate, and dominantly assertive. Buckner was third in seniority, technically proficient, but an unwilling participant.[1] Bushrod Johnson was there, too, but was for the most part silent.

Reports suggested that 15,000 to 20,000 new Federal troops had arrived, making a total of some 40,000 men, with possibly more on the way.[2] Actually, some sixteen transports had arrived in the last twenty-four hours, bringing only about 6,000 Federal troops. These were the Hoosier and Buckeye troops of Thayer's brigade, which were at this time unloading from the boats in a miserable four-hour operation. The Confederate senior officers had no way to really know the accurate count, but the inflated numbers deflated their hopes and resolve to defend the fort.

Accordingly, the brigadiers decided to break out of what was increasingly perceived as a trap, then march southeastward to Charlotte and then to Nashville to join Albert Sidney Johnston. Pillow was designated to lead the assault, and Buckner the rear guard. General Floyd sent no requests for reinforcements, nor did he update General Johnston of his plans. Floyd was, in effect, forfeiting any chance for outside help or support. The decision made, couriers carried orders through the bitter cold night to the brigades and regiments to assemble for an attack.

The morning dawned cold and cheerless upon men already severely tired by hunger, exposure, and endless watching and labor, yet they rose promptly to the duties of the day. The rising sun finally brought light and only slight relief to the bitterly cold soldiers of both armies. Fires were lit, coffee brewed, and the men thawed themselves as best they could. With daylight, though, the sharpshooters became active. The blue marksmen worked their way forward through the underbrush, and some took to the trees. Those in gray typically remained behind the breastworks, resting their rifles upon them to steady their aim.

The Confederates had more in mind this morning besides sharpshooting, as the regiments and brigades slowly began their movements to their assault points. With luck, they would make a hole in the Federal line, and the garrison could pass through to Nashville. Hours were spent getting the regiments into position, but for reasons unknown, the word to commence the attack never came. As more hours passed, the Confederates stacked arms and built fires to keep warm. After noon, Pillow and his staff finally rode to the head of the column and prepared to give the order to advance. Mounted officers typically drew the fire of sharpshooters, and this case was no exception. At the head of the assault column, Pillow in his resplendent uniform made a fine target. A sharpshooter took aim and fired, but instead of hitting Pillow, the bullet painfully wounded one of the infantrymen near him. Pillow then turned to one of Floyd's aides and reportedly said: "Captain, our movement is discovered. It will not do to move out of our trenches under the circumstances." The young officer disagreed, but Pillow would have none of it. "No, I am satisfied that our movement is discovered. Ride in haste and tell General Floyd that I think so and that the attack had better be deferred till morning."[3]

This abortive sortie thus stalled in place, and by midafternoon, the chance to launch the attack had passed, since there were only three to four hours of daylight left. After standing in the snow for hours, the troops eventually received word from Pillow to return to the trenches. Floyd was finally found back at headquarters in Dover, where he lost his composure when his aide told him of Pillow's order. He did eventually calm down, and in any case, it was far too late to countermand the order. Why Floyd was in Dover instead of supervising this critical action is a mystery. But with the men marching back to their old positions, the Confederates lost another good chance to strike at Grant's army or evacuate the fort.[4]

With the gunboats on station and the army heavily reinforced since his attack on Fort Henry, Grant appeared confident of victory. He had been in place for two days, which he had used to conduct a reconnaissance of the battlefield. Large amounts of supplies were on hand at the landing and in piles a short distance behind the lines. His naval colleague was ready with his ironclads, and so far General Halleck in St. Louis had not called off the operation. Furthermore, Grant knew that Floyd and Pillow were calling the shots across the way in Fort Donelson. The only general officer there that he respected, Simon Bolivar Buckner, was third in the chain of command. Other than the foul weather, everything was pretty much going according to plan.[5]

At first light, Grant left his headquarters and boarded the flagship *St. Louis* to confer with Flag Officer Foote. With Foote on hand, Grant could proceed with the next phase of his plan. The gunboats would proceed up the river and shell the Confederates out of their entrenchments and the water batteries. At the same time, McClernand's division would sweep around on the right and take possession of a portion of the trenches and possibly the town of Dover. This would cut off the Confederates from most of their supplies and force them back upon the Federal left and center, which were in position to block any escape.[6] But before the regiments moved, the gunboats would reduce the water batteries. Or that was the plan at least.

On the right of the line, General McClernand tried to fulfill this mission and continued to shift his division farther to the right to complete the trap. Although he blocked the roads out of Dover, there was still a considerable gap between his right flank and Lick Creek. McClernand dispatched a detachment of cavalry under Capt. Warren Stewart, supported by some infantry, to reconnoiter in that direction. Their report, later confirmed by a patrol of the 4th Illinois Cavalry, showed McClernand that he did not have enough men to effect an investment of the Confederates all the way to the Cumberland River. Until reinforcements arrived or he was relieved of maintaining contact with Smith's division on the left, he planned to anchor his right flank against the flooded Lick Creek.

McClernand arrayed his forces opposite the enemy defenses, with Oglesby's brigade on the right still some 400 yards short of Lick Creek, W. H. L. Wallace's brigade in the center, and Morrison's, now commanded by Col. Leonard Ross, on the left. Four artillery batteries were positioned along the divisional front in support. Three of these covered the Wynn's Ferry Road, which was the Confederates' most likely avenue of escape.[7] The cavalry assigned to the division was placed to the right and rear of the line, where it guarded the flank and rear of the army. Except for the occasional sharpshooter or artillery shell, the rest of the day passed fairly quietly for McClernand and his men, who were blissfully unaware that the Confederates had massed a large attack force against them but had withdrawn on General Pillow's order.

Grant needed more infantry quickly to add strength to his dangerously thin line around Fort Donelson. He was in constant communication with

Brig. Gen. G. W. Cullum, Halleck's chief of staff, who had gone some days earlier to Cairo to oversee the reinforcement of the expedition. An indispensable element in the success or failure of the operation, Cullum tightly managed the transportation assets and sent urgent telegrams to Halleck on the matter of the short supply of ammunition.[8] Grant was told that more units were on the way but it would take time to get them up the Cumberland. With a dangerous gap growing between his two divisions, Grant needed them now. But he did have an untapped source of manpower at his immediate disposal, which he now put to use.

Over on the Tennessee, a courier arrived at Fort Henry in the early morning hours. He carried orders for a delighted Gen. Lew Wallace to bring the bulk of his brigade up to Fort Donelson. Thanks to Wallace's foresight and preparations, this move was completed rapidly. Leaving behind the 23rd Indiana at Fort Henry and a detachment of the 5th Iowa Cavalry at Fort Heiman, Wallace led his column over the Telegraph Road, then crossed over to the Dover Road, where guides met him to show the way. The brigade arrived at Grant's headquarters near 11:00 A.M. and was reattached to Gen. C. F. Smith's division on the left of the line.

Wallace was then relieved of command of his beloved brigade and assigned the task of forming a new division from the regiments arriving by steamboat. He organized the seven available regiments into a division of two brigades under command of Colonels John Thayer and Charles Cruft. This unit became the 3rd Division of Grant's army at Fort Donelson. Wallace was given the same orders passed to McClernand and Smith: to resist all attempts of the enemy to break through and under no circumstances bring on a general engagement.

Around 2:00 P.M., the new 3rd Division left the Crisp house in column, the 31st Indiana in the lead, with the object of taking its place in the line. For quite a distance, the heavy woods and ravines screened this movement from the enemy. The route, however, eventually exposed the column for about 300 yards to Confederate gunners who did not let the march go unchallenged. As General Wallace's men came under shell fire for the first time, someone suggested that the men cross the open terrain at the double-quick. Declining that option, since it could degenerate into a run, Wallace instead sent word to the regiments to play all of their fifes and drums as if on parade. He reasoned that it was better to inspire contempt of shells from the beginning, rather than demoralize the men with fear of them. The music began, and the troops' resilience was magical. Many shells were lobbed at the regiments as they made the passage, yet not a man was killed or wounded.[9]

Once Wallace was in his assigned sector, Grant's aide-de-camp halted the new division. Here the ground was level, but to the front the dense trees and hills blocked the view of the Confederate defenses. Wallace learned to his astonishment that McClernand's division was still about a half mile farther off to the right, and Smith's was a quarter mile to the left. With no lateral roads, communication with either required a rider to take to the woods. It became very clear to Wallace why Grant had sent for his brigade. Until his arrival, there had been a real danger that the Confederates might attack in this virtually empty sector and split the army in two. Failure to do so was another example of the confusion and ineptness among the Confederate command.

Wallace placed his regiments in the line and sent pickets forward for security. Small fires were allowed on the sides of the hills away from the enemy, and the men took care not to create enough smoke to attract the attention of the enemy gunners. The snow here was a few inches deep, and it was bitterly cold. The men walked about and beat their bodies to maintain circulation, their teeth chattering like castanets. Yet there was nothing to do but wait and be ready.

There was one last significant movement on land that day. Apprised that McClernand could not close the 400-yard gap between his flank and Lick Creek, Grant sent McArthur's brigade, which had been positioned as a reserve for Smith's division on the right. Arriving well after dark, the brigade was not put into the line, but was held a short distance to the rear. The movement of novice troops at night was a risky endeavor; no one wanted another incident of friendly fire or to have a regiment wander into the Confederate defenses. Instead, the plan was for the brigade to rise at first light, move forward, and anchor the right flank of McClernand's division on Lick Creek. With this done, the Federal line would be almost continuous, though very thin. It also would be ready to take advantage of any diversion the gunboats provided.

As General Grant's army marched about the hills and gullies beyond the trenches, a new development caught the full attention of the Confederates at Fort Donelson.

Captain Culbertson watched intently from the lower river battery as columns of black smoke rose from an unknown number of vessels behind the line of trees downstream. He sent word for General Pillow, as well as a request for permission to fire the long-range Columbiad and 6.5-inch rifled gun. In a short time, Pillow arrived from the aborted attack on the left. He initially denied permission to fire. After some discussion, General Floyd allowed Culbertson to begin lobbing shells at the enemy forward debarka-

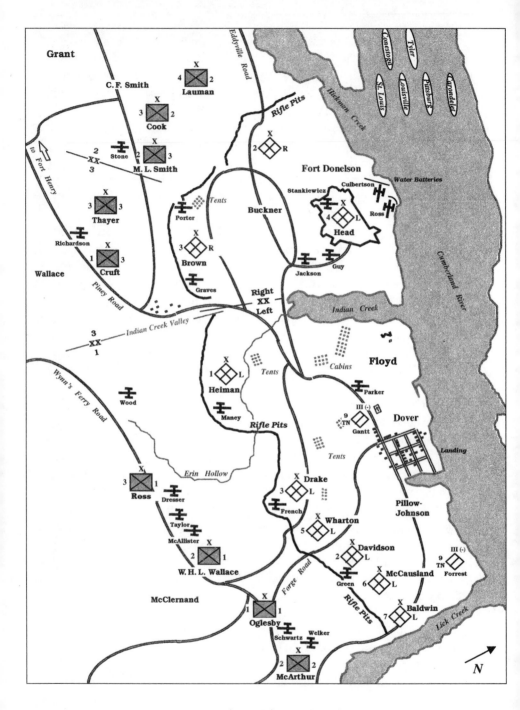

Fort Donelson, February 14, 1862

tion point. A half dozen shots were fired, which had more effect than the Confederate gunners could see from their angle. As the shells splashed into the water, the unarmored steamboats hastily slipped their lines and steamed downstream and out of range.[10]

The movement of boats observed by the Confederates was actually the planned departure of the gunboats. Flag Officer Foote's officers had detailed instructions for the battle, including placement of each boat in the formation and prearranged signals. At 1:00 P.M., Foote signaled his boats to follow the motions of the commanding officer. Twenty minutes later, as falling shells scattered the transports, the Flag Officer gave the signal, and just after 2:00, the flotilla churned slowly up the river in formation. As at Fort Henry, the ironclads formed the first division. On the western bank of the river, the *Louisville* was at the right of the formation. The *St. Louis,* with Foote on board and serving as the flagship, was next, and adjacent was the *Pittsburg.* The *Carondelet* was on the eastern bank, at the left of the line. The wooden gunboats *Conestoga* and *Tyler* formed the second division and trailed the first by several hundred yards to avoid enemy gunfire. The movement was not altogether without problems. In the stiff current, the *Pittsburg* and the *Louisville* had difficulty keeping their place in the line, and Flag Officer Foote signaled them to steam up. At 2:35, the fleet reached the end of a long tract of woods to the right and came within sight of the fort.[11]

Andrew Hull Foote was not as confident of success as he had been at Fort Henry. He had witnessed firsthand what a heavy gun could do to his lightly armored fleet. His boats were vulnerable to plunging fire, although the crews had done what they could to protect them. To minimize exposure to fire, Foote planned to close the distance against the strong current of the Cumberland to point-blank range and silence the guns as quickly as possible. As before, the timberclads' role was to lob shells at extreme range.[12]

Upstream, Captain Culbertson was directing his gun crews to adjust their fire on the debarkation point when the Union flotilla rounded the bend and came into full view. Shells were replaced by solid shot, and the Confederate gunners waited for the boats to come within effective range. The gunners had been taught to fire at given ranges and had their calibrations ready. Around 3:30 P.M., Culbertson's two heavy guns in the fort opened fire on the approaching boats. Splashes in the water showed the first salvo of Southern projectiles falling short. The gunners would have plenty of opportunity to improve their aim.[13]

When within a mile of the water batteries, the bow guns of the *St. Louis* opened fire, followed quickly by the other eleven bow guns of the ironclad division. Their first rounds also fell short, but as the gunners found their range, Foote signaled his squadron to steam up faster to close the distance. The ever-frugal skipper also ordered the boats not to fire so fast to avoid wasting ammunition. Commander Walke of the *Carondelet* particularly felt the flag officer's wrath for a breach of ammunition conservation. On board the *St. Louis,* Foote stood in the pilothouse watching the effect of every shot from his boat as well. When he saw a shell burst inside the fort, he instantly commended the deliberate aim of the marksman by a message through his speaking tube. When the shots fell short, he expressed his dissatisfaction.[14]

Onward the gunboats came, but by General Pillow's order, the 32-pounder smoothbores did not fire until they reached nearly point-blank range. This was against Captain Culbertson's judgment, as it again showed the enemy the positions of the two heavy guns. The gunboats did not exploit this information, however.

Although the water batteries were not damaged by enemy fire, a mishap cost the Confederates the use of one of these most effective guns for much of the battle. After the third or fourth round, improper loading caused a priming wire to become lodged in the vent of the 6.5-inch rifle. The gunners of Ross's Battery had but two days' experience on this cannon, and mistakes such as this were common to green crews. For the time being, only the heavy Columbiad offered resistance to the gunboat advance, and with its damaged traverse mechanism, it still had a severely restricted arc of fire.

The gunboats did not seem to recognize this development and did not concentrate on the single gun firing. Instead, the oncoming boats seemed to fire almost at random. Most of the shells passed over the water batteries and into the hills beyond. When the boats finally reached the point of the submerged tree obstacle, which was about 400 yards from the gun line, Culbertson ordered the crews of the 32-pounders to open up with everything they had. Reminiscent of Fort Henry, to the gunboats it looked as though a sheet of flame erupted from the water batteries.

Inside the gunboats, the crews could hear the deafening cracks of the bursting shells, the crashes of solid shot, and the whizzing of fragments of ammunition, metal, and wood as they ricocheted through the vessels. Smoke filled the boats' interiors, and near chaos ensued as orders were shouted, wounded men screamed, and guns thundered.

On the hill overlooking the river, the Confederates worked their guns with astonishing intrepidity and skill. When the naval shells blasted large amounts of dirt into the positions, the men coolly took shovels and threw the dirt back over the parapet. The supply of wadding gave out for Lt. John S. Martin's 32-pounder in the water battery, which had been firing as rapidly as possible. Undaunted, Martin pulled off his coat and rammed it down his gun as wadding, and thus kept up the fire.[15] The Confederate gunners had noticed the two wooden gunboats loitering in the rear but focused their attention on the ironclads.

By 4:00, the battle raged with all its horrors. When the ironclads reached a point about 350 yards from the water batteries, the heavy shot began to take effect. A 128-pound ball from the Columbiad hit the *Carondelet,* which smashed the anchor and sent the deadly pieces flying. The shot then bounded over the casemate, taking away part of the smokestack and one of the boat davits. Another ripped a section of iron plating, and yet another smashed into the pilothouse, mortally wounding a man. In the heat of the battle, the gun crew of the port bow gun failed to ram a projectile all the way down the barrel. When fired, the pressure in the chamber exploded the cannon, wounding over a dozen men and spreading panic and confusion throughout the gun deck. A fire started in the debris and two more shots entered the bow ports, killing four men and wounding several others. The Confederates were also skipping their projectiles on the water in an effort to strike the vessels at or under the waterline. The *Carondelet* received two such shots, and only the sealed compartments below deck kept her from sinking. But despite the heavy damage, she continued in line, firing her remaining bow guns without intermission.[16]

The ironclads continued to advance steadily up to 300 yards from the Confederate guns. The short range somewhat improved the gunboats' marksmanship, but it also greatly added to the effectiveness of the Southern guns. Meanwhile, the 6.5-inch rifle in the upper battery was finally cleared of the bent priming wire and resumed firing. But then a projectile became jammed halfway down the barrel, and all efforts to drive it home failed. A dozen men were dispatched to find a log long enough to fit the piece. Finding one, and exposing themselves to hostile fire, they mounted the parapet and drove the projectile home. The gunner of the piece, Pvt. John G. Frequa, cried, "Now boys, see me take a chimney!" With a pull of the lanyard, the shot brought down the flag of the *Carondelet* and one of the smokestacks. Frequa threw his cap into the air and yelled defiantly, "Come on, you cowardly scoundrels; you are not at Fort Henry!" After firing, these same men took several minutes to clean the bore until it was again serviceable. Later, still another mishap occurred when the loading rammer was tossed over the parapet by accident, but the soldier responsible coolly walked over to retrieve it.[17]

Despite the gallantry of the gunners, all did not share their enthusiasm. Lieutenant Colonel Nathan Bedford Forrest briefly left his command at the

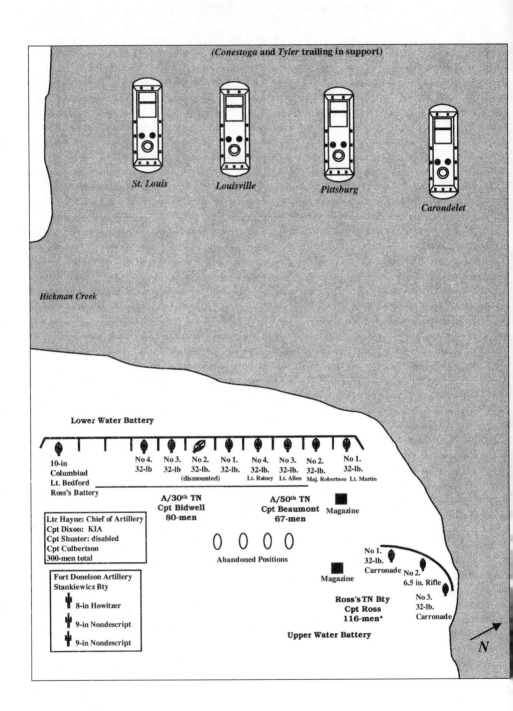

(Conestoga and *Tyler* trailing in support)

St. Louis   Louisville   Pittsburg   Carondelet

Hickman Creek

Lower Water Battery

10-in Columbiad
Lt. Bedford
Ross's Battery

No 4. 32-lb   No 3. 32-lb   No 2. 32-lb. (dismounted)   No 1. 32-lb.   No 4. 32-lb. Lt. Rainey   No 3. 32-lb. Lt. Allen   No 2. 32-lb. Maj. Robertson   No 1. 32-lb. Lt. Martin

A/30th TN
Cpt Bidwell
80-men

A/50th TN
Cpt Beaumont   Magazine
67-men

Ltc Hayne: Chief of Artillery
Cpt Dixon: KIA
Cpt Shuster: disabled
Cpt Culbertson
300-men total

O O O O
Abandoned Positions

No 1. 32-lb. Carronade   No 2. 6.5 in. Rifle

Fort Donelson Artillery
Stankiewicz Bty

Magazine

Ross's TN Bty
Cpt Ross
116-men*

No 3. 32-lb. Carronade

8-in Howitzer

9-in Nondescript

9-in Nondescript

Upper Water Battery

N

Fort Donelson Water Batteries, February 13–16, 1862

booming of the cannons and rode to a clearing overlooking the spectacle on the river. He watched as the naval shells plowed into the earthworks, sending dirt and debris flying in all directions. He was soon joined by his second, Maj. David C. Kelly, who had been a preacher prior to the war. Highly agitated, Forrest spun in his saddle and shouted, "Parson! For God's sake, pray; nothing but God Almighty can save that fort!"[18]

At 4:30, a naval shell struck the Confederate flagstaff, breaking it off close to the ground. An officer of the fort ran out and erected it near its former position. Scarcely had the fort's banner fallen when the flagstaff of the *St. Louis* was carried away. Without hesitation a handful of sailors exposed themselves to the deadly fire, seized the spar, and lashed it into place. Moments later the flagstaffs of the *Louisville,* and *Pittsburg* were also carried away in apparent retribution.[19]

The gunboats were taking a pounding and could withstand little more punishment. The *Louisville* received a heavy shot that was stopped just short of her boilers by the makeshift pile of hammocks and coal. A second swept the length of the vessel. Another struck her and severed her steering chains. Her pilot, Samuel McBride, ran out on the stern to rig a makeshift repair by hooking the relieving tackles and steering by them. His actions were halted by shells from the wooden gunboats, *Tyler* and *Conestoga,* which fired from a quarter mile astern. The shells were "exploding so fearfully and constantly" over the *Louisville* that McBride and his work party were driven into the shelter of the casemate. Commander Benjamin M. Dove, skipper of the *Louisville,* was compelled to let her drift out of the battle.[20]

The other gunboats were taking substantial damage, too. The flagship *St. Louis* was hit repeatedly, her armor cracked and casemate riddled. One 32-pound shot struck the pilothouse, sending splinters flying and killing the pilot, F. A. Riley. Foote was standing at his side and was wounded in the left ankle, but he took the wheel himself and continued the fight. He soon went below to urge the gunners and was wounded again in the arm as a shell struck the vessel. The *St. Louis* then lost her tiller ropes to enemy fire, and all efforts to steer her with the relieving tackle were unsuccessful. Being completely unmanageable, she was also compelled to drop out of the line of battle. Seeing the two ironclads fall back, the *Carondelet* and *Pittsburg* closed in to protect their heavily damaged sisters. The *Pittsburg* attempted to turn, and broke one of her rudders in a collision with the *Carondelet's* starboard quarter. The *Pittsburg* by then had been hit twice below the waterline and also fell back with the current, in grave danger of sinking.

The battered *Carondelet* was the last boat to withdraw and subsequently received the harshest treatment. A heavy shot struck her pilothouse and jammed the wheel, and with her starboard rudder disabled, she swung nearly broadside to the water batteries. The men on shore did not pass up such an inviting target. She received the full fury of the Confederate gunners, particularly the heavy Columbiad, which raked her side and tore away large chunks of her armor. She was terribly cut up, not a mast or spar left standing. All of the barges, boats, stanchions, and hammock nettings were cut to pieces. The pilothouse and smokestacks were riddled, the port side was cut open fifteen feet, and the decks were splintered. With four men killed and fifteen wounded, the *Carondelet* was also taking on water. She drifted toward shore to a point just below Hickman Creek and well within range of the enemy guns. To avoid grounding there and meeting certain destruction, the *Carondelet* was obliged to steam upstream under heavy fire to clear the point of land. Once clear, the acting pilot cut her engines, and she drifted downstream. As the *Carondelet* withdrew with the current and out of the battle, her two remaining bow guns fired defiantly until the range was too great.[21] For his gallant actions in serving the rifled bow gun in this action, Mathew Arthur later received the Medal of Honor.

It took about half an hour of drifting with the current, but once beyond the bend in the river and out of the range of the Confederate cannons, the gunboats anchored to assess the damage and casualties. The *Pittsburg* was taking on water and was tied up close against the bank to prevent her sinking. Makeshift repairs were begun on all of the vessels, and the dead were removed and buried near the landing. The damage inflicted was tremendous. The *St. Louis* had been hit fifty-nine times, the *Carondelet* fifty-four times, the *Louisville* thirty-six times, and the *Pittsburg* twenty times. At least eight men were killed and forty-four wounded. The Confederates had fired just under 500 rounds, the guns of the 32-pounders firing about 50 shots apiece. The fleet had fired just over 300, about 75 of which were heavy 8-inch shells.[22]

A journalist on the *Louisville* was not too impressed with the ironclads. "My curiosity is satiated. I have no particular desire to be on board a man-o-war when another battery is to be attacked, but, on the contrary, think I should prefer a land view."[23]

Some observers saw only three Confederate guns firing when the *Louisville* and *St. Louis* were disabled, and Flag Officer Foote thought the water batteries were ready to fall before disaster befell the flotilla. He wrote, "we have no reason to suppose that in fifteen minutes more could the action be continued, have resulted in the capture of the fort bearing on us, as the enemy was running from his batteries when the two gunboats drifted helplessly down the river from disabled steering apparatus."[24] Whether the

Confederate gunners were abandoning their guns or not, the repulse of the gunboats was a fact.

During the battle, every gun in the trenches remained silent and even the pickets paid deference to the fight between the gunboats and the river batteries. Though the water battle was out of sight, the troops could tell with unerring accuracy whether it was the gunboats or the water batteries that fired each shot. With each report from the naval guns, the hopes of the Federal troops were raised. But they knew with absolute certainty when the fleet stopped firing. Wrote Henry Hicks, who was posted on the far right of the Union line and had no way to ascertain firsthand how the fight was progressing: "After a little more than an hour of continuous firing, suddenly the roar of artillery ceased. Men spoke to each other quietly, almost in whispers, wondering what the ominous silence meant. After a few minutes of such silence, a yell burst from the throats of thousands, ringing from one end of the Rebel line to the other, and the mystery was solved."[25] There was no denying that the soldiers of Grant's army were discouraged by the news. Without the support of the gunboats, a protracted siege or bloody assault was a near certainty. Also, there was no telling what the Confederates, encouraged by their victory, might attempt that night or the following day. The pickets were reinforced, and commanders checked the men on the line. They would suffer another night of bitter cold but could take some comfort that the enemy on the next ridge who probably just as cold and miserable.

At the Widow Crisp's house, General Grant pondered his next move. The repulse of the gunboats and the heavy damage they had sustained were serious setbacks to his plan. With the water batteries intact, there was no possibility of running past the fort against the strong current. With only a slight edge in troop strength, it was not feasible to directly assault the fortified positions. At present, Grant concluded to make the investment of Fort Donelson as perfect as possible, partially fortify, and await repairs to the gunboats.[26]

This plan, too, would not go Grant's way.

The river battle over, the victors looked about them. Gone were the fine lines of the gun embrasures, as the naval shells had blasted chunks from them and heaped mounds of earth on the gun platforms. Even the snow on the hill behind the guns had been swept away as if by a whirlwind. The Confederate gunners took a well-deserved rest as Lt. Col. Alfred Robb of the 49th Tennessee passed around a bottle of liquor to the valiant crews. After their break, the gun crews readied for night firing in case the fleet tried to run the batteries in the rain and snow that were beginning to fall.

They also planned to fire at intervals in the night to let the enemy fleet know they were vigilant.

The vaunted ironclads that had made such short work of Fort Henry were badly damaged and beaten back, and morale in the Confederate trenches was at an all-time high. This was not the case at the senior command level, however. In fact, the Confederate command was in a state of confusion. During the gunboat assault, General Floyd kept Albert Sidney Johnston apprised via telegraph. The reports Johnston received should have caused him to question Floyd's competency and ability to command. In rapid succession, Johnston received the following dispatches, the second of which was sent by a man named Trabue, a panicked telegraph operator at Fort Donelson, the others from Floyd:

> "The enemy is assaulting us with a most tremendous cannonade from gunboats abreast the batteries, becoming general around the whole line. I will make the best defense in my power."

> "Operator at Donelson says gunboats passed and are right on him."

> "The fort holds out. Three gunboats have retired. Only one firing now."

> "The fort can not hold out twenty minutes. Our river batteries working admirably. Four gunboats advancing abreast."

> "The gunboats have been driven back. Two it is said seriously injured. I think the fight is over today."[27]

General Johnston had every right to question just what had happened on the river and the status of the fort. Combined, these messages did nothing to give Johnston confidence in Floyd. Gideon Pillow later sent a more coherent report directly to Johnston, confirming that the gunboats had been driven off and were severely damaged, as well as a report that the Confederates had received no casualties.[28] The fact that two of the brigadiers were sending messages to Johnston directly indicated that the chain of command was not clearly established or defined. But in spite of all the confusion, Johnston left Floyd in command.

That evening, the Confederate brigadiers met in Dover for another council of war. General Floyd apparently was convinced that Grant was reluctant to attack by land at the moment but could be reinforced over time to overwhelming strength. He also felt that after allowing Grant to completely invest the fortress, it was time for the Confederates to break out or they would have to endure a siege. He thought that the fort would not stand a prolonged siege and favored a breakout. He remembered one of Johnston's earlier telegrams: "If you lose the fort, bring your troops to Nashville if possible. If you can not hold the fort, at least save the army."[29]

The Confederates may have known that the transports were bringing reinforcements up the Cumberland, but they had no way to tell how many soldiers were landing. Particularly at this stage in the war, commanders typically inflated the strength of an enemy force, and this time was no exception. All of the Confederate brigadiers felt that they were greatly outnumbered by a force of over 40,000 organized into fifty-two regiments. The reality was just over half that.

General Pillow also favored an attack, but perhaps not an escape, feeling that Fort Donelson was a strong position. He too was incorrect in his assessment of the enemy force dispositions, however. He believed that enemy siege artillery was covering the roads and that the enemy was arrayed in three distinct encampments, which were separated by thick tangles of brush that prevented the movement of large bodies of troops. This describes the three divisions of Grant's army, and there were gaps in the Federal line, to be sure, but the units were not so badly cut off that they could not be moved to render support.[30]

When given the chance to speak, Pillow laid out his views in detail. His scouts reported that McClernand's division was astride both the Forge and Wynn's Ferry Roads leading out of Dover. Gideon Pillow was a man of action and proposed that his wing, reinforced by Buckner's elite 2nd Kentucky Regiment, hit this Union right flank and roll it back from the river and onto the Union center. Once this feat was accomplished, General Buckner would attack and catch the enemy in the flank and rear. Grant would then be pinned against the river and the garrison could escape at leisure.[31]

It was General Buckner's turn to speak next, and he immediately vetoed Pillow's use of his beloved 2nd Kentucky. He then proposed a modification of Pillow's plan. General Pillow would attack, but Buckner's division would play a more active role. The point of attack shifted to the left, with the goal of eliminating the Union artillery covering the Wynn's Ferry Road, thus reducing the load for Pillow's men. During a withdrawal, Buckner would then move in to protect the flank and rear as the garrison escaped to the south. Pillow agreed to Buckner's changes, and Floyd authorized the plan.

The Confederates would attack at dawn. With good preparations and timing, the chances seemed good for success.

In spite of his rank, Brig. Gen. Bushrod Johnson was not invited to the council of war.[32] He and the brigade commanders were summoned to headquarters after the meeting to receive their orders. At least one brigade did not send its commander or a representative. Floyd called the meeting to order, and Pillow briefed the officers on the plan, outlining its purpose and the role each unit would play. Floyd said little, if anything, to the assembled officers. What was not covered in the briefing was the process of withdrawing the garrison from the fort: details for rations, the carrying of blankets and knapsacks, the march order during the retreat, and how and when the actual retreat would commence were just a few of the procedural elements that were missing.

The council of war ended about an hour after midnight, and every officer left with a different impression of what was to transpire. General Pillow believed that his troops would return to their trenches after a victory so complete that they could retrieve their equipment at leisure. Buckner thought no one would return to the trenches after the battle commenced. Thus Buckner's units went into combat encumbered by their equipment and haversacks full of three days' rations, as did Baldwin's Brigade, although it was assigned to the left wing, indicating that Buckner and Baldwin consulted after the conference. Additionally, some brigade commanders returned to their units and failed to give detailed instructions at all to their subordinate regiments as to their role in the attack. For instance, one brigade sent word to its subordinate regiments only to be ready to move at an instant's notice in the morning. Time was running short, too, for the attack was scheduled for 5:00 A.M., and the brigades were to be on line by 4:30 in the early-morning darkness.

Major Gilmer confirmed this state of confusion in a report after the battle:

> The details of preparation for carrying out the plan decided upon, such as the number of rations that should be prepared; whether blankets and knapsacks should be taken or not; what should be the order of march on retreat for the different commands; who should take the advance, and who should protect the rear, were not arranged, to the best of my recollection. The decision of the council was in general terms . . . to attack the enemy, secure a retreat toward Charlotte, and if circumstances justified it, to follow up all advantages, and hurl the invaders back to their transports.[33]

If the Confederate commanders were confused and full of anxiety, not so the men. The Confederate brigade and regimental commanders returned to the trenches to find the morale of their soldiers high. Although they were isolated from Nashville, so far the battle had gone their way. The gunboats had been repulsed and direct infantry assaults against the trenches turned back over the past two days. The men were cold, wet, and bone weary, but they still had plenty of fight left in them.

In summary, the aborted early-morning sortie on the left of the line was a curiosity. It was uncharacteristic of Pillow to call a halt to an assault because of one shot from a lone sharpshooter. General Pillow could be described in many unflattering terms, but he was no coward in the physical sense. He had shown bravery to the point of rashness at Belmont and earlier in the war with Mexico. There was intermittent firing all along the line, as sharpshooters practiced their aim and artillery lobbed occasional shells. It is difficult to believe that the attack was called off for the reason Floyd's aide described some time after the battle. It is more likely, though pure conjecture, that Pillow sought to hold Fort Donelson to bring on a decisive fight more to his character. The sniper's bullet simply provided him with an excuse to halt the planned retrograde movement.

Had the assault taken place as planned, it may have stood a good chance of success. At this time, General McClernand's division was spread perilously thin trying to invest the left wing of the Confederate defenses. There was also a gap of some 400 yards between the Union flank and Lick Creek. The regiments of Gen. Lew Wallace's new division were as yet unavailable to reinforce McClernand, since they were either marching in from Fort Henry or unloading from the steamboats. A concentrated attack on McClernand at this moment would have enjoyed a substantial ratio of troops in the Confederates' favor.

Overall, the decision to undertake such a sortie may have had tactical merit, but it also was in conflict with the purpose for which Floyd believed Fort Donelson had to be held. Johnston's army was still not safely across the Cumberland, and breaking out at this time would allow the gunboats to destroy all of the bridges upstream. Floyd apparently had neither coordinated this effort with Johnston nor sought his permission.

As for the fight on the river, with the limitations of the Confederate water batteries clearly shown the day before, one can question Flag Officer Foote's tactics. If he had initial misgivings, they proved correct. Fort Donelson was indeed a tougher nut to crack. The heavy guns on the hill had an excellent position, and they were generally well served by the novice crews. The key 6.5-inch rifled gun was the glaring exception. Surprisingly, even when these guns exposed their positions, the gunners on the boats did not take advantage of that information.

Foote seriously misapplied the tactics he had used so effectively at Fort Henry. Fort Henry was essentially a water battery situated on a site that provided an unlimited field of fire, whereas Fort Donelson was placed on a hill with nearly all short-range guns. At Fort Donelson, the gunboats, with their weapons of superior range and effectiveness, had only to stand off and destroy the batteries at leisure, and then ascend the river and rake the garrison until it surrendered. By conducting a direct assault, the combined weight of the eight 32-pounders were added to the equation, resulting in an overwhelming volley of iron. The day before, the *Carondelet* had proven the worth of firing at long range. Although she fired a large number of projectiles, the naval fire dismounted one of the guns. Even if the combined fire of all the gunboats disabled but one gun apiece on February 14, that would have reduced the firepower of the water batteries by over fifty percent. This, in turn, would have made the prospect of a direct assault less costly at a future time.[34]

What may also have accounted for Foote's decision to close with the batteries was a limited supply of ammunition for the big guns. The availability of ammunition had plagued the gunboats since their completion. An accurate inventory is lost to history, but it stands to reason that Foote could not afford to expend hundreds of rounds at long range for an uncertain result.

Marksmanship during the river battle was also a lopsided affair. On a steady platform on the hill, the Confederates enjoyed a higher ratio of their shots striking home. On the boats, there was always a slight roll and the closing distance to compute. Many of the naval shells sailed over their intended targets to land in rear of the Confederate trenches, only a mere annoyance. Instead of increased accuracy as the range decreased, the opposite proved true. In fact, the fire from the gunboats was more accurate and destructive at maximum range than at 300 yards.[35] The shots from the wooden gunboats also did not have the same results at they had at Fort Henry. Instead of passing over the ironclads and landing with effect on their targets, many of the shells exploded far short of the intended distance. The *Louisville* and *Carondelet* reported shell fragment damage on their unprotected stern casemates attributed to the *Tyler,* and these shells prevented damage control parties from repairing the severed steering cables.

Commander Walke later asserted that the *Carondelet* had been in position during the attack to run the batteries but was prohibited by a standing order from Foote.[36] It is true that the Confederate guns had a limited field of fire, and unbeknownst to Foote, they were not able to swing about and face upriver. Had the gunboats run past the fort, they indeed would have effectively cut off the garrison from supply and reinforcements. Surrender probably would have quickly followed. Fate and good shooting did not allow this to happen, even if it had been the intent. Also, if the Union gunboats were to run the batteries, the time to do so was at night or under the cover of bad weather, not in the afternoon on a clear day. On the other hand, no one really knew what defenses the Confederates had upriver. The possibility of masked batteries was certainly considered. In addition, if the fort somehow stood defiant and Grant withdrew, any gunboat upstream would have to run past the fort again, exposing its unarmored stern to heavy fire. There also was no way to resupply the leviathans with coal or ammunition once past the fort.

Some may find fault with Grant for the haste with which he appeared to operate. The facts were that he needed to take Fort Donelson as quickly as possible. No one knew where Albert Sidney Johnston was or how many more reinforcements were on the way to Dover. The Confederates could also evacuate by river and once again slip out of the trap. Although Grant did not want the large number of casualties that would result from a direct assault, he also did not want to wait out a protracted siege.

As for the Confederate commanders, their operations planning and orders process left much to be desired. These would also be key factors in the fight ahead. General Pillow gave the mission briefing and left out many critical details, but Floyd was responsible for making sure the subordinates knew what was expected of them and for synchronizing the plan. He remained silent during most of the conference.

General Buckner's performance here, too, is questionable. If he really believed that the garrison was to evacuate immediately after the attack, would he not have insisted upon knowing the missing details? Buckner was trained at West Point and had either conducted or witnessed many such councils of war before. Analyzing the official records left by the commanders, one can surmise that the evacuation of the garrison was not a set decision at the time of the council of war, but one to be made later based on the results of the coming battle.

The Confederate senior leadership was also reacting to poor or erroneous intelligence reports, which tended to exaggerate the strength of Grant's army. The ground was rugged and wooded, which made such estimates difficult. Also, by allowing the enemy to invest the fort, Forrest's cavalry was pushed back within the perimeter by this time and was unable to reconnoiter. Captured Union pickets were not helpful, either. Even if they were talkative, they probably did not know the true strength of their own army, as reinforcements arrived by steamboat and from Fort Henry. The enemy picture drawn by the generals in gray grew beyond probability and ultimately led to despondency and defeatism.

Finally, it is interesting to see how much General Floyd deferred to Pillow. Perhaps it was understandable. In the last war, Pillow had been a major general and was apparently knowledgeable of what was needed to move an army and sustain it in the field. He was also aggressive and confident, and not afraid to make the occasional mistake. On the other hand, Buckner held no enthusiasm for defending Fort Donelson and probably made that fact known to all. Floyd must have known that Buckner had headed the Kentucky Guard as a brigadier general, but that post was purely administrative. Also, Floyd and Pillow were much closer in age and politics. Given the choice of taking advice from a brooding Buckner or an enthusiastic Pillow, it is no wonder Floyd, who was at Fort Donelson only because Johnston had ordered him there, deferred to Pillow so much.

CHAPTER ELEVEN

The Confederate Attack

Saturday Morning, February 15, 1862

THE NIGHT OF FEBRUARY 14 WAS ALMOST AS MISERABLE AS THE PREVIOUS two, as few units on either side had any shelter. There was little comfort from the quartermasters, either. For the Federals, the baggage left behind had not caught up with them. Rations were in short supply as the limited number of wagons hauled provisions all the way from Fort Henry or from the little makeshift landing three miles north of Fort Donelson. The proximity of the enemy's lines also hindered the delivery of supplies to the regiments on the line. Although in a static position, the Confederates fared little better for many of the same reasons. There were great heaps of supplies in Dover, but getting them to the troops was a difficult or impossible matter. As a result, many men on both sides had not eaten in a day or more.

By 4:00 in the morning, the Confederates prepared for an attack aimed at clearing a path to freedom down the Wynn's Ferry Road. In the winter cold and darkness, the Southern commanders struggled to get their tired and half-frozen men out of the meager shelter of the trenches and into a marching column. The confusion and haste of the planning process began to show as many officers and men learned for the first time that they were going to participate in a major attack. Some fortunate units with supplies of food were in the middle of preparing breakfast, and there was much chaos in the camps as the men packed up and fell into ranks.

The regiments and brigades were led through heavy underbrush and over snow-covered ground to their assembly points. General Buckner's men had the added requirements of carrying their knapsacks and crossing the icy waters of Indian Creek. Regiments jostled into formation just southwest of Dover, and even with the cold and sleet keeping the Federals heads down, it is amazing that the commotion did not alert the pickets.

Jackson's and Porter's artillery batteries were pulled off the line in Buckner's sector and moved to the left in support of the coming infantry assault. Curiously, though, no Confederate artillery was allocated to accompany the assault columns. (A section of Guy's Battery was initially detached to the assault column but was recalled before the advance began.) Fire support would be provided from the established positions in the outer defenses until the battle passed over the hills and beyond the sight of the gunners. Some accounts later reflected that the heavily wooded terrain negated the effective use of artillery, and for that reason the guns were left in place along the line. The result was that once the Confederate infantry was beyond the effective range of its artillery, it was on its own.

The Confederate assault was planned to begin at sunrise, but there was a problem. Colonel Davidson's Brigade was not at its assigned jumping off point, but remained in the trenches some distance off to the right, still in camp. Irritated, Pillow sent General Johnson off a gallop to ascertain just what the problem was. He found that Colonel Davidson, upon returning from the previous night's conference, had only instructed his regimental commanders to have their units held in readiness to move at first light. No word was given to the regiments to pull off the line and assemble for an attack. Moreover, Davidson was at the moment severely ill and incapable of leading his brigade in combat. When told of this development, Pillow placed Col. John M. Simonton of the 1st Mississippi in command of the brigade, which then began the movement toward the assigned assault position. Davidson's inactions delayed the attack by over one hour.[1]

As the errant brigade finally assumed its position, General Pillow drew his sword and gave the order to advance. Through the dense underbrush and bramble, the Southern infantry surged forward.

Lieutenant Colonel Forrest and his horsemen were by now positioned on the extreme left flank of the line southwest of Dover and along the banks of Lick Creek. The ground was low and swampy, and there was an abundance of trees and underbrush beyond the jumping-off point. The area was not particularly suited for cavalry operations, and this would become a factor in the next few hours. Forrest dispatched Capt. J. F. Overton's company to deploy forward as a screen, and the troopers found the enemy infantry of McClernand's division only some 500 yards distant. As the sun began to rise in the iron gray sky, the sharpshooters of both sides again opened a brisk fire along the entire front.

Back at headquarters, Grant received an invitation to confer on matters from Flag Officer Foote, the painful wound preventing the old sailor from mounting a horse to see him. The general was quite amenable to visiting

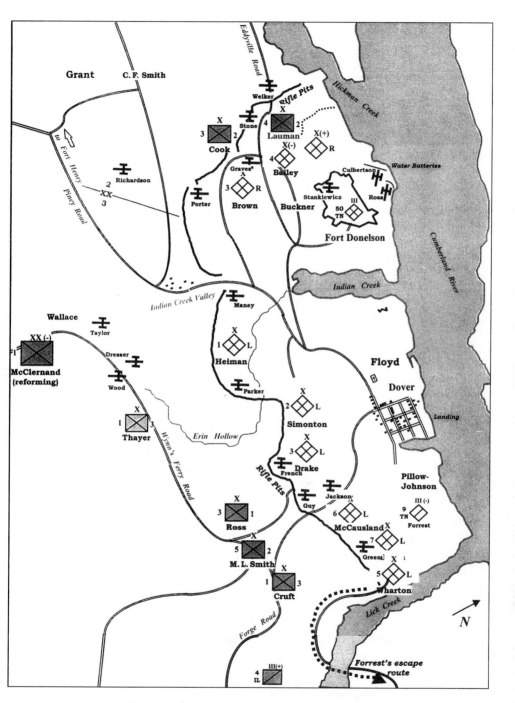

Fort Donelson, 6:00 A.M., February 15, 1862

Foote on the *St. Louis* and left the Widow Crisp's house with some of his staff just after sunrise. The rattle of musketry and the occasional boom of a cannon were heard off to the right of the line as they rode off. McClernand, Lew Wallace, and C. F. Smith were all under orders not to bring on a general engagement, but both sides had been sniping and intermittently lobbing shells at each other for the past two days. On this morning, the level of firing sounded no different than it had been, and Grant continued down to the steamboat landing for his meeting with Foote.

Colonel Whittlesey's 20th Ohio was camped near Grant's headquarters that morning. He wrote later that there was nothing in the sound that came through the several miles of intervening forest to indicate anything more serious than General McClernand's previous activities. No messengers appeared from that sector, either.[2]

Meanwhile, the Confederate infantry moved onward, closing the distance between the outer trenches and the enemy just beyond. Baldwin's Brigade marched by the right flank out of a narrow and obstructed byroad, crossed the valley in front of the trenches, and reached the foot of the opposite slope. This terrain feature was known at the time as Dudley's Hill, which was easily recognizable and was designated as the Confederate's first objective. The crossing of the valley produced no more than the occasional shot from a sharpshooter and a few pickets who turned to fire before running back to their own lines. As Baldwin's Confederates began to ascend the slope, they encountered what they initially believed to be a line of pickets lying on their bellies on the cold, hard ground. Much to their surprise, the men in blue uniforms rose almost in unison, revealing their true numbers. These were no pickets, but the main line of Oglesby's brigade of McClernand's division.[3] Chilled by the miserable weather, these and other Union troops were just rousing when the attack came. Stiff and shivering, they took their places in line of battle and began to fire at the approaching gray ranks.

A short distance away, the heavy firing alerted Col. John McArthur to the Confederates' position and intentions. Held to the rear of the line since last evening, he saw the immediate need to move forward to close the 400-yard gap from the Union right flank to Lick Creek. Without awaiting orders from General McClernand, McArthur ordered his men forward in the line of battle and aligned on the right of Oglesby's brigade. As the last of these regiments reached its place in line, Colonel Oglesby came riding along in front, inquiring what command this was. Upon receiving the reply "12th Illinois," Oglesby coolly remarked, "Excuse me, Colonel, I believe I am out of my brigade." He then suggested that the regiment move a little farther to the right and rode back to his own command.[4] Even after this movement, there was still a noticeable gap between the army flank and the swollen creek.

Once committed to battle, the Confederate formations attacked mostly in columns throughout the morning. Although considered a clumsy tactical formation, the column tended to keep troops effectively massed and allowed for rapid movement. When a column made contact, it would then change its formation into a line of battle using standard drill movements. Most of the gray brigades on the left wing were committed in this fashion, with only a few starting off deployed on line. Although some attacks were made piecemeal and poorly coordinated, the general assault was continuous. Units became intermingled as the distance increased, but this overall tactic allowed the Confederates to maintain the initiative as they drove each attack home.[5]

Here the men of the western theater first heard the famous "Rebel yell" during the Confederate advance. In the attack, the Confederates crouched, fired, and rushed forward, fighting like Indians. Their uniforms blended with the bark and leaves, making it difficult for the Federal soldiers to see them until they got very close. Therefore the men in blue acted on the principle of hitting a head wherever it could be found, and with the Confederates now swarming upon them, there was no shortage of targets. As for accuracy, the Federals tended to overshoot their intended targets, while the Confederates shot lower and more accurately.

For the first half hour of the engagement, Colonel Baldwin had difficulty getting the regiments of his brigade in position to close with the enemy. The 26th Mississippi deployed a company forward to screen the advance and came under heavy fire from Oglesby's brigade. Under a blistering hail of lead, a second company was immediately thrown forward to support the first, but both were soon driven back, confirming the presence of a considerable force. Sending in the balance of the regiment, the Confederates were initially thrown into confusion as they attempted to deploy into a parallel line with the enemy to the front. Falling back a short distance, they rallied and moved forward, but they were thrown again into disorder under heavy fire and pushed back before a line was formed. By adapting his tactics to the terrain and heavy vegetation, Colonel Baldwin was finally able to get his units into line. The Confederates advanced once again, this time with the 26th Tennessee in support. Both sides opened and maintained a brisk fire, and a tenacious face-to-face battle ensued. To many, it seemed so stationary that its termination seemed more a question of endurance than ammunition.[6]

As Baldwin's Brigade made decisive contact to the front, General Pillow was everywhere, directing units forward and urging officers and men to fight. His tactics were simple and suited for the situation at hand. He would generally try to wheel the trailing regiments and brigades around Baldwin's and get behind the enemy. Pillow also executed this maneuver to the right with McCausland's Brigade, followed quickly by Simonton's. The other brigades then moved to the left, using a depression for cover in order to get around the flank of McClernand's entire division. As more units made contact, the roar of battle was deafening in the hollows outside the Confederate outerworks.

These flanking movements did not go unchallenged by the enemy. Wheeling to its front moved the 20th Mississippi forward, but it suffered so severely that General Pillow ordered it withdrawn to shelter behind a ridge. Five companies of this regiment did not hear the order and lost several more men before retiring. The other regiments advanced up the slopes to within 50 to 100 yards of the foe with determination and valor, but in the end the Federals beat off the first organized wave of the attack. After an hour of constant fighting, the Confederate sortie retired a short distance to reorganize.[7] When the ranks were aligned they moved forward again.

As the Confederate regiments moved toward and through the gap between McArthur and Lick Creek on the right, the howitzers of McAllister's battery opened a scathing fire upon them. This provoked a response from the enemy guns in the trenches. As the artillery batteries traded shots, the brisk skirmishing and sharpshooting in this sector gave way to general battle as large masses of infantry collided.

McArthur's brigade put up a dogged resistance, but as more Confederate regiments were added to the attack, it came under extreme pressure. This was particularly true on the right flank, which was never strong, nor anchored on Lick Creek. Here enemy regiments were able to push back the Illinoisans and pour through the gap. Finding Confederates to his rear, Colonel McArthur begrudgingly allowed his right flank to bend back. Compounding the difficulties for the defense, after an hour or more of sharp fighting the ammunition supply was running low.

Off to the left, the men of Oglesby's brigade witnessed the Confederate attack striking the flank of McArthur's brigade but could not yet fire due to the lay of the land and fear of hitting their own comrades. As McArthur's brigade was pressed farther around to the rear of the Federal line, the men in blue had all the Confederates they ever cared to see before them. Colonel Oglesby shifted the 18th Illinois to the right to fill the gap between his and McArthur's brigades and formed a sort of hinge as the line bent backward. The 30th Illinois was brought up from its place in reserve to fill in the space vacated by the 18th Illinois. Oglesby also brought Schwartz's battery forward to support the defending infantry.

The Confederate attacks by columns of regiments poured onto Oglesby's brigade from no less than three directions. Every regiment in the Federal brigade found itself opposed by three, and in many cases four, of the enemy. The regimental commanders dashed among the ranks, waving hats and cheering their men to the conflict. "Suffer death men," cried Col. John A. Logan of the 31st Illinois, "but disgrace never. Stand firm." And well they heeded him. But conspicuous in their gallantry, the commanders were inviting targets. Many fell dead and wounded.[8] Undaunted by the greatly superior force of the enemy, Oglesby's brigade not only held its own for the moment, but upon two occasions actually counterattacked and drove the Confederates back a short distance.

Officers and men dropped on both sides, their blood staining the new snow. When field officers were borne killed or wounded from the battle, their next in command coolly took their place and continued the fight. As ammunition ran low, the cartridges were removed from the dead and wounded and distributed to the men still up and firing. An officer in the fight recalled that the scene defied description. "So thickly was the battle-field strewn with dead and wounded, that I could have trekked acres of it, stepping almost every step upon a prostrate body."[9]

Wounded men were often left where they fell, and those that were pulled off the line were taken to makeshift hospitals in the rear. Overrun in the chaos of battle, hundreds of men from both sides would spend hours and some even days bleeding and freezing on the battlefield. Many would die before they could receive medical attention.[10] The Federals had set up a mobile field hospital to the rear, where many of the wounded were carried, and local houses and barns were filled beyond capacity. Much to the cha-grin of the surgeons, many of the men who helped wounded comrades to the hospital did not return to their units, but gathered into groups or milled about the area. These armed malingerers in such proximity made the hos-pitals legitimate targets under the rules of war.

Miraculously, Colonel Oglesby held his precarious position for nearly an hour, shifting forces to meet the onslaught and nearly exhausting his supply of ammunition. In fact, the 8th Illinois had no ammunition at all at this point, but bravely held its ground though unable to return fire. Oglesby considered a bayonet charge to drive off the waves of Confederate infantry, but this would have been difficult in the heavy brush, and the command would have been exposed to excessive risk of casualties from the raking fire of the gray-clad soldiers.

When a particularly heavy barrage of fire descended on the 18th Illinois, Col. Michael K. Lawler was seriously wounded and carried from the field. He was one of the last officers of this regiment still on his feet. Shaken but not broken, the 18th Illinois doggedly held its ground until all of its ammunition was expended. It then retired under fire to replenish its supply, leaving some 50 dead and nearly 200 wounded on the field.

By now General McClernand knew he needed help against the mass of Confederates assailing his exposed right flank. Knowing McArthur's precarious ammunition situation, he ordered the brigade to hold its position as long as possible. He also finally sent an aide to General Grant's headquarters to apprise him of the situation and ask for immediate reinforcement. But Grant was still away conferring with Foote on board the *St. Louis,* and no one on his staff would take the responsibility of acting in his place. They relayed a message back to McClernand that the request would be presented to the commanding general upon his return.[11] Help would have to come from another quarter.

In the center of the Union line, Gen. Lew Wallace heard the burst of musketry off to the right shortly after sunrise. In a short time, the rising crescendo confirmed his assessment that this was no skirmish, but a major push by the Confederates. Mounting his horse, the general rode to Cruft's and Thayer's headquarters and directed them to have their brigades eat breakfast quickly and stand by their arms. Colonel Cruft was also told to call in his extra guard details. Here, Wallace found a moment to regret leaving his cavalry detachment at Fort Heiman, as he could have sent it to find out what was happening in McClernand's sector. Like the other division commanders, Wallace was under strict orders not to bring on an engagement, and presently this left him with nothing more to do but keeping his place in line, letting come what may.[12]

As the Confederate infantry of the left wing assailed Oglesby's and McArthur's brigades, the supporting cavalry was not idle. Nathan Bedford Forrest's mission was to get around the flank and rear of the enemy, but there had been difficulties. Along the bank of Lick Creek, the undergrowth was so thick that the horses could scarcely get through it. The only way he was able to commit his forces at all was to dismount them as infantry. With the Federal line bent back, Forrest initially thought there was now more suitable ground to his front. Ordering his men to mount their horses, he led them forward but was halted by impassable marsh. Until a wider gap was made between the backwaters of Lick Creek and the enemy, Forrest positioned his men to protect the flank of the assaulting infantry and looked for an opportunity to strike. He also sent details of his men back to the trenches to bring up more ammunition for the infantry to his front.[13] This rather unconventional quartermaster mission for the cavalry allowed many regiments to keep fighting without faltering.

General Pillow continued to ride across the battlefield, urging his men to the fight. Although the dead of battle were strewn across the ground, the inspired Confederates re-formed whenever they were repulsed, and charged again and again.

Against the combined weight of the infantry assault, the supporting fire from the artillery in the trenches, and Forrest's cavalry on the flank, the men of McArthur's brigade at last yielded their position and fell back into Oglesby's brigade, the next unit in line. The Confederates wanted to roll up Grant's army like a carpet, and they had just tucked in the edge and given it a push.

In the process of forcing the position, the Confederates were able to capture Schwartz's battery, which had served admirably but had also received severe punishment. An enemy shot had passed through three horses, and another had smashed the wheel of a howitzer. The trail of another howitzer had broken by its own recoil on the frozen ground. Despite these mishaps, the guns had repulsed the enemy's many attempts to drive the battery off. By now, though, the battery had fired all of its ammunition, and Lt. George C. Gumbart had tried in vain to get a new supply from the rear. Under heavy fire, and without ammunition or infantry support, Gumbart and his men were hitching six horses to the last serviceable howitzer to haul it off when Forrest's troopers arrived. After a short but brisk fight, the artillerymen were compelled to abandon the guns and fall back. Disorder and confusion grew in the Federal ranks, and the area became thickly strewn with hundreds more dead and wounded.

About a mile away in the center of the Federal line, the noise of battle rumbled on without lull or interruption. The suspense was torturous for the men. At last an officer galloped up to Gen. Lew Wallace's headquarters from the 1st Division. "I am from General McClernand, sent to ask assistance of you," he told Wallace. "The general told me to tell you the whole rebel force in the fort massed against him in the night. Our ammunition is giving out. We are losing ground. No one can tell what the result will be if we don't get immediate help." Mindful of his orders to remain in place, Wallace sent an officer to Grant's headquarters to ask permission to help the embattled McClernand. The officer shortly returned, confirming that Grant was on board the *St. Louis* conferring with Foote and nobody at headquarters felt authorized to act. Wallace then declined to aid McClernand at this time.

A second messenger from McClernand soon arrived, a gray-haired colonel with tears in his eyes. "Our flank is turned. The regiments are being crowded back of the center. We are using ammunition taken from the dead and wounded. The whole army is in danger." Wallace's decision to finally send help was reinforced by the arrival of a second messenger bearing similar news. The general realized that if McClernand's division broke completely, a panic might ensue. Although ordered not to bring on an engagement, now that one had been thrust upon him, Wallace took the initiative to help his fellow brigadier to his right.

By 8:30 A.M., Wallace ordered Cruft's brigade to march to the aid of McClernand's battered division. The brigade was moved by column of companies, with the 25th Kentucky in advance. Inexplicably, the guide from McClernand's division left his assignment and had given improper directions to the lead regiment. As a result, the brigade groped along the floor of a ravine toward the sound of the heaviest fighting, unsure of its location. Eventually, McClernand found this wayward column and directed it to relieve Oglesby's embattled brigade.

The relief of Oglesby's brigade did not go well. When Cruft's brigade came upon the rear of this unit around 9:30, its regiments were lying down and firing over the crest of a hill. Sighting the column to their rear, Oglesby's men rose, not knowing whether the men marching toward them were friend or foe. The relief column was also unsure of the allegiance of the soldiers to their front. As the green 25th Kentucky came forward, it did not take the time to find out for sure and fired a volley into the 8th Illinois, a portion of the 29th Illinois, and their supporting artillery. The error was quickly realized, but it caused some disorder and a great deal of consternation in the ranks. Large segments of the 8th and 29th Illinois broke and fell back, some men throwing down their guns and fleeing. In their haste, these men poured over Cruft's brigade, nearly destroying unit cohesion in the stampede. In one case, a regimental commander was swept away in the mass of men and remained separated from his unit for the rest of the day. The few roads soon were filled with stragglers, some of whom fled all the way to Fort Henry. The foreboding and despair were contagious, and the officers of adjoining units were hard-pressed to keep their remaining men in line.[14]

When Cruft's brigade finally assumed its position in the line, the organized remnants from Oglesby's and McArthur's brigades briefly withdrew a short distance to the rear to regroup and replenish their supply of ammunition. These soldiers did not see themselves as vanquished. When the last cartridge had been expended and orders given to retire, soldiers, grim with smoke and powder, angrily inquired why and begged to be allowed to use the bayonet.[15]

With McArthur's and Oglesby's brigades temporarily out of the way, the Confederates wheeled to their right and began to push in a direction parallel to their outer defenses. If their success continued, they would roll up the entire Federal line.

Having formed a line of battle on what was left of the Federal right flank, the men of Cruft's brigade prepared to block this attempt to roll up the line. Here the brigade held its position for about an hour, receiving and making charges and exchanging volleys with a determined foe. Against the mass of Confederates, and left exposed and without support, Colonel Cruft saw that he was in danger of being flanked and surrounded. He ordered his men to fall back to the next ridge, about half a mile to the rear.[16] For the second time, the Federal line had given way, but it was not broken. It was, however, continuing to roll back upon itself.

Although it was a devastatingly brutal struggle, the battle was generally going the Confederates' way over on the left wing. The same could not be said of General Buckner's sector, and his troubles started early.

In the early-morning darkness, the regiments on the Confederate right wing were to pull off the line and be replaced by the singular 30th Tennessee. This regiment was late in arriving, however, and the slippery road across Indian Creek prevented a rapid march to the assembly point to make up for lost time. It was some time later that Buckner positioned his forces in the center of the line and was ready to begin an assault to support Pillow. This delay actually proved insignificant, due to the late arrival of Simonton's brigade in Pillow's sector. It did heighten Buckner's tension, however, and indicated too that all would not go as planned.

The first significant change in plan came from Buckner himself, who did not begin his assault on time or in the place agreed upon the previous evening. Instead, he deployed his regiments in the defense and brought up two artillery batteries for the purpose of counterbattery fire. When he heard Pillow's units begin to fire shortly after dawn, Buckner ordered his artillery to open up on the Federals on the next ridge. After several volleys, the fire from the enemy guns slackened somewhat, possibly indicating that they were neutralized.

Around 7:00 A.M., Buckner sent only three regiments, the 14th Mississippi and the 3rd and 18th Tennessee, forward to finish the job and decisively dislodge the enemy battery, which was about 400 yards distant. The men moved from the cover of the trenches with spirit and advanced steadily through the brush, bramble, and snow.

The 14th Mississippi moved off by the right flank until it reached the outer entrenchments and led the advance on line as skirmishers. Major Alex Casseday of Buckner's staff directed these movements. The line of march took the gray ranks in front of their own supporting artillery, which had to hold its fire in order to avoid hitting its comrades. As the assault force disappeared into a depression, the Confederate artillery began to fire again. Coincidentally, the advancing Mississippians came under fire from the opposing infantry and artillery at this very moment. The shock of receiving smoke, flame, and lead from what seemed all directions sent the rank and file into confusion. Badly shaken, the men withdrew about 200 yards, where Casseday then gave the order to retire all the way back to the trenches.[17]

Directly opposite Buckner's position, Col. W. H. L. Wallace had been instructed by his hard-pressed division commander, General McClernand, to "rely upon himself and maintain his position at all hazards." As Buckner's attack materialized, the artillery of McAllister's, Taylor's, Dresser's, and a section of Welker's batteries massed their fire on the gray ranks. After the withdrawal of the 14th Mississippi, the 3rd Tennessee continued to advance under pressure and at one point came so close to McAllister's battery that the crews were compelled to leave their guns. Only a quick advance by a detachment from the 45th Illinois saved them from capture. But under heavy fire from the blue infantry and artillery, the Confederate advance was halted, and for about an hour, Buckner's vanguard traded volleys with the Federal infantry, a short distance away. Caught in a murderous crossfire, the Confederates also received a counterattack from the 20th Illinois, led by Col. Carroll C. Marsh.

Their ranks broken from pushing through the fallen timber, and unable to stand the heavy fire, the balance of the Confederate assault force was finally broken. The men fell back to the trenches, where apparently their despondency infected all of Buckner's regiments. General Buckner rode over to the 14th Mississippi and pointed to the advancing troops under General Pillow: "Mississippians, look at those Virginians driving the enemy from our soil. Is it possible that you are going to leave them to do the fighting? No, never, your general will lead you." The troops rallied but needed time to reorganize their shattered ranks and to overcome the dispiriting effects of the repulse. The effect was that Buckner's sector fell relatively quiet except for the occasional artillery shell and sharpshooter bullet. The gun crews of McAllister's Illinois battery were then able to come forward, claim their guns, and resume firing.[18]

Buckner later wrote why he deviated from the plan to launch a full-scale attack: "In view of the heavy duty which I expected my division to undergo in covering the retreat of the army, I thought it unadvisable to attempt an assault at this time in my front until the batteries were to some extent crippled and the supports shaken by the fire of my artillery."[19] Meanwhile, Pillow's division of about 6,500 rifles was up against roughly

15,000 Federals of McClernand's and part of Wallace's divisions. Buckner's decision to launch merely a feeble attack placed the entire operation at extreme risk.

To the Confederates on the left wing, it appeared as though every time one enemy regiment was driven away, another rose up to take its place. When the Federals were compelled to give ground, they did so very stubbornly and slowly, firing as long as they had ammunition. Over the course of the day, this scenario replayed over five succeeding ridgelines.

Colonel John A. Logan of the 31st Illinois re-formed the pieces of his regiment that were left from the early-morning fights, knowing it was imperative to hold his position at all costs to prevent a calamity. Logan ordered his regiment a short distance forward from the crest of a ridgeline, to prevent his men from being silhouetted against the sky and becoming conspicuous targets. There the 31st Illinois fought like veterans, defending the position against repeated assaults by the howling Confederates. The situation soon became perilous as the 25th Kentucky to the right started to fold under the onslaught of Drake's brigade. When the 31st Illinois ran out of ammunition, Colonel Logan approached Lt. Col. Thomas E. G. Ransom of the 11th Illinois, and asked, "What shall I do? I have not another cartridge." Ransom replied, "You have the best position. File out and I will take your place." This was done immediately, and the 11th Illinois continued the fight. In the process of this maneuver, however, Logan was severely wounded and carried from the field.

Under enormous pressure from three sides, W. H. L. Wallace's brigade was in danger of encirclement and annihilation and was ordered to fall back fighting, but in the confusion of battle, the 11th Illinois did not get the word and maintained its position. Although the rest of the brigade withdrew in good order, the 11th Illinois remained in position, alone and nearly surrounded.

Nathan Bedford Forrest seldom missed an opportunity, and he saw this one clearly and took full advantage of it. He had been moving steadily around the Federal right until he had gotten almost behind it. Wheeling to his right, his troopers fell upon the exposed flank and rear of the lone Illinois regiment, which already had its hands full trying to repel a charge made by thousands of yelling Confederate infantrymen to its front. Captain James O. Churchill of the 11th Illinois remembered: "My attention was drawn to the fact that our men were being shot in the back, and on looking to the rear saw the cavalry and notified Colonel Ransom. He at once ordered the regiment to 'Face to the rear and charge cavalry,' which we did on the run, he in advance." Regimental cohesion disintegrated as companies and squads fought their way through Forrest's cavalry and fell back to the next ridgeline east of the Buford Hollow Road. Meanwhile, as W. H. L. Wallace's brigade withdrew, some regiments were able to maintain a semblance of unit order, but many others simply melted away under the onslaught. The Confederates pursued their foes, but soldiers stopping to pick up a new musket or to loot the dead or occasional campsite slowed the pace.[20]

The pursuit was made over some very rough ground and through dense thickets. When the Confederates eventually reached an open field, they could see across to the Federal right flank, which again was exposed and in disorder. Forrest attempted a cavalry charge across the field to scatter the enemy, but the ground proved to be too marshy and soft to carry the horses. This short reprieve allowed McClernand's division to rally somewhat and form a line along the woods, from which position it could enfilade the advancing Confederates. Forrest gave up trying to get behind the enemy for the moment and moved his cavalrymen to a point of dry ground directly facing the foe to his front. Together with the gray infantry, Forrest prepared to advance again.

By 9:30 A.M., Nathan Bedford Forrest sensed that Oglesby's and Cruft's brigades were close to routing and asked Gen. Bushrod Johnson, who was nearby, for an all-out attack on the disorganized mass of troops to his front. At this critical point, Johnson feared an ambush and clearly remembered Pillow's wrath for overstepping his authority a few days back. Uncertain, Johnson withheld his permission for a general assault. He did agree, though, to push the infantry ahead slowly. Forrest later wrote that had they attacked in strength, a victory on the magnitude of Bull Run was possible.[21] The lull in this sector allowed the enemy brigades to consolidate on their new line.

The regiments and brigades of the left wing under General Pillow were by this time badly intermixed and short on ammunition from the long hours of constant fighting. In deploying and trying to envelop the right flank of the Federals, the frontage of the Confederate units was increased, making it more difficult to mass attacks. Although it had cost many casualties and much effort, the first phase of the operation was complete. Grant's army was bent back upon itself in an L shape and close to breaking. The decisive blow Forrest wanted from Johnson, or even one from Buckner's sector, could indeed tip the scales.

Forrest came upon General Pillow, who had been leading and directing the infantry attacks all morning. Pillow inquired as to the whereabouts of General Buckner, remarking that he as yet had heard no sound of battle from that part of the field. When Forrest replied that he had been too busy to know of the movements of units in that sector, Pillow asked, "Well then, Colonel, what have you been doing since I saw you last?" "Obeying orders, general, by protecting your left flank," Forrest replied, presenting the captured guns and prisoners as proof. Forrest no doubt also passed on his opinion that the attacks should resume. After a few kind words of commendation to the cavalryman, Pillow turned his attention to his right, namely General Buckner.[22]

Pillow saw that the assault against the Federal right had succeeded up to this point, and that there were indeed signs that the whole enemy line could give way. The men in gray around him were shifting about as they rejoined their units and re-formed into a cohesive line of battle. But this would take some minutes, and while the gray line was adjusting, the blue across the way must surely be trying to re-form too. What was needed at this moment was the planned attack by Buckner to hit the enemy line sharply bent at an angle to his front. In concert with an attack by Pillow's men, this could break the enemy, inflict a major defeat upon Grant, and lift the siege on Fort Donelson. This was the critical moment of the whole operation. Pillow spun his horse about and galloped off in search of his old nemesis, Simon Bolivar Buckner.

When General Pillow, with the engineer Major Gilmer, reached Buckner's command, to their surprise, they found the men still in the trenches, immobile. Pillow located General Buckner, and both managed to hold their temper in check. Buckner was obviously irritated and considered Pillow's presence an intrusion. In Buckner's view, Pillow was a fellow commander of a division, nothing more. He took orders from General Floyd, who in fact had been conspicuously absent all morning. Buckner explained the delay: He had just conducted a probing attack and was bringing up artillery to silence a Union battery. This attack had occurred almost two hours earlier, however, and since then, the battle had swept far enough away to make the planned assault point irrelevant. Applying his seniority, Pillow revised the attack plan and instructed Buckner to attack farther to the right, using Erin Hollow for cover, and to maneuver additional forces into the flank and rear of W. H. L. Wallace's Illinois brigade. Within a few minutes, the regiments of Buckner's command were on their feet and advancing.

The 14th Mississippi deployed as skirmishers and advanced again toward McAllister's battery, some 300 yards distant, which had up to this time prohibited the advance of Buckner's division. The advance of the 3rd Tennessee under Maj. Nathaniel Cheairs and the 18th Tennessee under Col. Joseph B. Palmer supported this movement. Pillow then ordered the 32nd Tennessee under Col. Edmund C. Cook to join the advance on the right flank and in support. This regiment previously had the mission of guarding a length of trench, but with the Federals so heavily pressed in this sector, the danger of an attack was slight.

The ground over which the Confederates advanced was typical of the area, with deep ravines, timber, and thickets, all covered with snow. The men again had to contend with the abatis of felled trees. Originally designed to break up and hinder an enemy assault, it now had the same effect on Buckner's units as they passed through the interlocking branches. For this attack, Graves's Battery was ordered forward in support, but it was soon discovered that it could do little good in this terrain and was ordered back to the trenches.[23]

Buckner's advance instantly came under heavy musket and cannon fire from the waiting Federals. The combination of the rough ground and heavy fire threw many regiments into confusion, but this time the men continued to press on. In one of the few recorded instances of General Floyd's whereabouts during the morning of February 15, as the 2nd Kentucky prepared to attack, Floyd got up on the breastworks, took off his hat, and shouted, "Now, charge 'em boys!" They jumped off with a start and immediately came under galling fire from W. H. L. Wallace's Federals on the next ridge. Someone had the wisdom to pull the general off the breastworks because he was so exposed.[24]

The Confederates advanced at the double-quick, using the deep ravine of Erin Hollow for cover. Becoming disoriented, the lead regiment soon stopped to send out skirmishers to ascertain just where the enemy was. Colonel Cook of the 18th Tennessee and Colonel Palmer of the 32nd Tennessee went forward also and found some blue-coated troops about 100 yards away. They returned to their commands to align the attack and had just done so when the Southern regiments again came under a combined fire of enemy muskets and artillery.

At the edge of the hollow, the Southern ranks loaded and fired their weapons on one knee to avoid casualties, and much of the deadly fire passed overhead. Both sides maintained their rate of fire, and Colonel Palmer advanced his regiment another fifty paces. After sustained firing, however, many of the weapons were becoming fouled and wet, particularly the many flintlocks carried by the Confederates. As a result, both Cook and Palmer felt compelled to withdraw their respective regiments about 100 yards to the rear, where they had the men clean their weapons and tend to the wounded.[25]

The other regiments under General Buckner continued to fight, but in the chaos of battle, Col. Thomas M. Gordon of the 3rd Tennessee was wounded. Falling in pain, he called out for his regiment to fall back to the trenches. Thereupon two other regiments also withdrew a short distance. But Buckner was close enough at hand to see the error and quickly countermanded the order before disaster occurred. Although the advance was rife with misfortune and uncoordinated, it was closing the gap between the lines and putting more pressure on W. H. L. Wallace's brigade of Illinois troops.[26]

Having left Buckner to conduct his assault, General Pillow rode to the artillery positions to direct their fire in support of the operation. The guns of Porter's, Graves's and Maney's batteries soon concentrated their fire, sweeping the ground in advance of Buckner's infantry. Continuing his ride, Pillow observed an enemy shell explode and fell every man at a gun from Guy's Battery. Pillow galloped to another gun of the battery and inquired of the men, "Where are you from?" When he was informed that they were Virginians, he asked them, "Will you follow me?" They replied that they would follow him anywhere. "Come on," he commanded, and they followed him at the double-quick across an open field under heavy fire to the deserted gun. There General Pillow at once directed the piece himself and, after a few shots, silenced the enemy fire.[27]

By this time, the fire of the left wing was heard advancing by the men of Buckner's command, while the fire from enemy artillery had slackened. This had an encouraging effect on all of Buckner's men as they formed and made a determined charge. W. H. L Wallace's brigade was now heavily pressed on his center and left by Buckner, and his right flank by the advancing regiments under Pillow's command. As had happened so many times already this morning, the men in blue maintained their position until their ammunition gave out, then begrudgingly fell back to the next ridgeline to form a new line. The victorious Confederates regrouped and prepared to pursue and attack again.[28]

Some of the most dramatic fighting of the morning occurred as Forrest left a small force to guard the left flank and took the bulk of his command toward the center of the advancing Confederate line. There he met General Pillow again, who pointed to McAllister's battery, which was formidably planted at the head of the ravine and in position to sweep it with lethal fire. It was supported by the 45th and 48th Illinois regiments. The battery had helped repulse General Buckner's attempts to advance and had caused Pillow's men a great deal of trouble in their own progress. Pillow asked the cavalryman if he could take it, noting that several other attempts by the infantry had failed. Obviously proud of the accomplishments of his regiment so far, Forrest confidently answered, "I can try," and turned to draw his men up in column of squadrons.[29]

About to order a charge, Forrest noticed a gray regiment to his rear. It turned out to be the 2nd Kentucky under Col. Roger W. Hanson, from

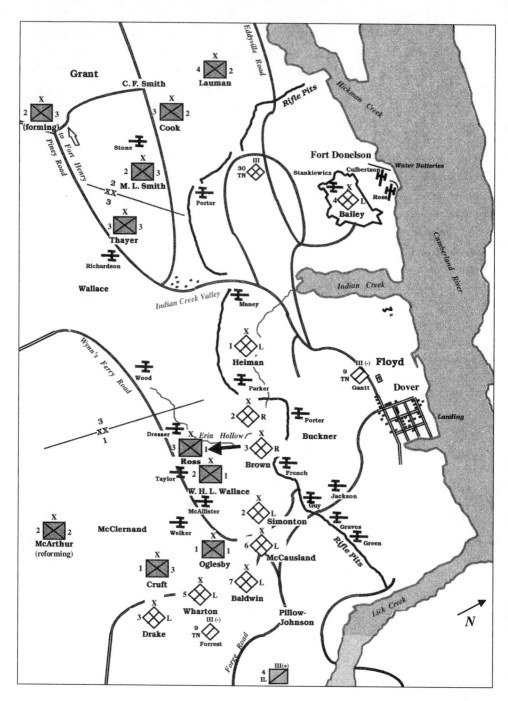

Fort Donelson, 10:00 A.M., February 15, 1862

Buckner's command. Forrest asked their cooperation: The Kentucky infantry would conduct a supporting attack as the Tennessee horsemen charged the guns. This action would also assist McCausland's Brigade, which had been fighting for four hours and was now stalled up against a persistent defense. Colonel Hanson sent a request to General Buckner for authorization to pull out of position in order to conduct the assault. When he learned that Buckner had ridden to the right and was unavailable, Hanson took the responsibility on himself. With no time to delay, the 2nd Kentucky marched across the abatis of fallen trees and a quarter mile beyond. Using a ravine for cover, Hanson came alongside Nathan Bedford Forrest's cavalry and joined in the fight.[30]

Coincidentally, General Buckner also sent the 3rd Tennessee in support and ordered Green's and Maney's batteries to fire in advance of the infantry attack, concentrating their fire on the enemy battery under the command of Captain McAllister.

The gray cavalry and infantry swarmed into the ravine, Hanson riding among his men. He ordered them not to fire their muskets, but to rely on their bayonets. Forrest's cavalry and Hanson's infantry descended the slope and crossed the ravine, stopping to re-form short of the crest of the opposite hill. From this position, they were protected from the fire of the enemy by the contour of the ground. When given the signal to charge, the Confederates dashed over the summit and into the Federal position.

Forrest led his men in the wild charge against McAllister's battery, and a volley sent many of the artillerists who were not killed or wounded running for cover. The cavalrymen were quickly among the guns and engaged in hand-to-hand combat. Swords, pistols, carbines, and ramming staffs were used in the melee. The blood of the fallen was thick enough that the horses' hooves splashed in the gore. In the chaos, a crew was able to drag the last serviceable howitzer for a short distance, but it became mired in the mud. The crew reluctantly cut the harness, and the horses, limbers, and empty caissons continued to the rear. The guns and a number of prisoners were left to their fate.[31] Meanwhile, the supporting 45th and 48th Illinois infantry fell back under the pressure of the combined arms of Confederate infantry, artillery, and cavalry. A little farther on a hospital tent was captured and about sixty Confederate prisoners recovered. Graves's Battery was then brought forward again from the outer defenses and into position here to help hold the line against any Federal counterattack.[32]

The Confederates of the left wing continued to give their enemy no respite as they pushed westward along the Wynn's Ferry Road, through the tangled thickets, and up the slopes of the next ravine. As the Southern infantrymen closed with their foe, Forrest and his cavalry regrouped from the capture of McAllister's battery and again fell upon the flank and rear of the Federal infantry. Pressed on three sides, Cruft's brigade and the few viable remnants of McClernand's division fell back once again to the next ridge to form a new line of battle.

As this attack concluded, Colonel Hanson was approached by Colonel Baldwin, who had fought under Pillow's command during the morning. Baldwin's men were completely out of ammunition. Hanson immediately directed him to a nearby wagon, and the ammunition was soon replenished. A staff officer also approached Hanson, directing him to detach two companies in support of Baldwin's Brigade, and they entered a thick fight that was brewing off to the left. Colonel McCausland asked for help, too.

Off on the far left of the line, and oblivious to everything but his front, Gen. Bushrod Johnson continued to keep the pressure on the fighting remnants of Cruft's brigade. Unable to communicate with General Wallace, Colonel Cruft had withdrawn his brigade again and occupied a position along a wooded ridge beyond the tents of the large field hospital. This left the facility between the battle lines and subject to capture, but Colonel Cruft occupied this position on the ridge with a view of protecting it by fire.

In this sector, the Confederate advance was now losing steam after several hours of bitter fighting, and attacks were uncoordinated. The 15th Arkansas, under Col. James M. Gee, advanced unsupported beyond the current line of battle and up against a hastily reassembled segment of Cruft's brigade. The men from Arkansas charged but were repulsed with heavy losses. Heartened by their success, the Hoosiers and Kentuckians then counterattacked. Alerted to the danger, Nathan Bedford Forrest quickly moved to the scene and deployed a cavalry squadron to help check the enemy advance. The Confederate infantry from Arkansas then rallied and pushed the opposing lines back to where they had been a half hour before. The entire line then settled into a desultory firing.

Over the course of the morning, Nathan Bedford Forrest's horse had received as many as seven wounds, but it only now collapsed from exhaustion and loss of blood. Forrest mounted a captured horse and rode forward to reconnoiter. He found the Federal line along a ridge, and the enemy had an intense interest in him as well. Drawing the fire of an entire regiment, Forrest dashed down a ravine, and in the process, his horse received a wound in the thigh. Out of danger for the moment, he rode his mount slowly back toward the trenches. As he crossed another ridge, he exposed himself to an enemy battery, which fired a solid shot in his direction. The shot passed through his horse just behind his legs, covering his feet with blood. This loss was the second of twenty-nine horses shot out from under him during the course of the war. Now afoot, he made his way back to his lines, where he found his men and General Pillow waiting for him. A count showed that Forrest's overcoat had no less than fifteen bullet marks on it.[33]

At what used to be the center of the Union line, General Wallace nervously awaited the developments of the fight in McClernand's sector. At length, Capt. John Rawlings of Grant's staff met up with him. While Wallace updated the officer on the situation, many of the survivors of McClernand's division soon appeared on the run. The mass of men streamed through Wallace's lines, thoroughly demoralized and yelling, "We are cut to pieces!" A mounted colonel of an Illinois regiment, who had utterly lost his composure, was also lamenting that all was lost. Disgusted, Rawlings drew his revolver and would have shot the man had Wallace not intervened.[34] A far more coherent rider soon arrived from the storm on the right and reported: "The road back there is jammed with wagons, and men afoot and on horseback, all coming toward us. On the plains we would call it a stampede." There was no question—McClernand's 1st Division was badly cut up and defeated.

Captain Rawlings galloped back to headquarters to find General Grant and inform him of the developments on the right. Meanwhile, General Wallace ordered the drummers to beat the long roll, and the men of Thayer's brigade took up their arms. Receiving the command "by the right flank, file left," the brigade moved out of the way of the mass of retreating men and avoided being caught up in the panic. Wallace discovered that in his haste to the front, Colonel Cruft had neglected to call in his pickets and guards, which was done at this time, and the men incorporated into the brigade.

With the stampede of refugees past him, Wallace realigned and advanced his two remaining brigades toward the firing. Along the way, the column came across numbers of men separated from their units. Many were still organized in squads and companies, and remnants of regiments were still led by officers. These men were not in a hurry or in a panic like those before them. These men were mostly from Oglesby's and McArthur's brigades, and even though they were out of ammunition, they were not out of fighting spirit.

Presently an officer rode up slowly, one leg casually thrown over the horn of his saddle, with 400 or 500 men with a flag behind him. General Wallace trotted his horse over to meet him. He found that this man was

Col. W. H. L. Wallace, commanding the 2nd Brigade of McClernand's division. He had just been pushed off his position by the combined weight of Buckner's and Pillow's legions. General Wallace directed this outfit and the others trailing to go down the road to where two wagons with ammunition were held in reserve. These remnants of McClernand's division then marched by to fill their cartridge boxes and regroup into a cohesive force. General Wallace then asked Colonel Wallace where the enemy was, and if they were following his men. "Yes," the colonel replied, "and you will have time to form a line of battle here."[35]

The general took his advice, and Wood's battery was ordered to cover the Wynn's Ferry Road at all possible speed. It did so at a full gallop, with guns and caissons bouncing over the roots and ruts, the men clinging to their seats. The guns were unlimbered quickly, and the horses and limbers were moved back a short distance.

General Wallace then deployed Thayer's and Morgan Smith's brigades, consisting of a total of nine regiments, astride the road and to the left of the disintegrating regiments of Cruft's brigade. There they were directly in the path of the triumphant Confederates. As soon as the line was formed, the men halted and waited for additional ammunition. It was issued just before the first gray wave hit.

The two Federal brigades came under fire of the advancing Confederates, which materialized through the brush no more than fifty paces away. Instead of advancing in line of battle, however, the Southern infantry had marched up the narrow road cramped in files of four to make the best possible speed. Encountering Thayer's brigade was completely unexpected, and the gray ranks tried to deploy on line. It was a tactical mistake that they paid for in blood. The Union muskets rose and fell steadily, sending sheets of lead into the attacking foe. The firing soon became constant, each man firing as fast as he could reload. Wood's battery joined the chorus of death by firing double-shot grape and canister at nearly point-blank range.

Additional regiments of Wallace's division arrived on the scene and were deployed to either side of the road. The pressure of the emergency was too great to worry about seniority of rank, and some of these regiments were given to Colonel Thayer's brigade as an additional reserve. The fight continued for almost an hour, but due to the confines of the terrain, it was concentrated in the sector of the 1st Nebraska and occasionally elements of the 76th Ohio, which fired obliquely into the Confederate ranks. The gray artillery fired at extreme range and uphill, and most of its shot and shells flew overhead. Three times the Confederate infantry deployed and attacked, but each time it was repulsed with heavy loss.[36]

The assaults were vigorous, but the blue line held steady and delivered a well-aimed and deliberate fire. The stout defense successfully held this ridge astride the Wynn's Ferry Road and frustrated Confederate attempts to further turn the right flank. After their final repulse, the Confederates retired about a half mile to a subsequent ridge. By 12:30 in the afternoon, the door to freedom was open wide, and total victory was close at hand. If this stubborn line broke like the others, a total rout of Grant's army would be the probable result.

It was a dire situation for Grant's army, but it was not hopeless. Holding the Union left was Brig. Gen. C. F. Smith, who had not been attacked that morning. His troops were rested and supplied with ammunition. On the right was Gen. Lew Wallace with his division, which was heavily engaged but holding its own. The worst was to the right and rear, where Gen. John McClernand's men were desperately short of ammunition, and unit cohesion was found only in small pockets of men.

An uneasy lull came over the battlefield as both sides paused to regroup. The morning clearly saw the culmination of the Confederate attack. Until the regiments could regroup and refit, they were spent as an offensive force. The Confederates had fought gallantly, but their senior leaders had not served them as well.

The lack of artillery support for the attacking columns seriously cut the firepower available to the Confederate assault forces. The Illinois regiments of McClernand's division would have found it difficult to rally and hold as long as they did had they come under the fire of a field battery. A handful of guns could have formed a strong point in order to seriously hamper any Federal counterattack, and there were many places on the attack axis where artillery could have been put to good use. Had the ground truly been found unsuitable for artillery, the batteries could have been withdrawn back into the lines easily. This was shown in the case of Graves's Battery in support of Buckner's second attack, and in the constant use of artillery by the enemy in this same area.

The Confederates also failed to commit all of the available cavalry to the operation. As Forrest's 3rd Tennessee was cutting its way into the history books, Lt. Col. George Gantt's 9th Tennessee Cavalry Battalion remained near the Dover cemetery all day. Forrest was technically in command of all Southern cavalry at the fort, but Gantt apparently refused to serve under him. Commitment of this outfit would have doubled the impact and firepower of the cavalry engaged.

Buckner's initial supporting attack was dismal, a reflection of his lack of resolve to defend Fort Donelson. The three regiments committed were

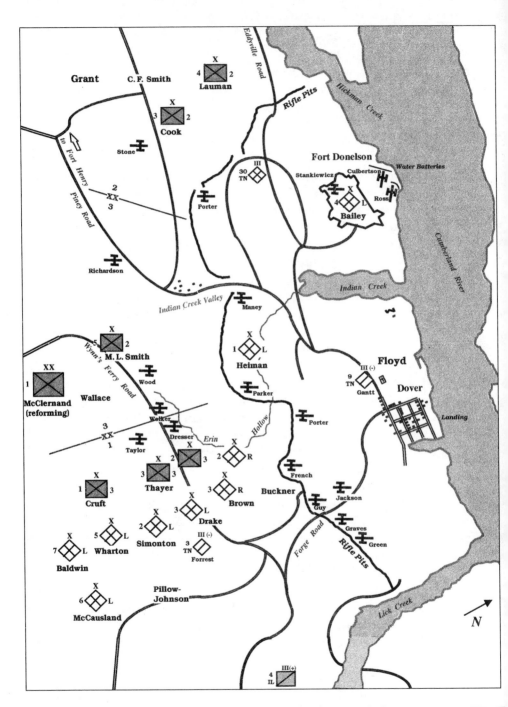

Fort Donelson, 12:00 P.M., February 15, 1862

about half of his available assault force. When conducting an infantry assault, the rule of the day was to mass forces and strike quickly and hard. This he did not do. When the attack stalled under the heavy fire of artillery and musketry, Buckner neither shifted the available artillery nor maneuvered additional units in support. Instead, he allowed these regiments of his command to get cut up and repulsed.

The initial reliance by Buckner upon his batteries to silence their Union counterparts is highly questionable. The Southern guns were short-range smoothbores, while the Federals opposed them with mostly long-range rifled guns. As a result, the Confederate gunners suffered severely under the furious return fire from an enemy it could not effectively hit. Again, the tactics of the day in this situation would have been to sweep away the opposing artillery with a determined infantry assault, not sit and endure it.

Buckner's failure to make a determined attack according to the plan resulted in a general lack of activity for Gen. Lew Wallace's division for the first several hours of the battle. This gave Wallace the freedom to shift forces to aid McClernand's division and ultimately halt the Confederate advance. The success in halting the Confederates by such a very small margin shows that had Buckner tied down Cruft's brigade before it shifted to the right, General Pillow may well have achieved the rout of the enemy he sought.

In his official report, Buckner reasoned that he expected his division to bear the brunt of holding the escape route open later in the day and night, and therefore wanted to keep it as fresh as possible. His unsanctioned delay put the entire operation at risk, however. The men of the left wing were making progress, but at the cost of going up against one fresh brigade after another; the resultant casualties and ammunition expenditure were severely weakening the assault force. A timely supporting attack by Buckner at the critical moment when Pillow's attack halted would have had far greater effect than after the Federals had regrouped somewhat during the short lull in the fighting.

It is clear, too, that General Grant's army was not functioning optimally. Over the past two weeks, it had been learning how to operate as one entity instead of separate regiments, but it still had a long way to go. During the battle, there was no coordinated effort at the brigade or regimental level to logistically sustain the troops as they fought. Units ran out of ammunition as boxes of it lay a short distance away. There was no adequate system in place to take it forward to those in need. As a result, units that were otherwise intact sometimes fell back only in order to replenish their supply of cartridges, thus giving up the very ground the Confederates needed in order to make their escape. This nearly brought catastrophe to Grant's army.

Federal logistical problems were not confined to ammunition. Provisions were also in short supply. Some units went for two days without issued rations. In the cold, bitter weather, this did nothing to improve the fighting abilities of the soldiers. Logistical lessons would be learned over time, but this was the first real test. Over the coming months, these individualistic regiments would be forged into the Army of the Tennessee.

Whereas the Confederate command in this campaign usually receives a great deal of scrutiny, command and control were very much a problem for the Federals as well. When General Grant left in the early-morning hours to see Flag Officer Foote, he had no reason to suspect that a major assault was under way. There was no discernable increase in enemy activity, and no messengers had arrived from any sector with threatening news. By 8:00 A.M., however, it was clear to every soldier on the right flank that the Confederates were serious in their intent. When McClernand sent aides to seek out Grant, they met with staff officers who were quite content to allow General Grant to return at leisure and make the appropriate decisions. A staff officer should have been immediately dispatched to the *St. Louis* to inform Grant of the situation at hand. McClernand's own officers could have bypassed Grant's staff and gone to the flagship themselves. Neither was done, and Grant remained in the dark.

Part of this fiasco may be attributed to the attitude of many officers in Grant's army toward General McClernand. A political appointee with no prior military training whatsoever, McClernand was known more for his eloquent speeches and being an irritant during councils of war. As a novice, many officers often did not take him too seriously. This included Grant, whose attitude no doubt had transferred to his own staff. It is quite probable that Grant's staff just did not give McClernand's reports much credence until confirmed by other officers.

As for troop dispositions, McClernand's right flank was never securely anchored on Lick Creek, which allowed the Confederates to attack the flank and rear of the army. Even with the addition of McArthur's brigade, there was still a gap in this critical area of the battlefield. Colonel McArthur attempted to fill this void by extending his flank regiment, the 12th Illinois, but the coverage was far too thin. This was where the brunt of the initial Confederate attack hit and where the flank of McClernand's division was turned. From that point on, the battle assumed a pattern in which successive regiments were hit on three sides and forced to retire. This domino effect continued for several hours, until General Wallace's division repositioned itself to successfully receive the Confederate onslaught.

McClernand had almost two regiments of cavalry at his disposal, totaling 800 or more men. Being on the extreme and very exposed flank of the army, it was logical to have the bulk of the cavalry assigned to this sector. McClernand positioned them to the right and rear of the line to take part in any "grand pursuit," but as his division fought for its life, he did not commit them to battle. This cavalry apparently was in an excellent position to strike Forrest's cavalry as they rode around the flank and rear of the Federal infantry. Why he did not unleash the 4th Illinois Cavalry and the other independent companies is a mystery. Did McClernand have no faith in their combat abilities? As it represented virtually all of General Grant's cavalry, was he afraid it would sustain heavy casualties and be unavailable for subsequent operations? Was it simple oversight? Neither McClernand nor Grant, nor any of the cavalrymen, left any hint as to the rationale. One can only guess the outcome had the Federal cavalry struck the Confederates on the flank while they were occupied fighting to their own front.

General Lew Wallace saved the day for the entire army. Although he hesitated, his initiative in detaching Cruft's brigade helped buttress McClernand's defense. And his foresight in bringing additional ammunition allowed a rapid resupply of Col. W. H. L. Wallace's brigade. The deployment of Thayer's brigade and the additional regiments that arrived on the scene made an effective stand against the Confederate attack. After three successive charges, the offensive power of the Confederates was finally spent.

CHAPTER TWELVE

The Afternoon of Decision

Saturday, February 15, 1862

SO FAR, THE CONFEDERATES HAD EXCEEDED ALL EXPECTATIONS. IT WAS AN achievement worthy of the highest praise for Southern arms. Although miserably armed and poorly trained, the Confederate soldiers had pushed their counterparts back over a mile or two of rugged, timbered, and snow-covered terrain. Not only had the sortie opened the roads to Nashville, but also, under General Pillow's direction, his men had maintained pressure on the enemy and pushed them back an extra ridgeline or two for good measure. As it stood by 1:00 P.M., the Union right flank was forced back onto the center, and General Buckner held the route of escape open. All that was left of the plan was to extract all available men and as many supplies as they could carry.

The morale of the men was at an all-time high, and many were pressing their officers to be allowed to continue to attack. But there were serious problems. In six hours of continuous fighting, the Confederate regiments and brigades were intermixed, and in many cases unit cohesion was gone. Some regiments of the left wing had degenerated into armed mobs, held together only by the common objective of closing with and killing the invader. Ammunition was in short supply for the Confederates as well as the Federals. The Southern troops had left the trenches in the morning with forty rounds or so, and most of the cartridge boxes were now empty. The nearest supply of ammunition was back in the camps a mile or more away. Captured weapons were used, but since the Federals were also fighting in short supply, there was little or no ammunition for them either. The wide variety of weapons of different calibers found among the Southern ranks further complicated the issue of rapid resupply.

As a result, the offensive power of the Confederate left wing was spent, at least until the regiments received ammunition and organized their jumbled ranks. So General Pillow made a fateful decision. Acting on his own, without consulting Floyd or Buckner, Pillow ordered his men back to their original lines in what he considered part of the prearranged plan. There they would draw ammunition and collect their knapsacks, blankets, and rations. That was the plan, at least.

Off to the right, General Buckner watched the retrograde movement of the Confederate left wing in disbelief and rode to confront the Tennessee general. The conversation was anything but civil.

As throughout most of the day, General Floyd was not located at the decisive place at the right time. By the time he arrived, the movement by Pillow's men was almost completed, while Buckner's men stood in the snow awaiting orders. The senior brigadier exploded: "In the name of God, General Pillow, what have we been fighting all day for? Certainly not to show our powers, but solely to secure the Wynn's Ferry Road, and after securing it, you order it to be given up." Pillow pointed out that his command had fought throughout the morning, and meanwhile twenty boatloads of troops were believed to have reinforced Grant. The soldiers were exhausted, cold, and short of ammunition. Units were mixed and disorganized, and generally in no condition to meet such a host of fresh enemy troops. The men had not brought their knapsacks, as had Buckner's men, and so they were not ready to begin a march to Nashville.[1] Note that Floyd did not chastise Pillow for not conducting an evacuation, but for giving up the road needed to execute one. Even at this point, it is not clear just what the final objective for the operation was. Was it to effect an escape or just to secure the means to do so when they wished?

Major D. C. Kelley of Forrest's cavalry witnessed the exchange and later wrote: "It was General Pillow's inflation of the idea of an easy victory the next day, which led to the change of the plans after the Confederates had won the ground necessary for the evacuation of Fort Donelson. It is equally true, however, that General Pillow but represented the feeling of the whole army, perhaps with the exception of General Buckner." It was not until later that the mood of the Confederate command would swing.[2]

If Kelley's observations were correct, Pillow may have thought the day's victory was complete enough to allow an escape at leisure. The Confederates had inflicted over 1,000 casualties and routed four enemy brigades, and both Pillow and Forrest would say later that they believed the Federals were too shaken to reinvest the fort quickly. Nevertheless, here was an opportunity to evacuate the fort, and it was still early enough in the day to do so. But Pillow thought it could wait until morning, giving his men a chance to collect the wounded, their equipment, and rations. Whole units went all the way back to the trenches and neglected to leave a security screen to keep the escape route open.[3]

As the three generals continued to argue, Pillow noticed some movement of Federal troops off to the right and ordered Buckner to hasten to his old lines. Only the greatly extended 30th Tennessee held these at the moment. Buckner refused to obey, as he did not consider Pillow his superior in command, and pressed Floyd to carry out an evacuation. After some delay, and a good deal of vacillation on the part of Floyd, the senior officer either agreed with or acquiesced to Pillow's order to return to the trenches. After even more delay, Buckner finally directed his division to reoccupy its old position in the trenches on the right. So most of the men returned to the very positions they had occupied the previous day, which called for Buckner's regiments to march over a snow-covered mile with full knapsacks.[4] The delay and distance combined to exacerbate a calamity that would soon occur.

General Bushrod Johnson was on the front lines on the far left and was completely unaware of the situation beyond his direct front. Riding to his right, Johnson found that there were no longer any fighting troops between him and the outer trenches. In fact, he could see Baldwin's and McCausland's brigades actually withdrawing back toward the rifle pits. Perplexed, Johnson sent an aide to ask for reinforcements but instead received orders to retire back into the trenches himself. Johnson sought out his fellow generals and suggested a continuation of the battle, but he was overruled. Uncharacteristically, he argued with his seniors, but he was again told to stop his attacks. After some discussion, though, it was decided to leave Drake's Brigade, supported by the 20th Mississippi, in position on a ridge some 300 yards in front of the outer defenses as a screen, keeping a section of the Wynn's Ferry Road open for the moment. This was actually a logical choice, for most of the men of this brigade had gone into battle with their knapsacks and blankets and were essentially ready to take up the march to Nashville. Work parties were detailed to collect the spoils of war and recover the wounded from the field of battle.[5]

As Pillow was making his fateful decision, the scattered and beaten remnants of McClernand's division were attempting to regroup. The men were out of ammunition, and the separate regiments and companies were mixed and spread across the hills and ravines beyond the battlefield. The few remaining officers did their best to reorganize their commands, but it would take hours. Essentially, McClernand's division was out of the fight, with the exception of a handful of scattered commands.

In the former center of the line, Gen. Lew Wallace took note of the morning's fight. In this sector, only three men had been wounded in Wood's battery and three killed and seven wounded in the 1st Nebraska. He surmised that these light casualties were due partly to the advantage of position, and partly to the desultory and uphill work of the enemy. The Confederate loss to his front was much greater, and many of the wounded enemy soldiers were recovered and cared for as if they were his own. He noted that the Confederates carried off a number of wounded men as they broke contact. Wallace sent pickets to cover his front and reestablished contact with Cruft's brigade, which had fought under General McClernand for most of the morning. He also readjusted many of the units within his division, which had grown to what he called the "pretentious proportion" of twelve regiments.[6] Generals McClernand and Wallace soon met on the battlefield to confer, and as they talked, the unseen Confederates made their way back to the trenches.

By now General Grant had returned from his conference with Foote, and an aide told him of the morning's catastrophe. He set off with Colonel Webster of his staff, galloping to the right of the line, stopping briefly at Gen. C. F. Smith's headquarters to alert his division. In a short time, Grant arrived on the scene of the Wallace-McClernand discussion. Lew Wallace later noted that the mud on Grant's horse and uniform showed the haste of his ride. He remembered, too, that Grant tightly held some papers in his right hand, and that he was obviously trying to keep his irritation and anger in check. Both division commanders saluted their senior and gave him instant attention.

General Grant clenched his jaw hard and said in a low tone: "Foote must go to Cairo, taking his ironclads, some of which are seriously damaged. We will have to await his return; meantime, our line must be retired out of range of the fort." The idea was detestable to him, and seeing this, Wallace made a suggestion: "We have nobody on the right now, and the road to Clarksville is open. If we retire the line at all, it will be giving the enemy an opportunity to get away tonight with all he has."[7] Were the Confederates to pull off an escape of any magnitude, it would be a grave and irrevocable embarrassment for Grant. Something had to be done, and quickly.

One can only imagine what went through Grant's mind at this moment of crisis. His army had been savagely thrown back upon itself, and there were signs that the men were on the verge of a rout. Soldiers were standing about in small groups talking in an excited manner, and no officer seemed to be giving directions.

The Confederates had just ended what was to be their final assault, but no one in the Union line knew that at the time. They had been repulsed only to return again and again, and as far as anyone here knew, they still could return at any moment. Grant probably believed with some truth that the former politician General McClernand would find some way to fix blame on him if a final defeat was in fact inflicted on his battered army. No one knew how many men were killed and wounded, but all indications were that the day had been a rather singularly bloody one. He would have to answer for the casualties, and relief of command was the likely result. Compounding this was the probable charge that Grant had been derelict in his duties by being absent from the field while in conference with Flag Officer Foote. All of Grant's efforts to crawl back from the obscurity of Galena, to make good, rested on what he would do next.

Ulysses S. Grant was desperate, and he had few options. The most expedient and perhaps wise thing to do, given the drubbing received, was to withdraw the army a distance away to regroup and refit. He could then renew his attack at the time and place of his choosing, and perhaps catch the Confederates in the open if they attempted to escape overland. Smith's division was still intact and was in position to guard the steamboat landing on the Cumberland River. From here, reinforcements and supplies would continue to flow to the army. Yet this option admitted defeat and risked the loss of what little morale remained in the ranks. This move also invited the wrath of General Halleck, who, unbeknownst to Grant, was conspiring to replace him anyway. The Confederates were not likely to cooperate with Grant and could use the opportunity to escape by the river or maybe overland. General Johnston near Nashville could also change his plans and heavily reinforce Fort Donelson or maneuver against Grant's flank and rear. This option of regrouping was what Grant was considering when he encountered McClernand and Wallace.

Another possibility was to remain in his current positions and regroup and refit in place. This option would keep pressure on at least part of the Confederate line and would not necessarily destroy the soldiers' morale. Again, reinforcements and supplies could continue to arrive at the steamboat landing north of the fort. Yet for Grant, this course of action would probably result in his relief of command, and again the Confederates were just as likely to escape by river or land. It was also far out of character for Grant to sit idle while the enemy was so close at hand. What he needed was a clear-cut victory, not a stalemate, to save his reputation and career.

The option remaining was to attack. The question was where. The Confederates had attacked on their left against McClernand's division. Grant surmised that this assault force was worn out, perhaps more so than his own right wing. The Union troops were short of ammunition, but supplies of it were close at hand. The Confederates must be in short supply too, and they had to haul it over the wooded hills and ravines, which were covered with snow. And it was the Confederates that had withdrawn in this sector.

Another thought occurred to Grant. In order to achieve such mass on the Confederate left, General Floyd must have stripped the defenses on the right, leaving it weakly held. Facing the Confederate left was Gen. C. F. Smith's division, which had not yet been committed and remained fresh.

The final deciding factor may have been what a young soldier pointed out to his commanding general. The man said the enemy had come out with knapsacks and haversacks filled with rations. It was an oddity that men would be committed to battle so encumbered. Not only would the added weight slow any soldier, but also the straps would hinder the arm movements necessary to load and fire the muzzleloading weapons of the day. Grant saw the significance immediately. The Confederate attack was an attempt to escape the fort. With their personal equipment and food, they were prepared to march for Nashville or some other point.

Turning to his chief of staff, Col. J. D. Webster, Grant said: "Some of our men are pretty badly demoralized, but the enemy must be more so, for he has attempted to force his way out, but has fallen back. The one who attacks now will be victorious and the enemy will have to be in a hurry if he gets ahead of me."[8]

General Grant was upset, and it is not difficult to imagine the frustration and near panic that anyone in command would feel at the brink of such a disaster. But by all accounts, he displayed a coolness that would become his trademark. He gave orders in a quiet tone that was in stark contrast to the emergency at hand. Grant's face reddened perceptibly, and he set his jaw. Without a word, he looked hard at McClernand, who began one of his long explanations. Grant interrupted him. "Gentlemen," he said, "that road must be recovered before night." Gripping the papers in his hand, he continued: "I will go to [Gen. C. F.] Smith now. At the sound of your fire, he will support you with an attack on his side."[9]

Grant then turned his horse and rode off at an ordinary trot, leaving McClernand and Wallace behind. Passing groups of men, Grant and Colonel Webster called out to them: "Fill your cartridge-boxes, quick, and get into line; the enemy is trying to escape and he must not be permitted to do so." This acted like a charm. The men only needed someone to give them a command, and they sprang to life.[10]

To further divert the Confederates' attention and to lift his army's morale, Grant wanted the gunboats to make a demonstration against the water batteries. He had spent the morning with the flag officer and had a deep appreciation of how badly damaged the boats were, but this was a critical moment. Grant wrote a dispatch to Foote:

> If all the gunboats that can, will immediately make their appearance to the enemy, it may secure us a victory. Otherwise we may be defeated. A terrible conflict ensued in my absence, which has demoralized a portion of my command, and I think the enemy is much more so. If the gunboats do not show themselves it will reassure the enemy and still further demoralize our troops. I must order a charge to save appearances. I do not expect the gunboats to go into action, but to make appearance, and to throw a few shells at long range.[11]

At the time, the battered *Carondelet* was the only boat capable of moving under her own power, so she built up steam and proceeded up the river toward the batteries that had wrecked havoc the day before. She did not dare come into range of the heavy guns but held a position and lobbed a few shells toward the fort. She had no measurable physical effect on the coming events, but no doubt she had the full attention of the Confederate command and the gunners at the batteries.

Little had occurred in Gen. C. F. Smith's sector during the morning except some shifting of forces, such as sending the 13th Missouri to the right to support Stone's and Richardson's batteries. The 52nd Indiana was also dispatched to the extreme left to prepare to repel any Confederate sortie from that area. This left only elements of Lauman's and Cook's brigades, with a battalion of Birge's Sharpshooters, to guard a front of about a half mile. These men did not know it, but they were facing only the thin line formed by the 30th Tennessee, and it had no intention of leaving the trenches.

Even by the afternoon, the men of Smith's division knew nothing of the battle on the right, except for hearing the constant thunder of cannons and rattle of musketry. What the losses were or who the victor was could only be guessed from the incomplete stories of the wounded men or passing stragglers who wandered into camp with stories of repulse, defeat, and disaster. Throughout the day, no orders came to these units except to stay near camp.

By 1:00 P.M., the roar of battle on the right had ominously ceased, and Grant had told the men to be ready to move in an instant.

Around 2:00, after his conference with McClernand and Wallace, Grant returned to Smith's headquarters, where he explained the situation. Smith was directed to charge the enemy's works to his front with his whole division. Grant was confident that Smith would find only a token force to contend with. The regiments and brigades were quickly assembled and fell into formation.

Smith rode along the front of his division and addressed each regiment. It was not a speech, as such, but it impressed the men greatly. He told them to rely on the bayonet and not to fire a shot until the enemy works were reached and his line broken. Members of the 2nd Iowa learned that they were to lead the attack. If they had any lingering doubts of possible defeat in the coming assault, their former brigade commander dispelled them. "Second Iowa, you must take the fort. Take the caps off your guns, fix bayonets, and I will lead you!"[12] Each man took up his gun, dressed the lines, and waited for the command to move forward. Most of the men stood silently in contemplation of what lay before them. Many would never return.

Smith's plan was simple. Each man of every regiment would fix his bayonet and remove the percussion cap from his musket to prevent firing. Without any artillery preparation, the blue infantry would use the speed and shock of a bayonet attack to gain the objective. Once in the enemy works, the regiments would then exploit their success. Lauman's brigade, consisting of the 2nd, 7th, and 14th Iowa, and the attached 25th Indiana, would conduct the assault. The 52nd Indiana, previously assigned to guard a gap in the line, was also brought up for the assault and attached to Lauman's brigade. Stone's battery was positioned in support, and elements of Birge's Sharpshooters were deployed on each flank as skirmishers. Colonel Cook's brigade would follow to the right and rear in support. This brigade was ordered to feign an attack to draw the enemy fire away from Lauman's brigade, which was designated as the main effort.

The assault force of Lauman's brigade formed in column of battalions of five companies each. The 2nd Iowa was in the center with General Smith, followed by the other regiments. Surrounded by his staff, Smith rode to the head of his division, and the command to advance came at last. The columns moved silently through the ravine without firing scarcely a gun. After a slight alignment in the march, Lauman's brigade, with the 2nd Iowa in the lead, came squarely into open view of the Confederate earthworks

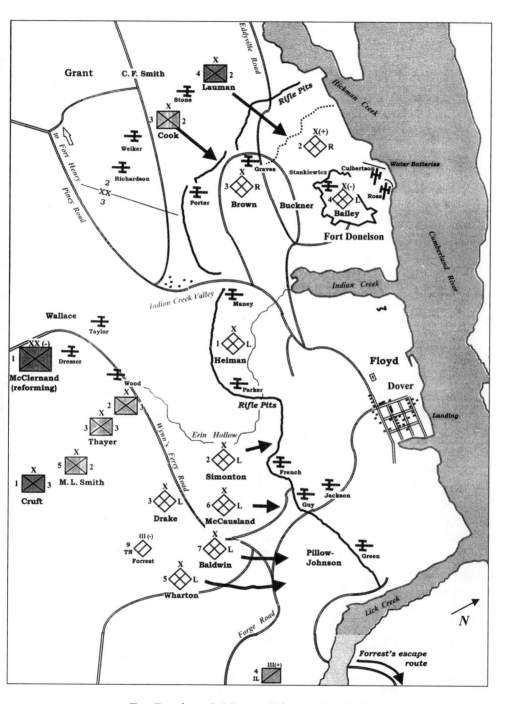

Fort Donelson, 2:00 P.M., February 15, 1862

some 200 yards away. The first of many hostile volleys passed over the attackers' heads. As the range closed, the Confederate fire became more accurate.

The blue waves flowed through the tangle of felled trees and covered the distance between them and the enemy. As the men cleared the obstacle, the 2nd Iowa received the concentrated fire of the defending Confederates. At the first volley, nearly 200 men fell dead or wounded, among them many company officers. The 25th Indiana soon suffered almost as many casualties, but without a perceptible halt, the blue ranks closed and moved steadily on.[13] One soldier remembered years later: "It appeared incredible that troops could go up that hill and keep any kind of lines of organization. It looked as if a rabbit could scarcely get through the brush and logs, and fallen timber, but broken as the lines were by such obstructions, and the storm of lead poured from the enemy, the regiment faltered not, but what was left of it pressed on over the earthworks."[14]

The Confederate right wing had, in fact, been stripped of almost every regiment. Colonel John W. Head's 30th Tennessee had defended this sector during the day, and it was spread very thin. Three companies under the command of Maj. James J. Turner held the point immediately assaulted. They were all that stood between Smith's division and the vital water batteries on the river.[15]

Meanwhile, the supporting attack of Cook's brigade commenced off to the right. The men eagerly went to the work assigned them and kept up a warm fire on the Confederates, focusing their attention on Porter's Tennessee Battery. They also advanced rapidly by the left flank and charged over the downed timber, but were then met by a rapid fire of canister and musketry that wounded several men. A charge was ordered to take Porter's Battery, but apparently due to a failure on the part of the individual regiments to cooperate in the venture, this produced no advantage except a slightly advanced position on the field. Cook's brigade, however, kept pressure on this section of the Confederate line as Lauman's brigade advanced onward toward its objective.[16]

The objective was getting closer, but the price for it was high. Lieutenant John G. Greenwalt of the 2nd Iowa, on the left wing of the regimental assault, reported: "Just as I saw my captain fall I sank down, and for the first time realized that the balls were flying pretty thick. I heard one or two strike the log I fell on, and only remember crawling down on the lower side of it, when all consciousness passed from me. When I recovered, I found myself a half-mile to the rear, the surgeon cutting a ball out of my right hip."[17]

The colors of the 2nd Iowa were positioned with the left wing of the regiment. Early in the action, four musket balls felled Sgt. Harry B. Doolittle, who carried the flag. Corporal Scehencius G. Page took up the colors but soon fell dead. Corporal James M. Churcher carried them further but received a wound that would cost him his arm. Corp. Harry E. Weaver was killed next, and Corporal Benjamin Robinson was shot in the face. The last man of the color guard on his feet, Corp. Voltaire P. Twombly, then took up the colors without hesitation but was knocked down by a spent ball. In spite of the pain, he got up and carried the flag, and it was the first to be planted inside the defensive works. For his actions that day, Twombly later received the Medal of Honor.[18]

The 2nd Iowa paid dearly for its place of honor on the field. Over half its men became casualties during the assault.

The 450 men of the 30th Tennessee held out as long as they could before retiring under fire to the next ridge, where they renewed the fight. When the 2nd Iowa gained the outer trenches, it pursued the Confederates into the ravine below. There it prepared to ascend the next hill to push on to the water batteries. The 25th Indiana then mounted the ridge just won by the Iowans. In the smoke and chaos of battle, the Hoosiers commenced a continuous fire into the blue ranks down below in the ravine. The ensuing confusion stopped the Union attack in its tracks. It was several minutes before the men of the 25th Indiana were persuaded to cease their fire. General Smith quickly arrived on the scene, assessed the situation, and recalled the 2nd Iowa to the captured trenches. Smith wanted to continue the attack, but he wished to concentrate his forces and coordinate them to prevent another case of fratricide among the raw troops.[19]

Coincidentally, at this time the battered 2nd Kentucky and other regiments of Buckner's command returned from their day of fighting on the Confederate left. The Kentuckians found their length of old trenches occupied by the men of the 7th Illinois and charged to drive them out. The men in blue did leave the trenches, in a sense, jumping over the other side of the rifle pits, where the earth had been thrown up as a breastwork. They did not fall back farther. Repulsed, the Kentuckians re-formed and charged two more times before withdrawing back onto the 18th Tennessee, which had formed a line of battle on the succeeding ridge.[20]

The Confederate field batteries were not silent during the affair and lent a hand in the defense, and Fort Donelson fired its few guns facing landward against Smith's attack. The 8-inch howitzer, under the command of Lt. Peter K. Stankiewicz, lobbed some well-placed rounds into the ranks of Federal infantry. A gun crew of one of the obsolete 32-pounder carronades in the upper river battery also made an appearance. These men made their way into the fort proper and manned one of the 9-inch nondescript railroad guns that had earlier been rejected due to their inferior quality. They apparently sent some shots over the heads of their comrades and in the direction of Smith's attacking regiments, but they could not tell to what effect.[21]

In a desperate attempt to stop Smith's attack and hold the final ridge before the water batteries, the 49th Tennessee and four companies from the 50th Tennessee left the confines of Fort Donelson proper and fell into position on the line held by the decimated 2nd Kentucky. The 42nd Tennessee, under Col. William A. Quarles, was also dispatched. Its men ran at the double-quick through the freezing mud and snow and took a place in the new line. The 14th Mississippi, 3rd Tennessee, 41st Tennessee, and parts of other commands moved into positions of support. A section of Graves's battery was shifted to this sector and placed at the hinge between the old and new lines. Ironically, and in hindsight, the new line was actually a better natural position of defense than the one previously held.[22] Here the Confederates were able to check any further advance by Smith's division, and they undertook limited counterattacks to drive the enemy from the captured trenches. These attacks were unsuccessful, and the Confederates had to be content with holding the new line. After nearly two hours of bitter fighting, it was after 4:00 P.M., and darkness was quickly approaching. Orders were given to entrench, but there were few shovels and the ground was frozen.

Meanwhile, General Smith sent for Cook's brigade to come up to the summit, as well as two additional 10-pounder Parrott guns of Stone's battery. The Federals occupied a fortified position, which had an elevation as high as any point in the line. The section from Stone's battery was also in position to fire in enfilade along a good portion of the enemy positions.

Smith made his way on horseback through heavy fire to the 7th Illinois. Reining up to Lt. Col. Andrew J. Babcock, he ordered: "Charge that battery [Porter's]! Charge it with your steel and silence its work of death!" The regiment's bayonets were soon up and bristling. Smith turned his eyes to the west, and seeing the sun fast sinking toward the horizon, he returned to Babcock and said: "I countermand the orders to charge that battery. It is now too late; I would leave that work for you to do tomorrow."[23]

Porter's Battery had put up a tough fight, being well positioned to fire in enfilade upon Smith's division as it swarmed upon the outer trenches. But with no protective works yet erected around the guns, the active crews made an inviting target. While the guns were brought into position, most of the horses were shot down and guns had to be run into place by hand. When the Federal infantry carried the trenches down the line, Stone's battery subjected Porter's men to a hail of deadly canister and shell fire. Under such punishment, the gray cannoneers took heavy casualties. Captain Porter himself was wounded in the thigh. Carried away bleeding from the position, he exclaimed to the only officer left, Lt. James H. Morton, a mere lad of nineteen, "Don't let them have the guns, Morton!" In spite of the heavy losses in men and horses, the battery continued to fire until darkness fell.[24]

Smith's attack cost the assault force some 61 killed and 321 wounded, the 2nd Iowa bearing the cost for over half of these numbers.[25] This attack, though, did succeed in wresting a long segment of the Confederate outer defense line and put Fort Donelson and the key water batteries in extreme jeopardy. Unless there was some change during the night, the morning would also find the blue ranks in good position to renew the attack.

News of the success of Gen. C. F. Smith's 2nd Division spread like wildfire throughout Grant's army. The importance was not lost on Grant's chief engineer, Lt. Col. James B. McPherson, who wrote: "The news that General Smith had captured the rebel entrenchments on their right, was borne along the lines, cheering and stimulating the men. We had secured a key to the enemy's position, obtaining a point having about as great an elevation as any portion of his works and where we could plant our artillery."

While Smith's attack was in process, another advance was brewing on the Union right. Grant's orders were to retake the lost ground of the morning and complete the investment of the Fort Donelson garrison. He gave this mission to General McClernand, and General Wallace was to support him.

After Grant's departure, McClernand and Wallace discussed their mission to reoccupy the ground lost during the morning and block the route of escape for the garrison. The Illinois politician lamented: "The road ought to be recovered—Grant is right about that. But Wallace, you know that I am not ready to undertake it."[26] His brigades and regiments had been shattered by the Confederate onslaught and needed time to reorganize and receive a new supply of ammunition. The Wynn's Ferry and Forge Roads did run through McClernand's sector, but it was clear that McClernand was now asking Wallace to relieve him of the burden.

The two officers worked out the brigade and division organizations, shifting them about a bit, but mostly returning units to their parent organizations. Cruft's brigade was reassigned to Wallace, and McClernand detached Ross's (Morrison's) brigade as well. In addition, the fortuitous arrival of Morgan L. Smith's brigade from the 2nd Division gave Wallace a total of ten relatively fresh regiments for the operation at hand, while the remainder held the center of the original line. After a brief personal reconnaissance of the ground to the front, Wallace sent orders to the brigades to advance. He calculated that he had but two hours of daylight left.

Morrison's old brigade, with Colonel Ross now in command, formed on the left. Colonel Smith's brigade was in the center and was considered the main attack. Cruft's brigade was posted on the far right, and Thayer's brigade was kept in reserve. The attacks were to be made in columns of regiments, the same tactic the Confederates had used all through the morning. Although this formation did not provide for flexibility in maneuver, the mass of men formed a human battering ram in the assault.

Cruft's brigade was the last into attack position, and when it formed, it came under fire. Hearing the rattle of musketry, General Wallace turned to Colonel Smith and said that it was time to move. Morgan Smith replied, "Wait until I light a fresh cigar." With that small task done, the regiments advanced and were soon under fire.[27] The advance was carried over the stretch of land left unoccupied by the Confederates when they withdrew earlier, and it drove in the thin line of remaining pickets.

On a ridgeline some 300 yards outside of the trenches, Drake's Brigade was deployed earlier with the idea of holding the Wynn's Ferry Road and halting any Federal advance. Here the ground was covered in patches of snow with clumps of shrubs and few trees. There were no entrenchments, but it was a relatively good defensive position.

The two lead regiments of Colonel Smith's brigade, the 11th Indiana and 8th Missouri, used their rudimentary "Zouave" training by loading and firing in the prone position. They also moved forward and up the steep slope in small groups by rushing, falling to the ground, and repeating the process. During the attack, Smith remained on horseback with his fresh cigar, a perilous feat under the most favorable of circumstances. When a bullet clipped the cigar off close to his lips, he coolly took out another. "Here," he shouted, "one of you fellows bring me a match." The match was brought, and after lighting a new cigar, Smith spurred on and up. Except for the skirmishers, there was little firing by the attackers, who meant to close the distance and keep the momentum of the assault going. Only the voices of the officers were heard. The exception to this rule was the Confederates on the ridge, who taunted: "Hi, hi there Yanks! Why don't you come up? What are you waiting for?"[28]

When the attackers were about two-thirds up the slope, the gray infantrymen of Drake's Brigade added lead to their jeers, which compelled Smith's brigade to lay prone and deliver its first ragged volley. The Hoosiers and Missourians then began to advance on their hands and knees, and that they would take the position was no longer in question. Scaling the hill, the infantry in blue pushed Drake's Brigade off the crest. The attacks in the other brigade sectors also attained their objectives, and the ridgeline was cleared of

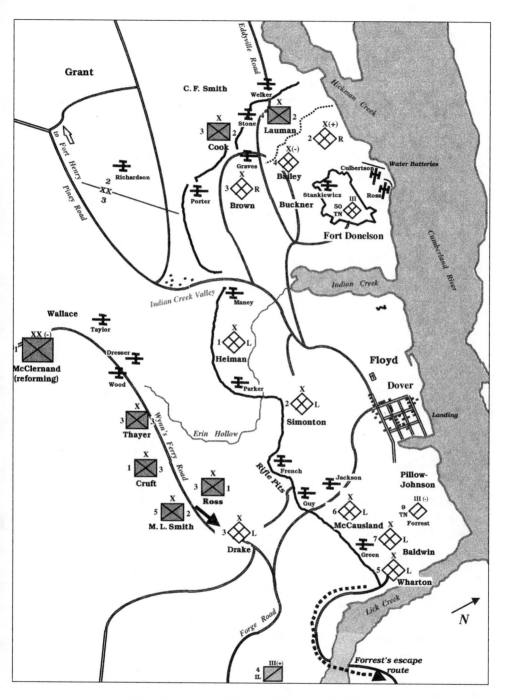

Fort Donelson, 3:00 P.M., February 15, 1862

Confederates, who by and large withdrew all the way back into the trenches guarding Dover. The brigades under General Wallace's command pushed forward with just enough resistance before them to keep their blood up.

Pushing on toward Dover, Wallace's men came upon the aftermath of the morning's fight. McAllister's howitzers were where they had been left, mired in the mud. Dead and wounded men lay where they had fallen. The latter were cared for no matter what color uniform they wore. General Wallace came across a Confederate sitting against the stump of a tree, sporting a coonskin cap. His eyes were wide open, and there was a broad grin on his face. Thinking the gesture was directed at him, Wallace stopped and told an aide, "Find out what that fellow means by grinning that way." The aide dismounted and shook the man. "Why, he's dead sir." He took the cap off to discover that a bullet had carried most of the man's skull away.[29]

Lew Wallace halted his men and instructed them to deploy skirmishers and adjust the line. Presently, Colonel Webster of Grant's staff returned with orders for him to retire his command out of range of the fort and throw up light entrenchments. Wallace gave it a moment's thought and replied, "Does the general know that we have retaken the road lost in the morning?" Receiving a negative reply, he added: "Oh well! Give him my compliments, colonel, and tell him *I have received the order.*" Webster gave the general a sharp eye and left. Lew Wallace had resolved to disobey orders again, which Grant subsequently justified.[30]

Wallace then aligned his forces, and Wood's battery was planted again on the Wynn's Ferry Road. Supposing the Federal movements indicated a retreat, the Confederates launched a counterattack. As the gray soldiers came yelling out of their works to the road, the Chicago battery blasted grape and canister rounds into the ranks. Additional fresh regiments in blue, which had not fired a shot during the day, were also brought forward too to stop this sortie dead in its tracks.[31]

The 3rd Division then continued to advance slowly until it came within sight of the outer defenses, and some say even Fort Donelson proper. Wallace did not have the authority to assault the works, nor adequate support to do so. Leaving a strong screen of skirmishers, he withdrew the bulk of the division 500 or 600 yards back and out of range of the Confederate trenches. He then contracted his lines in order to be in position for a divisional assault at first light. The men settled down to another night without fires and nothing to eat but hardtack, but not a murmur of complaint was heard. Fatigue parties were deployed forward to collect and look after the wounded. These work parties worked throughout the night, and the surgeons never rested.

By sunset, the 3rd Division had reoccupied most of the ground lost during the morning, but not all. How much of a gap the Confederates could still use to escape is a matter of speculation and conjecture to this day. Wallace was on terrain he had never reconnoitered, and darkness was fast approaching. He had also deployed his men to be in position to renew the assault in the morning, not to block every avenue of escape that the Confederates might use.

Back at his headquarters, General Grant mused on the operations for the next day. With the line mostly restored and a large part of General Smith's division holding a length of trenches, he could either renew the assault or lay down to a formal siege. Flag Officer Foote was emphatic that his flotilla was nowhere close to being ready to go head-to-head with the water batteries again. But the Confederates were weakened by their assault, and Grant's army was getting stronger as new regiments arrived by steamboat. Yet the Confederates still could effect an escape if the matter was not put to rest soon. Officers and men clamored for Grant to order an immediate assault—a night attack. Grant was very mindful of the risks of such an operation, difficult even with veteran troops. And even in broad daylight there had been far too many incidents of fratricide among the green regiments. Events show that he wisely postponed the final push, which was planned for the morning instead.

All along the line, the armies lay down to rest pretty much where they had stopped fighting. Most of the Confederates in the trenches tried to get all the rest they could, confidently anticipating the renewal of the battle in the morning, whatever their role may be. Morale was still high. In the past two days, they had beaten back the ironclads and driven aside the investing enemy force from the entire left wing of the defenses. There was little doubt in the Confederate soldiers' minds that they would be victorious yet again in the morning, come what may.

The night was clear with a full moon, but the temperatures again plunged to about ten degrees. No fires were officially allowed, but a few scattered men and small units pulled back beyond ridges to build small ones to warm themselves. Some lucky Union units even received their baggage trains through the efforts of their energetic quartermasters. But for the most part, the men of both armies shivered throughout the night.

Every farmhouse in the area was filled with the wounded. When soldiers died, their bodies were laid in neat rows on the ground. For those wounded men between the lines, it was a night of frozen hell. Those men who were able built fires to prevent freezing to death. Those unable to build one lay on the cold ground as their life ebbed away. In Dover, nearly

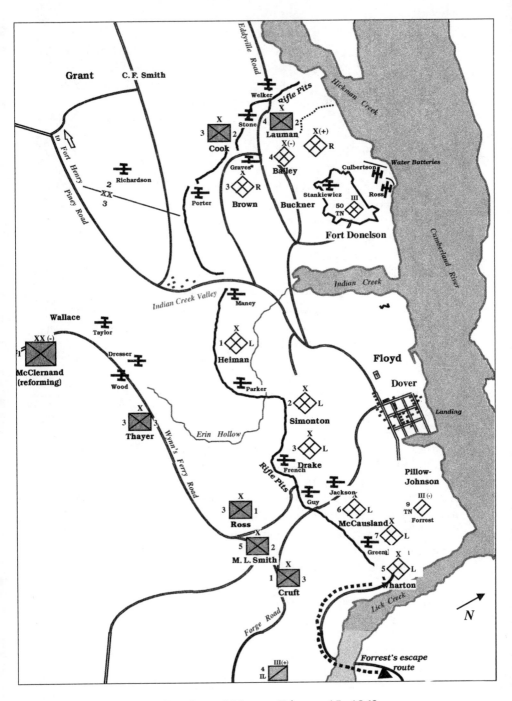

Fort Donelson, 6:00 P.M., February 15, 1862

every building was used as a makeshift hospital, and the number of casualties overwhelmed the limited number of trained medical personnel. In an effort to relieve the suffering, General Floyd directed that the wounded and 300 or so prisoners be evacuated to Clarksville, using the two available steamboats. He and many others would deeply regret this order.

Back in St. Louis, General Halleck continued to debate strategy and options with McClellan and Buell. He had not received any word from Grant since the day before and had no idea of what had transpired on the Cumberland. Halleck wired McClellan to ask for more troops to face the 30,000 Confederates he believed were in Fort Donelson. He also wired General Buell, asking him to reconsider an overland advance on Bowling Green, and that he instead bring his army to Dover to help with the siege. McClellan sided with Buell's assessment, believing a march on Bowling Green would tie down Albert Sidney Johnston and divert pressure from Grant. As the generals debated and conferred, events were well beyond their knowledge and control.

The Confederate high command was also active during this day. By now, Albert Sidney Johnston had set up headquarters in Edgefield, and most, if not all, of his army was safely across the Cumberland. At 5:00 P.M., he wired Richmond: "The attack at Fort Donelson this morning renewed by the enemy at dawn with great vigor and continued until 1 o'clock, when conflict was still raging. We had taken some 200 prisoners, forced their positions, and captured four pieces of artillery. At that hour the enemy was still bringing up reinforcements for the attack. Our arms were successful, the field having been carried inch by inch, with severe loss on both sides. There is no intelligence since 1 o'clock."[32]

That night, he got more. At 9:00, Forrest's cavalry patrols reported that there were as yet no enemy forces blocking the route of escape to Nashville. By all appearances, the garrison could get away clean at daybreak. Before calling his senior officers together for another council of war, General Floyd took time to pen an update to his department commander:

> The enemy having invested our lines, it was determined to attack them. . . . The enemy maintained a successful struggle, which continued for nine hours, and resulted in driving him from the field, with a loss on his part of 1,240 killed and wounded, of whom 1,000 were killed. About 300 prisoners, six pieces of artillery, and 1,000 stands of arms were captured. Our own loss amounted to about 500 killed and wounded. They have a force of forty-two regiments.[33]

One can only imagine the relief felt by Johnston. From his perspective, the ironclads had been repulsed, and now the Fort Donelson garrison had inflicted a major defeat on Grant. Meanwhile the army had evacuated Bowling Green and safely crossed the Cumberland into Nashville. Perhaps the string of disasters in the West could now be reversed. This was the very moment when Johnston needed to provide Floyd with his intent and subsequent orders. Was Fort Donelson to be held or abandoned? Floyd did not ask for guidance or reinforcements, and Johnston did not give any of either. Now that the route to freedom was open, just what was the next move?

Back at Fort Donelson, the brigade and regimental commanders were summoned to Pillow's headquarters in Dover. There they received instructions to march their units out of the trenches and bring them to the jumping-off positions they had occupied that morning. The men were to have their knapsacks, blankets, and four days' rations in their haversacks. The plan explained to them was to escape, cutting their way out if they had to.

The commanders returned to their units and began their preparations. Around midnight, Gen. Bushrod Johnson assumed the arduous task of supervising the massing of the regiments into their positions. This time, though, Colonel Heiman's brigade was present and fresh, having been relatively uncommitted during the day.[34] As a final precaution, General Pillow ordered the commissary stores burned at 5:30 A.M. to prevent their capture after the garrison's departure.

After the brigade and regimental commanders left the room, Floyd, Pillow, and Buckner remained to discuss their options. Bitter memories of this meeting would linger for many years in the minds of the participants and observers.

General Floyd began the meeting by asking, "Well gentlemen, what is best now to be done?" Pillow and Buckner immediately joined in a heated discussion about the conduct of the battle. Buckner argued that the object of the operation was attained when the road was open and that the army should have made good its escape. Pillow maintained that the agreement was to return to the camps to retrieve their equipment and withdraw under cover of night. He also proposed that it be done now, while there was still a chance to do so.

Yet there were complications. The Cumberland was at flood stage, and with the bitter cold, there was no other way to cross it except by boat. Also, scouts reported that the waters of Lick Creek were three feet deep or more, and the surgeons felt that the cold water and air would result in an extremely high death rate for the infantry.[35] It was assumed that Grant was receiving reinforcements, the number of which was unknown but wildly exaggerated. There were other reports that the Federals had once again blocked the road, intelligence based mostly on the number of fires seen in that direction. Furthermore, it was surmised that Grant was pushing units eastward past Lick Creek in an effort to get cannons to bear on the river above Dover to cut the river traffic. (He had wanted to but did not have enough men.) The Confederate brigadiers needed more information, and additional scouts were sent to determine the state of the roads out of Dover and the location of the nearest enemy forces that could block them.[36]

John B. Floyd was already considering the need to cut a way out and needed the cavalry to help if it came to that. Sometime after midnight, a courier awakened Nathan Bedford Forrest and summoned him to the conference being held in Dover. Arriving at Pillow's headquarters, the weary cavalryman strode through the door and witnessed a conversation he could not believe. After a day of such success, the senior officers were no longer discussing cutting their way out, but the possibility of surrendering the garrison!

Apparently the mood of the council of war had quickly degenerated upon receiving reports that the Wynn's Ferry Road appeared to be blocked. If escape proved impossible, then surrender was inevitable. It was at this moment that Forrest entered the room.

The wily cavalryman was adamant in his opinion that the roads were clear of the enemy. His scouts had reported that the way to Nashville was open and supposed that the fires seen in the woods were those of the hundreds of wounded soldiers left between the lines trying to stay warm. Forrest had himself recently ridden over the area in question and also found only dead or wounded men. Floyd and Buckner, however, had heard from other scouts that a line of Federal infantry was astride the road. Nothing Forrest could say would convince them otherwise, and he left to arrange another reconnoiter.[37]

Major Kelley, of Forrest's cavalry, remained on the battlefield with a large detachment of troopers to gather up arms and the wounded until after sunset. He also left the area in question without seeing any movement on the enemy's part to regain the position *east* of the Wynn's Ferry Road in order to block the river with artillery.[38] Two cavalry scouts soon returned to report, however, that the enemy had indeed blocked the Wynn's Ferry Road. Other scouts were sent to another escape option and reported that where the Charlotte Road crossed Lick Creek, the mud was about half-leg deep and the water was about saddle-skirt deep to the horses. The whole obstacle was some 200 yards wide. Major Frank Rice, a member of Pillow's staff and a local resident of Dover, confirmed this last item of information.[39]

General Pillow did not like any thought of surrender and offered yet another option. The two steamboats that had been sent to Clarksville by

Floyd with wounded were expected back in the morning. He proposed to hold the fort in the meantime, and then use the boats to ferry as many men as possible to freedom. Forrest also offered to cut a path with his cavalry and hold it open until the infantry passed, and then cover the rear of the column as it made its way to Nashville.[40] Both of these options had some merit, and a combination of the two may have allowed a substantial number of Confederates to escape Fort Donelson. If the three brigadiers could finally reach an agreement, a bold and coordinated operation could save something out of this yet.

But the three brigadiers were neither bold nor in agreement.

General Buckner would not commit to either plan and became stubbornly fixated on surrendering the garrison. He was certain that Smith's division would attack him at first light, and he felt his men could not last for thirty minutes. Pillow promptly asked: "Why can't you? I think you can hold your position; I think you can sir." General Buckner retorted: "I know my position; I can only bring to bear against the enemy some 4,000 men, while he can oppose me with any given number." He added that his men were so exhausted that they could not march more than ten miles, even if they made good their escape. The ammunition was nearly expended, and the men had been several days without regular or sufficient food. Therefore, regarding the proposed operation as hopeless, he felt that any attempt to escape would be a fruitless massacre, estimating that three-quarters of the men would be lost. He maintained that no commander had the right to sacrifice so many for the sake of so few. The men had all fought nobly and well, and General Johnston and the army were certainly safe across the Cumberland by now. Duty and honor required no more. With that said, General Floyd indicated to the group that his opinions coincided with Buckner's.[41]

In the end, Buckner's defeatism infected all present. Even Gideon Pillow lost his confidence in fighting on. "Well gentlemen," he said, "what do you intend to do; I am in favor of fighting out, [but] if we cannot cut our way out nor fight on there is no alternative left us but capitulation, and I am determined that I will never surrender the command nor will I ever surrender myself as a prisoner. I will die first."[42]

John B. Floyd had no intention of staying around for the surrender, either, believing that as the former secretary of war, he would be tried for treason and hanged. Buckner chided him and said that if he were in command, he would share the fate of the army in accordance with regulations.[43] Then occurred one of the most amazing examples of the collapse of a command in the annals of American warfare.

Taking Buckner's comments as volunteering for the job, General Floyd asked the junior brigadier, "If the command should devolve on you, would you permit me to take out my little brigade?" To which Buckner replied, "Yes, if you leave before the terms of capitulation are agreed on." Floyd turned to Pillow and told him, "General Pillow, I turn the command over sir." Pillow said, "And I pass it." Buckner said, "I assume it."[44]

After this ugly business was settled, Pillow asked if it would be improper for him to make his own escape. Floyd replied that each man would have to decide for himself, but that he would be glad for everyone to escape that could. Pillow said, "Then I shall leave this place."[45]

When Nathan Bedford Forrest heard of the final decision, he returned to headquarters. There he found the brigadiers and expressed his dissatisfaction by declaring, "I did not come here with the purpose of surrendering my command, and would not do it if they would follow me out; that I intend to go out if I saved but one man." Forrest was thoroughly convinced that he could escape and make his way to Nashville, and added that he had promised the parents of many of his young troopers to protect them when in his power to do so. Growing more agitated as he spoke, Forrest asserted that he would prefer that the bones of his men should bleach on the surrounding hills rather than that his troops be carried to the North and cooped up in open prison pens during midwinter. Forrest then leveled at General Buckner, "I think there is more fight in our men than you think, but if you will let me I will take out my command." At this, General Pillow suggested that Forrest be allowed to escape. The authorization was given on the express condition that he would do so before the flag of truce was raised. Forrest turned to Pillow and asked, "General I fought under your command, what shall I do?" Pillow answered, "Cut your way out," to which Forrest replied, "I will by God!" At this Forrest stomped out of the room in disgust.[46]

Pillow also left the room, but he returned a few moments later just to make sure everyone understood his rationale. "Gentlemen . . . I differ with you as to the cost of our cutting our way out, but if it were ascertained that it would cost three-fourths of the command, I agree that it would be wrong to sacrifice them for the remaining fourth."[47] Floyd and Buckner replied that everyone was in understanding, and Pillow left the room. Gathering his staff in the darkness, Pillow prepared to escape, presumably with Forrest's cavalry.

After the council of war, Floyd sent another message to Nashville, but with a distinctly different tone from those sent previously: "Last evening there arrived in the river near Fort Donelson eleven transports, laden with troops. We are completely invested with an army many times our own numbers. I regret to say the unanimous opinion of the officers seems to be that we cannot maintain ourselves against these forces."[48] As the Dover telegraph operator tapped out this message, his counterpart in Edgefield was already sending a message to Richmond with a far different message. This dispatch was from Albert Sidney Johnston to the secretary of war. Its three sentences repeated Floyd's earlier posts telling of the bloody yet brilliant victory of Fort Donelson. Within hours, the bitter truth would catch up to the department commander in time for him to eat those words for breakfast.

Meanwhile, Simon Bolivar Buckner sent for a bugler and writing materials and began the process of surrender.

The day of February 15 had seen victory and near disaster for both sides, but at the brink of defeat, it was clearly the person of Ulysses S. Grant that decisively turned the tide. In a cool and determined manner, he took control of the situation, stiffened the resolve of his army, and went on the offensive. Had the expedition been commanded by a man of the caliber of Buell or McClellan, the outcome probably would have been far different. In retrospect, it was truly remarkable how clearly Grant could think when calamity surrounded him. This was one of Ulysses S. Grant's finest moments in the war.

It will never be clearly known why Grant's staff did not alert him to the catastrophe on the right flank sooner that they did. Many of the staff officers did not have a high opinion of General McClernand, and perhaps they simply discounted the initial reports of an all-out Confederate attack. Also, many were new to their position and perhaps felt intimidated about disturbing the army commander while he was in the middle of an important conference. Rumors abounded after the battle that Grant had been drinking, but this was untrue. Besides, Flag Officer Foote was notorious for his temperance and would not have permitted Grant to drink any liquor without comment, private or official.

Undeniably, Grant's subordinates, notably Lew Wallace and Charles F. Smith, averted disaster by using their own initiative in his absence. Sending reinforcements to the embattled McClernand helped slow and finally check the Confederate advance. The mutual trust and common goals among the Federal senior officers were in sharp contrast to the distrust and division among the Confederate leaders. For example, when General Wallace received orders from Grant to pull back and regroup, Wallace disobeyed the order with the knowledge that doing so would further the aim of victory. His confidence that Grant would see this too was confirmed when his commander later backed him up fully. On the other hand, when Bushrod

Johnson considered pushing the attack without orders, he feared Pillow's wrath, hesitated, and lost a grand opportunity.

General Pillow's decision to return to the trenches is almost universally proclaimed to be the worst decision made in his career. It also exemplifies Pillow's personality—full of energy, brash, but lacking focus. In his report on October 10, 1862, Pillow belatedly offered an explanation for his orders to withdraw back into the trenches. Citing the council on the night of February 14, Pillow asserted that there was never any intention of retreating from the battlefield. The plan of the battle was, in fact, to inflict a decisive defeat upon the enemy and keep Grant from investing the fort. This was the reason why Pillow had not ordered his troops into battle encumbered with haversacks, rations, and blankets. He also pointed out that if the plan was to escape, then General Buckner would have reported that he was in position to cover the army as it commenced its retreat, which he apparently did not. It is highly unlikely that Buckner would have sought out Pillow to render any report whatsoever, but it again shows that General Floyd was never where he should have been to exercise effective control. As for the senior officer, once Floyd was reminded of the day's objectives by Pillow, he backed the decision to return to the trenches.[49]

Later in his campaign, to salvage his career, General Floyd stated that it was not his original intention to withdraw back to the trenches. To explain his absence from the scene where the decision was made, he said that after conferring with Buckner and subsequent to his second attack, he then departed to check the condition of the line on the far right. If he found it was secure, Floyd intended to move the whole army southward and into the open country. After Floyd rode away, Pillow and Buckner met and had their heated discussion in which they decided to order all of the troops to return to their former positions. Floyd did not become aware of this until the movement was almost completed. The timing is subject to question, but the right of the line was far from secure, as Gen. C. F. Smith's division was at that very moment massing for an assault in plain view. Thus Floyd's plan to withdraw uncontested was made moot once Smith's men were in motion. The retrograde would have degenerated into a footrace between Smith's and Wallace's fresh divisions, and the exhausted Confederates were not in a position to win.

Although Pillow's contention that a withdrawal was not the day's objective flies in the face of conventional thoughts on this subject, it seems to hold up to some scrutiny. For instance, the 32nd Tennessee did not enter the battle encumbered by haversacks, even though it was assigned to Buckner's command. When the regiment was committed to battle during General

Buckner's second attack, the men left their haversacks in the trenches.[50] The regimental commander obviously made this decision on his own, but had he thought an immediate withdrawal was in the works, it is unlikely he would have left them behind.

At the time of the reports found in the *Official Records,* Pillow was fighting desperately to salvage his career. However, his point ironically was substantiated by General Buckner's report of August 11, 1862, which also implied that withdrawal was not a given, and that the decision for a retreat would commence after a victory on the left. Buckner stated that the objective was "to make an immediate attack on their right, in order to open our communications with Charlotte, in the direction of Nashville." General Floyd unwittingly also confirmed Pillow's assertions by writing, "I thought we should at once avail ourselves of the existing opportunity." So prior to launching the assault on the morning of February 15, apparently the generals had no set plan to retreat from Fort Donelson; they would wait for an opportunity to do so as the situation unfolded. It is obvious, though, that General Buckner preferred to retreat no matter the outcome of battle, but it was not a clearly stated objective of the operation.[51] That these divergent views existed in the first place once again shows how fractured the Confederate command was and the inadequacies of the council on the night of February 14.

Other senior officers echoed General Pillow's contention that there was no plan to retreat. The fourth general officer at the fort, Bushrod Johnson, offered a defense in his report after the battle: "There was no proposition made in the conference [of February 14] to retreat from the battlefield and no determination made to do so. If a proposition had been made for a retreat from the field of battle, it would at once have suggested the necessity of making proper provisions for the march, of food and clothing for the intensity of the cold weather, and an additional supply of ammunition; and such preparation made previously to the battle would have greatly loaded down and encumbered the men in the fight."[52] Nathan Bedford Forrest and Colonel Quarles of the 42nd Tennessee, both of whom were present at the operational briefing, gave similar appraisals.

The Confederate withdrawal back into the trenches without establishing an adequate security screen to maintain an escape route virtually guaranteed that they would have to fight their way out once again. Pillow knew the Federals were being reinforced, so he also could guess that he would face fresh troops. By now, the enemy realized fully that this was the key terrain for any Confederate escape by land. Combining these observations, Pillow could surmise that Grant would greatly reinforce this sector of the battlefield with everything he could spare. So if the garrison was going to escape the next morning, he had to hold the road open throughout the night. Drake's Brigade alone was not enough to do this, as confirmed when it was attacked by three brigades and pushed back into the trenches. The only way the Confederates could ensure that the route stayed open was to leave the bulk of the brigades to hold the road and send small groups to the trenches to retrieve the knapsacks, ammunition, and rations.

Most historians agree that had the Confederates started their withdrawal after the Wynn's Ferry Road was clear they would have made good their escape. On the surface, it seems very plausible. By 1:00 P.M., McClernand's division was smashed. Wallace's division held its own but showed no signs yet of going on the offensive. The issue here is timing, and the myriad of personal accounts confuse it. General Wallace puts very little time between the final repulse of the Confederates and the arrival of Grant. If this were true, the withdrawal of the garrison would have been discovered as Wallace advanced, and appropriate measures taken. If there was an hour or more gap between the shock of the attack and Grant's recovery, then maybe there was a good possibility that the Confederates could have formed a column and commenced a march toward Nashville.

The Confederates probably did have a good chance to effect their escape as late as 1:00 that afternoon, and at least some of the garrison could have made their way out before the gate was closed. As the regiments cleared the perimeter, however, they had a long march over a country sparsely populated and offering little in the way of provisions. With the fort evacuated, the operational gunboats would freely roam the Cumberland, forcing the Confederates to avoid it, thus necessitating the use of the meandering backcountry roads. Also, General Grant had the equivalent of two regiments of cavalry, which would have relished the idea of running down a long, thin column of exhausted gray infantry. It is likely the retreat would have degenerated into a rout. Later, both Forrest and Major Gilmer of the engineers wrote that they believed a large part of the army could have escaped. If they were correct, and even if it arrived in Nashville a squad at a time, it was a far better result than to lose the whole army by surrender.

If an escape was not to occur on the afternoon of February 15 or even the next morning, then General Pillow probably made the right decision to withdraw back to the safety of the defensive works. If Fort Donelson held, General Grant's army was immobilized in a siege operation. In this position, it was vulnerable to a movement against its flank or rear, as General Johnston struck it while Buell was still slogging through the mud in Kentucky. For the next several days, Albert Sidney Johnston still could have massed against Grant, then turned on Buell. This strategy would be tried in about six weeks at Shiloh, but by then the Confederates were weaker and both Grant and Buell heavily reinforced. Also, as long as Fort Donelson and the water batteries held, Foote's fleet was not going anywhere near Nashville. The Confederates had no way of knowing it, but Grant was in imminent danger of being replaced by Halleck, and each day they delayed him made it more of a possibility. A change of command at this moment could have provided the Confederates with the needed time to either evacuate or be relieved by General Johnston.

The Confederate troops had fought long and hard that day, and they were cold, tired, hungry, and without ammunition. Without their knapsacks they were also without provisions and shelter. Their morale was high, however. In hindsight, Pillow's men should have brought their knapsacks along, as had Buckner's, or at least made provisions to retrieve them quickly. This way the Confederates would have been in a good position to continue their breakout. This precaution would not have solved the ammunition problem, though. The soldiers' cartridge boxes were empty, and there was no rapid way to get more to the front lines from the steamboat landing at Dover, except by pulling the units back to shorten the distance.

Holding the escape route open also had its risks. The Union right was heavily reinforced, and the Confederates no longer enjoyed a much higher ratio of soldiers in this sector. Also, the arriving Northern regiments were fresh and had ample ammunition. If General Pillow had established a defensive live covering the Wynn's Ferry Road, there were no entrenchments, and the supporting artillery was still in the old trenches to the rear. In such a situation, the Confederate forces holding the new line could have been under an extreme disadvantage and caught relatively in the open. Clearly, this option required generalship and luck of the magnitude exhibited later in the war by such men as Robert E. Lee. It was not found in John B. Floyd or any other general officer at Fort Donelson.

Although Simon B. Buckner advocated surrendering and was left behind to carry it out, the final decision to surrender was made by General Floyd. Floyd's letters in the *Official Records* are of a man desperate to salvage his career. The primary reason he gave for surrendering Fort Donelson was that it faced a massive enemy army that would surely overwhelm it in the morning. He claimed that he was facing 50,000 men in eighty-three Union regiments. There were actually 23,000 men in thirty-eight regiments of infantry and two of cavalry facing him, compared with his 16,000 men in twenty-eight regiments of infantry and the equivalent of one cavalry regiment. Floyd was outnumbered, but as long as he remained in his trenches, the Confederates were in a strong position.

To counter this argument, General Floyd attempted to show how the odds were just stacked too high against the garrison. He did this by blaming the placement of the fort and outer defenses:

> The position of the fort, which was established by the Tennessee authorities, was by no means commanding, nor was the least military significance attached to the position. The entrenchments, afterwards hastily made, in many places were injudiciously constructed, because of the distance they were placed from the brow of the hill, subjecting the men to heavy fire from the enemy sharpshooters opposite as they advanced or retired from the entrenchments.[53]

True, the defenses were hastily made and far from perfect, but on February 13, they held up against two separate determined assaults. Even Gen. C. F. Smith's divisional attack was held up for a time by a single regiment holding the line on the afternoon of February 15. Fort Donelson was indeed a strong position when it was manned and ready.

In his official report, Floyd also explained his reason for not asking for reinforcements or assistance: He had assumed that General Johnston knew full well that the garrison had no chance of standing up to the invading army, even if the whole force at Bowling Green were present. Thus he supposed the main object of holding Fort Donelson was to buy time for the evacuation of Bowling Green and the safe crossing of the Cumberland by Johnston's army. These arguments are remarkable when remembered in light of how close the Confederates came to total victory. Had some 10,000 more troops been thrown into the assault there is no doubt of the outcome.[54]

There seems to have been no compelling reason to surrender the fort in the morning, except for General Buckner's defeatism. His division was in a good position that was actually on more favorable ground than his initial line. In fact, this position had already repulsed determined attacks by Smith's division at the close of the day. Buckner's men had not entrenched yet, but that task was not impossible. The garrison was in no danger of starving if the quartermasters could get organized. Regiments arrayed in position and resupplied still had a good chance of repelling direct assaults.

It is clear that Simon Bolivar Buckner never supported the idea of any credible defense of Fort Donelson, going there only to remove his troops on February 12. During the fateful council of war on the night of February 14, it was Buckner who made the assumption that the purpose of the assault was to effect a retreat. His attacks on the fifteenth were half-hearted and poorly coordinated, and his delay in launching the assault in order to "keep his men fresh" put the entire operation at serious risk. During the final council of war, Buckner doubled the numbers of Federals opposing him and cut the estimate of his own command nearly in half. He also greatly underestimated the resiliency of his men.[55] In short, throughout the campaign, it was Simon Bolivar Buckner who hamstrung and resisted every attempt to decisively engage the enemy, particularly whenever his old nemesis Gideon Pillow had anything to do with the plan. History remembers Pillow as a petty and vain officer, but it was Buckner who was willing to risk the lives of thousands and allow the Federals to gain the Cumberland with only a token show of resistance. Contempt and hatred toward Pillow most certainly affected Buckner's decision-making abilities, and it cost the South dearly. General Buckner's soldierly conduct in remaining with the army after its surrender has, in the eyes of history, redeemed him from the just censure that belongs to him for his inaction during the day and defeatism during the night of February 15, 1862.

Still, Buckner held only part of the blame for the disaster. It is clear just how little effect Gen. John B. Floyd had on the battle, particularly at its most critical moments. Little is known regarding where Floyd was after riding the line with Pillow and Buckner that morning. He was certainly not communicating with Pillow and Buckner to ensure that the attack was coordinated or acting as an arbiter between the two headstrong brigadiers. When Pillow made his momentous decision, Floyd was not in the area, even though this was obviously the most critical point on the battlefield at that time. Considering the timing, he was either off on the right flank or back in Dover writing the dispatch to Albert Sidney Johnston describing the glorious victory of the day, which was sent around 1:00. Because of Floyd's absence, Pillow was able to order the fateful withdrawal on his own, which was not even noticed by the senior brigadier until it was almost completed. Had General Floyd been directing the fight, he could have prevented the withdrawal in the first place and carried on with the evacuation of the fort if indeed that was the plan. Whatever he decided, both Pillow and Buckner would have been present and in agreement. The operations presumably would have been coordinated and had a set purpose.

John B. Floyd was in way over his head at Fort Donelson, and he probably knew it. When Johnston placed him in command, Floyd initially had only Buckner's timid counsel. After he arrived at Fort Donelson, Floyd still had Buckner, but he also had Pillow's aggressive and often rash advice. His bombastic and confident personality probably was the primary reason deference was paid to Pillow, as well as the fact that Pillow had the rather dubious prior experience of commanding large numbers of troops in battle during the Mexican War. To his credit, Floyd repeatedly called on Albert Sidney Johnston for guidance and even asked for a personal visit to the fort. Each time, General Johnston wired back with irritation that Floyd should see to the defenses as he saw fit. Johnston was just too busy supervising the unopposed withdrawal from Bowling Green to attend to an enemy army knocking down his back door. In the end, Floyd listened first to Buckner's timid counsel, then to Pillow's rash advice, and ended up doing nothing that was right.

The lack of a single strong commander for the Confederates is a central theme for the entire campaign, and the tragedy is that many men of ability were available. Beauregard and Hardee were both competent generals who clearly outranked the four brigadiers at Fort Donelson. Without such a leader, and with Floyd nominally in command, the way was paved for Gideon Pillow to step in to fill the power vacuum.

Without a doubt, though, credit for the successful defense of Fort Donelson and the Confederate attack to clear the Wynn's Ferry Road belongs to Gideon Pillow. He had organized the defenses, seen to the mounting of the heavy cannons, and sent reinforcements and supplies to the threatened bastion. In combat, he was everywhere, directing, prodding, and pushing the men forward. But also without a doubt, he made some highly questionable decisions, which forfeited opportunities the Confederates would later regret.

CHAPTER THIRTEEN

A Disgraceful Surrender

Sunday, February 16, 1862

AFTER LEAVING PILLOW'S RICE HOUSE HEADQUARTERS IN DISGUST, LT. COL. Nathan Bedford Forrest sent for his field and company officers and updated them on the situation. He declared that he would never surrender and would lead forth all who desired to accompany him. All present gave Forrest a unanimous answer that they would follow him out of Fort Donelson. Companies prepared to move at once, and Major Kelley was dispatched to alert Lt. Col. George Gantt of the 9th Tennessee Cavalry Battalion, who was not present. The cavalry encampment was soon stirring with drowsy troopers who had been riding and fighting constantly over the past four days. When they became aware of their plight, they moved with an intense eagerness.[1]

As the cavalrymen saddled up, General Floyd once again summoned their fiery commander. Floyd had arranged with Buckner to escape prior to the surrender, and the only way to get his brigade out at the moment was by the same route Forrest had in mind. Since they were both going in the same direction, Forrest was designated to lead Floyd's old brigade out of Fort Donelson. Meanwhile, the separate regiments were called to assemble near the town of Dover. This task was extremely difficult, as the units of Floyd's command were spread over almost the entire length of the line, and many of the field officers apparently were absent from their units for one reason or another. A few regiments were already out of the trenches and marching in good order to the assault positions on the left wing in preparation of renewing the battle in the morning.

While he was writing the necessary orders, Floyd received word that the steamboats *General Anderson* and *John A. Fisher* were returning and would be at the landing by sunrise. This appeared to be a safer and faster route out of Fort Donelson, so Floyd released Forrest of his escort mission.

During the flurry of activity in headquarters, Capt. Robert M. Hughes of Floyd's staff was awakened from a fitful sleep. He now learned, to his surprise, that a surrender of the garrison was in the works. He later wrote that he believed the Confederates could have beaten the Federals back again in the morning. "Had it been the last instead of the first year of the war, we would have done so."[2] But that was later. At this time, he was directed to gather up the staff and collect the Virginia units and the 20th Mississippi for evacuation.

Gideon Pillow had made good his escape from Fort Donelson some time earlier, but without most of the shenanigans of Floyd or the audacious gallantry of Forrest. Virtually unnoticed, Dr. J. W. Smith, a native of Dover, procured a twelve-foot flatboat from the other side of the river and rowed General Pillow and his staff over to the north bank of the Cumberland. Major Gilmer of the engineers was with the group. The find of this craft was remarkable, for some months back Colonel Heiman had supposedly ordered all small boats in the area disabled to prevent visits to "Lady Peggy" on the opposite shore. On the north side of the Cumberland, Pillow later recovered his horse, baggage, and servant, which were brought over by steamboat. The little column then made its way to Clarksville and subsequently reached Nashville on February 18.

By 4:00 on Sunday morning, February 16, Nathan Bedford Forrest and about 400 men were ready to depart. Gantt and the 9th Tennessee had not yet come up, and Major Kelley was sent for a third time to hasten their arrival. But Gantt and his men responded to each offer in the negative. Two of the Tennessee companies felt differently, though, and cast their lot with Forrest, but two of Forrest's own companies, under the command of Captains James K. Huey and M. D. Wilcox, inexplicably failed to rejoin the regiment. They would never serve with him again. As the gray column passed through Dover, Forrest learned that General Pillow, whom he had expected to escort, had already crossed the Cumberland by boat an hour before. When the column made its way through the camps toward the outer line of pickets, men who were lucky or resourceful enough to find a horse joined with Forrest. Artillerymen unhitched their horses from their limbers and joined the column, which swelled to over 500 men.

Forrest led this column onto the Forge Road with the objective of Cumberland City and then on toward Nashville. Four men were sent forward to reconnoiter and returned after riding three-quarters of a mile with disturbing news: Federal infantry was deployed in a line of battle that was moving around and across the road. Forrest ordered another reconnoiter, but no one volunteered. Turning command over to Major Kelley, Forrest announced his intention to make a reconnaissance himself. If he should be killed, Kelley was to do the best he could to get the men out.

Forrest called for his youngest brother, Lt. Jeffrey Forrest, and rode to the point where the enemy was reported to be. There they scanned the area and listened closely but heard and saw nothing of any hostile force. They advanced farther, and out of the mist and gray atmosphere of that early hour appeared a line of fencing, formidably staked with short rails and somewhat resembling of a line of infantry. Forrest later asserted that it was this very fence, which the scouts mistook for the enemy, that had such weight in producing the capitulation.[3]

After making this important discovery, Forrest and his brother rode ahead and came upon some small fires where a number of Federal wounded had gathered to keep warm. This had been the scene of savage fighting the previous morning, but the wounded men told Forrest that only a few scouts from either side had been among them that night. Thus assured that the road was still open, Forrest returned to the column. The men then made their way to the ford of Lick Creek, just east of Dover, without a shot being fired at them.

Lick Creek on this morning was expanded by swirling backwater to about 100 yards in width. The banks were lined in ice. Calling for someone to test the depth of the water, and again finding no volunteers, Forrest spurred his horse into the icy flow. As he passed entirely across, the elated men saw that the water was no deeper than the saddle skirts. The whole command now crossed over quickly and filed onto the road to Cumberland City. Major Kelley and a detachment stayed at this point to cover the withdrawal. They remained there two hours without seeing any Federal soldiers.

Up the road, Forrest established a slow pace, with advance, rear, and flank guards. The men and horses were exhausted, and he eventually stopped the column at a small village to rest and to reshoe some of the mounts most in need. The column was soon on the march again and was next heard of when it arrived in Nashville.

The cavalry of Fort Donelson had escaped, and the legend of Nathan Bedford Forrest was born.

Major Kelley recalled the flight from Fort Donelson in his later years. He was among many Confederates who believed the garrison could have made good its escape:

I know that in riding out with the cavalry and artillerymen over the frozen ground—many of whom in closing up brought their horses to a gallop, so that the hoof-beats could have been easily heard a mile in the stillness of the night—no Federal gun, even a picket, was heard to break upon their march. Further, the writer paused at day-break within half a mile of the ground occupied by McClernand's headquarters, and remained till 8 o'clock in the morning without seeing or hearing any indicators of the passage of any Federal forces. There was not a captain in the Confederate service at the close of the war, with four year's experience, who would have hesitated in deciding that the army from Fort Donelson could have begun its march at any time from 4 o'clock in the afternoon to midnight without having attracted the notice of the Federal forces, and could have been eight to ten hours in advance before an enemy would have discovered the movement or began in earnest a pursuit.[4]

General Buckner returned to the Dover Hotel and penned a letter of surrender. This message was to be taken by an officer to the nearest picket of the enemy and on to General Grant. The officer was to request where further communication could occur and to inform Grant that his headquarters was in Dover. The dispatch read:

Sir: In consideration of all the circumstances governing the present situation of affairs at this station I propose to the commanding officers of the Federal forces the appointment of commissioners to agree upon terms of capitulation of the forces and post under my command, and in that view suggest an armistice until 12 o'clock today.

I am, very respectfully, your obedient servant
S. B. Buckner
Brigadier General, C.S. Army[5]

General Bushrod Johnson had spent most of the night assembling the brigades of the left wing into their attack positions in preparation to resume the fight at first light. True to form, he was completely oblivious to the proceedings at the Rice house, and was astonished to see McCausland's brigade and other Virginia units suddenly pull out of position and march toward Dover. Learning from a staff officer of Buckner's rise to command, he also found that the new commander wanted to see him immediately. Johnson mounted his horse and rode into the streets of Dover, which were packed with excited and confused soldiers. Arriving at the Dover Hotel, he found that Buckner had just left, but learned what had transpired over the last few hours. An aide instructed General Johnson to return the freezing men to the trenches and send a truce party out to ask the Federals for a cease-fire. As his frozen men shuffled back to their old positions, he and Maj. William E. Rodgers of the 3rd Mississippi rode out of the trenches with an improvised white flag to find the nearest Union general officer, preferably Ulysses S. Grant.[6]

At dawn, the two steamboats arrived at the landing at Dover, returning from their trip to Clarksville. One boat carried a supply of corn, the other supplies and ammunition. There were also 400 additional reinforcements that many reports called "raw troops." The new men were unceremoniously disembarked and most of the cargo dumped into the river to make room for the men of Floyd's Brigade. The regiments had assembled as ordered, but there were stragglers from other units that wanted to get on board also. To prevent a mob from storming the boats, Floyd assigned the 20th Mississippi to form an arc around the landing, with bayonets fixed. Thus his regiments embarked on the steamers in their standard order of march, meaning that the Mississippians planned to board last.[7] It was understood that they would be carried to safety once the Virginia regiments had boarded.

Time was running short for any chance of escape, though. When General Buckner heard that Floyd's command was still within the perimeter, he threatened to blow the steamers out of the water lest he violate the protocols of surrender. Whether he would or even could have done this is debatable, but no one wanted to put him to the test.

As Forrest, Floyd, and Pillow made their escapes, most of the Confederate soldiers in and around Fort Donelson still had no idea of the decision made by their leaders during the night. Private Charles Riddell of Guy's Battery awoke in the early morning and immediately noticed that the trenches in front of his battery were deserted. He and his comrades were informed by his captain that they were to proceed immediately to the wharf at Dover lest they be left behind. Upon his arrival, Riddell found a large assembly of excited soldiers watching a steamer pull from the bank. Many had thrown their weapons into the river to prevent their capture.

Riddell watched as the returning *General Anderson* nosed up to the wharf and a throng pressed forward to get onboard what could be their last chance of escape. Being on the outside edge of the mass of soldiers, Riddell had no hope of making his way through to the gangway. In desperation, he stepped into the freezing swirling waters of the Cumberland and waded to the waiting steamer. Exhausted and near freezing, Riddell was pulled aboard. He procured a cup of whiskey from a barrel, just opened by a bayonet, and took a position by the engines to get warm and dry his clothes.[8]

The boats made enough trips to ferry two Virginia regiments across the river, and then Floyd boarded the *General Anderson* and took a position on the top deck. There he drew his sword and exclaimed, "Come on my brave Virginia boys!" The steamer was soon almost filled to capacity. Apparently Buckner's threat to fire on the loitering boats had not yet caused him alarm, but news that the enemy gunboats *St. Louis* and *Louisville* were sighted steaming up the river surely did. The boat's engineer was immediately ordered to put on a full head of steam and proceed up the river as quickly as possible. Unfortunately for the men of the 20th Mississippi and Floyd's own aide, this act stranded them and condemned them to capture. They would never forgive this act of betrayal. With the perceived threat of a gunboat chasing them down, the *General Anderson* and *John A. Fisher* did not stop until they reached Nashville the next morning.

On the far left of the Union line, the men of Lauman's brigade heard the notes of a bugle advancing from the fort. The instrument announced the arrival of a Confederate officer who bore a message for General Grant. The officer was held on the scene while a courier swiftly made his way to Grant's headquarters.[9]

Earlier that evening, General Grant had sent an orderly with the message "Fort Donelson will surrender in the morning" to the nearest telegraph office. Dr. John H. Brinton of his staff wondered aloud if this was not just a bit premature. "Doctor, they will do it," Grant answered. "They were fighting to get away and now that they have failed, they will surrender. I knew generals Buckner and Pillow in Mexico, and they will do as I have said." With that, Grant crawled into his featherbed in the kitchen of Widow Crisp's house by the fire.

An orderly announcing that Gen. C. F. Smith had arrived on urgent business awakened the commanding general. The gray-haired former instructor entered and made his way to the fire to warm his backside. He handed a parchment to Grant, and as the Union general unfolded the paper, Dr. Brinton poured Smith a drink from his "medicinal" flask. Smith thanked him, then began complaining that he had earlier burned his boots sleeping too close to the fire.

The note Grant read was from Buckner. "What answer shall I send to this general?" "No terms to the damned Rebels!" barked Smith. Grant smiled and wrote out his reply. He took but a few moments, but these few lines would make him a national hero.

> Sir: yours this date, proposing armistice and appointment of com-missioners to settle terms of capitulation is just received. No terms except unconditional and immediate surrender can be accepted. I propose to move immediately upon your works.
>
> I am, very respectfully, your obedient servant,
> U. S. Grant,
> Brigadier General Commanding[10]

Grant passed the note to his former instructor to read. Smith read the passage and snarled, "It's the same thing in smoother words." Grant smiled again and gave it to a messenger for its delivery to General Buckner. Thanks to the press and a play on his initials, Ulysses Simpson Grant would become "Unconditional Surrender" Grant.[11]

Simon Bolivar Buckner never had much stomach for a fight at Fort Donelson, but the movement of regiments off the line during the night and their subsequent return did nothing to improve the fighting posture of the Confederates. Allowing the spiking of the artillery and the escape of the cavalry also greatly diminished the ability of the defenders. While in such a poor state, Buckner was now completely unable to carry on the fight and had forced himself into a position in which he had to accept any terms that Grant proposed, including no terms at all. Stunned and disappointed by the reply from his old friend, all Buckner could do at this point was to send a snippy reply:

> Sir: The distribution of the forces under my command incident to an unexpected change of commanders and the overwhelming force under your command compel me, notwithstanding the brilliant success of the Confederate arms yesterday, to accept the ungener-ous and unchivalrous terms which you propose.
>
> I am, very respectfully, your obedient servant
> S. B. Buckner
> Brigadier General, C.S. Army [12]

General Buckner sent a courier to Col. Cyrus A. Sugg, commander of Fort Donelson proper, with a message to raise a white flag. No one had such a banner, but Ordnance Sgt. R. L. Cobb had a white sheet, which was run up the fort's flagpole at daylight.[13]

Opposite the town of Dover, Gen. Lew Wallace, in command of the 3rd Division, began to wonder when the order to attack would come. In the faint light of sunrise, the Confederate flag flew defiantly over the defenses on his right. His men were ready; they just needed the order to advance and carry the works by storm. Riders came bearing a message, but they were not from General Grant. Instead, two mounted Confederate officers appeared over the breastwork and rode to the picket line carrying a flag of truce. Informed by an aide of their intentions, Wallace mounted his horse to meet them. After stiff and ceremonious introductions, he found the men to be Brig. Gen. Bushrod Johnson and Major Rodgers, who had in their possession a copy of Buckner's proposed cease-fire. Wallace pressed for details. "Do I understand gentlemen that the surrender is perfected?" Johnson replied: " I do not know if a formality will be required, but with that exception it is a surrender. . . . The troops are drawn up in their quarters, arms stacked."[14]

Lew Wallace lost no time on this historic event. He sent the Confederate major on to Grant's headquarters with an additional message: "I am in possession of the fort and all belonging to it." To another aide, he prematurely directed that the brigade commanders prepare to move the whole line forward and take possession of the Confederate defenses. With this business done, the wily Hoosier gave in to an impulse. "General Johnson, I will ride to General Buckner with you. General Buckner and I are personal friends. I have the highest respect for him, and it may be I can do him a good turn." Johnson borrowed the white flag from his associate but was not worried about being shot by the Federals. As for the men in gray, it was a different matter. Johnson said to Wallace, "Our people are in a bad humor; but I will be glad to have you go with me."[15]

General Wallace made his way through the lines and into Dover, coming to the hotel at the landing. Wallace was led down a narrow hallway and was shown to General Buckner, who sat at the head of a table with eight or ten of his officers. The two silently shook hands, and the staff officers cordially did the same. Buckner summoned a simple breakfast for his guest, and the two old friends talked about the war and the battle they had just fought. The Confederate commander was particularly interested in how he and his men were to be treated. Wallace was uncertain, but he did not believe either General Grant or President Lincoln would be vindictive.[16]

Upon receiving Buckner's memorandum accepting his terms, General Grant ordered the entire army to move forward and take possession of the fort, trenches, and the town of Dover. He wanted to get them taken before the Confederates could destroy their weapons, equipment, and supplies or change their minds. Also, and most importantly, Grant wanted to get to Buckner before the navy did. He did not want the navy to upstage him on this operation.

And the navy almost did get ahead of him again. The gunboats *St. Louis* and *Louisville* saw the white flags appear and were steaming upstream as General Floyd made his escape. As Buckner and Wallace talked things over, they were interrupted by a knock at the door. It was a naval officer, resplendent in a dress uniform with gilding and a sword. Stunned that a Federal officer was already there, the intruder stammered an apology for interrupting, spun on his heel and quickly departed. The comical scene was intensified when Buckner said to his guest: "He is not one of ours. I assume he belongs to your Navy." General Wallace replied that he had never seen the man before. Buckner then addressed one of his aides, "You better follow him captain, and see that no harm comes to him." Lew Wallace later recorded that the navy must have been looking for souvenirs of the victory.

Actually, the navy had much more in mind than collecting mere trinkets from the battlefield. Commander Benjamin Dove, skipper of the ironclad *Louisville,* had been sent up to Dover by Foote in order to upstage the army by receiving Buckner's surrender.[17] Unlike events at Fort Henry, though, this time the army did not let the navy get ahead of it. Unfortunately for Commander Dove, the navy brass was upset enough over his tardiness that he was suspended for a short time. Although the display at headquarters was comical, the movement of the gunboats did have the positive effect of halting any further evacuation by the river. Neither ironclad, however, was swift enough to catch the steamers carrying Floyd's men.

When announced that they were surrendered, the Confederate rank and file were greatly surprised, particularly those on the left wing who felt they had not been beaten. Bushrod Johnson, who subsequently lived through the horrors and tribulations of the war, later wrote: "The fatigue, cold, and privation endured by the men were equal to anything I have known; but there was no repining." That is, except at the hard fate of surrendering after such successful fighting the day before.[18] Many other recollections of the veterans of this fight echo these sentiments. When they learned of the events at headquarters and the steamboat landing, their surprise and dismay turned into bitterness and anger toward their senior commanders. Their hatred for Floyd and Pillow was keen, since they felt the generals had deserted them. Buckner earned it for officially surrendering them. The men were completely demoralized and had no further confidence in their leaders.

As General Grant took to hand the business of settling the surrender, the men of his army were awake and alert, but as the sun rose, they still had no orders, which were currently making their way down the chain of command. Most everyone on both sides of the trenches assumed that a Federal assault was planned against the rifle pits, yet no one had given the order to advance. As the men along the line pondered the absence of orders, white flags appeared from the fort and trenches. There then arose, far off from the left, a shout that grew louder and more powerful until it rolled along the entire line. Although Grant's orders were to the contrary, there was no holding back the combined shouts of over 20,000 men in the elation of victory.

When Grant's movement orders arrived, the various regiments and brigades from all over the Midwest advanced from their positions and camps held during the night and occupied the entire length of the Confederate trenches, the town of Dover, and Fort Donelson proper. The 2nd Iowa was given the honor of leading General Smith's column, marching with colors flying and the regimental band playing.[19] Once inside, the men stacked arms and took in the scenes around them. A clear sky and a warm sun began to melt the snow, increasing the depth of the universal red mud, which was over knee-deep in many places. Everywhere were lying fragments of shells and round shot, half buried in the frozen ground. Tents were torn to pieces, gun carriages broken, and blood scattered about. Deserted wagons, with living and dead mules attached, were mired in the roads. In the valleys and fields, the dead of both armies were strewn across the ground where they had fallen. The wounded men lay intermingled with the dead, many having lain there for over twenty-four hours. The raging battle had prevented the recovery of the dead and wounded, but work details were now busy caring for them.[20]

The national flag was soon flying from Fort Donelson and over the courthouse in Dover. Meanwhile, Grant ordered that all prisoners be rounded up and collected as rapidly as possible. They were to receive two days' rations in preparation for their transport to Cairo and were allowed to keep their clothing, blankets, and such private property as may be carried on their person. Officers were even allowed to keep their side arms.[21]

The Confederate soldiers of Fort Donelson were dejected, exhausted, hungry, cold, and wet. Their clothing was thin and ragged, and many were without hats. The colors of gray and butternut were dominant, but virtually every color of apparel was seen. For blankets, they carried an assortment of homespun material pieces or carpet; a few even carried featherbeds across their backs. The men of the South stacked their arms without complaint but objected to giving up their pistols and knives. By the proclamation of General Grant, the enlisted men were allowed to keep their private property, but the knives in question were mostly homemade affairs, some over eighteen inches long and looking just as deadly as their owners. Claiming that they were part of their general apparel, the men were initially allowed to keep them. It did not take long for this order to be countermanded as some of the unruly prisoners began using their knives on their guards. But most of the Confederate soldiers simply huddled together waiting to be officially counted on the rolls and issued the two days' rations.[22]

An interesting story passed down through the years illustrates just how high emotions were running that morning. A Federal staff officer approached the trenches occupied by Baldwin's Brigade and was shown to the quarters of Col. John C. Brown, temporarily in command. Meeting the commander, the staff officer announced that he had been sent forward by General Grant and would return with him shortly. Arriving in short order, Grant greeted the Confederate brigade commander: "Colonel Brown, it gives me great pleasure to take by the hand an officer who has made such a gallant defense."

After a few minutes, Grant's party passed on toward Dover, leaving Colonel Brown standing before his tent. As he turned, the colonel saw approaching a Confederate lieutenant mounted upon a splendid horse and riding at breakneck speed. His hat was drawn tightly down, and a full-size "navy six" was particularly noticeable in his right hand. Colonel Brown seized the horse's bridle and asked, "Where are you going sir?"

"To shoot that damned Yankee officer, and now let loose my bridle or I'll shoot you." After a brief exchange, Brown drew his own pistol and aimed it at the lieutenant, commanding "Drop that pistol." The lieutenant hesitated and then did just that. Ordered to dismount, the young officer was taken away safely under guard. Unaware of the incident, General Grant probably never knew how close he had come to death that day.[23]

Grant made his way through the trenches and to the Dover Hotel, where he met Lew Wallace and the captured Simon Buckner. He took temporary possession of the first floor as his headquarters. Most accounts of the meeting and days afterward tell of General Buckner being quite chivalrous and polite, giving rise to the esteem felt toward him in years to come, but the perception was not universal. Colonel Charles Whittlesey of the 20th Ohio felt differently after an encounter later in the morning. "On our arrival at the Confederate headquarters we found General Buckner and his staff. With two exceptions, their officers were courteous, endeavoring to make the best of their situation. The exceptions were General Buckner and a lieutenant of his staff, whom it soon became necessary to snub." It must be remembered that emotions were still very high among the exhausted and defeated Confederates.

With the formal surrender executed, the two commanders talked of the battle. In the course of the conversation, which was very friendly, Buckner said to Grant that had he been in command, he would have made it far more difficult to be surrounded. Grant replied that had Buckner been in command, he would not have tried it the way he did. Grant asked his old friend how many men he had. Buckner replied that in the chaotic state things were in, he could not be certain, but there could not be less than 12,000 and no more than 15,000. Buckner also asked for permission to send out parties to collect and bury the dead, to which Grant immediately agreed. In a short time, Confederates were freely passing to and fro between the lines, and many took the opportunity to escape.[24]

When the meeting was over, Grant pulled his old friend aside to return a favor done some eight years earlier when life gave him a hard knock. "Buckner, you are, I know, separated from your people, and perhaps you need funds; my purse is at your disposal." Buckner thanked him for his thoughtfulness but politely declined.[25]

Ironically, as Buckner was entertaining Grant at his former headquarters, Richmond received a telegram Albert Sidney Johnston had sent at midnight the previous night: "We have had to-day at Fort Donelson one of the most sanguinary conflicts of the war. Our forces attacked the enemy with energy and won a brilliant victory. I have the satisfaction to transmit the dispatch after nightfall, of General Floyd, who was in command of our forces."[26]

As President Davis read these telegrams, Johnston was reading Floyd's far more current and accurate dispatches. Undoubtedly it was a painful and humiliating task to forward them and a retraction on to Richmond.

It is difficult to arrive at a precise number of Federal soldiers who fought at Fort Donelson. Reinforcements came in at a rapid rate and were committed to battle in extreme haste. Grant may have had up to 27,000 by the late afternoon of February 16, but only about 22,000 were on the field to see action. Casualties were heavy for this phase of the war, numbering approximately 500 killed, 2,000 wounded, and 200 missing.

Accurate numbers of Confederates at Fort Donelson are lost to history, if they were ever known. Regiments arriving at Fort Donelson were already reduced in number by the sick and lame who had been left behind in cities like Clarksville and Nashville. Records were incomplete or nonexistent in the rush to prepare for deployment to Fort Donelson and during the subsequent battle. After the surrender, Buckner submitted a list to Grant containing a little over 9,000 names. This list was compiled in great haste, as units were scattered over the battlefield, and it was wildly inaccurate by Buckner's own admission. It is widely accepted that there were approximately 21,000 Confederate troops within the works during the battle. About 300 were killed and 1,200 wounded. By noon on February 16, over 12,000 soldiers of the Fort Donelson garrison surrendered unconditionally to the Union forces.[27] The balance of the forces made their escape with Floyd or Forrest's cavalry or simply walked through the Union lines during the hours of confusion after the surrender. Few units did not have at least a handful of soldiers who failed to take an opportunity to flee. For further confirmation of this higher number of captives, 14,623 rations were issued to the Confederate prisoners at Cairo on their way to Northern prison camps.[28]

The amount of munitions, logistics, and booty taken was also immense and beyond the capabilities of General Grant and his staff to control. He issued orders against plundering from the inhabitants or stealing property taken in battle, but the temptation for many was too great.

Over 20,000 stands of arms of all types were stacked up along River Street in Dover. This did not include the weapons thrown into the river by their owners to prevent capture. Men detailed from the gunboat crews later fished these out of the water. Of the sixty-five captured artillery pieces that had not been spiked, most were generally new and in good order. Over 1,200 boxes of beef and a large amount of other provisions also were piled up near the docks.[29] There was such abundance of material that many of the weapons and slabs of beef were strewn across the roads of bottomless mud to form a causeway over which the troops and wagons moved. Grant's precarious supply situation was over for the moment.

The Confederates had also thrown most of the mail into the river to prevent its capture. Colonel A. H. Markland, Grant's postal director, succeeded in snagging a number of mailbags and went through their contents. He kept some letters supposed to contain important military information.[30]

As the initial excitement died down, General Grant began the process of evacuating the Confederate prisoners and consolidating his command. In the next two days, all but about 250 Confederates were loaded onto the steamboats and sent to the North. This group was held for a time at Fort Donelson to exchange for a like number of Federal prisoners that were shipped out by General Floyd in the late hours of February 15.[31] The divisions and brigades were also assigned sectors of the old defenses, and General Wallace was ordered in the afternoon to return with his division to Fort Henry.

Grant's army began preparing for its next push, and the navy wasn't idle either. Foote dispatched an ironclad to ascend the Tennessee, and a detail of men burned the Tennessee Rolling Mills. These works had been used by the Confederates to manufacture shot, shell, and other war materiel. The way to the heart of the Confederacy was laid bare, and Grant and Foote wanted to press on. Grant wrote to Halleck, "I am proud to inform the department commander of our success at Fort Donelson, and that the way was now open to Clarksville and Nashville, and that unless I receive orders to the contrary I should take Clarksville on the 21st [of February], and Nashville about the first of March."[32]

In St. Louis, Halleck had not yet heard of the victory and was worried about a possible counterattack. He wrote to General McClellan in Washington:

> It is said that Beauregard is preparing to move from Columbus either on Paducah or Fort Henry. Do send me more troops. It is the crisis of the war in the West. Have you fully considered the advantage that the Cumberland River affords the enemy at Nashville? An immense number of boats have been collected, and the whole Bowling Green force can come down in a day, attack Grant in the rear, and return to Nashville before Buell can get halfway there. . . . I must stop the transports at Cairo to observe Beauregard. We are certainly in peril.[33]

When the glorious news arrived, Henry Halleck did not miss a beat as he changed his tune. "Make Buell, Grant, and Pope major-generals of volunteers, and give me command in the West. I ask this in return for Donelson and Henry."[34] Promotions were quickly approved over the next few weeks, but command in the West would have to wait for the moment.

Even in victory, Halleck was not through trying to usurp Grant. He added: "Make General Smith major general. He by his coolness and bravery when the battle was against us, turned the tide and carried the enemy works." Had Halleck been successful, Smith would have been senior to Grant. And even two days after the victory, he continued to ask Buell to come over to the Cumberland and assume command of the operation. On February 19, Halleck also believed Maj. Gen. Ethan Allen Hitchcock was on his way and told McClellan of his plans to place him in command at Dover.[35]

Happily for Ulysses S. Grant, he had just earned the respect and thanks of Abraham Lincoln by being the first general to make a major advance in the West and, more importantly, the first to win a significant victory for the Union. General Grant had led the Fort Henry–Fort Donelson campaign, and it was he who was recognized first. The President immediately submitted Grant's name to the Senate, which unanimously endorsed his promotion to major general on February 19, giving him clear seniority to Buell, Sherman, and the brigadiers of Fort Donelson. These other gentlemen would also receive their own promotions and increased commands in the days and weeks to come, but "Unconditional Surrender" Grant became the national hero of the day.

By noon of February 17, the bulk of Confederate prisoners and the meager guard of the 20th Ohio were on board steamboats destined for prison camps scattered across the North. The field officers were sent to Fort Warren in Boston Harbor, and the company officers were incarcerated at Johnson's Island in Lake Erie. The enlisted men were sent to Camp Morton, near Indianapolis; Camp Butler, near Springfield, Illinois; or Camp Douglas, near Chicago.

Curiously, Gen. Bushrod Johnson was not among them, essentially having been forgotten again by friend and foe alike. After the surrender, Johnson did not indulge in any of the social mixing with the enemy that was so common. He avoided Grant, whom he had known at West Point and during the Mexican War. He also shunned C. F. Smith, his former instructor. For three days at Fort Donelson, he watched the soldiers and officers loaded onto steamers and shipped north. By February 18, all of the men he had led in battle were on their way to prison, and he reasoned he "could not be of any more service to them." Near sunset, Johnson and Capt. John H. Anderson of the 10th Tennessee walked from Heiman's old trenches and kept going. No Federal pickets challenged them, and they eventually obtained horses and reached Nashville. For the next few weeks, Johnson had to explain his violation of his parole of honor and wrote of his desire for an investigation to clear his name, but in the crisis of the times, nothing official ever came of this misdeed. Johnson would serve again under Simon Bolivar Buckner, who often praised his service. His receipt of a serious wound at Shiloh on April 6 may also have curtailed any further mention of the incident.[36] Johnson would survive the war, enduring the hell of trench warfare again at Petersburg.

When General Pillow arrived in Nashville, he sought out Albert Sidney Johnston for a new command. In this he was refused, for there were no commands to give. He was told instead to complete his official report of the disaster at Fort Donelson. Over the next ten months, Gideon Pillow waged a long and bitter campaign to clear his name and for reinstatement of command. He would eventually get a small command and finish the war as a brigadier general, but he was forever linked to the disaster at Fort Donelson.

General John B. Floyd made good his escape to Clarksville and proceeded on to Nashville. After a brief meeting with Albert Sidney Johnston, he was given the task of supervising the withdrawal of all the military stores from the city warehouses. The people of Nashville were becoming agitated and called for the distribution of the government supplies stored there. As Johnston led the bulk of the army south to Murfreesboro, General Floyd was left to deal with the explosive situation, with the added threat of an approaching enemy army or the arrival of gunboats. Not surprisingly, under his dubious supervision, the whole operation broke down and mobs began looting the warehouses.

Nathan Bedford Forrest's cavalry column rode into Nashville on February 18 and found the city in a panic. Most of Johnston's army was gone, and the enemy was expected to arrive at any minute. The city was utterly defenseless. People and vehicles of every description crammed onto the roads. Other citizens boarded the remaining trains heading south. Forrest came upon General Floyd, who promptly passed the responsibility for the safety and transport of government supplies to him and left town. Forrest characteristically set upon the given task with determination. He organized the movement of government property and brought the mobs under control. Through his determined and at times ruthless actions, he was able to save large quantities of war materiel and machinery from Nashville.

As the Confederate army marched southward, Floyd found time to write his account of the battle. Richmond wanted answers and wanted them now. He had some explaining to do and knew his career was on the line. In his report, Floyd laid a great deal of praise on the fighting ability of the Southern soldier. He also praised the actions of both Pillow and Buckner, downplaying the despondency of the latter on the night of February 15. The War Department promptly rejected this and other reports as unacceptable. It seems that Floyd could not adequately justify why he had decided to surrender the fort, flee for his own safety, and take only his Virginia brigade along. After several months, though, Floyd apparently had cleared his name enough to return to active duty. He was given command of the Virginia State Line but died of disease on August 26, 1863.

As Albert Sidney Johnston and his little army fell back from Nashville to Murfreesboro without even a show of resistance, the Union armies were now advancing on the Tennessee capital. Energized by the fear of being eclipsed by Grant and Halleck, General Buell picked up the pace and finally reached Nashville on February 24. He arrived to find that the city was already occupied by the troops he had sent by boat to reinforce Grant after the fall of Fort Henry.

Since Grant did not hear from Halleck or headquarters to refrain from taking Nashville, he acted. On February 19, a detachment under Gen. C. F. Smith, escorted by the gunboats *Cairo* and *Conestoga,* ascended the river to Clarksville. There they found the scanty defenses abandoned and the bridges burned, and they occupied the city on February 22. General Grant later lamented that he should have sent troops on up to Nashville, but his transport was then limited by the requirement to send prisoners up north.[37]

Nelson's division from Buell's army finally arrived at Dover a week after the surrender. Wanting to return the unit to Buell and also take Nashville, Grant forwarded it on up the Cumberland, and it occupied that city just hours before Buell's arrival. Grant himself went to Nashville the next day, where he had an icy meeting with the usurped Don Carlos Buell. Buell thought Nashville was in imminent danger, but Grant correctly disagreed. The fighting was only a minor rear-guard action north of Murfreesboro. Buell also felt that Grant was intruding into his department and no doubt lodged a complaint with Halleck afterward.

Meanwhile, General Halleck complained to McClellan that he had not heard from Grant in more than a week, charging that he had left his command without permission and gone to Nashville. The army at Fort Donelson was supposedly demoralized, though it actually was still euphoric after its decisive victory. Based on the tone and severity of Halleck's telegram, General McClellan authorized the arrest and replacement of Grant for the good of the service if he felt the need. In less than three weeks, Grant went from national hero to under virtual arrest and relief of command. The first Grant knew that there was trouble was when he received the letter of his removal on March 2. Two days later, Halleck added fuel to the fire by claiming that general had "resumed his former bad habits" of drinking.

President Lincoln in a short time found out that his winning general was being shelved by political maneuverings. The adjutant general's office wrote to General Halleck on his behalf:

> It has been reported that soon after the battle of Fort Donelson Brigadier-General Grant left his command without leave. By direction of the President the Secretary of War desires you to ascertain and report whether General Grant left his command at any time without proper authority, and, if so, for how long; whether he has

made to you proper reports and returns for his force; whether he has committed any acts which were unauthorized or not in accordance with military subordination or propriety, and if so, what.[38]

Henry Halleck now had to submit hard evidence or drop the matter. By now he knew that the lack of communication between him and Grant was due to a telegraph operator with Confederate sympathies and Halleck's own chief of staff not forwarding Grant's reports from Fort Donelson. Also, a glance at a map confirmed that Nashville was indeed on the western bank of the river, and thus technically in Grant's department. Halleck had gone too far, and he knew it. He quickly restored Grant to command on March 13 and sent a dispatch to Washington exonerating his subordinate from all charges. He then forwarded a copy of this message to Grant but neglected to tell him that it was his own telegrams that had created all of the trouble in the first place. "Instead of relieving you, I wish you, as soon as your new army is in the field, to assume immediate command, and lead it to new victories."[39]

By this time, General Buell had some 50,000 men at Nashville, and the newly named Army of the Tennessee was reinforced to about 40,000 at Fort Henry and Fort Donelson. Once again, though, overestimations of Confederate strength slowed the advance of the Union armies, as Halleck and Buell spent the next several weeks consolidating and planning strategy, handing the initiative to the Confederates. Grant had no input in these matters; for much of this time, he was relieved of command. By the time he returned, the next phase of operations had already been decided upon.

As for Albert Sidney Johnston, the Fort Donelson disaster certainly knocked him further off balance. In Murfreesboro, he could hardly muster more than 20,000 men. The fortifications around Columbus were abandoned by now, and he had no thought of making any offensive movements in the department—at least, not yet. What Johnston was looking for was a place to regroup and make a stand. He found that place in Corinth, Mississippi. Calling all available troops to that rail center, Johnston would look for a time and place to strike. Perhaps with a bold stroke he could yet restore the defenses in the West.

In summary, the fact that Nathan Bedford Forrest had been able to escape Fort Donelson unscathed makes it clear that Federal forces were not positioned to block such a movement. General Lew Wallace had occupied his sector as darkness approached and had not been able to reconnoiter. Because of this, he was not familiar with the local terrain. As the sun rose on Sunday morning, he spotted the white flags of surrender where the outer trenches cut across the Wynn's Ferry Road. This meant Wallace was positioned more to the center of the Confederate line, not to the far left.[40] In defense of Wallace, his mission that evening was to prepare to resume the assault in the morning. To do this, he naturally massed his soldiers against a narrow sector of the line, not spreading them out to cover a large area. But unfortunately for the Confederates, by the time Forrest confirmed that the road to freedom was clear, it was too late to change the course of events.

Grant's "unconditional" surrender terms actually turned out to be quite magnanimous. That officers were able to retain their sidearms and soldiers their personal property were very lenient provisions and became a trademark of Grant throughout the war. Security of the prisoners was very lax, allowing many of them to escape. The effect of this in providing manpower to the South was minimal, however, since the numbers were not exorbitant and men escaped as individuals and not units. The escapees also carried word of their good treatment to their homes and to any unit they were later attached to. Confederates did indeed learn that they would be well treated by Grant if they surrendered to him. This was to be seen again, and on large scales, after Vicksburg and finally at Appomattox Court House.

Grant's army subsisted on the stores captured at Fort Donelson for several days. This showed that the Confederates, in considering whether to surrender the fort, did not need to fear starvation in the short term. An extensive effort, however, would have been required to move the supplies from the landing to the troops in need.

Only after the campaign did the fractures in the Union high command negatively affect the operations on the Cumberland. This was due to the slow methods of communication and the secret and conspiratorial nature of many of the messages. By the time most of Halleck's micromanaging dispatches arrived, they generally had already been overcome by events or were impossible to carry out. Also, Grant was oblivious to the danger of being relieved of command and thus could simply focus on the task at hand.

CHAPTER FOURTEEN

The Final Analysis

THE FALL OF THE TWO FORTS SENT WAVES OF SHOCK ACROSS THE SOUTH, the reaction comparable to the North's after the debacle at Bull Run. For the Confederates, the loss of this campaign was not only a tactical disaster, but a strategic one as well. In one stroke, the vital city of Nashville and most of Tennessee, including its iron deposits, were lost forever. Albert Sidney Johnston also lost an entire army and gave up two rivers upon which the enemy would advance into the heart of the Confederacy. The South would never recover from this disaster. The war in the West was on a slow and agonizing path from which it would not deviate until the final collapse of the South.

The Fort Henry–Fort Donelson campaign provides a unique and interesting insight into a breakdown in command. In the course of the war, there was no other parallel of such incompetence and incapacity. The campaign was lost not by the defeat of a Confederate army, but through its mismanagement and surrender by blundering leaders while it still had the will and the means to fight.

The merits of the Confederate objective of holding as much territory as possible instead of using tactics similar to those of Washington during the Revolution are arguable points. In truth, Jefferson Davis could not afford to lose territory if he were to maintain an independent nation and its institution of slavery. The strategy of holding all ground was a necessity for the South, and generals such as Albert Sidney Johnston were charged to conduct their operations in compliance with it. Johnston's reliance on fortifications along likely avenues of approach was necessary for such a static defense. Several major mistakes were made, however, for which Johnston or his immediate subordinates were ultimately responsible.

The first mistakes by the Confederate command were in the placement and design of the forts guarding the Tennessee and Cumberland Rivers, and the low priority given them. Unlike the forts along the Mississippi, neither Fort Henry nor Fort Donelson was assigned a dedicated engineer officer to oversee construction until late October 1861. This was not because none was available. General Polk had three engineer officers at Columbus alone and held them there even when the fortifications were all but complete.[1] Fort Donelson did not suffer as much as Fort Henry, since the high bluff along the river and the flooded creeks on the landward side provided some natural defense. After deciding to rely on the deficient Fort Henry to hold the Tennessee, the Confederates then made no serious attempt to fortify any other point of the river. There were no secondary or subsequent defenses along the length of the river to slow an enemy if the fort fell. The same was true in relying on Fort Donelson to hold the Cumberland: The Confederates made no substantial effort to fortify Clarksville, Nashville, or any other point on the river. When these two forts fell, Foote's gunboats had free passage up to the heads of navigation.

The key mistake of the engineers was the placement of Fort Henry. Located at it was on the floodplain, no amount of work would have made it tenable. Building began in the summer, when the waters were low, and the engineers obviously failed to take into account the winter floods. It is generally agreed that few people were expecting a long war at that point, but certainly a structure that took so much effort should have been placed in position to be in service throughout the year. In spite of the reports of its inadequacy, General Polk and later General Johnston ordered work on the fort continued, instead of building one elsewhere. Fort Heiman was ordered built in November, but it was not a replacement for Fort Henry, just a supplement. In the end, Fort Henry was defeated just as much by the Tennessee River as by ironclad gunboats. Yet, had it been formidable, the possibilities become interesting. Eight thousand additional men were sent to Fort Donelson between February 7 and 14, and more were on the way at the time of surrender. Had Grant been required to lay siege to Fort Henry, a reinforced garrison at Fort Donelson would have been a serious threat to his rear. Perhaps Grant would have had to wait additional weeks for reinforcements or have been defeated at Fort Henry.

Despite the location and construction of the forts, the Confederate soldiers accounted for themselves in an extraordinary manner. Outmanned and outgunned by a mixed array of experienced and novice troops, the garrisons of both forts did extremely well. The ninety men of Fort Henry were able to severely damage the ironclad flotilla even while the floodwaters were flowing into the gun embrasures. The ill-trained and poorly armed force at Fort Donelson pushed Grant's army to the brink of a rout on the magnitude of Bull Run. So if the Confederate soldiers were able to overcome the odds, what kept the victory from them? Again, it was the Confederate command, namely Albert Sidney Johnston.

When General Johnston assumed command of the Western Department in September 1861, he had but five months to prepare for Grant's offensive. It was a daunting task, and he used considerable energy in procuring arms, supplies, and troops from the individual states in his command as well as appealing directly to Richmond. He had to be a soldier, diplomat, and politician to raise the army he needed to defend his department.

Jefferson Davis also gave Johnston a great deal of discretion on where to locate his headquarters. For some unfathomable reason, he chose Bowling Green, which was actually the front line, instead of a more central location. As a department commander, it was Johnston's job to coordinate its defense with the states' governors and secure arms and equipment from widely scattered sources. A central location is highly desirable to facilitate this. Locating the headquarters on the periphery of the department reduced Johnston's ability to coordinate his defenses by extending the distances needed to travel or communicate. More telling, in Bowling Green, Johnston's attention and priorities became fixed on the situation to his immediate front. He then tended to act more as a mere army commander than a department commander.

General Johnston received a number of conflicting reports on the state of affairs at the two forts. Many were quite accurate in pointing out the deficiencies in labor, materials, ordnance, and placement. Notable exceptions, particularly one by Senator Henry, stated that Fort Henry was a strong position, ready to repel the invader.[2] Like all general officers, Johnston had a full schedule, and he never found the time to inspect these key positions. He did send subordinates to collect information for him from time to time, but when the crisis began, he had no personal knowledge of either fort. This lack of knowledge forced him to rely on the officers at the scene to accurately report their status and recommend courses of action. Johnston's lack of firsthand knowledge is evident. For example, he did not learn that construction of Fort Heiman had not begun until two months after he issued orders to do so. He also believed Fort Henry was a stronger position than Fort Donelson.[3]

In an era when commanders had to totally rely upon the good judgment of subordinates to make sound decisions at great distances from headquarters, Albert Sidney Johnston erred badly in his selection of subordinate commanders. Considering the officers he sent to the forts, reliance on their input was asking for disaster. The first general officer to command the forts was Lloyd Tilghman. Interestingly enough, he was not Johnston's first choice; that was a Maj. A. P. Stewart, whose selection was not approved by the War Department. Until reminded by the secretary of war, Johnston apparently had forgotten or was not aware that Tilghman was in his command.[4] Yet he entrusted this man to prepare the twin river defenses without benefit of a direct meeting or subsequent command inspection. Furthermore, Johnston continued a command climate in which whatever senior officer just happened to be present would be in command. When Tilghman was captured, Johnston again followed this precedent. The man who happened to have seniority of rank as a brigadier on the Cumberland was now the incompetent John B. Floyd.

In January 1862, Johnston had a number of other generals under his immediate control available to command the forces at Forts Henry and Donelson. Most notable was the "Hero of Fort Sumter" himself, P. G. T. Beauregard. As a full general, he was clearly senior to the brigadiers who had commanded there in rapid succession. He was an experienced engineer who could have applied his talents well. Beauregard also had the faith and trust of the Southern people, and the soldiers held him in high esteem. But Beauregard was suffering from a chronic throat ailment and declined command of Fort Donelson, citing that he could not effectively lead in such a condition. It did not prevent him from accepting command of Columbus a few days later, however. Perhaps he, too, felt the fort could not stand up to the ironclads. If so, he probably wanted no part in what he perceived was a no-win scenario.

Another distinguished officer was William J. Hardee, technically commanding the army at Bowling Green. Hardee was a West Point graduate who had served with distinction in the Mexican War. He was respected and widely read. He had, in fact, revised and updated the U.S. Army's tactics manual after the Mexican War, a work held as the standard for the current conflict. As a major general, Hardee was also clearly senior to the brigadiers at Donelson.[5] Johnston could have led the retrograde from Bowling Green himself, as he did, or given this fairly simple task to the senior remaining general officer. Either way, both of these distinguished general officers were not needed at Bowling Green.

As it happened, General Johnston simply sent as many forces as he could spare toward Fort Donelson and left it up to the senior man on the scene to worry about how to use them. And unfortunately that man was John B. Floyd. General Floyd proved easy to manipulate, first by Buckner at

Cumberland City, and then by Pillow at Fort Donelson. In fairness, Johnston may not have known of this weakness, since there was not enough time for this characteristic to have been exposed in the weeks prior to the assignment. Johnston may have known little about the military abilities of Floyd, but incoming telegrams did little to inspire faith. General Floyd often contradicted himself, and the dispatches found in the *Official Records* show a man who was anything but confident. Yet even on the eve of battle, when Johnston appeared to have lost faith in Floyd, he did nothing to alleviate the command situation.

Alongside General Floyd was the dominant and often insubordinate Gideon Pillow. Johnston at the very least knew Pillow by reputation and had dealt with him when the latter commanded briefly at Columbus. However, General Pillow stands as the unlikely hero of the campaign on the Confederate side. After Fort Henry's fall, he consistently saw Fort Donelson as the place to defend Nashville and possibly inflict a defeat on the invader. For fleeting moments, Albert Sidney Johnston also saw this, but his actions never matched his rhetoric. As the commander of the depot at Clarksville, it was Pillow who sent ammunition, supplies, and every unit he could find to the endangered Fort Donelson. Upon his arrival there, he tirelessly organized the defenses down to the smallest detail. If it were not for Pillow, no credible defense of Fort Donelson would have been possible.

Obviously, Pillow had his faults. He had no formal military training and, often arrogant, was prone to insubordination and going over the head of his commander. In the months leading up to the campaign, he had thrown away what little credibility he had in clamoring for various offensives and other schemes. He also lacked judgment at some critical moments. The abortive attack on the fourteenth and the decision to withdraw all the way back into the trenches on the fifteenth are but two examples. During the fateful council of war, Pillow gave a poor operations briefing whose lack of clarity and detail directly resulted in confusion and delay. In fairness to Pillow, General Floyd, as the senior officer, was the one responsible for ensuring that all of the subordinate commanders understood the mission. General Buckner was a West Point graduate and had considerable experience. He, too, could have positively contributed to the critical meeting.

What magnified the inadequacies of the brigadiers at Fort Donelson was the bitter personal feud between Gideon Pillow and Simon Bolivar Buckner. This feud was virtually known to all, and it is hard to believe that Johnston thought they would be able to put their personal feelings aside. It is also difficult to believe that Johnston thought Floyd was capable of dealing with such an explosive situation. The bitterness between the two caused friction and resulted in enough vacillation and hesitation during key times to have cost the battle.

General Buckner most certainly became an acquaintance of Albert Sidney Johnston during his months in Bowling Green. Although many see Buckner as the most proficient of the brigadiers at Fort Donelson, he had a reputation for being slow and deliberate in making decisions. And Buckner's hostility toward Pillow affected his decision-making abilities at the expense of his men and country. The first incident of this occurred on February 12, as Buckner persuaded Floyd to allow the removal of troops to Cumberland City, leaving Pillow and the Fort Donelson garrison to their fate. As Grant's army approached Fort Donelson, Pillow was compelled to leave the fort to settle the matter. Just when a determined commander was needed to prevent an uncontested investment, Pillow was fifteen miles upstream. Meanwhile, General Buckner made no effort to improve the defenses or hinder the enemy advance, since his only interest in the fort was in getting his own men out. Throughout the morning of February 15, it was Buckner who hesitated to attack, allowing Pillow's assault to culminate. This hesitation quite possibly prevented the Confederates from routing and maybe even destroying Grant's army. Finally, it was Buckner's infectious defeatism late that evening that convinced Floyd and Pillow that they should surrender, even though there were options to escape or even renew the fighting. Buckner's arguments that his troops were too exhausted to fight or unable to march toward Nashville were weak at best. If he truly believed them, he had no appreciation of just how tough Confederate soldiers could be. Seen by many historians today as a chivalrous hero, Buckner was in fact far from it. His hostility toward Pillow, poor battlefield performance, and low morale were key factors in the debacle at Fort Donelson.

No one can envy the position of any of the brigadiers at Fort Donelson. None of them had a good opportunity to see the terrain, guidance from above was vague, and the size and composition of the enemy were essentially unknown. Fort Donelson had had a long string of commanders, and the units forming the garrison had never fought together or had time to gain confidence in their commanders. The Confederates were in a precarious position, but they had chances to stave off disaster and attain victory.

The Confederate command did not suffer only from the highly individualistic and temperamental personalities of the general officers and the lack of a common vision. The senior commanders also quite simply became shaken by the use of a relatively new technology. The introduction of ironclad gunboats dated back to the Crimean War, but this was their first appearance in North America. When Fort Henry fell to a purely gunboat attack in but two hours, General Johnston himself became convinced that Fort Donelson had no hope of standing up to them. From that point, it seems that Johnston lost his will to put up a determined resistance. Had Johnston seen for himself just how poorly Fort Henry was constructed, he would have realized that its fall was not due simply to the ironclads, and that though they were powerful, they were not invincible. Surprisingly, Johnston's outlook did not appreciably improve with the repulse of the ironclads on February 14.

Of the Confederate commanders involved, it is Albert Sidney Johnston who deserves the harshest criticisms. As department commander, it was he who was given the task and responsibility of establishing the Confederate defenses in the West. Although the placements of Fort Henry and Fort Donelson were decided before he took command, he was negligent in their construction and manning. He also allowed for no strategic reserves in the theater, since all available troops were sent to the forward strongpoints.

In positioning himself at Bowling Green, Johnston lost the ability to act as a department commander, becoming fixated on the threat of Buell's army moving south from Louisville. Although this was a possibility, Buell showed few signs of making any serious movement until after the evacuation of Bowling Green. Events showed that Grant's army was the most immediate threat during the winter months. But with his attention focused on Bowling Green, Johnston did not develop a coherent strategy for the defense of his department, nor did he adequately share his views with his subordinate commanders. When the defenses began to crumble, his actions and decisions were of an *ad hoc* nature, leaving his officers confused and unsure.

With the benefit of hindsight, it seems clear that the Confederacy's best chance of defeating Grant was at Fort Donelson, not at Cumberland City or anywhere else south of the Tennessee border.[6] Gideon Pillow saw this, and for once he was right. Grant gave opportunities to the Confederates to defeat him, but they were missed or not taken. The Confederates might have made a determined attack on the Federals as they were strung out along the twelve miles of road between Fort Henry and Fort Donelson. Grant would never be weaker than during this campaign, for later Lew Wallace's division and elements of Buell's army would reinforce him. Grant himself later wrote: "[Johnston] should have left Nashville with a small garrison under a trusty officer, and with the remainder of his force gone to Donelson himself. If he had been captured the result could not have been worse than it was."[7]

With the defeat of the gunboats on the fourteenth, the Confederates had other options they chose to ignore. The river and rail transportation network was still intact to Bowling Green and Nashville. Johnston could have brought up more reinforcements for a decisive battle with Grant. Hardee was moving south from Bowling Green with about 14,000 men. Had they been added to Fort Donelson or struck the flank and rear of Grant's battered army, there was a good chance for its defeat. With that, General Buell most certainly would have retreated back to the Ohio River, and Tennessee would have been saved for the South.[8] But this option proved too bold for Albert Sidney Johnston, who then lost it all.

Ulysses S. Grant, on the other hand, was a bold commander, almost to the point of recklessness. At the beginning of this campaign, he landed a petty force of about 15,000 in the midst of nearly 45,000 enemy soldiers who could have massed against him. After the fall of Fort Henry, Grant moved his army up against a fortress that he thought may have had more men than he did. Trusting his instincts and his disdain for Pillow and Floyd, he continued his investment of the fort, hoping that the men he had and any reinforcements that happened to come up would be enough to contain the garrison.

Grant's superior, Gen. Henry Halleck, also contrasted with his counterpart. Unlike Johnston, Halleck was in constant communication with his subordinates in the field, not only receiving reports, but also giving his thoughts and strategies. Grant was bombarded with new and sometimes impossible tasks, but he knew what Halleck wanted as a measure of success. Halleck was not infallible, though, and missed some opportunities as well. Even with the Confederates reeling from the defeat, he did not quickly follow up his victory. Grant described it so in his memoirs:

> My opinion was, and still is, that immediately after the fall of Fort Donelson the way was open to the national forces all over the southwest without much resistance. If one general who would have taken the responsibility had been in command of all the troops west of the Allegenies, he could have marched to Chattanooga, Corinth, Memphis, and Vicksburg with the troops we then had, as volunteering was going on rapidly all over the North, there would have been force enough at all these centers to operate effectively against any body of the enemy that might be found near them.[9]

Maybe the Union army could have pushed on, but perhaps not quite as far as Grant envisioned. On the other hand, Halleck did put the brakes on any major advance and handed the initiative back to the Confederates. The pressure off, Albert Sidney Johnston would mass his forces and strike back at the battle of Shiloh six weeks later.

Naturally the victory at Fort Donelson made Ulysses S. Grant an overnight hero. "Unconditional Surrender" Grant caught the eye of President Lincoln, who admired his persistence and eagerness to fight. Of all the generals up to that time, General Grant was unique in his willingness and ability to advance. More importantly, he showed that he could win victories. During the course of the war, Lincoln helped shield Grant from his enemies and eventually promoted him to command of all Union armies. Grant also caught the public eye. A sworn pipe smoker, he was seen by many journalists riding the battlefield with a cigar clenched between his teeth. This colorful detail was added to the newspaper dispatches, and soon boxes of cigars came from grateful people across the country. A mud-splattered Grant with the stub of a cigar would become one of the best-known images of the war.

The lessons learned from this campaign are still relevant for today. The Fort Henry–Fort Donelson campaign shows clearly the importance of a sound command structure, based on each commander understanding the higher echelon's vision. The senior commander must also be in direct charge of events and impose his will upon his unit. The subordinate commanders must know the plan in order to make decisions on the scene that will support this plan. If there is a conflict of a personal nature among the senior leaders, this situation must be quickly resolved to avoid any chance of its affecting the mission. And senior commanders must get to know their subordinates and ensure they are competent.

A commander must also know his enemy and the capabilities of his own soldiers. General Johnston thought the most immediate threat was from Buell in Louisville. He did not have a good picture of Grant's forces and failed to learn the lesson of Belmont, which was that Grant could use transports to move any time of the year. Because he did not know the actual conditions at Fort Henry, Johnston vastly overestimated the capabilities of the Federal ironclads. Conversely, the lack of intelligence about the enemy must not render the command impotent. In these situations one must know the strengths and weaknesses of his own forces. General Grant is perhaps an extreme example of knowing his men and taking calculated risks.

This campaign also shows that commanders must have the moral courage to do what is right. The surrender proceedings at Fort Donelson are an obvious example, but there are others. Both Pillow and Buckner failed to put personal feelings aside to defend against a common enemy.

Floyd failed to effectively command these two men, and he did not adequately press Johnston for the guidance and support he needed. Johnston failed to alleviate the command situation at the forts regardless of political and individual sensitivities involved.

The Fort Henry–Fort Donelson campaign is not often associated with the great battles of the war, such as Gettysburg, Vicksburg, or Chancellorsville. It was fought so early in the war, and in comparison, the casualties sustained there were light. Neither side used dynamic tactics, which became required study at military academies. The military advantages the campaign brought about were truly significant, but the full advantages of the victory were not quickly achieved, since Halleck stopped the advances and temporarily passed the initiative to the Confederates. The great victory faded from memory as bloodier battles were fought for less result. The campaign, though, did give the nation and the world confident assurance of the United States' ability to restore the national union. It lifted the spirits of that nation, which had seen little but defeat, and showed that the nine months of continuous drilling and disciplining of troops and preparing them for war were not spent in vain.[10]

A few short weeks after Fort Donelson's surrender, Albert Sidney Johnston died of his wounds on the battlefield of Shiloh. In a desperate attempt to surprise and destroy Grant's army before Buell's could join it, he had used a variation of the strategy that he should have used at Fort Donelson. But by this time, Grant's army was heavily reinforced, and many of his troops were now veterans. In the bloodiest fight on the continent up to that time, the raw Confederate soldiers were at the brink of victory when Albert Sidney Johnston was mortally wounded. One can only speculate upon the outcome of that battle, and indeed the war, had the bulk of the 21,000 soldiers of Fort Donelson also been present.

Order of Battle and Casualties

THE ORDER OF BATTLE FOR BOTH SIDES IS NOT A MATTER OF PRECISE SCI-
ence, but an art form of sorts. Neither commander appears to have kept
meticulous records; if there were any, they have been lost to history.

Grant's headquarters left a list of regiments assigned to brigades that
actually took part in the battle. Those commanders who were able wrote
postbattle accounts, which were eventually placed in the *Official Records.*
From these entries, one can determine the aggregate strength of the units
and their losses. Not included in the following tables are the several regiments that arrived at Fort Donelson too late to see action or be included in
the official reports, nor are the units sent to reinforce Fort Henry as Grant
enveloped Fort Donelson, since these regiments did not fire in anger.

Confederate records are sketchier, presumably because records were not
kept during the chaotic rush to reinforce Fort Donelson, or perhaps they
were destroyed to prevent capture. Confederate infantry units above regimental level were rarely given numerical designations. The Fort Donelson
campaign is an exception of sorts. When General Pillow organized the
defense, he assigned a number to each brigade. In practice, the brigades
were known as and recorded by the commanders' names. All narrative references to units listed here follow that procedure.

By and large, the *Official Records* have been used to tabulate strength
and losses, but personal accounts were used to fill in the gaps. Numbers
given in parentheses are approximations.

U.S. Army Order of Battle

Unit	Commander	Strength	KIA	WIA	MIA
1st Division	**BG McClernand, John A.**				
1st Brigade	**Col Oglesby, Richard J.**	**3,734**	**184**	**595**	**75**
8th IL Inf Rgt	Ltc Rhoads, Frank L.	613	54	186	10
18th IL Inf Rgt	Col Lawler, Michael K.	671	53	158	18
29th IL Inf Rgt	Col Reardon, James S.	542	25	61	13
30th IL Inf Rgt	Ltc Dennis, Elias S.	568	19	69	6
31st IL Inf Rgt	Col Logan, John A.	598	31	117	28
D Bty, 2nd IL Lt Art (Dressor)	Cpt Dresser, Jasper M.	113	0	1	0
E Bty, 2nd IL Lt Art (Schwartz)	Lt Gumbart, George C.	129	2	3	0
A Co, 2nd IL Cav★	Cpt Hotaling, John R.	105	(0)	(0)	(0)
B Co, 2nd IL Cav★	Cpt Larrison, Thomas J.	95	(0)	(0)	(0)
C Co, 2nd US Cav★	Lt Powell, James H.	(50)	0	0	0
I Co, 4th US Cav★	Lt Powell, James H.	(50)	(0)	(0)	(0)
Carmichael's IL Cav Co★★	Cpt Carmichael, Eagleton	(50)	(0)	(0)	(0)
Dollin's IL Cav Co★★	Cpt Dollin, James J.	(50)	(0)	(0)	(0)
O'Harnett's IL Cav Co★★	Cpt O'Harnett, Morrison J.	(50)	(0)	(0)	(0)
Stewart's IL Cav Co★★	Cpt King, Ezra	(50)	(0)	(0)	(0)
2nd Brigade	**Col Wallace, William H. L.**	**3,037**	**65**	**180**	**62**
11th IL Inf Rgt	Ltc Ransom, Thomas E. G.	579	19	41	31
20th IL Inf Rgt	Col Marsh, C. Carroll	758	19	66	0
45th IL Inf Rgt	Col Smith, John E.	615	5	26	0
48th IL Inf Rgt	Col Haynie, Isham N.	512	20	34	31
B Bty, 1st IL Lt Art (Taylor)	Cpt Taylor, Ezra	120	1	2	0
D Bty, 1st IL Art (McAllister)	Cpt McAllister, Edward	133	1	11	0
4th IL Cav Rgt	Col Dickey, T. Lyle	(500)	(0)	(0)	(0)
3rd Brigade	**Col Morrison, William R.**	**1,617**	**29**	**106**	**19**
17th IL Inf Rgt	Col Ross, Leonard F.	750	13	61	7
49th IL Inf Rgt	Ltc Pease, Phineas	627	15	44	12
H Bty, 1st MO Lt Art (Welker)	Cpt Welker, Frederick	(120)	1	0	0
K Bty, 1st MO Lt Art (Stone)	Cpt Stone, George H.	(120)	0	1	0
	1st Division Total:	**8,388**	**277**	**881**	**156**

The following were detached from their regiments to brigade command:

Col Oglesby 8th IL   Col Wallace 11th IL   Col Morrison 49th IL   Col Ross 17th IL

★ These four companies were under the temporary command of Col. Silas Noble of the 2nd Illinois Cavalry Regiment.

★★ When combined, these companies made up Stewart's Independent Cavalry Battalion. This unit was formally organized in July 1862 and later became part of the 15th Illinois Cavalry Regiment.

U.S. Army Order of Battle *(continued)*

Unit	Commander	Strength	KIA	WIA	MIA
2nd Division*	**BG Smith, Charles F.**				
2nd Brigade	**Col McArthur, John**	**1,612**	**70**	**344**	**20**
(to 1st Div Feb 15)					
9th IL Inf Rgt	Col Mersey, August	(500)	36	165	9
12th IL Inf Rgt	Col Chetlain, Augustus L.	612	19	62	8
41st IL Inf Rgt	Col Pugh, Isaac C.	500	15	117	3
3rd Brigade	**Col Cook, John**	**2,620**	**23**	**90**	**1**
7th IL Inf Rgt	Ltc Babcock, Andrew J.	(500)	18	2	0
50th IL Inf Rgt	Col Bane, Moses M.	(500)	0	12	0
12th IA Inf Rgt	Col Woods, Joseph J.	(500)	1	27	0
52nd IN Inf Rgt	Col Smith, James M.	(500)	4	48	0
13th MO Inf Rgt	Col Wright, Crafts J.	(500)	0	1	1
D Bty, 1st MO Art	Cpt Richardson, Henry	(120)	(0)	(0)	(0)
4th Brigade	**Col Lauman, Jacob G.**	**2,620**	**54**	**312**	**0**
2nd IA Inf Rgt	Col Tuttle, James M.	620	33	164	0
7th IA Inf Rgt	Ltc Parrott, James C.	(500)	2	37	0
14th IA Inf Rgt	Col Shaw, William T.	(500)	2	28	0
25th IN Inf Rgt	Col Veatch, James C.	(500)	16	75	0
14th MO Sharpshooter Rgt**	Col Compton, Benjamin	(500)	1	8	0
5th Brigade	**Col Smith, Morgan L.**	**1,180**	**11**	**69**	**0**
11th IN Inf Rgt	Col McGinnis, George F.	(500)	4	29	0
8th MO Inf Rgt	Col Smith, Morgan L.	680	7	40	0
	2nd Division Total:	**8,032**	**158**	**815**	**21**

The following were detached from their regiments to brigade command:

Col McArthur 12th IL   Col Cook 7th IL   Col Lauman 7th IA   Col Smith 8th MO

*The 28th Illinois was also part of the 2nd division and participated in the operation against Fort Heiman. It remained there on guard duty until March 6, 1862.

**Stand F, "Brigadier General Charles F. Smith's Division," at the Fort Donelson National Battlefield lists the 16th Missouri Infantry under Col. Benjamin S. Compton as having been present. This is an error; it should list the 14th Missouri, as shown here. Colonel Compton was authorized to raise the 16th Missouri, but it did not complete its organization, and its recruits were dispersed to other units. This may account for the confusion of the historian responsible for the sign.

U.S. Army Order of Battle *(continued)*

Unit	Commander	Strength	KIA	WIA	MIA
3rd Division★	**BG Wallace, Lew**				
1st Brigade	**Col Cruft, Charles**	2,137	35	180	18
31st IN Inf Rgt	Col Osborn, Thomas O.	727	9	51	1
44th IN Inf Rgt	Col Reed, Hugh B.	(500)	7	34	2
17th KY Inf Rgt	Col McHenry, John H. Jr.	510	4	34	3
25th KY Inf Rgt	Col Shackelford, James M.	(400)	15	61	12
2nd Brigade★★		2,852	6	15	12
46th IL Inf Rgt	Col Davis, John A.	(500)	0	3	0
57th IL Inf Rgt	Col Baldwin, Silas D.	975	1	0	6
58th IL Inf Rgt	Col Lynch, William F.	887	5	12	6
20th OH Inf Rgt	Col Whittlesey, Charles	490	0	0	0
3rd Brigade	**Col Thayer, John M.**	2,446	4	25	1
1st NE Inf Rgt	Ltc McCord, William D.	816	3	7	1
58th OH Inf Rgt	Ltc Rempel, Fred†	630	1	9	0
68th OH Inf Rgt	Col Steedman, Samuel H.	(500)	0	0	0
76th OH Inf Rgt	Col Woods, Charles R.	(500)	0	9	0
A Co, 32nd IL Inf Rgt	Cpt Davidson, Henry	(100)	0	7	0
A Bty, 1st IL Lt Art (Wood)	Cpt Wood, Peter P.	135	0	3	0
	3rd Division Total:	7,670	45	230	31

The following were detached from their regiments to brigade command:

Col Cruft 31st IN   Col Thayer 1st NE

★The 23rd Indiana was left behind to guard Fort Henry on February 14th, 1862. The 5th Iowa Cavalry Regiment was moved to Fort Henry from February 8 to 11, 1862. The regiment remained there as a garrison for one year.

★★The 2nd Brigade was attached to the 3rd Brigade on February 15, 1862.

†Rempel replaced Col V. Bausewein, who was ill during the campaign.

	Strength	KIA	WIA	MIA
Grant's Army Total:	24,090	480	1,926	208

U.S. Army Order of Battle *(continued)*

Unit	Commander	Crew*	KIA	WIA
Western Flotilla	Comm Foote, Andrew H.	1		1
USS *St. Louis*★★/†	Lt Paulding, Leonard	44/44	0/2	0/7
USS *Carondelet*★★/†	Cdr Walke, Henry	55/50	0/5	0/29
USS *Cincinnati*★★	Cdr Stembel, Roger N.	49	1	8
USS *Essex*★★	Cdr Porter, William	99	15	18
USS *Louisville*†	Cdr Dove, Benjamin M.	50	4	5
USS *Pittsburg*†	Cdr Thompson, Egbert	42	0	2
USS *Conestoga*★★/†	Lt Phelps, S. Ledyard	25	0	0
USS *Lexington*★★/†	Lt Shirk, James W.	36	0	0
USS *Tyler (Taylor)*★★/†	Lt Gwin, William	46	0	0
	Western Flotilla Total:	**441**	**27**	**70**

*This shows the number of crew on the official roster of 1862. The "city-class" boats had additional men to round out to approximately 175 personnel each. Most of these came from transferring men from boat to boat during the campaign.

**Veterans of the battle of Fort Henry.

†Veterans of the battle of Fort Doneslon.

C.S. Army Order of Battle

Unit	Commander	Strength	KIA	WIA	Surrender	Esccape
Left Wing	**BG Pillow, Gideon**					
1st Brigade	**Col Heiman, Adolphus**	**2239**	**14**	**44**	**2058**	**123**
27th AL Inf Rgt★	Col Hughes, Adolphus A.	280	0	1	279	0
10tn TN Inf Rgt★	Ltc McGavock, Randal W.	750	1	5	701	44
42nd TN Inf Rgt	Col Quarles, William A.	498	4	7	465	22
48th TN Inf Rgt★	Col Voorhies, William M.	291	1	11	(420)★★	9
53rd TN Inf Rgt	Col Abernathy, Alfred	420	8	20	344	48
2nd Brigade	**Col Davidson, Thomas J.††**	**1711**	**71**	**223**	**1355**	**62**
8th KY Inf Rgt	Ltc Lyon, Hylan B.	350	27	72	220	31
1st MS Inf Rgt	Col Simonton, John M.	352	19	66	267	0
23rd MS Inf Rgt	Ltc Wells, Joseph M.	624	5	46	573	0
7th TX Inf Rgt	Col Gregg, John	385	20	39	295	31
3rd Brigade	**Col Drake, Joseph**	**1041**	**51**	**61**	**929**	**0**
26th AL Inf Rgt★	Maj Garvin, John S.	72	0	0	72	0
15th AR Inf Rgt★	Col Gee, James M.	304	11	23	270	0
4th MS Inf Rgt★	Maj Adaire, Thomas N.	665	40	38	587	0
4th Brigade†	**Col Head, John W.**	—	—	—	—	—
5th Brigade	**Col Wharton, Gabriel C.**	**545**	**13**	**54**	**0**	**478**
51st VA Inf Rgt	Ltc Massie, James W.	275	5	45	0	225
56th VA Inf Rgt	Col Slaughter, Philip P.	270	8	9	0	253
6th Brigade	**Col McCausland, John**	**1242**	**43**	**173**	**454**	**572**
20th MS Inf Rgt	Maj Brown, William N.	562	19	59	454	30
36th VA Inf Rgt	Ltc Reid, Leigh W.	280	14	46	0	220
50th VA Inf Rgt	Maj Thorburn, Charles E.	400	10	68	0	322
7th Brigade	**Col Baldwin, William E**	**843**	**23**	**156**	**635**	**29**
26th MS Inf Rgt	Col Reynolds, Arthur E.	443	12	71	334	26
26th TN Inf Rgt	Col Lillard, John M.	400	11	85	301	3
	Left Wing Total:	**7,621**	**215**	**711**	**5,581**	**1,264**

The following were detached from their regiments to brigade command:

Col Heiman 10th TN	Col Wharton 51st VA	Col Head 30th TN
Col Davidson 3rd MS	Col McClausland 36th VA	Col Simonton 1st MS
Col Drake 4th MS	Col Baldwin 41st TN	

★Fort Henry veterans. At Fort Henry, Tilghman's report of February 12 says a battery led by Capt. Culbertson and Gantt's cavalry battalion was attached to the 1st Brigade. A battery led by Capt. Crain was attached to the 2nd Brigade. Crain's battery, an Alabama cavalry battalion, and Capt. Padgett's Spy Company were left on the west bank of the Tennessee to harass Gen. C. F. Smith's force.

★★Two companies of the 48th Tennessee arrived just prior to the surrender.

†The 4th Brigade was never employed as such. It was composed of the regiments assigned to the fort proper, which were deployed to the outer defenses individually and never fought together as a brigade.

††Simonton assumed command of the brigade on February 15, since Davidson was ill. Very much overweight, he could not keep up with his troops during the battle. Brigade command was soon nonexistent or fell upon Colonel Gregg.

C.S. Army Order of Battle *(continued)*

Unit	Commander	Strength	KIA	WIA	Surren	Esc
Right Wing	**BG Buckner, Simon B.**					
2nd Brigade★		**1,851**	**32**	**147**	**1,595**	**77**
2nd KY Inf Rgt	Col Hanson, Roger W.	618	13	57	500	48
14th MS Inf Rgt	Maj Doss, Washington L.	658	17	84	554	3
41st TN Inf Rgt	Col Farquharson, Robert	575	2	6	541	26
3rd Brigade	**Col Brown, John C.**	**2,021**	**25**	**139**	**1,848**	**9**
3rd TN Inf Rgt	Ltc Gordon, Thomas M.	750	12	76	658	4
18th TN Inf Rgt	Col Palmer, Joseph B.	685	10	38	633	4
32nd TN Inf Rgt	Col Cook, Edmund C.	586	3	25	557	1
	Right Wing Total:	**3,872**	**57**	**286**	**3,443**	**86**

The following were detached from their regiments to brigade/garrison command:
Col Baldwin 14th MS

★Attached to the 3rd Brigade.

Unit	Commander	Strength	KIA	WIA	Surren	Esc
Fort Donelson	**Col Head/Bailey**					
30th TN Inf Rgt	Col Head, John W.	751	9	10	730	2
49th TN Inf Rgt	Col Bailey, James E.	372	7	17	348	0
50th TN Inf Rgt	Col Sugg, Cyrus A.	650	2	6	547	95
1st TN Inf Bn	Maj Colms, Stephen H.	270	0	0	270	0
Stankiewicz's Bty★	Lt Stankiewicz, Peter K.	34	1	1	32	0
	Garrison Total:	**2,077**	**19**	**34**	**1927**	**97**

The following were detached from their regiments to brigade/garrison command:
Col Head 50th TN   Col Brown 3rd TN

★Stankiewicz's artillery battery was technically under the direction of Lt. Col. Milton Haynes, chief of the Tennessee Artillery Corps. It is listed here since it essentially was part of the organic garrison of the fort proper. It was originally a section of Taylor's Tennessee Battery, which was lost at Fort Henry.

C.S. Army Order of Battle (continued)

Unit	Commander	Strength	KIA	WIA	Surren	Esc
Artillery*	**Ltc Haynes, Milton**					
Culbertson's TN Bty	Cpt Culbertson, Jacob	300	0	0	300	0
French's VA Art Bty	Cpt French, David A.	54	0	0	0	54
Graves's KY Art Bty	Cpt Graves, Rice E.	70	0	50	19	1
Green's KY Art Bty	Cpt Green, Henry F.	76	0	1	40	35
Guy's VA Art Bty	Cpt Guy, John H.	58	0	0	0	58
Jackson's VA Art Bty	Cpt Jackson, Thomas E.	70	0	0	70	0
Maney's TN Art Bty	Cpt Maney, Frank	100	5	9	63	23
Parker's Art Bty	Cpt Parker. A. H.	134	0	0	34	0
Porter's TN Art Bty	Cpt Porter, Thomas K.	113	7	4	90	12
Ross's TN Art Bty	Cpt Ross, Reuben R.	116	2	2	110	2
	Artillery Total:	**1,057**	**14**	**66**	**726**	**185**

*For standardization purposes, all Confederate batteries are listed here by the commanders' names, which was the typical practice for the Confederates during the war. However, at this early stage, some of the batteries were also known by their regional names, such as the Goochland Artillery.

Unit	Commander	Strength	KIA	WIA	Surren	Esc
Cavalry	**Ltc Forrest, Nathan B.**					
3rd TN Cav Rgt	Ltc Forrest, Nathan B.	600	8	15	107	470
9th TN Cav Bn	Ltc Gantt, George	340	1	5	303	31
Co D, 1st KY Cav	Cpt Williams, S. B.	(85)	0	0	(45)	(40)
Co G, 1st KY Cav	Cpt Wilcox, M. D.	(85)	0	0	0	85
Co K, 1st KY Cav	Cpt Huey, James K.	112	0	0	112	0
Melton's KY Cav Co	Cpt Melton, James F.	52	0	0	52	0
Co E., 11th TN Cav Bn	Cpt Gordon, William N.	(85)	3	4	0	(78)
Co F., 11th TN Cav Bn	Cpt Martin, William (?)	(85)	2	1	0	(82)
	Cavalry Total:	**1,444**	**14**	**25**	**619**	**786**

		Strength	KIA	WIA	Surren	Esc
	C.S. Army Total:	16,171	327	1,127	12,392	2,418

Transports/Auxiliary Vessels

THE FOLLOWING IS A LIST OF SUPPORT VESSELS MENTIONED IN THE OFFICIAL and unit records. It is not necessarily all-inclusive. During the Fort Henry operation, there was an acute shortage of transports. More boats were available by the time of Fort Donelson. All of these boats were the backbone of the river trade prior to the war and the river operations during the conflict. Refer to *Way's Packet Directory* for their individual history.

*Adams	*Empress—HQ boat	Prairie Rose
*Alexander Scott	*Fairchild	R. M. Patton
Alps	*Fanny Bullit	*Rob Roy
*Baltic	Golden State	*Rose Hambleton
*Bee	*G. W. Graham	Silver Lake #1
*B. Emerald	*Hannibal—hospital	Silver Lake #2
*Birmingham	Havana	Southwestern
Boston	Hiawatha	Spitfire
Champion #3	*Illinois	Starlight
*Chancellor	*Iatan	Tecumseh
*City of Memphis—hospital	Izetta	Thomas E.
Dauntless—dispatch boat	*January	*Tutt
Des Moines	Maria Denning—receiving ship	V. F.
Diadem	McGill	War Eagle
Dictator	*Minnehaha	Warner
Doctor Kane	Missouri	W. H. Brown
Emma Duncan	Nebraska	*White Cloud
Emma Graham	New Uncle Sam—HQ boat	*Wilson

*These vessels were part of the initial lift of forces to Fort Henry on February 2, 1862.

NOTES

INTRODUCTION

1. Benjamin Franklin Cooling, *Forts Henry and Donelson: The Key to the Confederate Heartland* (Knoxville, TN: University of Tennessee Press, 1987), xii.
2. Steven E. Woodworth, *Jefferson Davis and His Generals* (Lawrence, KS: University Press of Kansas, 1990), 51.

CHAPTER ONE

1. Thomas L. Connelly and Archer Jones, *The Politics of Command: Factions and Ideas in Confederate Strategy* (Baton Rouge, LA: Louisiana State University Press, 1973), 88–92.
2. William P. Johnston, *The Life of Albert Sidney Johnston* (New York: D. Appleton and Company, 1878), 312–14.
3. Cooling, *Forts Henry and Donelson,* 1–3.
4. Typical letters of correspondence are found in U.S. War Department, *The War of the Rebellion: A Compilation of the Official Records of the Union and Confederate Armies* (Washington, DC: Government Printing Office, 1880–1901) (cited hereafter as *OR*; all references are to ser. I, vol. 64), 419–22. See also Johnston, *Albert Sidney Johnston,* 328–30, 341–42.
5. Stanley F. Horn, ed. *Tennessee's War, 1861–1865* (Nashville: Tennessee Civil War Centennial Commission, 1965), 19.
6. U.S. General Service School, *Fort Henry and Fort Donelson Campaigns Source Book* (Fort Leavenworth, KS; General Service Schools Press, 1923) (cited hereafter as *Source Book*), 783.
7. *OR*, 359–90. See also Horn, *Tennessee's War,* 20. Before their capture, Memphis and Nashville produced about six cannons a week and 3,000 pounds of gunpowder each day.
8. Woodworth, *Davis and His Generals,* 30–31.

9. Nathaniel C. Hughes, Jr., and Roy P. Stonesifer, Jr., *The Life and Wars of Gideon J. Pillow* (Chapel Hill, NC: University of North Carolina Press, 1993), 127. See also Woodworth, *Davis and His Generals*, 30.

10. Johnston, *Albert Sidney Johnston*, 328–33.

11. Ezra J. Warner, *Generals in Gray: Lives of the Confederate Commanders* (Baton Rouge, LA: Louisiana State University Press, 1959), xx–xxii.

12. Shelby Foote, *The Civil War, a Narrative: Fort Sumter to Perryville* (New York: Random House, 1958), 171. See also Horn, *Tennessee's War*, 21.

13. Joseph H. Parks, *General Leonidas Polk, CSA: The Fighting Bishop* (Baton Rouge, LA: Louisiana State University Press, 1962), 173.

14. Hughes and Stonesifer, *Gideon J. Pillow*, 172–74.

15. Woodworth, *Davis and His Generals*, 33.

16. Benjamin C. Brown, ed. *Regulations for the Army of the United States* (Albany, NY: Weep, Parsons and Company, 1825), 1–2.

17. *OR*, 306.

18. Charles B. Kimbell, *History of Battery "A," 1st Illinois Light Artillery Volunteers* (Chicago: Cushing Printing Company, 1899), 16.

19. Ulysses S. Grant, *Memoirs and Selected Letters*, edited by John Y. Simon (Carbondale: Southern Illinois University Press, 1990), 47.

20. Johnston, *Albert Sidney Johnston*, 300; Shelby Foote, *Civil War*, 86–87.

21. Arndt M. Stickles, *Simon Bolivar Buckner: Borderland Knight* (Wilmington, NC: Broadfoot Publishing Company, 1987), 33–34. Contrary to legend, Buckner did not give cash directly to Grant, which would have been extremely humiliating in nineteenth-century society. Buckner's Papers shed no light on this matter.

22. Stickles, *Simon Bolivar Buckner*, 40–41.

23. Ibid., 86–87.

24. Richard N. Current, *Encyclopedia of the Confederacy* (New York: Simon and Schuster, 1993), 238; Jon L. Wakelyn, *Biographical Dictionary of the Confederacy* (Westport, CT: Greenwood Press, 1977), 116.

25. Wakelyn, *Biographical Dictionary*, 172–73. Daniel S. Donelson was born on June 23, 1801, in Sumner County, Tennessee. He graduated from West Point in 1825 as a lieutenant of artillery but resigned the following year. Donelson served in the Tennessee Militia as a major from 1827 to 1829 and as a general from 1829 to 1834. He was a successful planter, a member of the state house, and a powerful force in the state Democratic Party. Donelson was appointed a brigadier general in the Confederate army in July 1861 and fought in West Virginia under Robert E. Lee. He went on to fight with Bragg at Perryville, Murfreesboro, and Shelbyville. Illness forced his transfer to east Tennessee, where he died on April 17, 1863.

26. James L. Nichols, *Confederate Engineers* (Tuscaloosa, AL: Confederate Publishing Company, 1957), 42–43.

27. Ibid., 43. See also Cooling, *Forts Henry and Donelson,* 46.

28. Cooling, *Forts Henry and Donelson,* 46–48.

29. Charles M. Cummings, *Yankee Quaker, Confederate General: The Curious Career of Bushrod Rust Johnson* (Rutherford, NJ: Farleigh Dickinson University Press, 1971), 171–75. See also Nichols, *Confederate Engineers,* 43.

30. Cummings, *Yankee Quaker,* 172.

31. Jesse Taylor, "The Defense of Fort Henry," *From Sumter to Shiloh: Battles and Leaders of the Civil War* (1956), 368.

32. *OR,* 253–54.

33. Connelly and Jones, *Politics of Command,* 91.

34. Ibid., 18–22.

CHAPTER TWO

1. *Source Book,* 2–3.

2. Ibid. The city of Pittsburgh did not add the "h" until 1882.

3. U.S. War Department, *The War of the Rebellion: A Compilation of the Official Records of the Union and Confederate Navies* (Washington, DC: U.S. Government Printing Office, 1908) (cited hereafter as *ORN;* all references are to ser. I, vol. 22), 281, 283.

4. Ibid., 283. See also Frederick Way, Jr., *Way's Packet Directory, 1848–1994* (Athens, OH: Ohio University Press, 1994) for individual ship history.

5. *ORN,* 291, 292.

6. Ibid., 283, 287.

7. Ibid., 343; also refer to Appendix B for more detailed descriptions of the boats and crew.

8. Ibid., 342, 283.

9. Ibid., 291, 299.

10. For a detailed description of Eads's life, see John M. Barry, *Rising Tide: The Great Mississippi Flood of 1927 and How It Changed America* (New York: Simon and Schuster, 1997), 22–31.

11. *ORN,* 279. After the war, Eads was active in clearing the rivers and building bridges. He built St. Louis's Eads Bridge.

12. Ibid., 278. The term "submarine" was often used to describe vessels for underwater work, although they operated on the surface. "Submarine boats" on the rivers were essentially barges that carried equipment for underwater salvage and removal of snags and obstructions.

13. John R. Spears, *The History of Our Navy, from Its Origin to the Present Day, 1775–1897* (New York: Charles Scribner's Sons, 1897), 245.

14. Myron J. Smith, Jr., *The U.S. Gunboat "Carondelet," 1861–1865* (Manhattan, KS: MA/AH Publishings, Kansas State University, 1982), 36. James Eads owned the company, which was also known as the Union Iron Works or Marine Railway. The city of Carondelet was later absorbed into the city of St. Louis. The gunboats *St. Louis, Carondelet, Louisville,* and *Pittsburg* were built at Eads's facility. Hamelton and Collier built the *Cairo, Mound City,* and *Cincinnati.*

15. *ORN,* 444. The *St. Louis* was built and commissioned by the War Department, whereas the *Monitor* was purely a navy project. Those who point out that the *Monitor* was the navy's first ironclad are technically correct, but she was not the United States' first ironclad.

16. Ibid., 384.

17. Spears, *History of Our Navy,* 246.

18. *ORN,* 307, 313, 387, 394, 429. His date of rank was November 13, 1861. See also F. H. Magdeburg, "Capture of Fort Donelson," in *War Papers,* Wisconsin MOLLUS, vol. 3 (Wilmington, NC: Broadfoot Publishing Company, 1993), 289–90.

19. *ORN,* 334.

20. Ibid., 323, 331.

CHAPTER THREE

1. Quoted from Woodworth, *Davis and His Generals,* 48.

2. Ibid., 49.

3. Lynda L. Crist and Mary S. Dix, eds. *The Papers of Jefferson Davis* (Baton Rouge: Louisiana State University Press, 1997), 7: 291–93. The letter of Thomas C. Reynolds, acting governor of Missouri, to Davis in August is typical. Parks, *General Leonidas Polk,* 179–80.

4. Woodworth, *Davis and His Generals,* 30; T. Harry Williams, *P. G. T. Beauregard: Napoleon in Gray* (Baton Rouge: Louisiana State University Press, 1995), 116.

5. Parks, *General Leonidas Polk,* 178–80.

6. *OR,* 287.

7. Hughes and Stonesifer, *Gideon J. Pillow,* 396–97. See also Parks, *General Leonidas Polk,* 40–41.

8. Stickles, *Simon Bolivar Buckner,* 40–41; *OR,* 255.

9. Woodworth, *Davis and His Generals,* 52–54. See also Johnston, *Albert Sidney Johnston,* 308–9.

10. M. F. Force, *Campaigns of the Civil War* (New York: Charles Scribner's Sons, 1881), vol. 2, *From Fort Henry to Corinth,* 24.

11. Ibid., 18.
12. John F. C. Fuller, *Grant and Lee: A Study in Personality and Generalship* (Bloomington, IN: Indiana University Press, 1957), 73–75.
13. Stanley F. Horn, *The Army of Tennessee: A Military History* (New York: Bobbs-Merril Company, 1941), 58–59. See also Johnston, *Albert Sidney Johnston,* 328–38. General Johnston wrote a prolific letter campaign imploring for weapons and all other means of equipment and supplies. However, most Confederate units in the campaign fought with muskets issued by the states, or more often, with what they brought with them from home.
14. Woodworth, *Davis and His Generals,* 53.
15. Cooling, *Forts Henry and Donelson,* 65–66.
16. Foote, *Civil War,* 175.
17. Force, *Campaigns,* 20.
18. Grant, *Memoirs,* 183–85.
19. *OR,* 346.
20. Hughes and Stonesifer, *Gideon J. Pillow,* 204–5.
21. *OR,* 345–46.
22. Ibid., 759.
23. John T. Hubbell and James W. Geary, eds., *Biographical Dictionary of the Union: Northern Leaders of the Civil War* (Westport, CT: Greenwood Press, 1996), 228.
24. Stephen E. Ambrose, *Halleck: Lincoln's Chief of Staff* (Baton Rouge, LA: Louisiana State University Press, 1962), 3–4. This is the definitive biography of Henry W. Halleck.
25. Ibid., 19.
26. Charles Whittlesey, *War Memoranda: Cheat River to the Tennessee, 1861–1862* (Cleveland: William W. Williams Publisher, 1881), 27; *OR,* 441.
27. Grant, *Memoirs,* 188.
28. Johnston, *Albert Sidney Johnston,* 412. Although Johnston neglected the forts, he knew of the danger. This is pointed out clearly in a dispatch to General Polk on October 31, 1861.
29. Horn, *Tennessee's War,* 30–31; Hall Allen, *The Center of Conflict* (Paducah, KY: *Paducah Sun-Democrat,* 1961), 61–62; *OR,* 711
30. *OR,* 711.
31. Nichols, *Confederate Engineers,* 44. See also Wakelyn, *Biographical Dictionary,* 202, 206, and Current, *Encyclopedia,* 686. Jeremy Gilmer was born on February 3, 1818, in Guilford County, North Carolina. He was commissioned a 2nd lieutenant of engineers after his graduation from West Point in 1839. Gilmer served a professor of engineering there and

helped construct Fort Schuyler, New York, from 1840 to 1844. He served in the Mexican War as chief engineer in New Mexico, and from 1853 to 1858, he was engaged in the improvement of rivers and fortifications throughout the South. He joined the Confederacy and was severely wounded at Shiloh. He was promoted to brigadier general in October 1862 and became head of the Engineering Bureau. Gilmer was promoted to major general and helped fortify Atlanta. After the war, he worked for a railroad and became president of the Gas Light Company. He died in Savannah on December 1, 1883. Gilmer's papers are part of the Southern Historical Collection at the University of North Carolina. See also Johnston, *Albert Sidney Johnston,* 414–15. Gilmer had thought a site at Lineport, some fifteen miles upstream, was better.

32. Johnston, *Albert Sidney Johnston,* 413.
33. Nichols, *Confederate Engineers,* 44; *OR,* 724, 739.
34. H. L. Bedford, "Fight Between the Batteries and Gunboats at Fort Donelson," *Southern Historical Society Papers* 13 (January-December 1885): 35.
35. *ORN,* 345, 397; *Source Book,* 12.
36. The park rangers at Fort Donelson gave the story of Lady Peggy to me. I have found no reference to her, even in the James E. Bailey Papers, but she falls well in the realm of possiblity.
37. *OR,* 699–700.
38. Ibid., 453, 689. See also Johnston, *Albert Sidney Johnston,* 413–15. Apparently, Tilghman was to report to General Polk in Columbus. A telegram met him in Clarksville with a change of orders to go to Fort Henry.
39. Warner, *Generals in Gray,* 306; *OR,* 485–86, 719, 723. These letters are typical.
40. Franklyn McCord, "J. E. Bailey: A Gentleman of Clarksville," *Tennessee Historical Quarterly* 23 (September 1964): 253; *OR,* 245, 308; Horn, *Tennessee's War,* 31.
41. Johnston, *Albert Sidney Johnston,* 416–17.
42. *OR,* 710, 735
43. McCord, "J. E. Bailey," 252.
44. Noel Crowson and John V. Brogden, *Bloody Banners and Barefoot Boys: A History of the 27th Regiment Alabama Infantry, CSA* (Shippensburg, PA: Burd Street Press, 1997), 3.
45. *OR,* 748.
46. Johnston, *Albert Sidney Johnston,* 412; Johnston's letter to Polk, October 31, 1862.

CHAPTER FOUR

1. *OR,* 521, 524, 526, 529. Buell believed he was up against some 60,000 Confederates. This letter from Buell to McClellan is typical.

2. *Source Book,* 369–70.

3. Daniel L. Ambrose, *History of the 7th Illinois Volunteer Infantry* (Springfield, IL: Illinois Journal Company, 1868), 22.

4. *OR,* 388.

5. This gun is often referred to as a rifled 32-pounder. It apparently was originally cast as a smoothbore but later bored out to produce rifling. An indicator of just how incomplete the forts were was the presentation of a flag to Fort Donelson on January 10, 1862, made by the ladies of Nashville.

6. Nichols, *Confederate Engineers,* 44. T. J. Glen of Clarksville used a chartered steamboat to complete the task.

7. *Source Book,* 273, 276–77; Cummings, *Yankee Quaker,* 184–85.

8. Foote, *Civil War,* 179.

9. Hughes and Stonesifer, *Gideon J. Pillow,* 206–7.

10. Alfred Roman, *The Military Operations of General Beauregard in the War Between the States, 1861–1865* (New York: Harper and Brothers, 1884), 1: 217.

11. Warner, *Generals in Gray,* 90.

12. W. S. Morris, *History of the 31st Illinois Volunteers, Organized by John Logan* (Herrin, IL: Crossfire Press, 1991), 29–30.

13. Williams, *P. G. T. Beauregard,* 89. See also Roman, *Operations of Beauregard,* 211. For a short biography on Beauregard, refer to Wakelyn, *Biographical Dictionary,* 94–95, or Jack D. Welsh, *Medical Histories of the Confederate Generals* (Kent, OH: Kent State University Press, 1995), 18–19.

14. Williams, *P. G. T. Beauregard,* 115.

15. *OR,* 508–11.

16. Ibid., 56; Grant, *Memoirs,* 147.

17. *OR,* 121, 561.

18. Ibid., 121.

19. Archer Jones, *Civil War Command and Strategy: The Process of Victory and Defeat* (New York: Free Press, 1992), 47.

20. Virgil Carrington Jones, *The Civil War at Sea* (New York: Holt Publishing, 1960), 1: 359. Foote's fanaticism is legendary and often quoted.

21. Lew Wallace, *Lew Wallace: An Autobiography* (New York: Harper and Brothers Publishers, 1906), 363. Three sources authored by Wallace were used with this work. They roughly repeat the same accounts.

22. General Floyd had a brigade of four regiments and three batteries. Later these were divided into two brigades and the artillery detached by necessity. This resulted in many accounts of "Floyd's division," although the number of regiments did not increase. All references here will maintain the official term "brigade" for consistency and clarity.

23. Johnston, *Albert Sidney Johnston*, 424–25.

CHAPTER FIVE

1. *Source Book*, 382.

2. *OR*, 172.

3. A running dialog is found in *OR*, 574–75. General Buell's excessive caution and his inability to overcome supply difficulties would eventually be his undoing. After the indecisive battle of Perryville, which halted a Confederate invasion that was already faltering, he failed to pursue the retreating enemy. He was relieved of command on October 24, 1862, and sent home to await orders that never came.

4. Charles D. Gibson and E. Kay Gibson, *Assault and Logistics: Union Coastal and River Operations, 1861–1865* (Camden, ME: Ensign Press, 1995), 73.

5. Ulysses S. Grant, *The Papers of Ulysses S. Grant,* edited by John Y. Simon (Carbondale, IL: Southern Illinois Press, 1970), 4: 129.

6. *OR*, 579, Grant's General Order No. 7, February 2, 1862.

7. Grant, *Papers,* 129.

8. Ibid., 128. Letter dated January 31 directing the shipment of forage is typical. Grant also took a personal interest in the shipment of ammunition, stores, and men as well, without delegating this to a subordinate staff officer.

9. Fortunately for James Eads, no city-class boat was sunk in this campaign. Due to the acceptable performance of the boats, and riding on the euphoria of victory, the government paid him the balance due, and Eads was then able to pay his creditors. He would build many more gunboats for the Union during the war.

10. J. F. C. Fuller, *The Generalship of Ulysses S. Grant* (New York: Dodd, Mead and Company, 1929), 80.

11. Grant, *Papers,* 146–47.

12. James P. Jones, *Black Jack John A. Logan and Southern Illinois in the Civil War Era* (Tallahassee, FL: Florida State University Press, 1967), 119.

13. *Source Book,* 313. A *New York Herald* dispatch reported that Grant's forces landed at Lyes' Landing, six miles below Fort Henry. This report also supposes that there were about 15,000 Confederates inside the fort.

Stewart's Cavalry Battalion consisted of three independent Illinois cavalry companies, which were eventually absorbed into the 15th Illinois Cavalry Regiment.

14. Edwin C. Bearss, "The Fall of Fort Henry," *West Tennessee Historical Society* 17 (1963): 5.
15. Grant, *Papers,* 145; telegram to Halleck.
16. Daniel L. Ambrose, 26–27. See also *OR,* 583–84.
17. *OR,* 149. Colonel Heiman includes in his official report that at 4:30 A.M., rocket signals were exchanged between the sentinels downstream and the fort, announcing the arrival of the Federal threat. It is inconceivable that Tilghman would have left Fort Henry on a routine inspection tour had this been accurate.
18. Ibid., *OR,* 145–46, Milton Haynes's official report.
19. Ibid., 149.
20. Henry Walke, *Naval Scenes and Reminiscences of the Civil War in the United States on the Southern and Western Waters* (New York: F. R. Reed and Company, 1877), 54.
21. Walke, *Naval Scenes,* 55, 62; Spears, *History of Our Navy,* 255.
22. Allen, *Center of Conflict,* 68; H. Allen Gosnell, *Guns on Western Waters* (Baton Rouge, LA: Louisiana State University Press, 1995), 49. This account says the torpedo was not thrown overboard.
23. Walke, *Naval Scenes,* 56. One can surmise that the *Essex* was chosen for this duty primarily because she had more powerful engines. While the city-class boats battled the current, the *Essex* was the most capable ironclad for the reconnaissance. Her crew also had served together for several weeks and was thus at least drilled.
24. Taylor, 371. Reports vary on the number of guns and their caliber. Some may have counted the 42–pounders, which apparently had no ammunition. Taylor maintains that the 42–pounders had no ammunition, yet Tilghman's and Gilmer's reports say a 42–pounder exploded. The Confederates were probably firing improvised ammunition. *OR,* 554–55, Tilghman's report of February 12, 1862. See also *OR,* 133, Major Gilmer's report.
25. *OR,* 581, General Grant's message to Halleck, February 4, 1862. The Confederates had not recently received any reinforcements at this time. Steamers plying back and forth between Fort Henry and Fort Heiman were merely shifting available forces.
26. Ibid., 126–27, report of General McClernand from February 10, 1862.
27. Grant, *Papers,* 148–49, letter to Grant from McClernand describing his action for the day.

28. *OR*, 128–29, McClernand's report to Grant dated February 10, 1862.

29. Randal W. McGavock, *Pen and Sword: The Life and Journals of Randal W. McGavock, 1826–1863* (Nashville: Tennessee Historical Commission, 1959), 583.

30. *OR*, 150, Colonel Heiman's report.

31. Ibid., 555, Tilghman's report of February 12, 1862. The artillery heard from Fort Donelson was the gunboats shelling the woods in support of the landing below Fort Henry some twelve miles away. Deployment of the 49th and 50th Tennessee was actually a bold move by Tilghman. These two regiments added up to about 750 men and consisted the bulk of the Fort Donelson garrison at this point. Removing them left only a small artillery detachment to defend this vital post. Tilghman also knew the condition of the roads. Large numbers of wagons and artillery would only slow things down. Incidentally, the 49th Tennessee was a very raw unit that had just finished its organization on January 2. Peytoma Furnace was built in 1846.

32. Ibid., 149, Colonel Heiman's official report.

33. Ibid., 858–59. It is interesting that Tilghman did not trust Albert Sidney Johnston for reinforcements.

34. Ibid., 554, Tilghman's report of February 12, 1862. The number of men in the fort varies widely from source to source. Tilghman's figures are generally used.

35. The two companies from the 51st Tennessee were miserably armed and had little or no training. At Fort Donelson, this unit was initially used as replacements for the artillery. It was known during the battle as "Browder's Artillery Battery." The 48th Tennessee was also a raw unit, with no more than 300 men.

36. Johnston, *Albert Sidney Johnston,* 351.

37. Williams, *P. G. T. Beauregard,* 117. See also Roman, *Operations of Beauregard,* 216–17. Roman's recollections can be suspect, for his agenda is to portray his former chief in the best possible light.

38. *OR*, 858, Tilghman's dispatches to Polk, February 5, 1862.

39. Ibid., 138. Also *ORN,* 554–55, Tilghman's report of February 12, 1862. See also *ORN,* 133, Major Gilmer's report.

40. Ibid., 555–56, Tilghman's report of February 2, 1862. See also Ibid., 129–30, McClernand's report of February 10, 1862.

41. McGavock, *Pen and Sword,* 140–50.

42. Taylor, "Fort Henry," 370.

43. *Source Book,* 340; *New York Herald* dispatch of February 7, 1862.

44. Grant, *Papers*, 152, letter from McClernand to Grant. He added this suggestion to a detailed description of the disposition of his forces.

45. Grant, *Papers*, 147. Also, Grant's letter to his wife Julia, 153. See also *ORN*, 141; McGavock, *Pen and Sword*, 584.

46. Grant, *Papers*, 160. Halleck believed that 10,000 Confederates were on their way from Bowling Green to Fort Henry under the command of General Beauregard. He was stripping his department of all available forces to support Grant and begging for more.

47. Force, *Campaigns*, 30. See also *ORN*, 556–58, Tilghman's official report.

48. *OR*, 129.

49. Wallace, *Autobiography*, 369–70.

50. *OR*, 150–151, Colonel Heiman's official report; *ORN*, 535–36. See also Taylor, "Fort Henry," 370.

51. Force, *Campaigns*, 30. This source says the attack commenced at 11:45. The other boats were ordered to hold their fire and consider the first round from the *Cincinnati* as the signal to commence firing.

52. Walke, *Naval Scenes*, 62–63.

53. Ibid., 63–64.

54. Richard S. West, Jr., *Mr. Lincoln's Navy* (New York: Longman's Green and Company, 1957), 165.

55. *OR*, 539; Walke, *Naval Scenes*, 67.

56. Arthur L. Conger, *The Rise of Ulysses S. Grant* (New York: Century Company, 1913), 10. Conger asserts that McClernand lost the will to fight and halted his column short of his objective, allowing the Confederates to escape. See also *ORN*, 557–58, Tilghman's official report. Tilghman also notes that McClernand's forces halted at a crossroads, apparently to avoid receiving fire from the gunboats should their rounds fly over their mark. Tilghman's assessment does not conform to the angle of attack and the location of the crossroads.

57. Force, *Campaigns*, 30–31, and Taylor, "Fort Henry," 370–71. See also *OR*, 134, 141, 146; *ORN*, 558–59. Gilmer reports that the men stopped serving some of the 32–pounders under the belief that their pieces had no effect upon the ironclads. Also, Tilghman never planned to surrender himself at Fort Henry, but to continue the fight at Fort Donelson.

58. Walke, *Naval Scenes*, 57. Also *OR*, 558, Tilghman's official report.

59. Taylor, "Fort Henry," 371.

60. *OR*, 146–47 and 152.

61. Taylor, "Fort Henry," 371.

62. Walke, *Naval Scenes,* 67. Commander Walke, who was near Foote at this time, later said that he probably never made such a reply. "He was too much of a gentleman to say anything calculated to wound the feelings of an officer who had defended his post with signal courage and fidelity, and whose spirits were clouded by the adverse fortunes of war." Whether or not Foote said it, he would have meant it if he had.

63. Charles Hubert, *History of the 50th Illinois Volunteer Infantry in the War of the Union* (Kansas City, MO: Western Publishing Company, 1894), 63; Allen, *Center of Conflict,* 71.

64. Walke, *Naval Scenes,* 57; McGavock, *Pen and Sword,* 585.

65. Force, *Campaigns,* 31; *OR,* 123, 538. Foote says sixty invalids surrendered in the hospital boat. Foote's and Walke's accounts describe the carnage inside Fort Henry right after the battle. They tell of bodies lying about and a number of wounded men. Other reports mention only five men killed. This lower number does match the number of graves known to exist at the battle site, but their names do not match those who fought on February 6.

66. Walke, *Naval Scenes,* 58. The *Essex* was the only ship present with a 9–inch gun. It was mounted on the center, bow position.

67. Grant, *Papers,* 159–60. Grant, *Memoirs,* 192, mentions only two guns captured. See also *OR,* 129–30, McClernand's official report.

68. Wallace, *Autobiography,* 370. Wallace sent the tent home as a souvenir, using it many times in hunting and fishing trips after the war.

69. Ibid., 371. This was not Colonel Heiman's dinner, since he had left Fort Heiman two days earlier. Apparently Hubbard's and Padgett's cavalrymen, left behind to harass the invaders, made themselves quite at home in the former commander's camp. See also Crowson and Brogden, *Bloody Banners,* 4. Virtually every man in the 27th Alabama carried a large Bowie knife, but when the order came to evacuate Fort Heiman, the men were ordered to take only their muskets and cartridge boxes. An inspection made the next day showed that there no more than half a dozen knives remaining among them. The other 400 or so were left sticking into trees where the soldiers had practiced throwing them or otherwise scattered throughout the camp.

70. *OR,* 586, Halleck's dispatch to Washington, February 6, 1862.

71. The guns of Culbertson's Battery were probably not the only ones lost. This disposition of the guns of Waller Crain's and Peter Stankiewicz's batteries are lost to history. They, too, could have been stuck in the

mud and retrieved later by either side. Crain's battery did not make it to Fort Donelson but appeared in Corinth in March. Stankiewicz's men did make it to Fort Donelson, but without any cannons. Also, some guns may have made it to Fort Donelson and been distributed out to the existing batteries. See also Crowson and Brogden, *Bloody Banners,* 6.

72. *OR,* 152, Heiman's report. The Confederates did not take the Ridge Road, which was the shortest route to Dover. Fearing an interception by a large body of Federals, the Confederates took a more southerly route that wound through the hills and across Standing Rock Creek. Their trek took them more than twenty-two miles over rough, wet, muddy terrain.

73. Conger, *Rise of Grant,* 10–11.

74. *OR,* 147, Lt. Col. Milton Haynes's official report. Gilmer would do the same thing at Donelson.

75. Ibid., 539.

76. Walke, *Naval Scenes,* 66.

77. Smith, *Carondelet,* 61–62, 64; *ORN,* 470; Walke, *Naval Scenes,* 424.

78. Taylor, "Fort Henry," 371.

79. *OR,* 131–32.

80. Ibid., 137–38, Tilghman's report, February 12, 1862. See also Johnston, *Albert Sidney Johnston,* 408–9.

CHAPTER SIX

1. Jay Slagle, *Ironclad Captain: Seth Ledyard Phelps and the United States Navy, 1841–1864* (Kent, OH: Kent State University Press, 1996), 163.

2. *ORN,* 572, Phelps's report.

3. Ibid., 572, Phelps's report. See also Slagle, *Ironclad Captain,* 166. The Confederates got a late start on their ironclad. The *Eastport* was not authorized until December 6, 1861. A study was made, but no ironclad was started for the Cumberland, with the lack of iron plate cited. This is ironic, as the region was a leader of iron production for the South, but much of it at this time was being sent to the armories in the East.

4. Ibid., 572, Phelps's report.

5. Ibid., 372–73, Phelps's report.

6. *Source Book,* 429, abstract deck log of the USS *Lexington,* August 16, 1861–April 11, 1862, Commander Rodger N. Stembel.

7. Slagle, *Ironclad Captain,* 169.

8. *ORN,* 573, Phelps's report.

9. James M. Crew was authorized to raise the 58th Tennessee Infantry Regiment but failed to secure enough companies to complete the

organization. The incident related here no doubt did little to encourage enlistments. After Shiloh, the battalion was consolidated into one company and eventually transferred to the 23rd (Neuman's) Tennessee Infantry Battalion. Lieutenant Colonel Crew subsequently was assigned to Nathan Bedford Forrest's staff in November and later commanded the 3rd (Forrest's) Tennessee Cavalry Regiment. For a full account, refer to Craig L. Symonds, *Tennesseans in the Civil War: A Military History of Confederate and Union Units with Available Rosters of Personnel*, part 1 (Nashville: Civil War Centennial Commission, 1864).

10. *ORN*, 573, Phelps's report.

11. *Source Book*, 430, abstract deck log of the USS *Lexington*, August 16, 1861–April 11, 1862, Commander Rodger N. Stembel.

12. *ORN*, 573, Phelps's report; Ibid., 575. Walke's report. See also *Source Book*, 361. The Confederate steamers were the *Sam Kirkman, Sam Boyd, Julia Smith, Samuel Orr*, and *Appleton Belle*.

13. *Source Book*, 361.

14. Ibid., 362.

15. *ORN*, 576.

16. Ibid., 588.

CHAPTER SEVEN

1. *OR*, 162, report of Lt. Col. J. B. McPherson, engineer on General Grant's staff, dated February 25, 1862.

2. Kenneth P. Williams, *Grant Rises in the West: The First Year, 1861–1862* (Lincoln, NE: University of Nebraska Press, 1997), 206.

3. *OR*, 596.

4. Grant, *Memoirs*, 173.

5. *OR*, 859–60, Pillow's telegram to Captain Pickett, February 6, 1862.

6. Hughes and Stonesifer, *Gideon J. Pillow*, 211. If the friction between Clark and Pillow was intense, it apparently did not cross the lines of friendship. When Pillow later went to Fort Donelson, Clark loaned him his horse.

7. The *Essex* was virtually rebuilt at a cost of $91,000. This sum was just under the price to build one city-class boat from the keel up. Commander Porter recovered from his burns and oversaw the project. He came under great suspicion and earned a rebuke when the bill for repairs was delivered to the War Department, but the colorful officer kept his command, and the *Essex* returned to service in time to see action at Island No. 10.

8. *OR,* 590, Halleck's and McClellan's telegrams.

9. Ibid., 587–88.

10. Ibid., 593, Buell's telegram to McClellan, February 7, 1862, 9:00 P.M.

11. Ibid., 602–3, Buell's telegram, February 10, 1862, 1:30 P.M., and McClellan's response at 7:00 P.M.

12. *Source Book,* 338.

13. *OR,* 135, Adj. P. Ellis's report to Gen. S. Cooper, February 8, 1862. This report states that Major Gilmer of the engineers was also captured. He, in fact, escaped Fort Henry before its investment by General McClernand's division.

14. Ibid., 864–65, Buckner's report, February 8, 1862.

15. Williams, *P. G. T. Beauregard,* 118.

16. Ibid., 214–16. A postwar account says Hardee went to Beauregard's room earlier in the day to break the news of Fort Henry's fall to the ailing general. Beauregard told Hardee then that the Confederate forces should concentrate at Fort Donelson with the aim of defeating Grant and turning on Buell. Hardee agreed to present these views to General Johnston later. See also *OR,* 818. The Confederates had 12 engines, 120 boxcars, and 55 flat cars at their disposal. At full capacity, there were two trains per day between Nashville and Bowling Green. This could have easily carried Johnston's army to Clarksville in the next five days.

17. James Hamilton, *The Battle of Fort Donelson* (New York: A. S. Barnes and Co., 1968), 41.

18. *OR,* 861, Johnston's Memorandum, February 7, 1862. See also Roman, *Operations of Beauregard,* 219–20, for a description of the meeting between the generals. Jeremy F. Gilmer Papers, letter to his wife dated November 14, 1861. See also Nichols, *Confederate Engineers,* 49.

19. *OR,* 861, Johnston's Memorandum, February 7, 1862.

20. Ibid., 861.

21. Ibid., 259, Johnston's report to Jefferson Davis, March 18, 1862.

22. Cummings, *Yankee Quaker,* 190. Hamilton, *Battle of Fort Donelson,* 42–43.

23. Williams, *Grant Rises,* 219, 498; Ethan Hitchcock, *Fifty Years in Camp and Field* (New York: G. P. Putnam's Sons, 1909), 434; *OR,* 578, 930–31.

24. *OR,* 130–31, A. S. Johnston's message to Hon. J. P. Benjamin, Secretary of War, February 8, 1862.

25. Ibid., 862–63, J. P. Benjamin's telegram to A. S. Johnston, February 8, 1862. Interestingly, Jefferson Davis desired this new command to be given to Simon B. Buckner.

26. Ibid., 865, Floyd's message to A. S. Johnston, February 8, 1862.

27. OR, 598–99, Grant's Field Orders 3 and 5, dated February 9, 1862.

28. Jesse Grant Cramer, ed., *Letters of Ulysses S. Grant to His Father and Youngest Sister, 1857–1878* (New York: G. P. Putnam's Sons, 1912), 81–82.

29. OR, 868, Pillow's Special Order No. 1, February 9, 1862. Of note, Major Rice's home was destroyed with most of the town during the battle of Dover on February 3, 1863.

30. Ibid., 279, Pillow's report, February 18, 1862.

31. Hughes and Stonesifer, *Gideon J. Pillow,* 216; OR, 869.

32. Johnston, *Albert Sidney Johnston,* 423–24.

33. OR, 870.

34. Ibid., 599.

35. Stickles, *Simon Bolivar Buckner,* 115–18.

36. OR, 599, 600.

37. Ibid., 600, Grant's telegram to Foote on February 10, 1862.

38. Ibid., 602, Field Order No. 7, February 10, 1862.

39. Ibid., 293.

40. Ibid., 869, Gilmer's report of February 10, 1862. Gilmer was well known to Albert Sidney Johnston and was assigned specifically to the Fort Henry–Fort Donelson project. His opinion was highly valued. See also *Source Book,* 376. A *Boston Journal* account is typical of those praising the accuracy and effectiveness of the Confederate gunners. Using simple math, however, another conclusion can be reached. The Confederates fired about 300 rounds at Fort Henry. About fifty-two hits were scored, for an approximate 17 percent of the total.

41. OR, 870, Pillow's messages, February 10, 1862.

42. Hughes and Stonesifer, *Gideon J. Pillow,* 216.

43. Grant, *Memoirs,* 212.

44. OR, 273.

45. Ibid., 604.

46. Force, *Campaigns,* 38.

47. William S. McFeeley, *Grant: A Biography* (New York: W. W. Norton and Company, 1981), 98–99; Wallace, *Autobiography,* 376–77.

48. OR, 161–62, McPherson's report.

49. Ibid., 170, McClernand's report, February 28, 1862. See also Ibid., 183, Colonel Oglesby's report and Ibid., 192, Col. W. H. L. Wallace's report.

50. Ibid., 605, Field Order No. 11, February 11, 1862.
51. William C. Church, *Ulysses S. Grant and the Period of National Preservation and Reconstruction* (New York: G. P. Putnam and Sons, 1897), 102.
52. *OR,* 259.
53. Hamilton, *Battle of Fort Donelson,* 41–42.
54. Bruce Catton, *Grant Moves South* (Boston: Little, Brown Publishing, 1960), 154.
55. *OR,* 591. Incidentally, even General Halleck would agree.

CHAPTER EIGHT
1. *Source Book,* 541–42.
2. Ibid., 543–44, and 580–81.
3. Ibid., 544–45, *New York Herald* dispatch of February 13, 1862.
4. Lew Wallace, "The Capture of Fort Donelson," in *Battles and Leaders of the Civil War* (1956): 1, 240; this anecdote is an enduring legend of the campaign.
5. *OR,* 183, Colonel Oglesby's report, February 20, 1862.
6. Thomas Jordan and J. P. Pryor, *The Campaigns of Lieutenant General Forrest and of Forrest's Cavalry* (New York: Da Capo Press, 1996), 62–63.
7. *OR,* 183, Colonel Oglesby's report, February 20, 1862; Grant, *Memoirs,* 212.
8. Walke, *Naval Scenes,* 73; Allen H. Gosnell, *Guns on Western Waters,* 59.
9. *OR,* 191, Captain Dressor's report. See also Ibid., 183, Colonel Oglesby's report.
10. Ibid., 211–12, Colonel Morrison's report.
11. Grant, *Memoirs,* 196–98.
12. *OR,* 162, Lt. Col. James B. McPherson's report, February 25, 1862.
13. Ibid.
14. Ibid., 183, Colonel Oglesby's report. See also Ibid., 191.
15. Ibid., 193, Col. W. H. L. Wallace's report,
16. Ibid., 171–72, McClernand's report, February 28, 1862; Ibid., 193, Col. W. H. L. Wallace's report.
17. Benjamin C. Brown, ed., *Regulations for the Army of the United States,* 99–105.
18. *OR,* 607, Halleck's message to Buell, February 12, 1862.
19. Ibid., 607–8, Buell's message to Halleck, February 12, 1862.
20. John S. Wilkes, "First Battle Experience: Fort Donelson," *Confederate Veteran* 14, no. 11 (November 1906): 500–501. Curiously, this man does not appear on the roster of either 48th Tennessee regiment. It is a good story, though.

21. *OR,* 868, 870–71, Pillow's message to A. S. Johnston, February 12, 1862.
22. Ibid., Floyd's report to General Johnston, March 20, 1862.
23. *Source Book,* 589.
24. John T. McAuley, "Fort Donelson and Its Surrender," in *Military Essays and Recollections,* Illinois MOLLUS, vol. 1 (Chicago: A. C. McClurg and Company, 1891), 70–71.

CHAPTER NINE
 1. Hughes and Stonesifer, *Gideon J. Pillow,* 217. See also Hamilton, *Battle of Fort Donelson,* 79.
 2. *Source Book,* 583. The 14th Missouri was redesignated as the 66th Illinois later in the year. Most of the men replaced their heavy Dimmick rifles with the new Henry repeaters, buying them with their own money.
 3. Jordan and Pryor, *Campaigns of Forrest,* 63–64.
 4. Walke, *Naval Scenes,* 73–76.
 5. *OR,* 388–89, Lieutant Colonel Haynes's report.
 6. Walke, *Naval Scenes,* 73.
 7. *OR,* 389, 393, 395, Haynes's, Culbertson's, and Bidwell's reports.
 8. Force, *Campaigns,* 41–42.
 9. *OR,* 173.
10. Ibid., 203–4, 211; Catton, *Grant Moves South,* 156.
11. *OR,* 172–173; Force, *Campaigns,* 43.
12. *Source Book,* 540–41.
13. Ibid., 541, *New York Herald* dispatches dated February 12 and 13, 1862.
14. Ibid., 591.
15. *OR,* 185.
16. Jeffrey C. Weaver, *Goochland Light, Goochland Turner, and Mountain Artillery* (Lynchburg, VA: H. E. Howard and Company, 1994), 26.
17. *Source Book,* 581.
18. The design of the ironclads did not include a cargo hatch. Ammunition, food, and coal had to be loaded through the gun ports, round by round, basket by basket, and scuttle by scuttle. Refueling was a tiresome and slow process that required all hands.
19. Cooling, *Forts Henry and Donelson,* 153.
20. Walke, *Naval Scenes,* 73–76.
21. McAuley, *Fort Donelson,* 71.

CHAPTER TEN

1. Cummings, *Yankee Quaker,* 193.
2. Cooling, *Forts Henry and Donelson,* 149.
3. Robert M. Hughes, "Why Fort Donelson Was Surrendered," *Confederate Veteran* 37, no. 8 (August 1929): 302–3.
4. Why the attack order was never given is a mystery. Perhaps Pillow was waiting for Floyd to give the order, while Floyd assumed Pillow would do the honors. Both of these officers failed to even mention this operation in their subsequent reports. Buckner, Forrest, Colonel Baldwin, and Major Brown of the 20th Mississippi all do in theirs, however.
5. *Source Book,* 560.
6. *OR,* 163, Lieutenant Colonel McPherson's report, February 25, 1862.
7. Ibid., 174–75. These were Dresser's, McAllister's, Schwartz's, and Taylor's batteries.
8. *Source Book,* 689.
9. Wallace, *Autobiography,* 390–91.
10. *Source Book,* 560.
11. Walke, *Naval Scenes,* 73–76; *Source Book,* 561.
12. *Source Book,* 689.
13. *OR,* 409.
14. *Source Book,* 566.
15. *OR,* 281.
16. Walke, *Naval Scenes,* 77. Walke adds in a footnote that the explosion of the bow gun was caused by reckless disregard of the standing order never to fire a gun until the cartridge and shell were well rammed down to the bottom of the barrel. The reason that no men were killed and so few were mortally wounded by this explosion is that the gun crew knew the shot was not seated properly and stood farther from the gun than usual. The gun was broken into four large pieces, the largest of which fell outside of the port.
17. Rueben R. Ross, "River Batteries at Fort Donelson," *Confederate Veteran* 4, no. 11 (November 1896): 395–98. The "chimney" quote is from Lew Wallace, "It Was Not Possible for Brave Men to Endure More," in *Battles and Leaders of the Civil War,* edited by Robert U. Johnson (New York: Century Publishers, 1887), 72.
18. Brian S. Wills. *A Battle from the Start: The Life of Nathan Bedford Forrest* (New York: HarperCollins Publishers, 1992), 100.
19. *Source Book,* 564, *New York Herald* dispatch dated February 21, 1862. The accuracy of this story is suspect, but it is interesting nonetheless. Another journalist did confirm the *St. Louis* incident.

20. Walke, *Naval Scenes,* 79. See also Henry Walke, "The Western Flotilla at Fort Donelson, Island Number Ten, Fort Pillow and Memphis" in *Battls and Leaders of the Civil War* (New York: Castle Books, 1992), 430–38, where Walke tells a virtually identical tale of the battle.

21. Walke, *Naval Scenes,* 77–78. See also *OR, 281.* Pillow heard from citizens living on the river below that one of the damaged ironclads sank and the others had to be towed to Cairo. The gunboats did take a severe pounding and were incapable of another direct assault, but the situation for them was not that grim. None of the boats was lost, and they all made it back to Cairo under their own power. Most likely other vessels escorted them though. Also, many Confederate reports claim that the boats swung broadside to fire. This was not the plan, nor was it intentional. They swung broadside because the steering mechanisms were damaged. See also *Source Book,* 578.

22. *Source Book,* 572.

23. Ibid., 574. Also, a number of official and newspaper reports tell of the Confederate gunners abandoning their guns under fire. This may or may not be true. The water batteries had a large number of spectators and volunteers from the fort to relieve the gunners, carry ammunition, take water to the guns, and so on. Men running up the hill from the guns probably had a number of legitimate reasons.

24. *Source Book,* 565–66.

25. Henry G. Hicks, "Fort Donelson," in *Glimpses of the Nation's Struggle,* Minnesota MOLLUS, vol. 4 (St. Paul: H. L. Collins Company, 1898), 447. See also George Hunt, "The Fort Donelson Campaign," in *Military Essays and Recollections,* Illinois MOLLUS, vol. 4 (Chicago: Cozzens and Beaton, 1907), 70.

26. *OR,* 159, report of General Grant, February 16, 1862. Most historians point out that Grant did not fortify his position. Grant's reference to fortifying probably was in regard to the artillery batteries covering the Wynn's Ferry Road. Otherwise there was little or no entrenching done by the Northern soldiers. McPherson's report on February 25 (Ibid., 163) says that there were no tools available and plans were made to unload them on Saturday morning.

27. Ibid., 880.

28. Ibid., 611–12.

29. Ibid., 800–801; Johnston, *Albert Sidney Johnston,* 453.

30. *OR,* 280–82, Pillow's report of February 18, 1862. What Pillow writes must be taken with a grain of salt. This was two days after the battle,

and he needed to justify his actions in the disaster. He was in trouble with the high command, and he knew it.

31. Hughes and Stonesifer, *Gideon J. Pillow,* 223–25.

32. *OR,* 265. Interestingly, Major Gilmer of the engineers *was* at the conference by invitation.

33. Ibid., 265–66.

34. Conger, *Rise of Grant,* 12–13.

35. Ibid., 395. Captain Bidwell of the water batteries made this observation.

36. Walke, *Naval Scenes,* 80.

CHAPTER ELEVEN

1. Colonel John M. Simonton was very much overweight, at approximately 300 pounds. When the advance began he could not keep up with his troops. Brigade command and control disintegrated or fell upon Col. John Gregg of the 7th Texas.

2. Hunt, "Fort Donelson Campaign," 71. See also Whittlesey, *War Memoranda,* 31–32.

3. Walter Geer, *Campaigns of the Civil War* (New York: Brentano's, 1926), 48.

4. Hunt, "Fort Donelson Campaign," 71.

5. Hughes and Stonesifer, *Gideon J. Pillow,* 226.

6. *OR,* 282, Pillow's report February 18, 1862. Also, Ibid., 339, Baldwin's report, March 12, 1862.

7. Ibid., 341, 380–81.

8. *Source Book,* 706.

9. Ibid.

10. James O. Churchill, "Wounded at Fort Donelson," in *Sketches of War History, 1861–1865,* Missouri MOLLUS, vol. 1 (St. Louis: Becktold and Company, 1892), 150.

11. *OR,* 177, General McClernand's report, February 28, 1862.

12. Wallace, *Autobiography,* 397–99. Why he did not send one of his staff is unknown.

13. *OR,* 387.

14. *Source Book,* 741.

15. Ibid., 772.

16. Ibid., 723.

17. *OR,* 345, see Buckner's and Major Ross's reports.

18. Ibid., 264–65, Gilmer's report, March 17, 1862; Buckner's quote from *Source Book,* 1350–51; *OR,* 331, Buckner's report of August 11, 1862.

19. *OR,* 331, Buckner's report of August 11, 1862.
20. Churchill, "Wounded," 148–50. Incidentally, General McClernand's headquarters was overrun and captured. Many Confederates after the battle believed it belonged to General Grant.
21. Cummings, *Yankee Quaker,* 178.
22. Jordan and Pryor, *Campaigns of Forrest,* 76–77.
23. Buckner, in his report, blames Pillow for ordering this battery to the rear, thus depriving him of artillery at a critical moment. Major Washington L. Doss of the 14th Mississippi and part of Buckner's command did not substantiate this.
24. Robert M. Hughes, "The Situation at Fort Donelson," *Confederate Veteran* 32, no. 12 (December 1929), 303.
25. *OR,* 352–53 and 356.
26. Jordan and Pryor, *Campaigns of Forrest,* 79, attribute this mishap to an aide to General Buckner. See also *OR,* 348.
27. *Source Book,* 1351, excerpt from the *Richmond Dispatch,* February 10, 1895.
28. *OR,* 263–64, Jeremy Gilmer's report, March 17, 1862.
29. Jordan and Pryor, *Campaigns of Forrest,* 82–84.
30. *OR,* 343.
31. Jordan and Pryor, *Campaigns of Forrest,* 778.
32. John K. Farris, "Sketch of Lieutenant General N. B. Forrest," *Southern Bivouac* 2, no. 7 (March 1884): 294. Also Jordan and Pryor, *Campaigns of Forrest,* 83.
33. Jordan and Pryor, *Campaigns of Forrest,* 83–84.
34. Cooling, *Forts Henry and Donelson,* 168–70.
35. Wallace, *Autobiography,* 403–5.
36. Ibid., 405–8.

CHAPTER TWELVE
1. *OR,* 290.
2. *Source Book,* 1360.
3. Hughes and Stonesifer, *Gideon J. Pillow,* 229–31.
4. Hughes, "Situation at Fort Donelson," 303.
5. Jordan and Pryor, *Campaigns of Forrest,* 84–85.
6. Wallace, *Autobiography,* 407–8.
7. Ibid., 410–11.
8. Grant, *Papers,* 181.
9. Wallace, *Autobiography,* 411–12.
10. Grant, *Papers,* 181.

11. *OR,* 618.

12. John G. Greenwalt, "A Charge at Fort Donelson, February 15, 1862," in *War Papers,* District of Columbia MOLLUS, vol. 2, paper 41, April 2, 1902.

13. Addison A. Stuart, *Iowa Colonels and Regiments: Being a History of Iowa Regiments in the War of the Rebellion. . .* (Des Moines: Mills and Company, 1865), 54.

14. Ibid., 346.

15. Jordan and Pryor, *Campaigns of Forrest,* 86. See also McAuley, *Fort Donelson,* 73.

16. Stuart, *Iowa Colonels,* 272.

17. Greenwalt, "Charge at Fort Donelson," 348. The next morning, Greenwalt was placed on a boat and sent downriver. He was discharged in July 1862 because of his wound but subsequently joined the 37th Iowa and survived the war.

18. Ibid., 347–48.

19. Stuart, *Iowa Colonels,* 65.

20. Frank Funk, "Fort Donelson," *Southern Bivouac* 1, nos. 9–10 (1883): 345; *OR,* 350, 401.

21. *OR,* 464, 514, 699. Since the two railroad guns had been rejected for service several weeks earlier, it is improbable that there was any stockpile of ammunition for these guns. The gun crew probably used 8–inch shot designed for the nearby howitzer, or some other expedient. Cannons of the era were fairly temperamental, and using ammunition not designed for the gun was downright dangerous, probably more so to the user than the target. Use of the 42–pounders at Fort Henry is an example.

22. Ibid., 344. Colonel Hanson of the 2nd Kentucky said as much in his report. Every effort was made to entrench that night, but the men were exhausted. The movement to assault positions and back also interrupted any work and sleep.

23. Ambrose, *7th Illinois,* 34.

24. Jordan and Pryor, *Campaigns of Forrest,* 86–87.

25. Geer, *Campaigns of the Civil War,* 57.

26. Wallace, *Autobiography,* 412.

27. Ibid., 415.

28. Ibid., 418.

29. Ibid., 420–21.

30. Ibid., 419.

31. *Source Book,* 723.

32. *OR,* 255.
33. Ibid., 255–56, Floyd's telegram to Johnston, February 15, 1862.
34. Jordan and Pryor, *Campaigns of Forrest,* 87.
35. Johnston, *Albert Sidney Johnston,* 469; *OR,* 273.
36. *OR,* 268.
37. Robert Selph Henry, *First with the Most: Nathan Bedford Forrest* (New York: Smithmark Publishers, 1991), 57–58; *OR,* 270.
38. *Source Book,* 1361.
39. *OR,* 287, 293.
40. Ibid., 295.
41. Ibid., 288, 298.
42. Ibid., 289.
43. Ibid. As a West Pointer, Buckner apparently knew these regulations well.
44. Geer, *Campaigns of the Civil War,* 59; *OR,* 299, 334. The various accounts of this event in the *Official Records* are remarkably similar.
45. *OR,* 300.
46. Jordan and Pryor, *Campaigns of Forrest,* 90–91; *OR,* 295.
47. *OR,* 300. The verbiage of this conversation comes from Hunter Nicholson of Pillow's staff. The content is substantiated by many of the official reports on the matter.
48. Ibid., 256, Floyd's telegram to Johnston, February 16, 1862.
49. Ibid., 318–19.
50. Ibid., 356.
51. Ibid., 328–36, General Buckner's report dated August 11, 1862.
52. Ibid., 327, 365, 387.
53. Ibid., 267, Floyd's report to A. S. Johnston, February 27, 1862.
54. Ibid., 271. Floyd's report to A. S. Johnston, March 20, 1862. Floyd was scrambling to justify his actions. Clearly he was overstating the strength of the Federal forces while minimizing the strength of Fort Donelson and the troops under his command.
55. Ibid., 328–36, Buckner's final report, dated August 11, 1862, is typical of the defeatist tone described in this paragraph.

CHAPTER THIRTEEN

1. Jordan and Pryor, *Campaigns of Forrest,* 91–92.
2. Hughes, "Situation at Fort Donelson," 317.
3. Ibid., 91–92. See also *OR,* 387.
4. *Source Book,* 1361–62.
5. *OR,* 160, Buckner's message to Grant, February 16, 1862.

6. Cummings, *Yankee Quaker,* 202–3. Pillow had established his headquarters at the Rice House. Floyd and Buckner used the Dover Hotel.

7. *OR,* 415. There is a great deal of speculation as to which unit these reinforcements were, but it is certain that two companies of the 48th Tennessee arrived that night. Most reports cite a "Mississippi regiment" unloading at the landing; however, no regimental history lays claim to this distinction. The most likely explanation is that these men were evacuated before the campaign with cases of sickness or were on leave and attempting to rejoin their regiments. The communications concerning the subsequent abandonment of the 20th Mississippi Infantry Regiment at the landing were probably unintentionally garbled, resulting in the mystery.

8. *Source Book,* 1354, excerpt from the *Richmond Dispatch,* February 10, 1895.

9. Force, *Campaigns,* 59–60.

10. *OR,* 161.

11. Allen, *Center of Conflict,* 93. This is the only reference to General Smith's dialog on the surrender that I came across. It is included here for color, although it could quite possibly be true.

12. *OR,* 161.

13. *Source Book,* 1373.

14. Wallace, *Autobiography,* 426–27.

15. Ibid., 427.

16. Ibid., 428–29.

17. *ORN,* 588–99; Jones, *Civil War at Sea,* 382–83; Jay Slagle, *Ironclad Captain: Seth Ledyard Phelps and the United States Navy, 1841–1864* (Kent, OH: Kent State University Press, 1996), 183. To make matters worse for Dove, he apparently landed at Fort Donelson and declined the surrender and sword of a Confederate major. He then proceeded up the river to Dover.

18. Jordan and Pryor, *Campaigns of Forrest,* 94; *OR,* 161, General Grant's reply to Buckner, February 16, 1862.

19. Greenwalt, "Charge at Fort Donelson," 350.

20. Whittlesey, *War Memoranda,* 38–39.

21. Force, *Campaigns,* 60.

22. Whittlesey, *War Memoranda,* 39–40.

23. This incident is from the *Columbia Herald,* July 1, 1870 and provided to me by Jill Garnet.

24. Grant, *Memoirs,* 184–85.

25. Stickles, *Simon Bolivar Buckner,* 173.

26. *OR,* 255, Johnston's telegram to J. P. Benjamin, February 16, 1862.

27. Johnston, *Albert Sidney Johnston*, 479.
28. *Campaigns*, 61.
29. *Source Book*, 724, 735.
30. Ibid., 725.
31. *OR*, 159, Grant's report, February 16, 1862.
32. Grant, *Memoirs*, 190.
33. *OR*, 628.
34. Ibid., 628, 652.
35. Ibid., 629.
36. *Source Book*, 206–11.
37. Ibid.
38. *OR*, 681–83.
39. Grant, *Memoirs*, 194; *OR*, 683.
40. *OR*, 46, 147, 151, 156. This is also discussed in Jordan and Pryor, *Campaigns of Forrest*, 98–97.

CHAPTER FOURTEEN

1. Woodworth, *Davis and His Generals*, 57.
2. *OR*, 459–62, dispatches shown here are typical; Ibid., 496–98, Senator Henry's optimistic letter to General Johnston.
3. Ibid., 528. Johnston sent a letter to the secretary of war dated November 8, 1861, stating that Fort Henry was a "strong work."
4. Ibid., 452–54, Senator Henry's letter to General Johnston.
5. Herman Hattaway and Archer Jones, *How the North Won: A Military History of the Civil War* (Chicago: University of Illinois Press, 1991), 75–76. See also Johnston, *Albert Sidney Johnston*, 353–54.
6. Roy P. Stonesifer, Jr., *The Forts Henry-Heiman and Fort Donelson Campaigns: A Study of Confederate Command*, Pennsylvania State University, Dissertation, 1965, 410–15. Stonesifer differs with this view. In his dissertation, he maintains that Buckner's plan to fix the Federals at Fort Donelson and maneuver against Grant's rear from Cumberland City was the correct option. Although intriguing, the force envisioned to hold Grant at Fort Donelson was only a fraction of that necessary. The plan also required a dynamic commander, which Floyd was not. Also, no preparations had been made at Cumberland City, and there were no stockpiles of supplies there. Simply put, at the time of conception, the plan had already been overtaken by events. The place to defeat Grant was at Fort Donelson.

7. Grant, *Memoirs,* 192.

8. Parks, *Gedneral Leonidas Polk,* 209–10.

9. Grant, *Memoirs,* 317.

10. *Source Book,* 78–81.

GOVERNMENT DOCUMENTS

Adjutant General of Iowa. *Report of the Adjutant General of the State of Iowa.* Des Moines: F. W. Palmer, 1868.

Adjutant General of Kentucky. *Report of the Adjutant General of the State of Kentucky.* Frankfort, KY: Kentucky Yeoman Office, 1867.

Atlas of American Wars. Vol. 1, 1689–1900. New York: Praeger Publishers, 1959.

Bearss, Edwin C. *The Fort Donelson Water Batteries.* Washington, DC: Division of History, Office of Archeology and Historic Preservation, 1968.

Brown, Benjamin C., ed. *Regulations for the Army of the United States.* Albany, NY: Weep, Parsons and Company, Printers, 1825.

Heitman, Francis B. *Historical Register and Directory of the United States Army, from Its Organization, September 2, 1789, to March 1903.* Washington, DC: U.S. Government Printing Office, 1903.

King, George L. *Campaign of Fort Henry and Fort Donelson, 1862.* Fort Benning, GA: U.S. Army Infantry School, Fourth Section, Committee "H", 1928.

Rietti, J.C. *Military Annals of Mississippi.* Spartansburg, SC: Reprint Company, Publishers, 1988.

Terrel, W. H. H. *Indiana in the War of Rebellion: Report of the Adjutant General.* Indianapolis: Douglas and Conner Printers, 1869.

U.S. General Service Schools. *Fort Henry and Fort Donelson Campaigns Source Book.* Fort Leavenworth, KS: General Service Schools Press, 1923.

U.S. Naval History Division. *Civil War Naval Chronology, 1861–1865.* Washington, DC: U.S. Government Printing Office, 1971.

U.S. War Department. *The War of the Rebellion: A Compilation of the Official Records of the Union and Confederate Armies.* 128 volumes. Washington, D.C.: U.S. Government Printing Office, 1880–1901.

———. *The War of the Rebellion: A Compilation of the Official Records of the Union and Confederate Navies.* 27 volumes. Washington, DC: U.S. Government Printing Office, 1908.

Vance, J. W. *Report of the Adjutant General of the State of Illinois.* Vol. 1. Springfield, IL: H. W. Broker, 1886.

PERIODICALS AND ARTICLES

Bailey, L. J. "Escape from Fort Donelson." *Confederate Veteran* 23, no. 2 (February 1915): 64.

Bearss, Edwin C. "The Fall of Fort Henry." *West Tennessee Historical Society Papers* Vol. 17 (1963).

Bedford, H. L. "Fight between the Batteries and Gunboats at Fort Donelson." *Southern Historical Society Papers* 13 (January–December 1885).

Burt, R. W. "Fort Donelson: Experiences of the 76th Ohio during the Siege." *National Tribune* (September 13, 1906): 14.

Casseday, Morton. "The Surrender of Fort Donelson." *Southern Bivouac* vol. 2, no. 11 (April 1887): 694–97.

Castell, Albert. "The Life and Sudden Death of General Albert Sidney Johnston." *Civil War Times Illustrated* vol. 34, no. 1 (March 1997): 30–37.

Churchill, James O. "Wounded at Fort Donelson." In *War Papers and Reminiscences,* Missouri MOLLUS, vol. 1. St. Louis: Becktold and Company, 1892.

Farris, John K. "The "Fighting" Forty-Eighth Tennessee Regiment." *Southern Bivouac* 2, no. 6 (February 1884): 36–45.

———. "A Surgeon's View of Fort Donelson." *Civil War Regiment: A Journal of the American Civil War* 1, no. 3 (1991).

———. "Sketch of Lieutenant General N.B. Forrest." *Southern Bivouac* 2, no. 7 (March 1884): 289–98.

Funk, Frank. "Fort Donelson." *Southern Bivouac* 1, nos. 9–10 (1883): 345.

Greenwalt, John J. "A Charge at Fort Donelson, February 15, 1862." In *War Papers,* District of Columbia, MOLLUS, vol. 2, paper 41, April 2, 1902.

Harrison, Lowell. "Simon Bolivar Buckner: A Profile." *Civil War Times Illustrated* vol. 24, no. 10 (February 1978): 36–45.

Hicks, Henry G. "Fort Donelson." In *Glimpses of the Nation's Struggle,* Minnesota MOLLUS, vol. 4. St. Paul: H. L. Collins Company, 1898.

Hudson, Mike. "The Civil War Adventures of Rice E. Graves of Daviess County and Graves' Battery, CSA." *Daviess County Historical Quarterly* vol. 24, no. 2 (April 1983): 26–33.

Hughes, Robert M. "The Situation at Fort Donelson." *Confederate Veteran* 32, no. 12 (December 1929): 300–303.

Hunt, George. "The Fort Donelson Campaign." In *Military Essays and Recollections,* Illinois MOLLUS, vol. 4. Chicago: Cozzens and Beaton, 1907. 61–82.

———. "Why Fort Donelson Was Surrendered." *Confederate Veteran* 37, no. 8 (August 1929).

Keller, Allan. "Admiral Andrew Hull Foote." *Civil War Times Illustrated* vol. XVIII, no. 8, (December 1979): 6–11, 43–47.

Magdeburg, F. H. "Capture of Fort Donelson." In *War Papers,* Wisconsin MOLLUS, vol. 3. Wilmington, NC: Broadfoot Publishing Company, 1993. 285–87.

McAuley, John T. "Fort Donelson and its Surrender." In *Military Essays and Recollections,* Illinois MOLLUS, vol. 1. Chicago: A. C. McClurg and Company, 1891. 69–74.

McCord, Franklyn. "J. E. Bailey: A Gentleman of Clarksville." *Tennessee Historical Quarterly* 23 (September, 1964): 246–53, 263–68.

Nye, N. S. "Jake Donelson: A 'Cocky' Rebel." *Civil War Times Illustrated* (March 1997): 28.

Paddock, George L. "The Beginnings of an Illinois Regiment in 1861." In *Military Essays and Recollections,* Illinois MOLLUS, vol. 2. Chicago: A. C. McLurg and Company, 1894. 253–67.

Ross, Reuben R. "River Batteries at Fort Donelson." *Confederate Veteran* 4, no. 11 (November, 1896): 393–98.

Selcer, Richard. "South's Feuding Generals." *America's Civil War* 12, no. 5 (November 1999): 34–40.

Spencer, Richard. "Diary Account at Fort Donelson." *Confederate Veteran* vol. 5, no. 6 (June 1897): 282–85.

T. D. J. "Fort Donelson Remembered." *Southern Historical Society Papers* 19, (1977).

Taylor, Jesse. "The Defense of Fort Henry." *From Sumter to Shiloh: Battles and Leaders of the Civil War* (1956): 368–72.

Tuttle, James. "Personal Recollections of 1861." In *War Sketches and Incidents,* Iowa MOLLUS, vol. 1. Kenyon, 1893. 18–24.

Van Vandt, K. M. "Seventh Texas at Fort Donelson." *Confederate Veteran* 18, no. 11 (November, 1910): 501.

Walke, Henry. "The Western Flotilla at Fort Donelson, Island Number Ten, Fort Pillow and Memphis." *From Sumter to Shiloh: Battles and Leaders of the Civil War.* New Castle Books, 1992.

Wallace, Lew. "The Capture of Fort Donelson." *From Sumter to Shiloh: Battles and Leaders of the Civil War.* 1 (1956): 398–428.

Whitfield, John H. "Maney's Battery at Fort Donelson." *Publication no. 21.* Waverly, TN: Humphreys County Historical Society, December 1990. 5–8.

Wilkes, John S. "First Battle Experience: Fort Donelson." *Confederate Veteran* 14, no. 11 (November 1906): 500–501.

BOOKS AND GENERAL SOURCES

Adair, John M. *Historical Sketch of the Forty-Fifth Illinois Regiment.* Lanark, IL: Carroll County Gazette Print, 1869.

Agee, Helen B. *Facets of Goochland County's History.* Richmond: Dietz Press Inc., 1962.

Allen, Hall. *The Center of Conflict.* Paducah, KY: *Paducah Sun Democrat,* 1961.

Amann, William F. *Personnel of the Civil War.* Vol. 2, *The Union Armies.* New York: A. S. Barnes & Company, 1961.

Ambrose, Daniel L. *History of the 7th Illinois Volunteer Infantry.* Springfield, IL: Illinois Journal Company, 1868.

Ambrose, Stephen E. *Halleck: Lincoln's Chief of Staff.* Baton Rouge, LA: Louisiana State University Press, 1962.

Anderson, Bern. *By Sea and by River: The Naval History of the Civil War.* New York: Alfred A. Knopf, 1962.

Avery, Phineas O. *History of the Fourth Illinois Cavalry Regiment.* Humboldt, NE: Enterprise Print Shop, 1903.

Barber, Flavel C. *Holding the Line: The Third Tennessee Infantry, 1861–1864.* Kent, OH: Kent State University Press, 1994.

Barker, Lorenzo A. *With Western Sharpshooters: Michigan Boys of Company D, 66th Illinois.* Huntington, WV: Blue Acorn Press, 1994.

Barnard, Harry V. *Tattered Volunteers: The 27th Alabama Infantry Regiment, CSA.* Northport, AL: Hermitage Press, 1965.

Barry, John M. *Rising Tide: The Great Mississippi Flood of 1927 and How It Changed America.* New York: Simon and Schuster, 1997.

Bearss, Edwin C. *Hardluck Ironclad: The Sinking and Salvage of the Cairo.* Baton Rouge, LA: Louisiana State Historical Press, 1966.

———. "John Calvin Brown." In *The Confederate General,* edited by William C. Davis, vol. 1. Harrisburg, PA: National Historical Society, 1991.

Blanchard, Ira. *I Marched with Sherman: Civil War Memoirs of the 20th Illinois Volunteer Infantry.* San Francisco: J.D. Huff Publishers, 1992.

Boatner, Mark M., III. *The Civil War Dictionary.* New York: David McKay Company, 1959.

Bohannon, Keith S. *The Giles, Allegheny, and Jackson Artillery.* Lynchburg, VA: H. E. Howard and Company, 1990.

Booth, Andrew B. *Records of Louisiana Confederate Soldiers and Louisiana Confederate Commands.* Spartanburg, SC: Reprint Company, 1984.

Brower, W. *Alabama: Her History, Resources, War Record, and Public Men, from 1540 to 1872.* Tuscaloosa, AL: Wilco Publishing Company, 1964.

Carroll, J. M., ed. *Register of Officers in the Confederate States Navy, 1861–1865.* Mattituck, NY: J. M. Carroll and Company, 1983.

Catton, Bruce. *Grant Moves South.* Boston: Little Brown Publishing, 1960.

———. *Short History of the Civil War.* New York: Knopf Publishers, 1962.

———. *Terrible Swift Sword.* New York: Dell Publishing Company, 1960.

Church, WIlliam C. *Ulysses S. Grant and the Period of National Preservation and Reconstruction.* New York: G. P. Putnam and Sons, 1897.

Clement, Evans, ed. *Confederate Military History.* Vol. 12. Atlanta: Confederate Publishing Company, 1899.

Cluett, William W. *History of the 57th Regiment, Illinois Volunteer Infantry, from Muster In December 21, 1861, to Muster Out July 7, 1865.* Princeton, IL: T. P. Streeter, 1886.

Commanger, Henry S. *The Blue and the Gray.* Vol. I. New York: New American Library, 1973.

Conger, Arthur L. *The Rise of Ulysses S. Grant.* New York: Century Company, 1931.

Connelly, Thomas L. *Army of the Heartland: The Army of Tennessee, 1861–1862.* Baton Rouge, LA: Louisiana State University Press, 1967.

Connelly, Thomas L., and Archer Jones. *The Politics of Command: Factions and Ideas in Confederate Strategy.* Baton Rouge, LA: Louisiana State University Press, 1973.

Cooke, Donald E. *For Conspicuous Gallantry: Winners of the Medal of Honor.* Mapelwood, NJ: C. C. Hammond Publishers, 1966.

Cooling, Benjamin Franklin. *Forts Henry and Donelson: The Key to the Confederate Heartland.* Knoxville, TN: University of Tennessee Press, 1987.

Cox, Douglas E. *Joint Operations during the Campaign of 1862 on the Tennessee and Cumberland Rivers.* Carlisle Barracks, PA: U.S. Army War College, 1989.

Cramer, Jesse Grant, ed. *Letters of Ulysses S. Grant to His Father and Youngest Sister, 1857–1878.* New York: G. P. Putnam's Sons, 1912.

Crist, Lynda L., and Mary S. Dix, eds. *The Papers of Jefferson Davis.* Vol. 7 of 9. Baton Rouge: Louisiana State University Press, 1997.

Crowson, Noel, and John V. Brogden. *Bloody Banners and Barefoot Boys: A History of the 27th Regiment Alabama Infantry, CSA.* Shippensburg, PA: Burd Street Press, 1997.

Crute, Joseph H., Jr. *Units of the Confederate States Army.* Midlothian, VA: Derwent Books, 1987.

Cummings, Charles M. *Yankee Quaker, Confederate General: The Curious Career of Bushrod Rust Johnson.* Rutherford, NJ: Fairleigh Dickinson University Press, 1971.

Current, Richard N. *Encyclopedia of the Confederacy.* New York: Simon and Schuster, 1993.

Davis, James A. *51st Virginia Infantry.* Lynchburg, VA: H. E. Howard and Company, 1984.

Davis, William C. *The Orphan Brigade: The Kentucky Confederates Who Couldn't Go Home.* Garden City, NY: Doubleday Publishing Company, 1980.

———. *Rebels and Yankees: The Commanders of the Civil War.* Edited by Tony Hall. New York: Smithmark Books, 1989.

Dawson, George F. *Life and Services of General John A. Logan, as Soldier and Statesman.* Chicago: Belford, Clarke, and Company, 1887.

Dryer, Frederick H. *A Compendium of the War of Rebellion.* Vol. 2. Dayton: Morningside Bookshop, 1979.

Eddy, Thomas M. *The Patriotism of Illinois: A Record of the Civil War and Military History of the State.* Vol. 2. Chicago: Clarke Printing Company, 1866.

Evans, Clement A. *Confederate Military History Extended Edition.* Vol. 4, Virginia. Wilmington, NC: Broadfoot Publishing Company, 1987.

Faust, Patricia L. *Historical Times Illustrated Encyclopedia of the Civil War.* New York: Harper & Row, Publishers, 1986.

Fish, Daniel. *The Forty-Fifth Illinois, a Souvenir of the Reunion Held at Rockford on the 14th Anniversary of its March in the Grand Review.* Minneapolis, MN: Byron and Willard, 1905.

Foote, Shelby. *The Civil War, a Narrative: Fort Sumter to Perryville.* New York: Random House, 1958.

Foraker, Joseph B. *Official Roster of the Soldiers of the State of Ohio in the War of Rebellion. 1861–1865. Volume II.* Cincinnati: Wilstache, Baldwin, and Company, 1886.

Force, M. F. *Campaigns of the Civil War.* Vol. 2: *From Fort Henry to Corinth.* New York, Charles Scribner's Sons, 1881.

Fuller, John F. C. *The Generalship of Ulysses S. Grant*. New York: Dodd, Mead and Company, 1929.

Geer, Walter. *Campaigns of the Civil War*. New York: Brentano's, 1926.

———. *Grant and Lee: A Study in Personality and Generalship*. Bloomington, IN: Indiana State University Press, 1957.

Gibson, Charles D., and E. Kay Gibson. *Assault and Logistics: Union Coastal and River Operations, 1861–1865*. Camden, ME: Ensign Press, 1995.

Gosnell, H. Allen. *Guns on Western Waters*. Baton Rouge, LA: Louisiana State University Press, 1995.

Grant, Ulysses S. *Memoirs and Selected Letters*. Edited by John Y. Simon. Carbondale, IL: Southern Illinois University Press, 1990.

———. *The Papers of Ulysses S. Grant*. Edited by John Y. Simon. Vol. 4 of 24. Carbondale, IL: Southern Illinois University Press, 1967–1984.

Hamilton, James J. *The Battle of Fort Donelson*. New York: A. S. Barnes and Company, 1968.

Hattaway, Herman and Archer Jones. *How the North Won: A Military History of the Civil War*. Chicago: University of Illinois Press, 1991.

Henry, Robert Selph. *First with the Most: Nathan Bedford Forrest*. New York: Smithmark Publishers, 1991.

Hitchcock, Ethan A. *Fifty Years in Camp and Field*. New York: Putnam's Sons, 1909.

Horn, Stanley F. *The Army of Tennessee: A Military History*. New York: Bobbs-Merrill Company, 1941.

Hubbell, John T., and James W. Geary, eds. *Biographical Dictionary of the Union: Northern Leaders of the Civil War*. Westport, CT: Greenwood Press, 1996.

Hubert, Charles. *History of the 50th Illinois Volunteer Infantry in the War of the Union*. Kansas City, MO: Western Publishing Company, 1894.

Huffstodt, James. *Hard Dying Men: The Story of General W. H. L. Wallace, General T. E. G. Ransom, and their "Old Eleventh" Illinois Infantry in the American Civil War*. Bowie, MD: Heritage Books, 1991.

Hughes, Nathaniel C., Jr., and Roy P. Stonesifer, Jr. *The Life and Wars of Gideon J. Pillow*. Chapel Hill, NC: University of North Carolina Press, 1993.

Horn, Stanley F. *The Army of Tennessee*. New York: Bobbs-Merrill Company, 1941.

———, ed. *Tennessee's War, 1861–1865*. Nashville: Tennessee Civil War Commission, 1965.

Johnson, Robert U. and Clarence C. Buell, eds. *Battles and Leaders of the Civil War*. New York: Century Publishers, 1887.

Johnston, William P. *The Life of Albert Sidney Johnston*. New York: D. Appleton and Company, 1878.

Jones, Archer. *Civil War Command and Strategy: The Process of Victory and Defeat*. New York: Free Press, 1992.

Jones, James P. *Black Jack: John A. Logan and Southern Illinois in the Civil War Era*. Tallahassee, FL: Florida State University Press, 1967.

Jones, Thomas B. *Complete History of the 46th Illinois Veteran Volunteer Infantry*. Freeport, IL: Bailey and Ankeny Printer, 1866.

Jones, Virgil Carrington. *The Civil War at Sea*. Vol. 1. New York: Holt Publishing, 1960.

Jordan, Thomas, and J. P. Pryor. *The Campaigns of General Nathan Bedford Forrest*. New York: Da Capo Press, 1996.

Kimball, Charles B. *History of Battery "A," First Illinois Light Artillery Volunteers*. Chicago: Cushing, 1899.

Lindsey, T. J. *Ohio at Shiloh: Report of the Commission*. Cincinnati: C. J. Krehbiel and Company, 1903.

Lindsley, John B. *The Military Annals of Tennessee (Confederate): A Review of Military Operations, Regimental Histories and Memorial Rolls, Compiled from Original Sources*. Nashville: Lindsley and Company, Publishers, 1886.

Logan, John A. *The Volunteer Soldier in America*. New York: Neale Publishers, 1887.

Logan, Mary S. C. *Reminiscences of the Civil War and Reconstruction*. Carbondale, IL: Southern Illinois University Press, 1970.

MacArtney, Clarence E. *Mr. Lincoln's Admirals*. New York: Funk and Wagnalls Company, 1956.

Mackey, James T. *Camp Life in Tennessee, Kentucky, Mississippi, Louisiana, and Alabama: The Diary of James T. Mackey*. Columbia, TN: Maury County Historical Society, 1990.

McFeeley, William S. *Grant: A Biography*. New York: W. W. Norton and Company, 1981.

McGavock, Randal W. *Pen and Sword: The Life and Journals of Randal W. McGavock, 1826–1863*. Nashville: Tennessee Historical Commission, 1959.

McPherson, James M. *Ordeal by Fire: The Civil War and Reconstruction*. New York: Alfred A. Knopf, 1982.

Moore, Robert H., Jr. *Graham's Petersburg, Jackson's Kanawha, and Lurty's Roanoke Horse Artillery*. Lynchburg, VA: H. E. Howard and Company, 1996.

Morris, W. S., L. D. Hartwel, and J. B. Kuykendall. *History of the 31st Illinois Volunteers, Organized by John Logan*. Herrin, IL: Crossfire Press, 1991.

Morrison, Marion. *A History of the Ninth Regiment Illinois Infantry.* Monmouth, IL: John S. Clark, 1864.

Nichols, James L. *Confederate Engineers.* Tuscaloosa, AL: Confederate Publishing Company, 1957.

O'Shea, Richard. *Battle Maps of the Civil War.* New York: Smithmark Publishers, 1992.

Parks, Joseph H. *General Leonidas Polk, CSA: The Fighting Bishop.* Baton Rouge, LA: Louisiana State University Press, 1962.

Powell, William H. *Officers of the Army and Navy (Volunteer) Who Served in the Civil War.* Philadelphia: Hamersly and Company, 1892.

Rawls, Walton. *Great Civil War Heroes and Their Battles.* New York: Abbeville Press, 1985.

Reid, Whitelaw. *Ohio in the War: Her Statesmen, Her Generals, and Soldiers.* Vol. 2, *The History of Her Regiments, and Other Military Organizations.* New York: Moore, Wilstauch, and Baldwin, 1868.

Ritter, Charles F., and Jon L. Wakelyn, eds. *Leaders of the American Civil War.* Westport, CT: Greenwood Press, 1998.

Rodenbough, Theophilus F. *From Everglade to Canon with the Second Dragoons, 1836–1875.* New York, NY: D. Van Nostrand, Publisher, 1875.

Roland, Charles P. *Albert Sidney Johnston: Soldier of Three Republics.* Austin, TX: University of Texas Press, 1964.

Roman, Alfred. *The Military Operations of General Beauregard in the War Between the States, 1861–1865.* Vol. 1. New York: Harper and Brothers, 1884.

Rowland, Dunbar. *Military History of Mississippi, 1803–1898.* Spartanburg, SC: Reprint Company, 1988.

Scott, J. L. *The 36th Virginia Infantry.* Lynchburg, VA: H. E. Howard, 1987.

Sifakis, Stewart. *Compendium of the Confederate Armies.* 10 vols. New York: Facts on File, 1992.

———. *Who Was Who in the Confederacy.* New York: Facts on File, 1988.

———. *Who Was Who in the Union.* New York: Facts on File, 1988.

Silverstone, Paul H. *Warships of the Civil War Navies.* Annapolis, MD: Naval Institute Press, 1989.

Slagle, Jay. *Ironclad Captain: Seth Ledyard Phelps and the United States Navy, 1841–1864.* Kent, OH: Kent State University Press, 1996.

Smith, John T. *A History of the 31st Regiment of Indiana Volunteer Infantry in the War of Rebellion.* Cincinnati: Western Book Concern, 1900.

Smith, Myron J., Jr. *The U.S. Gunboat "Carondelet," 1861–1865.* Manhattan, KS: MA/AH Publishing, Kansas State University, 1982.

Spears, John R. *The History of Our Navy, from Its Origin to the Present Day, 1775–1897.* New York: Charles Scribner's Sons, 1897.

Speed, Thomas. *The Union Regiments of Kentucky.* Louisville, KY: Union Soldiers and Sailors Monument Association, 1897.

Spencer, James. *Civil War Generals: Categorical Listings and Biographical Directory.* New York: Greenwood Press, 1986.

Starr, Stephen Z. *The Union Cavalry in the Civil War.* Vol. 1. Baton Rouge, LA: Louisiana State University Press, 1980.

Stickles, Arndt M. *Simon Bolivar Buckner: Borderland Knight.* Wilmington, NC: Broadfoot Publishing Company, 1987.

Stuart, Addison A. *Iowa Colonels and Regiments: Being a History of Iowa Regiments in the War of the Rebellion . . .* Des Moines: Mills and Company, 1865.

Symonds, Craig L. *A Battlefield Atlas of the Civil War.* Baltimore: Nautical and Aviation Publishing Company of America, 1983.

———. *Tennesseans in the Civil War: A Military History of Confederate and Union Units With Available Rosters of Personnel,* part 1. Nashville: Civil War Centennial Commission, 1864.

Tenney, W. J. *The Military and Naval History of the Rebellion in the United States.* New York: D. Appleton and Company, 1865.

Thompson, Edwin P. *History of the Orphan Brigade.* Cincinnati: Caxton Publishing House, 1898.

Thornbrough, Emma L. *Indiana in the Civil War Era, 1850–1880.* Indianapolis: Indiana Historical Society, 1989.

Twombly, Voltaire P. *The 2nd Iowa Infantry at Fort Donelson, February 15, 1862: Together with an Outline History of the Regiment from Its Organization at Keokuk, Iowa, May 27, 1861, to Final Discharge at Davenport, Iowa, July 20, 1865.* Des Moines: Plain Talk Printing House, 1897.

VanTassel, David D., ed. *The Dictionary of Cleveland Biography.* Indianapolis: Indiana University Press, 1996.

Wakelyn, Jon L. *Biographical Dictionary of the Confederacy.* Westport, CT: Greenwood Press, 1977.

Walke, Henry. *Naval Scenes and Reminiscences of the Civil War in the United States on the Southern and Western Waters.* New York: F. R. Reed and Company, 1877.

Wallace, Isabel. *Life and Letters of General W. H. L. Wallace.* Chicago: R.R. Donnelly, 1909.

Wallace, Lee A., Jr. *A Guide to Virginia Military Organizations, 1861–1865.* Richmond: Virginia Civil War Commission.

Wallace, Lew. *Lew Wallace: An Autobiography.* New York: Harper and Brothers Publishers, 1906.

———. *"It Was Not Possible for Brave Men to Endure More."* In *Battles and Leaders of the Civil War,* edited by Robert U. Johnson. New York: Century Publishers, 1887.

Ward, Geoffrey C. *The Civil War: An Illustrated History.* New York: Alfred A. Knoff, Inc., 1990.

Warner, Ezra J. *Generals in Blue: Lives of the Union Commanders.* Baton Rouge, LA: Louisiana State University Press, 1964.

———. *Generals in Gray: Lives of the Confederate Commanders.* Baton Rouge, LA: Louisiana State University Press, 1959.

Way, Frederick, Jr. *Way's Packet Directory, 1848–1994.* Athens, OH: Ohio University Press, 1994.

Weaver, Jeffrey C. *Goochland Light, Goochland Turner, and Mountain Artillery.* Lynchburg, VA: H. E. Howard and Company, 1994.

Weigley, Russel F. *The American Way of War: A History of United States Strategy and Policy.* Bloomington, IN: Indiana University Press, 1973.

Welcher, Frank J. *The Union Army, 1861–1865: Organizations and Operations.* Vol. 2, *The Western Theater.* Indianapolis: Indiana University Press, 1993.

Welsch, Jack D. *Medical Histories of the Confederate Generals.* Kent, OH: Kent State University Press, 1995.

West, Richard S., Jr. *Mr. Lincoln's Navy.* New York: Longman's Green and Company, 1957.

Whitelaw, Reid. *Ohio in the War: Her Statesmen, Her Generals, and Soldiers.* Cincinnati: Moore, Wilsatch, and Baldwin, 1868.

Whittlesey, Charles. *War Memoranda: Cheat River to the Tennessee, 1861–1862.* Cleveland: William W. Williams Publisher, 1881.

Williams, Kenneth P. *Grant Rises in the West: The First Year, 1861–1862.* Lincoln, NE: University of Nebraska Press, 1997.

Williams, T. Harry. *P. G. T. Beauregard: Napoleon in Gray.* Baton Rouge, LA: Louisiana State University Press, 1955.

Wills, Brian S. *A Battle from the Start: The Life of Nathan Bedford Forrest.* New York: Harper Collins Publishers, 1992.

Wilson, James G. *Biographical Sketches of Illinois Officers Engaged in the War against the Rebellion of 1861.* Chicago: James Barnet, 1862.

Woodworth, Steven E., *Jefferson Davis and His Generals.* Lawrence, KS: University Press of Kansas, 1990.

Wright, Marcos J. *Tennessee in the War, 1861–1865.* New York: Ambrose Lee Publishing Company, 1908.

UNPUBLISHED WORKS AND PAPERS

Bailey, James E. Bailey Family Papers, 1828–1878. #1307. Tennessee State Library and Archives, Nashville.

Brownlow, John P. Papers, April 1861–April 1862. Military Institute Manuscript Collection, Carlisle Barracks, Pennsylvania.

Buckner, Simon B. Papers. KYSX449–A. Manuscripts Section, Western Kentucky University, Bowling Green.

Chipman, Charles. Papers, 1853–1972. Military Institute Manuscript Collection, Carlisle Barracks, Pennsylvania.

Fletcher, Samuel H. "The History of Company A, 2nd Illinois Cavalry Regiment."

Foote, Andrew Hull. Papers, 1822–1890. 0626J. Library of Congress.

Gebhart, Carl D. "The 11th Illinois Infantry Regiment in the Civil War." Master's thesis, Western Illinois University, Macomb, 1968.

Gilmer, Jeremy F. Papers. #276. Manuscripts Department, Library of the University of North Carolina, Southern Historical Collection, Chapel Hill.

Hamilton, Edward P. "The Battle of Fort Donelson: The Technology and Significance." Master's thesis, Georgia Southern College, Statesboro, 1975.

Haynie, Isham N. Papers, 1848–1898. SC 673. Illinois State Historical Library, Springfield.

Hicken, Victor. "From Vandalia to Vicksburg: The Political and Military Career of John A. McClernand." Master's thesis, University of Illinois, Urbana: September 14, 1955.

Kincaid, Gerald Allen, Jr. "The Confederate Army, A Regiment: An Analysis of the 48th Tennessee Volunteer Infantry Regiment, 1861–1865." Master's thesis, U.S. Army Command and General Staff College, Fort Leavenworth, 1995.

Norton, John A. John Alston Norton Books. #2491. Manuscripts Department, Library of the University of North Carolina, Southern Historical Collection, Chapel Hill.

Pugh, Isaac. Papers. Special Collections Library, University of California, Riverside.

Stonesifer, Roy P., Jr. *The Forts Henry-Heinman and Fort Donelson Campaigns: A Study of Confederate Command.* Pennsylvania State University, Dissertation, 1965.

Stuwart, William D. Papers. MS #0108. Virginia Military Institute Archives, Lexington.

Walczynski, Mark. "The Battle of Fort Donelson." Master's thesis, California State University, Dominguez Hills, 1997.

Westbrook, Joseph W. Papers. Military Institute Manuscript Collection, Carlisle Barracks, Pennsylvania.

Note: Index subentries are ordered chronologically where appropriate. Page references in **bold italic** type indicate illustrations. The denotation "***pl.***" followed by a number indicates a plate in the series following page 158.

A

Abernathy, Alfred, 64

Alabama units
  26th Ala., 85, 101
  27th Ala., 54, 88, 100

Alps, 95, 145, 165

Ambrose, Daniel, 61

"Anaconda Plan," 8–9

Anderson, Adna, 16–18

Appleton Belle, 107

CSS *Arkansas,* 33

Arkansas units
  15th Ark., 88, 101, 210

Arthur, Matthew, 182

B

Babcock, Andrew J., 230

Bailey, James E., 53

Baldwin, William E., 194, 195, 210

"bandboxes." *see* "timberclads"

Beauregard, Pierre Gustave Toutant
  assigned to western theater, 67–68
  arrives Bowling Green, 86–87
  in battle of Fort Henry, 87
  and Fort Donelson defense plans, 122–23
  declines command of Fort Donelson, 274

Belmont, battle of, 43–44

Benton, 26, 70

Bird's Point, 13

Bowling Green, Ky., 38, 86, 124, 273

Brinton, Dr. John, 144, 256

Brown, I. N., 108

Brown, John C., 153, 261

Buckner, Simon Bolivar, ***pl.6***
  and Pillow, 14–15, 275–76
  joins Confederate army, 37–38
  occupies Bowling Green, 38
  personal misfortune, 131
  Cumberland City defense plans, 141
  at Fort Donelson, 161, 185–86, 201–3, 205–7, 213–15
  and surrender plans, 240–41, 247–48
  performance evaluated, 248, 276
  surrenders Fort Donelson, 254–62

Buell, Don Carlos
  troop strength of, 41
  assumes command of Depart-
    ment of the Ohio, 46
  plans to cut off Nashville, 68
  ineffectiveness of, 76
  overestimates Confederate forces,
    118–19
  Johnston fears advance by, 123
  dispatches Nelson's division to
    assist Grant, 152
  arrives Nashville, 267

C
Cairo, 27, 70, 78
Cairo, Ill., 9–11, 13, 77
Cameron, Simon, 26
Camp Boone, 15
Camp Halleck, 84
Camp Robinson, 15
Carondelet, pl.9, 27, 78, 95, 111,
    135, 145, 159–60, 167, 177,
    179, 182
Carondelet, Mo., 27
Casseday, Alex, 201
casualties, Union
  at Fort Donelson February 12,
    154
Cerro Gordo, Tenn., 108, 110
Cheairs, Nathaniel, 205
Churcher, James M., 229
Churchill, James O., 203
Cincinnati, 27, 78, 93, 95, 97, 117
city-class ironclads
  first construction of, *pl.9,* 25–28
  design and outfitting of, 28–29

Clark, Charles, 117
Clark, Edward, 86
Clarksville
  Pillow fortifies, 50
  bridges at, 126, 128, 131, 135
  Grant captures, 267
Cobb, R. L., 258
Coffee Landing, Tenn., 111
Columbus, Ky.
  Pillow occupies, 37
  Grant reconnoiters, 59–61
  fortifications, 73
  reinforced by Polk, 74
  Johnston abandons, 123
communications, 1–2
Conestoga, 22–23, 51, 63, 71,
    107–14, 143, 177, 181, 182
Confederacy
  defense problems, 1, 271
  recruitment and supplies, 3–4
  manufacturing facilities, 4
  political recognition of, 19
  economy of, 19–20
  Union support in, 113, 143–44
Confederate Army
  departmental organization, 2, 6
  recruitment, 3, 15–16, 40
  supplies and materiel problems,
    4–7, 40, 55–56
  election and appointment of offi-
    cers, 5–6
  communication challenges, 6
  seniority determinations, 8
Cook, Edmund C., 205
Cook, John, 161, 226
cotton-clad gunboats, 26

Crew, James M., 110–11
Cruft, Charles, 200–201, 210,
    231, 232
Cubine, W. J. B., 96
Culbertson, Jacob, 175–77
Cullum, G. W., 135, 174
Cumberland City, Tenn., 134, 141
Cumberland river, 2–3

D
Davidson, John, 117, 192
Davis, Charles H., 26
Davis, Jefferson
    defense problems of, 1–2
    emphasis on Eastern theater, 3,
        19, 20
    military strategy of, 19–20, 271
    appoints Johnston to Western
        Department, 36
    and P. G. T. Beauregard, 67–68
Dixon, Joseph, 49, 159, 168
Dollam, Major, 125
Dollins, James J., 88
Donelson, Daniel S., 16–18
Doolittle, Harry B., 228–29
Dove, Benjamin M., 181, 259
Dover, Tenn., 17, 148, 149, 260
Drake, Joseph, 221, 232
Dresser, Jasper M., 148, 150, 161,
    162
Dudley's Hill, 194
Dunbar, 86, 92, 107

E
Eads, James B
    builds first "city-class" gunboats,
        25–29
    unpaid at start of Fort Henry
        campaign, 78
Eastern theater, 3, 19, 20
Eastport, 108, 109, 111
England, 19
entrenching, 154
Erin Hollow, 205, 206
Essex, *pl.10,* 29–30, 60, 70
    in battle of Fort Henry, 78,
        82–83, 94–95
Essex, 117

F
1st Division (McClernand), 77,
    136
    1st Brigade (Oglesby), 77, 84,
        136, 148, 149, 161
    2nd Brigade (Wallace, W. H.
        L.), 77, 84, 136, 150
    3rd Brigade (Morrison), 136,
        164
Florence, Ala., 3, 110, 113, 114
Floyd, John B., *pl.6*
    arrives at Bowling Green, 65–67
    commands Cumberland River
        defenses, 127–28
    and Fort Donelson defenses,
        134–35
    Cumberland City defense plans,
        141
    ordered to Fort Donelson,
        153–54

assumes command at Fort
Donelson, 157
telegraph dispatches to Johnston,
184
council of war, 184–86
deferred to Pillow, 190
in Confederate attack, 206
confronts Pillow about troop
movements, 220
messages to Johnston, 237–38,
241–42
surrender plans, 240–41, 251–52
performance evaluated, 243,
246–47, 248–49, 274–75
escapes Fort Donelson, 255–56
after battle, 266
Foote, Andrew Hull, *pl.2*
assumes command gunboat
fleet, 31–33
and Grant, 47
in battle of Fort Henry, 78, 81,
93–95, 97, 104–5
Tennessee River Raid, 107–14
and Fort Donelson assault plans,
135, 138
launches from Paducah, 143
arrives at Fort Donelson,
167–69
launches naval bombardment,
177–83, *180,* 187–88
and Confederate surrender, 259
Forrest, Jeffrey, 253
Forrest, Nathan Bedford
delays Grant on road to Fort
Donelson, 144–45

at battle of Fort Donelson,
154–55, 158, 192, 198,
203–5, 207–11
surrender discussions and, 239,
241
escapes Fort Donelson, 251–54
after battle, 266
Fort Defiance, 50
Fort Donelson, *pl.13, pl.14*
established, 16–17
construction difficulties, 48,
49–51, 53
construction nearly complete,
62–64
design limitations, 73, 247
Columbiad gun, 83, 129, 159,
160–61
water batteries, *180, pl.12*
Fort Donelson, battle of, *pl.12,
pl.14–16*
Grant reconnoiters, 115–16, 128
Confederate preparations for,
120–25, 129–31, 132–35
Union preparations for, 125–26,
131–32, 135–38
Grant's advance on Fort Donelson, 144–50, *146, 151,* 154
casualties February 12, 154
Carondelet's bombardment,
159–60
initial Union probes and assaults,
161–65, *163*
attack on "Redan #2," 162–64
Confederate artillery in,
168–69, 213

Confederate command confusion during, 171, 184–86, 189–90, 243–49, 274–76

Confederates abort escape sortie Feb. 13, 171–72, 187

Grant reinforces with Wallace, 174–75, *176*

river battle of Feb. 14, 177–83, *180,* 187–89

Feb. 15, 6:00 A.M., *190*

Pillow attacks McClernand Feb. 15, 192–201, 203–4

Buckner attacks Wallace, 201–3, 205–7

Feb. 15, 10:00 A.M., *208*

Confederate attack stalls, 213–17

Feb. 15, 12:00 P.M., *214*

Union logistics problems, 215–16

Confederate resupply problems, 219–20

Grant returns to field, plans attack, 222–25, 242

Smith counterattacks on left, 225–31, 242

Feb. 15, 2:00 P.M., *227*

Wallace counterattacks on right, 231–35, 242

Feb. 15, 3:00 P.M., *233*

Feb. 15, 6:00 P.M., *236*

Confederate surrender plans, 238–42, 247–48

Confederate surrender, 254–62

troop strength in, 262–63

prisoners, 263–64, 265, *pl.13*

Fort Heiman, 54, 72, 88, 91, 100

Fort Henry, *pl.11*

siting of, 17–18, 48–49, 105–6, 272

Smith reconnoiters, 44

Union plans to advance upon, 45–47

construction problems, 48, 53

construction nearly complete, 61–62, 64

design limitations, 73, 272

floodwaters threaten to engulf, 80–81, 89

condition after surrender, 98–100

grave errors of Confederacy at, 114

Fort Henry, battle of, *pl.11*

Union plans and preparations for, 75–78

Union landings, 79–80, 83–84

position Feb. 4–5, *90*

naval bombardment, 94–95, 96, 139–40

land assault, 95

Tilghman surrenders to Foote, 97–98

maneuvers Feb. 6, *99*

Confederates withdraw to Fort Donelson, 101

importance and lessons of, 101–6, 114

Fort Henry–Fort Donelson campaign

Confederate order of battle, 286–88

effects of loss on Confederacy, 271

Johnston's command mistakes, 134–35, 139–40, 153–54, 272–75, 277, 279

lessons from, 280

transport/auxiliary vessels, 289

Union order of battle, 281–85

see also Fort Donelson, battle of; Fort Henry, battle of

Fort Holt, 13

Foster, William F., 16–18

France, 19

Frémont, John C., 44–45

Frequa, John G., 179

G

Gantt, George, 85, 101, 251, 252

General Anderson, 251, 254–55

Gilmer, Jeremy F.
  at Fort Henry, 49–50, 53, 97
  at Fort Donelson, 120–21

Gordon, Thomas M., 206

Goudy, Jason, 111

Grant, Ulysses S., *pl.1*
  pre-war activities, 11–13
  occupies Paducah, 38–39
  leadership style of, 39–40
  at battle of Belmont, 41–43, *42*
  and Halleck, 45, 47, 119–20
  and Foote, 47
  reconnoiters Columbus, 60–61
  Fort Henry attack plans, 69–71
  initial movement toward Fort Henry, 80–84, 90
  assault on Fort Henry, 92–93, 95–98, 99, 102–3

reconnoiters Fort Donelson, 115–16

preparations for assault on Fort Donelson, 125–26, 131–32, 135–38

command attributes of, 137–38

advance on Fort Donelson, 144–50, *146,* 151, 154–55

initial probes and assaults, 162–69

haste of operation, 189

meets with Foote, 192–94

returns to field, plans attack, 222–25, 242

and Confederate surrender, 256–62

promoted to major general, 265

takes Clarksville, 267

performance evaluated, 277, 278, 279

Greenwalt, John G., 228

Gumbart, George C., 199

gunboats. *see* ironclads; Western Flotilla

Gwin, William, 108, 111

H

Halleck, Henry, *pl.1*
  assumes command Department of the Missouri, 45
  and Grant, 45, 47, 119–20
  reconnoiters Columbus, 59–61
  and Fort Henry attack plans, 69–70
  reinforces Grant at Fort Henry, 118, 128

Buell uncooperative with, 118–19
and Clarksville bridges, 126, 128, 131–32, 135
and Grant's victory, 264
and Grant, 267–68
performance evaluated, 278–79
Hambrick, J. M., 144–45, 158
Hanson, Roger W., 161, 207–9, 210
Hardee, William J., 122–23, 274
Harris, Isham, 3, 16, 40
Haynes, Milton
trains artillery at forts, 48, 61
in battle of Fort Henry, 97
at Fort Donelson, 129, 159
Haynie, Isham, 162–64
Head, John W., 54, 85
heavy mortar boats, 33
Heiman, Adolphus, 18, 50
at battle of Fort Henry, 81, 83, 85, 96–97, 101
at Fort Donelson, 120
Hickman Creek, 121, 129, 130
Hitchcock, Ethan Allen, 126
Hubbard, David C., 88
Huey, James K., 252
Hughes, Robert M., 252
Hughes Creek, 81
Hunter, David, 45

I
Illinois Central Railroad, 9
Illinois units
1st Ill. Lt. Artillery
B Bty, 162, 202
A Bty, 212

2nd Ill. Cavalry, 144
2nd Ill. Lt. Artillery
D Bty, 148, 150, 161–62, 202
E Bty, 148, 199
4th Ill. Cavalry, 79, 91, 92, 101, 217
7th Ill., 61, 161, 229
8th Ill., 144–45, 150, 197, 200
11th Ill., 203
17th Ill., 162
18th Ill., 100, 196, 197–98
20th Ill., 202
21st Ill., 12
29th Ill., 150, 200
30th Ill., 144–45, 196
31st Ill., 79, 197, 203
45th Ill., 164, 202, 207, 209
48th Ill., 207, 209
49th Ill., 162
57th Ill., 143
McAllister's Illinois Battery, 145, 162, 202, 207–9
Wood's Illinois Battery, 11, 93
Indian Creek, 121, 129, 130
Indian Creek Road, 147
Indiana units
11th Ind., 232
23rd Ind., 174
25th Ind., 161, 228
31st Ind., 174, 232
52nd Ind., 226
Iowa units
2nd Iowa, 226, 228–29, 260
5th Iowa Cavalry, 174
7th Iowa, 161, 226
14th Iowa, 161, 226
Ironclad Board, 26

ironclads
    city-class, 25–29
    effectiveness of, 276–77
    generally, 30–31
    outfitted and crewed, 70–71
    see also Western Flotilla

J
Jackson, Thomas E., 192
John A. Fisher, 251, 254–55
Johnson, Bushrod, *pl.8*
    and site selection of forts, 16–18
    commands Fort Henry, 64
    brief command at Fort Donelson, 124
    at battle of Fort Donelson, 154, 204, 221
    and surrender, 254–55, 258, 259
    violates parole of honor, 265
Johnston, Albert Sydney, *pl.4*
    pre-war activities, 35
    appointed command Western Department, 36, 54
    builds troop strength and defenses, 40–41, 47–48, 55, 65
    never inspects forts, 56, 273
    and battle of Fort Henry, 87, 104
    and Fort Donelson defense plans, 121–24
    reinforced with twelve regiments, 127
    decisions in defense of area, 134–35, 139–40
    troop strength at Bowling Green, 138
    receives news from Fort Donelson, 237–38, 241–42
    performance evaluated, 245–46
    after battle, 268
    command mistakes, 134–35, 139–40, 153–54, 272–75, 277, 279
Jones, J. W., 125

K
Kelley, D. C., 220, 251, 252, 253–54
Kentucky
    neutrality of, 13–14
    recruitment in, 15–16
    neutrality violated, sides with Union, 37, 55
Kentucky units
    2nd Ky., 124, 161, 185, 209, 229
    25th Ky., 200, 203
    Graves's Ky. Artillery Battery, 206, 207, 230
    Kentucky State Guard, 15, 16

L
Lanning, James, 71
Lauman, Jacob G., 161, 226–31
Lawler, Michael K., 197
Leach, Elbert C., 101
Lexington, pl.8, 22–23, 63, 71, 78, 107–14
Lick Creek, 121, 175, 198, 216, 239, 253
Lincoln, Abraham, 59, 120, 265
Logan, John A., 197, 203

*Louisville, **pl.10,*** 27, 135, 143, 165, 177, 181, 182
Lovell, Mansfield, 127
Lynn Boyd, 86, 107

M
Magoffin, Beriah, 13, 37
maps
  Area of Operations, 1861, *10*
  Area of Operations, September 1861, *42*
  Area of Operations, January 1862, *66*
  Tennessee River Raid, *112*
  Grant's advance on Fort Donelson, *146*
  Fort Donelson, February 12, *151*
  Fort Donelson, February 13, *163*
  Fort Donelson, February 14, *176*
  Fort Donelson Water Batteries, February 13–16, *180*
  Fort Donelson, 6:00 A.M., February 15, *190*
  Fort Donelson, 10:00 A.M. February 15, *208*
  Fort Donelson, 12:00 P.M., February 15, *214*
  Fort Donelson, 2:00 P.M., February 15, *227*
  Fort Donelson, 3:00 P.M., February 15, *233*
  Fort Donelson, 6:00 P.M., February 15, *236*
Maria Denning, 70

Markland, A. H., 263
Marsh, Carroll C., 202
Martin, John S., 178–79
Maryland, 13
Maury, Matthew F., 108
May, Charles, 144–45, 158
McArthur, John, 175, 194, 196
McCausland, John, 196
McClellan, George B., 23, 26, 68, 118–19, 267–68
McClernand, John A., ***pl.2***
  moves toward Columbus, 60
  in battle of Fort Henry, 77, 80–81, 84, 92–93, 95, 100, 101
  marches on Fort Donelson, 136, 144–45, 147, 148–50
  in battle of Fort Donelson, 161, 162–64, 173
  meets Confederate attack, 194, 196–98, 199–200, 210, 216–17
  regroups, 221–22
McGavock, Randal W., 44, 50, 85, 92
McNeely, Dr. James, 167
McPherson, James B., 136, 231
Memphis, Tenn., 3, 4
Memphis & Charleston Railroad Bridge, 107–8, 111
Merritt, Thomas, 24
Mexican War, 12
Mill Springs, battle of, 64–65
Milner, Henry, 88
mines, underwater, 80, 81
Mississippi river, importance of, 2–3, 6

Mississippi units
  1st Miss., 192
  4th Miss., 85, 89
  14th Miss., 201, 202, 205, 230
  20th Miss., 196, 221, 252, 255
  26th Miss., 195
Missouri, loyalties of, 13
Missouri units
  1st Mo. Light Artillery
  Battery H, 202
  Battery K, 226
  14th Mo. (Birge's Sharpshoot-
    ers), 158, 161, 226
Monitor, 28
Morgan, James D., 77
Morrison, William R., 162–64,
  232
Morton, James H., 231
Mound City, 27
Mound City, Ill., 27
Mudd, John J., 144–45
Muscle, 109, 111

N
Nashville, Tenn.
  importance of, 3, 4, 139, 140
  fortified, 50
  abandoned by Johnston, 266–67
Nashville Railroad Company, 131
Nebraska units
  1st Neb., 212
New Era, 29
New Madrid, Mo., 36
New Orleans, La., 9
New Uncle Sam, 136
Noble, John, 115

O
Oglesby, Richard, 41
  in battle of Fort Henry, 77, 100
  in battle of Fort Donelson, 148,
    161, 162, 164–65, 173
  meets Confederate attack, 194,
    196–97
Ohio units
  20th Ohio, 194, 261, 265
  76th Ohio, 212

P
Padgett's Spy Company, 88, 100
Page, Scehencius G., 229
Paine, Eleazer A., 77
Palmer, Joseph B., 205, 206
Panther Creek, 81, 84
Parsons, Lewis B., 77
Paulding, Hiram, 26
Phelps, Seth Ledyard, 51
  reconnoiters Fort Henry, 63, 71
Phelps, Seth Ledyard, 107–14
  and plans to attack Fort Donel-
    son, 132
Pillow, Gideon J., *pl.7*
  appointed commander of Provi-
    sional Army of Tennessee,
    4–5
  subordinate to Polk in Western
    Department, 7–8, 18
  and Buckner, 14–15, 275–76
  occupies Columbus, Ky., 37
  encounters Grant's initial move-
    ments, 43
  at battle of Belmont, 43–44
  resigns, 44

commands Clarksville supply depot, 65

reinforces Fort Donelson, 116–17

improves defenses at Fort Donelson, 125, 129–31, 132–33, 141

council of war plans, 184–86

attacks McClernand, 192–201, 203–4

re-directs Confederate attack, 205, 207

pulls back troops to trenches, 220, 243

performance evaluated, 243, 244–45, 249

escapes Fort Donelson, 252

after battle, 265–66

Pittsburg, 27, 135, 143, 165, 167, 177, 182

Polk, James K., 4, 44

Polk, Leonidas

given command of Western Department, 6–7

and fort construction, 18, 36–37

and battle of Fort Henry, 86, 87–88, 104

troop strength, 138–39

Pook, Samuel, 22, 26, 28

Porter, Thomas K., 158, 192

Porter, William "Dirty Bill," 29–30, 94–95

prisoners/prisons, *pl.13,* 263–64, 265, 269

Provisional Army of Tennessee, 4–5

Q

Quarles, William A., 244

R

Ransom, Thomas E. G., 203

Rawlings, John, 13, 211

Reardon, James S., 150

"Rebel yell," 195

Rice, Frank, 129

Riddell, Charles, 255

Riggins, James, Jr., 111

Riley, Robert K., 95

rivers, inland

and "Anaconda Plan," 9

facilities and materials on, 21

for transportation, 1, 2–3, 74

see also Western Flotilla

Robb, Alfred, 183

Robinson, Benjamin, 229

Rodgers, John, 22–24, 31, 32

Rodgers, William E., 255

Ross, Leonard F., 232

Ross, Reuben, 129, 178

S

Sallie Wood, 109, 111

Samuel Orr, 107, 108

Scott, Winfield, 4

"Anaconda Plan," 8–9

in Mexican War, 14–15

2nd Division (Smith), 77–78, 137

2nd Brigade (McArthur), 175

3rd Brigade (Cook), 161

4th Brigade (Lauman), 161

5th Brigade (Smith), 232

Sherman, William T., 9

Shirk, James W., 111

siege warfare, 150, 154
Simonton, John M., 192, 196
Smith, Charles F., *pl.3*
  occupies Smithland, 39, 44
  reconnoiters Fort Henry, 63
  in battle of Fort Henry, 78, 91,
    92, 93, 100
  in battle of Fort Donelson, 161,
    213, 225–31
  and Confederate surrender,
    256–57
  Halleck attempts to promote,
    264
Smith, Dr. J. W., 252
Smith, Joseph, 26
Smith, Morgan L., 212, 231, 232
snipers/sniping, 157–58
St. Louis, 27, 28, 78, 95, 117, 135,
    143, 165, 177, 178, 181, 182,
    194
Stacker, Col., 54
Standing Rock Creek, 101
Stankiewicz, Peter K., 229
Stewart, A. P., 52, 274
Stewart's Hill, 54
Stewart's Independent Cavalry
    Battalion, 80
Stone, George H., 226
strategic importance of, 3
Submarine No. 7, 26
Sugg, Cyrus A., 54, 257

T
Taylor, 24
Taylor, Jesse, 48–49, 89, 93, 162
Taylor, Zachary, 35
Tennessee, recruitment in, 3–4

Tennessee river, 2–3
Tennessee River Raid, 107–14,
    112
Tennessee units
  1st Tenn. Artillery
    Company B, 89
  3rd Tenn. Cavalry, 85, 201, 133,
    205, 206–7, 209, 230
  9th Tenn. Cavalry Battalion, 85,
    251, 101, 213
  10th Tenn., 18, 50, 85, 86, 89,
    92, 129
  18th Tenn., 161, 201, 205, 229
  26th Tenn., 195
  30th Tenn., 54, 201, 221,
    228–29
  32nd Tenn., 205, 243
  41st Tenn., 230
  42nd Tenn., 244
  48th Tenn., 86, 153
  49th Tenn., 183, 53, 85, 230
  50th Tenn., 50, 54, 85, 230
  51st Tenn., 86
  53rd Tenn., 64
  Maney's Tenn. Battery, 50, 161,
    169, 207
  Porter's Tenn. Artillery Battal-
    ion, 158, 192, 207, 228, 230
  Ross's Tenn. Artillery Battery,
    178
  Tenn. Corps of Engineers, 18
Thayer, John, 166, 212
3rd Division (Wallace), 174,
    231–35
  1st Brigade (Cruft), 200
Thomas, Felix, 64–65
Tilghman, Lloyd, *pl.5,* 38

promoted and commands both
  forts, 52–54
at Battle of Fort Henry, 85–86,
  87–89, 92, 93, 96–97, 103–4
"timberclads," 23–25, 105
Time, 107
torpedoes, underwater, 80, 81
transportation, 1, 2–3
Twombly, Voltaire P., 229
Tyler, 22–24, 78, 107–14, 177, 181

U
Union Marine Works, 27
U.S. Army
  recruitment and supply, 9–11,
    15–16
  Department of the Missouri, 45
U.S. Navy
  vessels in, at outbreak of war, 21
  coal supply, 22

V
Van Dorn, Earl, 86
Virginia units
  Guy's Va. Artillery Battery, 166,
    192
  Jackson's Va. Artillery Battery,
    192

W
Walke, Henry, 97, 132, 145,
  159–60, 178
Wallace, Lew, *pl.4*
  reconnoiters Fort Henry, 71
  in battle of Fort Henry, 100
  remains at Fort Henry, 138, 149

Grant orders to Fort Donelson,
  174–75
and Confederate attack, 198,
  199–200, 207, 211–13, 217
regroups, 222
counterattacks on right, 231–35
and Confederate surrender, 258
Wallace, W. H. L., at Fort Donel-
  son, 150, 173, 202, 212
Washburne, Elihu B., 13
Washington, George, 19
Watts, Ornsby, 89
Weaver, Harry E., 229
Webster, J. D., 224, 234
Welles, Gideon, 23, 26
West Point, 20
Western Department (Confederate
  Army)
  features of territory, 2–3
  Polk appointed command, 7
  Johnston appointed command,
    36
  Johnston builds army strength
    and position, 40–41, 47–48,
    55, 65
  strength in February 1862,
    86–87
  see also Johnston, Albert Sydney
Western Flotilla
  planning for gunboat fleet,
    21–22
  Rodgers assembles fleet, 22–24
  recruitment for, 24–25
  Eads builds "city-class" gun-
    boats, 25–29
  Foote takes over command,
    31–33

outfitted and crewed, 70–71
in battle of Fort Henry, 78,
    81–82, 93–95, 104–5
in battle of Fort Donelson, 143,
    145, 165–67, 177–83, *180*
Whittlesey, Charles, 46, 261
Wilcox, M. D., 252
Wilkes, John S., 153
Wynn's Ferry Road, 164–65, 173,
    191, 209, 231

Y
Yates, Richard, 11, 12

Z
Zollicoffer, Felix K.
    occupies Cumberland Gap, 38
    and battle of Mill Springs,
        64–65